THE WORLD ENCYCLOPEDIA OF

SOCCER

To Aidan, Lyndon, Noel and Christy

First published in the United States by Sevenoaks in 2000

10 9 8 7 6 5 4 3 2 1

ISBN 1 86200 063 8

Project editor: Martin Corteel
Project art direction: Paul Oakley
Production: Sarah Corteel

Printed and bound in Dubai

AUTHOR'S ACKNOWLEDGEMENTS

Thanks are due to all those, seen and unseen, who worked so hard and with such enthusiasm to bring an ambitious project to fruition. Particular thanks to all my fellow writers for their contributions on the many and varied aspects of soccer considered in these pages; to Paul Gardner for his expert contribution on the history and development of soccer in the United States. Thanks also to Jack Shafer, Steve Dobell, Peter Arnold and David Ballheimer for their work on the text; and Lorna Ainger for picture research. Last, but not least, to Martin Corteel, Editorial Manager of Carlton Books, for keeping the show on the road from initial planning meeting to final print run.

OPPOSITE: WORLD CHAMPIONS
The USA team show off the World Cup and their medals to a delighted crowd at the Rose Bowl

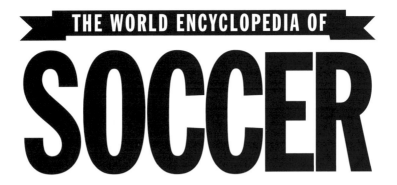

THE WORLD ENCYCLOPEDIA OF
SOCCER

The definitive illustrated guide

Keir Radnedge
Executive Editor of World Soccer magazine

SEVENOAKS

CONTENTS

6 THE HISTORY OF SOCCER IN THE UNITED STATES

Looks at the way soccer developed in the United States from the first recorded matches at Oneida School in Boston, through World Cup finals appearances, the ill-fated NASL and rival MISL to the Major League Soccer at the end of the 20th century. The chapter is broken down into four sections:

10 NASL
13 World Cup USA 1994
14 Major League Soccer
20 The U.S. on the world stage

22 THE MAJOR COMPETITIONS

Describes principal competitions for the national squads of the American and European continents and the major continental club competitions. Nine competitions are described together with the details of every final. For the World Cup finals, both men's and women's, every result in the final is recorded as well as each tournament's leading goalscorer and the teams' line-ups in the Final.

22 World Cup
38 Copa America
39 European Championship
40 Women's World Cup
44 World Club Cup
46 Copa Libertadores
48 European Cup
50 European Cup-winners' Cup
52 UEFA Cup

OPPOSITE: BROTHERS IN ARMS *Los Angeles Galaxy goalkeeper Jorge Campos (9) celebrates a goal with scorer Greg Vanney (20) as teammates Motajo (15) and Hurtado (23) look on*

54 THE GREAT CLUBS

Profiles of 43 of the most prestigious teams in Europe, Central and South America, from Ajax of Amsterdam, Holland, to Vasco da Gama of Rio de Janeiro, Brazil, plus listing of principal honors. In addition, there are brief biographies on some of soccer's most famous and innovative coaches.

54 Rinus Michels
58 Helenio Herrera
64 Giovanni Trapattoni
65 Bill Shankly
65 Matt Busby
73 Tele Santana

75 LEGENDS

Pays tribute to 10 of soccer's all-time greats.

76 Franz Beckenbauer
77 Bobby Charlton
78 Johan Cruyff
79 Alfredo Di Stefano
80 Eusebio
81 Diego Maradona
82 Stanley Matthews
83 Pele
84 Ferenc Puskas
85 Lev Yashin

86 THE GREAT PLAYERS

Profiles 228 of the game's famous names from "Trello" Abegglen of Switzerland to Andoni Zubizarreta of Spain, with a verdict on what made that player great.

127 US INTERNATIONAL RESULTS 1916–1999

COMPETITIONS *Madrid Champions Cup*

MLS *Carlos Valderrama (left)*

PLAYERS *England's Alan Shearer (left)*

THE HISTORY OF SOCCER IN THE UNITED STATES

THE NEW WORLD'S FIRST experience of football was in the seventeenth century, when it erupted as an alarming mêlée involving kicking and running and dribbling and handling: the very same roughhouse activity that was causing problems in England, in fact. Just as in England, the city authorities objected. In 1657 Boston issued an edict banning this primitive version of "football" as noisy and dangerous.

The game virtually disappeared, but – again following the English pattern – it was reborn 200 years later in schools and colleges. Records show the Oneida School in Boston with a four-year unbeaten record between 1862 and 1865 (a modest monument on Boston Common commemorates the feat).

At the National Soccer Hall of Fame in Oneonta, in upper New York State, it is now claimed that Oneida was America's first soccer team, but this is debatable. The original Football Association in London did not formulate its rules until 1863, and anyway the game played by Oneida permitted running with the ball. The inscription on the Boston monument – "the Oneida goal was never crossed" – makes it clear that scoring involved carrying the ball across the opponents' goal line.

In 1869, two leading colleges, Rutgers and Princeton, played each other on Rutgers' New Jersey campus, basing the game on the new FA rules. Rutgers took the game 6–4, but were trounced 8–0 in the return at Princeton. Alas, the University authorities were not delighted by this diversion from studies, and they managed to ban the third and deciding game. But the games had proved very popular with the students, and for a short while, it looked as though football would become the autumn sport in the colleges.

That did not happen. By 1877 football had vanished from college fields. Americans did not want to play sports imported from England. Cricket had been replaced by baseball, and the colleges soon abandoned football for rugby which in turn was Americanized into gridiron football.

Football, now bearing an un-American label, faded into the background, but did not disappear. European immigrants – British, German and Irish mostly – kept it alive. The United States Football Association was formed in 1884, and the following year put itself into the record books by staging the first-ever international game played outside the British Isles. The occasion was slightly marred by the result, the

6

U.S. losing 0–1 to Canada.

There was even a pro league in 1894. It was formed by baseball owners (who had been running their own pro league since 1871) and their idea was simply to get more use, and money, out of their stadiums, which lay idle after the baseball season finished in October.

The American League of Professional Football Clubs was limited, as was baseball, to the northeast corner of the U.S. It failed miserably, and ceased operations after only three weeks. The nineteenth century ended with more gloom when, in 1899, the USFA closed down.

Brighter news came with the new century. The colleges rediscovered the sport in 1902, while tours by the English amateur teams Corinthians and Pilgrims rekindled enthusiasm. In 1906 the USFA was reborn, and the Intercollegiate Association Football League was formed.

The game had by now spread to the midwest, and in 1910 Stanford University, way out in California, took up the sport. In 1914 Spalding's Soccer Guide claimed that "no sport in America is making more rapid strides than soccer." Possibly it was true. That same year a national Open Cup competition was launched, while the USFA had been admitted to FIFA in 1913. But there were already signs of the organizational problems that were to plague American soccer for decades.

Gaining FIFA's approval had not been easy. In 1912, two separate organizations, both claiming to represent the sport in the US, had turned up at the FIFA meeting in Sweden. FIFA sent them back home to work out their differences. This was done, but a pattern of divisiveness had been set. It was to surface again in the 1920s.

A new pro league, the American Soccer League, was formed in 1921, with backing from major commercial companies – particularly Bethlehem Steel – and a number of top professionals from Britain were imported. They included the Scot Alec Jackson, who later returned to Britain to play for Huddersfield Town – and to score a hat-trick for Scotland's Wembley Wizards in their 5–1 trouncing of

WORLD CUP *The U.S. Team's best performance came in the 1930 World Cup when it lost to Argentina in the semi-final.*

England in 1928.

There was logic behind this British soccer drain to the U.S.: international transfer regulations could be ignored because the British had walked out of FIFA in 1920, while the money in the U.S. was better than the almost slave-wages allowed a pro player in England. But when Britain rejoined FIFA in 1924, trouble was brewing for the United States Soccer Football Association, as it now called itself. In 1927 FIFA threatened it with expulsion for encouraging British players to jump their contracts.

The matter was smoothed over but the USSFA was soon embroiled in another squabble with a decidedly modern ring to it. The pro ASL ordered its clubs not to take part in the Open Cup, claiming it disrupted the league schedule. Three clubs ignored the ban, including the powerful Bethlehem Steel FC. The ASL suspended all three, but the USSFA

refused to recognize the suspensions.

The three clubs then formed the nucleus of a rival pro league, the Eastern Professional League. The fight between the ASL and USSFA-backed EPL lasted a year, during which there was talk of setting up a national body to oppose USSFA. While that never materialized, the bitter internecine struggle did untold damage to the sport. The wealthy backers of the ASL, disillusioned, withdrew and the league dwindled to semi-pro status.

The college game, too, after a false dawn in the early 1900s, stagnated – though it did claim an American first when it played a game under floodlights in 1939.

Foreign – usually British – teams were frequent visitors to the U.S. in the 1920s and these tours, plus its membership of FIFA, encouraged USSFA to enter international competition. In 1924 it sent a team to

the Olympic Games in France. It made a creditable beginning: after beating Estonia 1–0, the US went down 0–3 to Uruguay, the eventual gold-medallists. But in the 1928 Games, the U.S. was outclassed 11–2 by Argentina.

When the first World Cup arrived in 1930, the US was eager to participate – good news for FIFA, which was having trouble finding enough teams to make the long journey to Uruguay. The American team, which included a number of naturalized British players, had a sturdy physical look to them – the French dubbed them "the shot-putters."

However 3–0 wins over both Belgium and Paraguay put the Americans into the semi-finals, where they were taken apart 6–0 by the Argentines, who had mauled them in the Olympics two years earlier. The American press paid little attention to the achievement of the Americans in reaching the semi-finals of the first world football championship. But not too much can be read into that. European countries – most of whom had refused to participate – virtually ignored the event that was to become the greatest attraction in world sports.

By the outbreak of the Second World War in 1939, football in the U.S. was still very much a minor sport. Its attempts to start a pro league, or to capture the interest of the American public or media, had all ended in failure. And because it was played and controlled largely by immigrant groups from Europe it had an image problem: it was widely seen as a foreign sport. This led to unfavorable comparisons with the home-grown sports of baseball and gridiron football. There was even a hint that playing soccer was somehow unpatriotic.

Nothing much seemed to change in the immediate post-war years. Football was no longer limited to the north east, but was now played

all over the United States, with St Louis emerging as the sport's new capital. But important changes were on the way, brought about by the war and advancing technology. The war had brought waves of new European immigrants to the US, and their passion for football injected dynamism into the game in the New York area.

Admittedly, it was unashamedly ethnic soccer. Teams now proudly bore names such as Philadelphia Ukrainians or Brooklyn Italians or the German-Hungarians of New York. But they drew good crowds. It was those same fans who responded when the advent of air travel made it easier for foreign teams to tour the US. In 1948 England's Liverpool played Djurgardens of Sweden at the stadium of the Brooklyn Dodgers baseball team. It was billed as the first-ever meeting of two foreign teams on American soil and more than 18,000 turned out to celebrate the occasion.

Then, seemingly out of the blue, came an event that should have given

football in the U.S. a tremendous boost. It started with the U.S. qualifying for the finals of the 1950 World Cup. The team of part-timers boasted a lively assortment of professions: a carpenter, a teacher, a couple of mailmen, a machinist ... and an undertaker.

Off they went to Brazil, there to pull off one of the great sporting upsets. The football world was shocked to read the scoreline from Belo Horizonte: U.S. 1, England 0. A goal from the Haitian-born Joe Gaetjens had given the American no-hopers, players that no one had ever heard of, an unlikely win over an English side which included the likes of Billy Wright, Tom Finney, Alf Ramsey and Stan Mortensen.

The Brazilian fans, delighted by a win for the underdogs, raced on to the field at the end of the game and chaired the American players off. But back in the U.S. the achievement was barely noticed. Only one U.S. newspaper (from St Louis) even had a reporter

at the tournament in Brazil. All the rest gave minimal space to wire service reports, and then forgot about the World Cup when the US was eliminated in its next game.

Clearly football still had a long way to go if it was to become part of the mainstream of American sports. One man who believed in that dream was promoter Bill Cox, who had learned his trade in the most American way possible, as the owner of a baseball team. He watched throughout the 1950s as big-name foreign teams such as Real Madrid, Manchester United, Celtic, and Vasco da Gama played exhibition games in the US before large crowds.

Reasoning that the games would be even better attended if a trophy and prize money were on offer, in 1960 he organized the International Soccer League. Playing in the summer in New York, the ISL featured eleven teams from Europe and, significantly, South America – for the Hispanic fans were beginning to make their presence felt. The ISL – it lasted until 1964 – consistently drew five-figure crowds, and helped prepare the ground for the next step in the development of football as a spectator sport: the birth of a truly national pro league.

By 1965, the word was out: pro soccer just might be the next great American sport. Part of the reasoning had little to do with soccer. The American pro sports scene was thriving as never before, in particular the gridiron game where the value of franchises had been increasing feverishly with every year that passed. Football was seen as a superb opportunity for spectacular capital gains: a start-up league in which the franchises would cost little, but would soon be worth untold millions.

Indeed, such was the attraction of a fledgling soccer league that top corporations and rich businessmen were falling over each other to get in on the ground floor. Not just one, but three groups of potential owners sprang up, willing to put their money into pro soccer. Just as in 1928, the USSFA was presiding over a surplus of pro leagues.

UNBELIEVABLE *Alf Ramsey (dark shirt) watches Larry Gaetjeans' header slip through the legs of goalkeeper Gil Merrick for what turned out to be the only goal as the U.S. beats England 1–0 in the 1950 World Cup at Belo Horizonte, Brazil.*

THE NORTH AMERICAN SOCCER LEAGUE

THE BUSINESSMEN WERE used to American ways: if you wanted to start a sports league, you just did it. But they quickly discovered, to their surprise, that they needed the sanction of the USSFA if they wanted their new leagues to be part of world-wide football. This they very definitely did want, it was part of the sport's appeal. So USSFA found itself being courted by all three groups.

USSFA, a small-time body run mostly by immigrants, was hardly ready for the coming clash with American big business. It set up a committee – consisting of a Scot, a German and a Rumanian – that tried to get the three groups to combine. A forlorn hope. Forced to choose, USSFA sanctioned the group that eventually called itself the United Soccer Association, with the patriotic acronym USA.

The two groups which had been left out in the cold decided that they could, after all, combine and they formed the National Professional Soccer League (NPSL). Not being sanctioned by USSFA meant that NPSL was also not recognized by FIFA, which meant international isolation. As a pirate league, it would have huge problems signing foreign players – which surely meant its league was doomed before it even started.

Such was the USA's thinking, and

it was roundly shocked when the NPSL succeeded in signing a significant number of foreigners, enough to stock its ten teams, and announced that it would start play in the summer of 1967. Not only that, it secured a national television contract from CBS.

Alarm bells clanged loudly over at the headquarters of the USA, which had been complacently planning to begin in 1968. Scared to give the NPSL a one year unopposed start, it had to act quickly. The only answer was to sign up eight entire teams, one for each of its franchised cities, to play "on loan" during the summer of 1967.

Eight mediocre teams were signed: England's Stoke City became, temporarily, the Cleveland Stokers, Uruguay's Cerro were transformed into the New York Skyliners, and so on. And the 1967 season was a disaster for both leagues.

When it was over, when the losses were seen to amount to several million dollars, reason prevailed. The owners said the problem was that the public had been confused by two leagues. They agreed to merge (the decision was undoubtedly nudged along by the NPSL's lawsuit accusing the USSFA and the US league and – by implication, FIFA – of being an illegal monopoly).

The new combined league was

named the North American Soccer League, NASL. It operated in 1968 with 17 teams. Fifteen were in American cities ranging from Dallas and Houston in the south to Boston in the north, with three clubs – Los Angeles, San Francisco and San Diego – out west in California, plus two Canadian entries in Vancouver and Toronto.

But 1968 was another disaster. All the clubs lost money, and for most of them, the commitment to football evaporated. It was evidently not a satisfactory investment after all. Massive defections followed, and the NASL was soon down to a mere five clubs.

That it did not fold was due largely to the efforts of two Brits. Former Wales international Phil Woosnam took over as commissioner of the shrivelled league, backed up by ex-Fleet Street football journalist Clive Toye. Slowly they rebuilt the league – something that would never have happened had not one of the surviving owners been Texas oil-millionaire Lamar Hunt with his Dallas Tornado club. Unshakeable in his faith in football, Hunt was to be a key figure in the sport for many more years. As long as Hunt backed football, it was not easy for its detractors to write it off.

PHIL WOOSNAM *Welsh international and Commissioner of the NASL.*

By 1971, the NASL had eight clubs, including New York Cosmos, owned by Warner Brothers, with Toye as the general manager. And it was the Cosmos and Toye who made

LAMAR HUNT *Owner of the Dallas club and other sports franchises too.*

the crucial move in 1975. By then there were 15 clubs. Woosnam and Toye had often talked of the league's need for a superstar – and both had agreed that Pele was the only soccer player well-enough known in the U.S. to fill the role. Now Toye, backed up by Warner's money, convinced Pele to come out of retirement and play in New York.

It was a masterstroke. From the moment of Pele's arrival, press and television coverage of the league and the sport soared. Pele turned up at the White House with President Ford, Pele was a guest on the late-night Johnny Carson show, articles on Pele appeared in the chic magazines.

Wherever Cosmos went, the fans poured into the stadia to see Pele. In the 15 games he played in 1975, six were sell-outs, ten set club records. In Washington he set a league record of 35,620. Pele gave instant credibility to the NASL, and suddenly top stars from around the world wanted to play in the U.S. Giorgio Chinaglia and Franz Beckenbauer followed Pele to Cosmos, while George Best and Johan Cruyff played in Los Angeles. They were joined by Bobby Moore, Eusebio, Gordon Banks, Trevor Francis, Geoff Hurst, Roberto Bettega, Teofilo Cubillas, Kaz Deyna, Elias Figueroa, Rodney Marsh, Gerd Muller, and others.

When Cosmos moved, in 1977, to the new Giants Stadium in New Jersey, they consistently outdrew the local baseball teams, the Yankees

PELE *The New York Cosmos filled Giants Stadium when the Brazilian played, outdrawing New York's two baseball teams, the Yankees and the Mets.*

and the Mets, climaxing in a massive crowd of nearly 78,000 for a playoff game against the Fort Lauderdale Strikers.

With other NASL clubs such as Tampa Bay Rowdies, Minnesota Kicks, Portland Timbers and Chicago Sting drawing well, euphoria was in order. In 1979 came the crowning touch, the one thing necessary for the NASL, now boasting 24 teams, to be considered

a major league sport: a television contract with the ABC network.

A climactic championship game called Soccer Bowl (modelled on the hugely successful gridiron Super Bowl) had been inaugurated in 1975. "By 1982," predicted Woosnam, "Soccer Bowl will have the same importance as the Super Bowl has today." The years of the NASL's greatest success – between 1977 and

FRANZ BECKENBAUER *Having won everything as a player with Bayern Munich and West Germany, Der Kaiser showed off his skills to the American market.*

1982 – were also Cosmos years. The New York club won the Soccer Bowl in four of those six years.

Americans, allegedly resistant to soccer's charms, seemed at last to have succumbed. Admittedly, some ground had been ceded by the sport. The worldwide practice of awarding two points for a win and one for a tie had been modified: a winner got six points and (in a move to encourage scoring) an extra point for each goal scored in the 90-minute game, up to a maximum of three. There were no tied games. If the score was tied at 90 minutes, two 7 1/2-minute sudden-death overtimes were played. If the scores were still level, a shootout was used to determine a winner. But not with standard penalty kicks. The NASL version had the kicker dribbling the ball in from 35 yards, with the goalkeeper coming out to meet him. The kicker had 5 seconds to get off his shot.

If soccer purists were willing to suffer this new-fangled shootout procedure, they were much less happy with another NASL innovation, one that modified the offside rule. This sounded much too much like the dreaded "Americanization." Offside calls had been identified as a major culprit in stopping the game at exciting moments, guilty of frustrating scoring opportunities.

Americans will never take to soccer until there's more scoring went the refrain, heard especially from marketing people. There were suggestions that the offside rule should be abolished altogether. The NASL found a compromise. All its playing fields carried two field-wide lines, 35-yards in from each goal line. The NASL rule was that players could not be offside in the entire central area of the field, between the two 35-yard lines.

Unlike the shootout, which was tacked on at the end of a game, this was a law change, something that fundamentally affected the way that the game was played right from the opening whistle, that called for changes in the players' way of thinking, and in team tactics.

The change was, in fact, an experiment for which FIFA permission had been obtained. It began in 1973 and went on for seven years until, in November 1980, FIFA suddenly

CRUYFF *Joined the exodus from Europe.*

remembered about it, and issued an ultimatum to the NASL that it drop the experiment. It was also told to use two, instead of three, substitutes and to "comply fully with the official Laws of the Game." After four months of testy exchanges between FIFA and NASL, the league was allowed to continue the 35-yard line experiment for one more year. But it was dropped before the 1982 season.

GEORGE BEST *Collected one final big payday with the Tampa Bay Rowdies.*

Just as the NASL seemed poised to take its place as America's fifth pro sport (alongside baseball, basketball, gridiron football and ice hockey) the wheels started to fall off. The outward glamor of the league was not reflected on the balance sheets. All the clubs, including the high-spending Cosmos, were losing money. Cosmos, backed by Warner Brothers' millions could afford the losses. The other clubs could not. In 1981, three clubs folded, and ABC, dissatisfied with stagnant ratings, did not renew its television contract.

Those old nemeses of American soccer, internal strife and competing leagues, surfaced again. The competing league came in the form of the MISL – the Major Indoor Soccer League.

The NASL had only itself to blame for this one, for it had started the indoor ball rolling with its own tournament in 1975. For the owners it had been a simple matter of getting full value from their players, most of whom were on year-round contracts. The NASL season lasted only six months, and paying their players for half a year's idleness did not appeal to the clubs. A short two-month indoor season, starting in January, seemed one way to ease the problem.

Some NASL clubs liked the sport, some did not, and not all the clubs played in the indoor soccer championship, which was always a half-hearted affair. But it stirred the interest of yet another group of promoters. Led by Earl Foreman, they formed the MISL in 1978. They shrewdly leveled the "foreign sport" accusation at football, pointing out that it was run by FIFA, a bunch of foreigners in Switzerland, who could – and did – block attempts by the NASL owners to modify the rules to suit American tastes.

Indoor football was different. FIFA barely acknowledged its existence, so that the MISL owners could do what they liked. Scoring was high (low-scoring was a constant target for critics of the outdoor game), all sorts of show-biz gimmicks could be added, and the sport could be swamped in statistics, supposedly another American essential. "Indoor soccer is the game Americans want," said Foreman. The MISL owners did not have to

divide their attention between indoor and outdoor football – a split that was to fatally weaken the NASL in the coming struggle. Foreman summed it up: "I don't give a shit about outdoor soccer." As the NASL floundered, the MISL grew in strength.

According to some, the NASL's main problem was not the MISL, but the extravagant ways of its own flagship team, Cosmos. They were spending too much money, and smaller clubs like Rochester, Philadelphia and Memphis had gone bankrupt trying to keep up. No doubt there was some truth in that, but it seemed a curious criticism to be made in the US, the heart of competitive capitalism.

Another reason for the NASL's woes was said to be over-expansion. Too many teams had been added too

MAJOR INDOOR SOCCER LEAGUE *Heralded the demise of the NASL because it fed the American public's enjoyment of scoring and continuous goalmouth action.*

quickly. Commissioner Phil Woosnam was blamed for this and for not ensuring that all of the new team owners had the necessary money. Another odd criticism, coming as it did from the owners who had themselves approved all the additional teams.

Yet a third reason emerged: the NASL was too wedded to using foreign players. It needed more Americans. The owners, struggling with their losses, found this idea acceptable, as American players were decidedly cheaper than foreigners.

Conforming to the pattern of the other pro sports, football had introduced a draft of college players in 1972. It turned into an almost comical opera-

tion as NASL coaches desperately tried to find out something, anything, about a college scene which they had until then largely ignored. It was also a somewhat futile operation, with only eight college players considered good enough to be signed. Of those, only two made it as first-team starters.

A quota system was introduced, requiring all teams to have a certain number of Americans on the field – by 1984 it was five. Sadly, the American youngsters – most of them coming straight from college soccer – were not good enough. The caliber of play in the league went into a noticeable decline.

Seven more teams folded in 1982, among them Lamar Hunt's Dallas Tornado, the only team that had been present right from the start in 1967. Phil Woosnam was ditched as Commissioner in 1983. In his place, the league appointed Howard Samuels, a successful businessman who knew nothing of soccer and was supposed to restore financial health to the league and to the clubs.

But as NASL clubs struggled to hold down player salaries, the MISL gleefully jumped in to offer top players better money in the indoor game. When, in 1983, Rick Davis, the most trumpeted young American player of his generation, jumped from Cosmos to join the MISL's St Louis Steamers, the writing was surely on the wall for the NASL.

The task of saving the league proved beyond Samuels. When he

died, in late 1984, he left a league that was down to nine clubs. Clive Toye took over, but his difficult task was rendered impossible in March 1985 when he was forced to expel Cosmos for failure to pay their membership fees. There would be no 1985 season for NASL. The league was dead.

Yet the NASL had accomplished much. In a few short years it had done what the USSFA had spent decades trying, and failing, to do. It had spread the sport of football nationwide, taking it far beyond the boundaries of the big-city ethnic enclaves. This had been part of a deliberate plan to encourage America's kids to take up the game. Targeted were the affluent white suburbs, families that would form the NASL's future fan base.

The plan was remarkably successful – even though the NASL collapsed before it could benefit from it. Instead, the big beneficiaries turned out to be the colleges. Clubs for youth football proliferated all over the country. A measure of the growth was provided by the Dallas–Fort Worth area of Texas, which in 1967 had just 150 boys playing soccer. A decade later there were 43,000 boys and 7,000 girls playing.

This astonishing growth took place in an area considered the very citadel of the super-macho gridiron sport. It was the same story up in Portland, Oregon: from 200 boys in 1972 to 11,850 boys and 900 girls in 1977. The colleges responded to the rapidly growing stream of young soccer players by adding soccer to their sports menu. In 1963 the National Collegiate Athletic Association (NCAA) soccer guide listed 225 schools offering the sport; the 1981 guide had over twice that number.

The boys coming out of the youth clubs – white middle-class Americans – were destined for college anyway, but their parents now saw the possibility of getting that education paid for with one of the increasingly numerous soccer scholarships on offer, providing a further boost for the youth game. (For the moment, football was still primarily a game for men. The great explosion of women's soccer was yet to come.)

WORLD CUP USA 94

THE COLLAPSE OF THE NASL left an ominous vacuum at the center of the sport in the U.S. Who was now to take the lead? There were only two candidates, neither of them really qualified to provide the leadership and direction necessary.

The United States Soccer Federation (USSF – it had finally bowed to reality and dropped the word "football" from its title), though no longer the unambitious group of 15 years earlier, remained a largely volunteer organization full of internal bickering, and lacking any sign of decisive leadership.

The other nationally organized body was college soccer, which had problems of its own. Not the least of them was that all of its important decisions were made for it by the NCAA, which had no particular interest in the sport of football. Indeed, it had a formidable reputation for making decisions that favored gridiron football (from which it made a lot of money) and often damaged college football.

The college coaches were told how many games they could play, when they could play them, how many scholarships they could give and, based on aca-demic records, which players they could have on their teams.

There was also, among the college coaches, a lack of pro experience: very few of them had ever played the game at the top level. In compensation they tended to emphasize theoretical aspects of the game, and to be very big on tactical planning and rigid schemes and systems.

This propensity for the "academic" side of the game made college coaches the natural instructors for the USSF's coach in schools, which awarded (after testing) A, B and C licenses. The courses, inevitably reflecting the theory-dominated approach of the instructors, left much to be desired.

Fortunately for the sport there was, during this 12-year period without a pro league, a project that kept the U.S. in touch with the wider world of football: the campaign to stage the World Cup in 1994.

The idea of the U.S. playing host to the world's top sports event had been around for some time. In 1978 an application was made to FIFA proposing that the U.S. host the 1990 World Cup. That got nowhere, but the idea

was revived in 1982 when Colombia announced that it was pulling out of hosting the 1986 tournament. FIFA invited bids and the U.S. – along with Mexico and Canada – responded.

The NASL was the driving force behind the bid, believing that the staging of the World Cup could save their already faltering league. Gene Edwards, at that time the president of USSF, was lukewarm, so the NASL turned to vice-president Werner Fricker as their front man.

The USSF bid was not taken seriously by FIFA, which never bothered to inspect the U.S. facilities, and accused the Americans of over-playing their hand when they enlisted Franz Beckenbauer, Pele and Henry Kissinger to bolster their case.

The 1986 World Cup went to Mexico (Fricker later came to believe that the bid process was mere window-dressing, and that FIFA had already struck a deal with the Mexicans before it even began). With the 1990 tournament already allocated to Italy, the Americans went to work on the 1994 edition. Under the leadership of Werner Fricker, now the USSF president, a meticulously detailed bid

TAB RAMOS *(left) and Brazil's Leonardo*

document was presented to FIFA. On July 4, 1988, FIFA gave its approval.

There followed two years of increasingly difficult "co-operation" between FIFA and USSF. Fricker, determined to have his own way in everything, proved a formidable obstacle to FIFA, which regarded the World Cup as its own tournament.

Things got so bad that FIFA began to consider taking the World Cup back. Instead, it blatantly intervened in the internal politics of the USSF by

promoting the candidacy of lawyer Alan Rothenberg as an opponent to Fricker in the 1990 presidential election. At 6.20 a.m. on the morning of the election, Paul Stiehl, a third candidate, took a telephone call in his hotel room. It was FIFA's public relations director with the suggestion that

Stiehl withdraw to avoid splitting the anti-Fricker vote. Stiehl did not stand down but Rothenberg romped to victory anyway, and took over the organization of World Cup 94.

The rest of the world was sceptical about giving football's crown jewel to a country widely seen as having no tradition in, or feeling for, the sport. Many believed that FIFA's interest was merely commercial, the opening up of the world's richest nation to football, with all that meant in bringing aboard new corporate sponsors. FIFA, of course, denied the accusation and made it clear that World Cup 94 was not to be simply a one-off money-making bazaar. There had been a trade-off: in return for the right to host the World Cup, the USSF had agreed to back the formation of a pro league.

"The World Cup will be played in half-empty stadiums," had been the jibe of a leading English journalist. He could not have been more wrong. The stadiums were jammed – so jammed, in fact, that the attendance figure of 3.5 million was more than one million beyond the previous World Cup record, set in Italy in 1990.

When all the accounting had been done, when each team had been paid $685,000 for each game that it had played (another World Cup record), there was still a profit of some $60 million. This was put into a specially created foundation, to be used only to promote the development of the sport within the U.S.

Rothenberg himself had done pretty well, too, pocketing $4 million in salary, plus a $3 million bonus. These huge sums were viewed askance by the USSF's membership, which was very aware that the World Cup organizers had used over 10,000 volunteer workers. When Rothenberg stood for re-election in 1994, his World Cup triumph almost blew up in his face, as he just squeaked home on the second ballot.

PROUD MOMENT *The U.S. was the surprise team of the 1994 World Cup finals, reaching the second round, losing to eventual champion Brazil 1–0.*

MAJOR SOCCER LEAGUE

TONY MEOLA *(left) and Alexi Lalas were two home-grown stars of the fledgling Major Soccer League.*

WITH THE WORLD CUP NOW history, Rothenberg could turn his attentions full time to the matter of a pro league. Given the depressing history of failed pro leagues in the U.S., it was never going to be easy to find investors. The new league – to be called Major League Soccer, MLS – was therefore cast in a unique format, the so-called single-entity structure.

This called for many of the activities usually performed by individual clubs to be taken over by the league. The chief aim was to avoid clubs engaging in bidding wars, or paying ruinously large salaries. Under the system – dubbed "socialized soccer" by its critics – the league, not the clubs, negotiates and retains all player contracts, thus giving it close control over expenditure.

The commercial stability of the league was the overriding consideration, but the process of finding investors and sponsors was a slow one, and the scheduled 1995 start for MLS had to be postponed. Television exposure was considered essential for success, and two contracts were negotiated: one with the ESPN network ensuring the transmission of at least 35 live games, the other for 26 matches on the Spanish-language Univision network. All this before the league had signed any players!

By April 1996 everything was in place for the kick-off. Clubs had been formed in ten cities: Boston, Columbus, Dallas, Denver, Kansas City, New York, San Francisco, San Jose, Tampa, and Washington DC. Seven of the clubs were run by wealthy owner-operators each investing $10 million (they included Lamar Hunt, in Columbus) and committing themselves to at least a five-year involvement in the league. This guarantee was considered vital to avoid the constant defections that plagued the NASL – a league that only once, in its 18-year history, fielded the same line-up of clubs in consecutive seasons.

There was a late surprise, a shock almost. The assumption that Alan Rothenberg would run the show was suddenly proved incorrect. The new group of owners decided against him, and appointed as Commissioner Doug Logan, a businessman with a background in sports and entertainment promotion, but who admitted that he did not know much about football.

The three MLS teams for which owners had not been found – San Jose, Dallas and Tampa – were to be run by the league.

Under the guidance of its deputy commissioner, Sunil Gulati, MLS made a point of trying to sign creative, attacking players – particularly Latin-Americans. This was logical, and reflected the huge change that had taken place in the American soccer community since the NASL days. This change was, in turn, the result of changing immigration patterns, with vast numbers of new immigrants arriving from Mexico and Central America. Hispanic fans were expected to account for at least a third of MLS attendances. Among the first signings were Colombia's Carlos Valderrama and Mexico's flamboyant goalkeeper Jorge Campos (who could also perform as a very good centre-forward), and Italy's Roberto Donadoni.

The clubs were obliged to adhere to a maximum team salary cap of $1.3 million, with no player receiving more than the permitted maximum annual salary which, in 1996, stood at $175,000. But special deals with sponsors allowed the stars to earn more – Donadoni's annual salary was around $1 million.

CARLOS VALDERRAMA *The two-time South American Player of the Year gained a new lease of life with Tampa Bay Mutiny.*

JORGE CAMPOS *Southern California's Hispanic population in had a local hero in Mexico's flamboyant national goalkeeper ... until he signed for Chicago.*

FOUNDING FATHERS *(left to right) Alan Rothenberg, Doug Logan and Sunil Gulati helped to ensure that the MLS began operations on a firm financial footing.*

It was not the intention to have foreigners dominate MLS and each club was limited to four. Top American players then with overseas clubs – for example, Tab Ramos in Spain, John Harkes in England, Alexi Lalas in Italy – were lured back home.

The bulk of the league players would be Americans, most of them products of college soccer. The caliber of such players was undoubtedly better than it had ever been, but there were serious doubts whether there would be enough good players to populate ten teams.

In its first season, MLS acknowledged what NASL had only come to realize towards the end of its life: that college soccer could not serve as the supplier of pro players. In college, players played only between 20 and 30 games a year, many of which were not at all competitive. And, crucially, the players were all between the ages of 18 and 22; there were no games against or alongside older, more experienced players.

Project 40 was the title given to a program set up by MLS under which it signed up promising high school players or college underclass men, and assigned them to MLS clubs; each player was awarded scholarship money to enable him to continue his education. Significantly, the USSF, which had traditionally gone along with college soccer's many deficiencies (including its persistent refusal to adhere to FIFA rules) lined up alongside the pros.

Such opposition as there was from the college coaches to a scheme that would deprive them of their best players, was half-hearted. The case against the colleges was overwhelming: their players were still inadequately prepared for the pros.

MLS – with an average attendance of 17,673 and a final that, despite being played at a neutral site in pouring rain, attracted 34,643 – had a pretty successful inaugural year. The winner of the soggy final was DC United, clearly the class of the league, with two Bolivians as their stars: Marco Etcheverry and Jaime Moreno. Carlos Valderrama of the Tampa Bay Mutiny was voted the league's Most Valuable Player.

The success of the Hispanic players provided ample justification for the league's policy of signing them. The league's own surveys showed that nearly 40 per cent of their fans were of Hispanic origin. The Latin hotbed was Los Angeles, where the debut of the Los Angeles Galaxy, featuring Mexico's Jorge Campos and Ecuador's Eduardo Hurtado, drew 69,255 fans to the Rose Bowl.

Soccer purists had feared that MLS would want to play around with the game's laws, that it would try to "Americanize" things. With one exception, MLS resisted the temptation to do this. Just as the NASL had done, MLS banned tied games. Any game that ended with the score level at 90 minutes went straight into a shoot-out. Not standard penalty kicks, but the 35-yard/5-second version that had been used in the old NASL.

The reasoning was the old one that "Americans want a result, they don't like tied games." It was never a totally convincing argument, for there were tied games in the pro ice-hockey league. Why not play sudden-death overtime before the shoot-out? Because of the demands of television: MLS games had to fit into a two-hour slot, and overtime might mean the game being blacked out before a result was reached.

Events at the coaching level made it clear just how much had changed in the U.S. during the 12 years since the demise of the NASL. With MLS teams containing a majority of Americans, a sound knowledge of the American game was now necessary.

The two foreign coaches who were brought in both did poorly: Englishman Bob Houghton's

FRANKIE HEJDUK *Reversed the trend by leaving the MLS for a club in Europe.*

Colorado Rapids finished bottom of the West Division, Irishman Frank Stapleton's New England Revolution were bottom of the East Division. Neither coach lasted the season.

Significantly, the most successful coaches, the men who took their teams to the final, were Americans: DC United's Bruce Arena, and Los Angeles Galaxy's Lothar Osiander, German-born but a U.S. resident since 1962.

Arena's case was particularly instructive, as he arrived in MLS with no experience of the pro game. He had come straight from college soccer, where he had coached the University of Virginia to five Division 1 titles. His DC roster included no fewer than eight players from his former college.

In its second year of operation, 1997, MLS saw its attendance level slip slightly to 15,315, but television ratings, described as "comparable

TONY SANNEH *One of the rising stars of Major League Soccer, Washington D.C. United's midfielder scored the winner in the first MLS Cup Final in 1996.*

to college basketball and pro ice hockey", held their ground. DC United again took the honors, beating Colorado Rapids 2–1 in Soccer Bowl 97 before a crowd of 57,431.

Expansion to 12 teams was the big MLS move in 1998. The newcomers were Chicago Fire (owned by Philip Anschutz, already the owner of Colorado Rapids), and Miami Fusion, owned by newcomer Ken Horowitz who paid MLS $20 million for the rights to operate the team.

Attendances edged slightly upward to 16,083 per game, and there

was good news on the television front. A new deal, worth $5 million to MLS, was signed with ABC and ESPN for the live transmission of 59 games. In its first two years, MLS had been purchasing time from the networks, producing its own programs, and hoping to make money by selling commercial time. For the two-hour slot for MLS Cup 97, it had paid ABC $450,000.

The success story of the season was undoubtedly Chicago Fire. Breaking with the league's Latin player policy, Chicago filled its foreign slots with three Poles (including former national team captain Peter Novak) and a Czech. Strong attendances (the Fire finished third, with a game average of 17,887) were matched by success on the field as the team took MLS Cup '98 by defeating DC United 2–0. Much less pleasing was the manner of Chicago's win, which was based on defensive,

counter-attacking tactics, particularly in the playoffs. Chicago won two of its four playoff games in shootouts, and scored a total of only four goals, two of them from penalty kicks. A trend toward defensive play was the last thing that MLS needed – a league struggling to establish itself in the face of the by-now almost traditional criticism in the media that the sport didn't feature enough scoring.

During the first two MLS seasons, the league had been not only negotiating contracts, but actually picking players. Now the situation was much

closer to the standard worldwide procedure: club coaches were selecting their own players (the league still did the contract negotiations). And the coaches were evidently more cautious in their selections.

A festering problem for MLS was the continued lackluster performance of the New York/New Jersey MetroStars. It has long been held that one of the essentials for the success of any pro sports league in the U.S. is a strong team in New York. This is not simply a matter of the vast audience in the area, but because the city is such an important focus for the advertising and television industries and other major corporate activities.

By the end of 1998, the MetroStars had already used up four coaches, including Carlos Alberto Parreira, who guided Brazil to its 1994 World Cup win. In 1996 they squeaked into the playoffs, but were knocked out immediately; in 1997 they failed to qualify. At the end of the 1998 season, the MetroStars again just managed to make the playoffs; at this late stage they fired coach Alfonso Mondelo, and brought in Bora Milutinovic, who had been coach of the US national team during the 1994 World Cup. There were no miracles from Milutinovic and the MetroStars were promptly eliminated, badly beaten by Colorado Rapids in the first two games of the three-game series.

For MLS, 1999 was to prove a troublesome year. In February, Commissioner Doug Logan suddenly fired his deputy, Sunil Gulati. The circumstances were unclear, but it seemed that MetroStars owner Stuart Subotnick felt that Gulati had misled him over the re-signing of Tab Ramos.

Internal politics were at work, too. For three years Logan had operated in Gulati's shadow. Inevitably, because Logan knew no soccer, and Gulati was the league's highly articulate and knowledgeable soccer person. Logan had now removed his rival, but Gulati's enforced departure meant that MLS would enter the season without anyone at the top level who had any understanding of the sport.

Logan now had to deal with soccer matters, and his efforts were predictably ill-informed. Confronted at the start of the season by a rash of low-scor-

ing games that went to the shoot-out, Logan said that maybe the cold weather was keeping the scoring down.

What did seem to be happening was that clubs were aping the defensive success of the Chicago Fire. Certainly, the impression gained ground that MLS had lost its early glamour. The new foreign-player signings were no longer top stars. Everything seemed to be stagnating. Logan could offer no leadership, and half way through the season he was fired.

His replacement was Don Garber, a marketing executive who moved over from the National (Gridiron) Football League. Again, some one with no knowledge of football. MLS admitted that it had some problems. "We started with a bang, it levelled off and we're creeping up again," said Subotnick. "That's OK if you want a middling business. We don't." But the answer was seen in terms of better marketing. Many critics considered that a misguided approach, and that more attention should be paid to improving the level of play.

Nor did Garber's early, sweeping statement that he intended to "be an advocate of the game to the fans" help matters. Coming from some one whose knowledge of football was zero, it sounded like arrogance.

An immediate problem for Garber to solve was the continuing awfulness of the MetroStars. When the team had played its first ever game in 1996 – a new team full of players unknown to local fans – it had drawn a crowd of 46,826 to Giants Stadium. By the end of the 1999 regular season, it was drawing around 6,000, it had the worst record of all 12 MLS teams, had set a league record by losing 12 games in a row, and failed to make the playoffs.

Possibly, help was on the way. It was announced that Lothar Matthäus would join the MetroStars in 2000. A superstar signing that would certainly help the league's credibility. But the notion that a single player – a 39-year-old at that – could turn things around at the MetroStars seemed fanciful.

On the brighter side for the sport, the league, and for Garber were events in Columbus. Columbus Crew had had stadium problems right from the start, being forced to play on a field barely 62 yards wide. In this, they symbolized a huge problem that had bedevilled American pro football from its earliest days in the 1920s: a total absence of professional-quality football-specific stadiums. Pro football was always forced to play either in baseball stadiums (which are the wrong shape, and where the field often has to include the dirt infield of the baseball diamond) or gridiron football stadiums, which are usually too narrow, might be of artificial turf and are likely to bear a maze of confusing gridiron markings.

When a referendum to build a new civic stadium was turned down by the Columbus taxpayers, the owner of the Crew decided to act. Fortunately, the owner was Lamar Hunt, whose 30-year faith in the future of pro soccer had never wavered. A site was selected on the outskirts of Columbus, and Hunt spent $28.5 million building the US's first pro-football stadium. The capac-

CHAMPIONS *John Harkes (middle) and D.C. United won the inaugural MLS Cup.*

ity was 22,500, and the design included features that would allow future expansion to 40,000.

Columbus fans responded by purchasing over 9,000 season tickets for the 1999 season, by far the largest total in MLS. There was talk that other MLS clubs might follow the Columbus lead. Among them were the MetroStars, who for four years had born the cost of laying down a grass field in Giants Stadium, and then when gridiron football took over late in the season, having to take it up and play on plastic.

Another positive sign for MLS was the encouraging performance of young American players, with a number of Project40 players holding down starting spots.

But even the success of American players had its drawbacks, and MLS began to discover a problem that had long worried clubs elsewhere in the world, particularly in South America. When the league produced an exceptional player, it risked losing him to a European club, where the rewards were greater. DC United's Tony Sanneh joined Hertha Berlin, Tampa's Frank Hejduk went to Bayer Leverkusen, Marcus Hahnemann to Fulham. Eddie Pope (DC United) turned down offers from Germany, and top-scorer Stern John (Columbus) – a Trinidadian international – signed for Nottingham Forest in fall 1999.

The problem was not limited to senior players: the U.S. team that participated in the 1999 under-17 World Cup in New Zealand included two players already signed with German pro clubs.

MARCO ETCHEVERRY *Ejected in the first game of USA '94, the Bolivian (right) has enjoyed happier times as a full-time player with D.C. United in the U.S.*

THE U.S. ON THE WORLD STAGE

JOHN SOUZA *One of the best players in post World War 2 U.S.*

BRUCE ARENA *The U.S. national coach who took over from Steve Sampson in 1998 defeated Germany twice and Argentina once in his first year in charge.*

DESPITE THE EARLY START – that 1885 game against Canada – it took the U.S. more than a hundred years before its national team began to make an impact at the international level.

Of course, there were those early World Cup adventures. In the first-ever tournament in 1930 the U.S. reached the semi-finals with a team that included a number of naturalized Brits, but also featured two of the first stars of the American game – Bert Patenaude and Billy "Piano Legs" Gonsalves, both from the Portuguese community in Fall River, Massachusetts.

In the 1950 World Cup came the famous 1–0 win over England, with most of the team consisting of American born-and-bred players. There were the Souza brothers, John and Ed, from that traditional hotbed, Fall River. But St Louis was now making its claim to be the centre of American football, and five of the squad, including defenders Harry Keough, Charley Colombo and goal-keeper Frank Borghi were from the midwest city. There was, however, considerable doubt whether three foreign-born members of the team (including goal-scorer Joe Gaetjens, holder of a Haitian passport) were eligible to play for the U.S.

After 1950, the U.S. experienced 40 years of futility when it came to the World Cup. Every four years it entered the qualifying rounds, and every time – nine times in all – it flopped badly. Usually it was Mexico that took the one place available to the Concacaf region, though in 1974 little Haiti proved that Mexico could be beaten. Even when the Concacaf allotment was increased to two in 1982 the U.S. still couldn't make it in either 1982 or 1986.

Ironically, the span took in the years when the U.S. had its strongest-yet pro league, the NASL. The failure of the national team lent credence to the criticism that the NASL employed too many foreigners and was doing nothing for the development of the domestic game.

At last, in 1990, the US returned to the World Cup finals. It was not a happy return. Coach Bob Gansler's experience was primarily in coaching the college game; he built a young team based on college players which proved far too green to cope with the rigors of World Cup play in Italy. After being wiped out 5–1 in its first game against Czechoslovakia, defense took over, and the team played two unimaginative but narrow losses, 1–0 to host Italy, and 2–1 to Austria.

When the U.S.' moment in the sun came round four years later, when it staged the World Cup, only six of the players from 1990 were on the team. Gone, too, was coach Gansler, replaced by Bora Milutinovic, who had coached Mexico in the 1986 tournament, Costa Rica in 1990.

The changes reflected a massive change in the sport. A new, professional USSF was in the making, upgrading itself from the rather sleepy volunteer organization that it had always been. Gone were the days when the national team was assembled only a day or two before a game, or even at the airport itself!

Money was no longer a problem; sponsors, lured by the glamour of the World Cup, were falling over themselves to buy into the national team.

Because the absence of a pro league presented a problem in training the players, the USSF purchased

ON TOP OF THE WORLD *Ernie Stewart (middle) celebrates his goal which clinched U.S. team's famous 2–1 upset victory over one of the tournament's favored teams, Colombia. The victory vindicated FIFA's decision to bring the tournament to the U.S. and led to an upsurge in interest in soccer.*

the contracts of a number of players, and set them up in a permanent training centre in Mission Viejo, California. On the final 22-man U.S. roster, 12 players were under contract to the USSF. The other ten were playing for foreign teams including Tab Ramos (Betis, Spain), John Harkes (Derby County, England), Cle Kooiman (Cruz Azul, Mexico), Eric Wynalda (Bochum, Germany). The team included five naturalized players, among them the captain Thomas Dooley, a German-born son of a US serviceman and a veteran of the Bundesliga with Bayer Leverkusen.

Milutinovic's US played inconsistently throughout a heavy series of exhibition games – recording wins over Uruguay, Mexico, England,

Romania and Ireland, but losing to the likes of Iceland, Honduras, Australia and Japan.

The aim for 1994 was modest: to get into the second round, something that no host team had ever failed to do. It was accomplished – just. With a tie against Switzerland and a victory over Colombia, the US advanced as a third-place team. Its next opponent, eventual champions Brazil, proved far too strong, and, despite playing with ten men for the entire second half, beat the U.S. 1–0.

After USA 94 it was clear to the USSF that it needed to concentrate on building up a nationwide system of player development. Milutinovic's international experience was no longer needed, and his contract was not

renewed. His assistant, the American-born Steve Sampson, was appointed as a stop-gap while the USSF searched for the right man. But Sampson came up with a string of excellent results – in particular a fourth-place finish in the 1995 Copa America (the U.S. played as a guest team) that included a 3–0 win over Argentina. He was confirmed as coach but only for the qualifying games for World Cup 98. When the U.S. did qualify, there was a long pause before Alan Rothenberg, the USSF president, announced that Sampson would coach the team in France.

The doubts about Sampson were evidently justified. His sensational decision suddenly to omit captain Harkes from the final roster was unsettling. Sampson felt that Harkes

could not play in midfield with the rising star of US soccer, Claudio Reyna. Sampson's team selections led to open dissension in France. The team's performance was well below its best level – it lost all three game, and finished in last place among the 32 teams. Sampson was fired as soon as the US was eliminated.

The new coach was Bruce Arena. In his three seasons (1996–98) with the MLS club DC United he had taken them to the final each year, winning two of the championships. He was widely hailed as someone who knew how to get the best out of American players.

His appointment marked the opening of a new era, as the veteran players of the past two World Cups passed from the scene. With serious games – i.e. qualifiers for the 2002 World Cup – still two years away, Arena set to work blooding younger players. In this he had a vital tool that was denied to Sampson: the existence of a pro league, the MLS.

Most of Arena's newcomers were MLS players such as Eddie Lewis (San Jose), Chris Armas and C.J.Brown (Chicago), Tony Sanneh and Ben Olsen (D.C.Utd), Frankie Hejduk (Tampa Bay). Two – Jovan Kirovski (Cologne, Germany) and John O'Brien (Ajax, Holland) – were examples of a new trend: Americans who had gone to Europe while still of high school age and matured with European clubs. But on one point at least, Arena clearly agreed with Sampson: the key man on his team was to be Claudio Reyna.

While Arena experimented quietly with the men's team, a new phenomenon exploded noisily on the scene: women's football. There was a huge irony here. For the very thing that had for so long held the men's game back – college football – was what gave the American women their lead over the rest of the world. In no other country was the sport given the attention and the backing that it received in the American colleges. It greatly benefited from the government's Title IX regulations, which made it an offense not to provide equal sports opportunities for men and women. In 1974 the total of officially recognized women's teams in NCAA colleges had been ... none. By 1998 it was 791, more than the men's figure of 718.

The staging of the 1999 Women's World Cup, with the victory of the US team, proved a stunning success, with huge crowds and high television ratings (see pages 40–43). But many felt that the enthusiasm engendered owed more to feminism and patriotism than to any devotion to football. It remained to be seen whether the sudden popularity of the women's team would have any lasting effect on the popularity of the sport itself.

BORDER RIVALS *Alexi Lalas (22) and John Harkes (6) try to stop a Mexican forward during a 1996 international.*

THE MAJOR COMPETITIONS

International soccer has grown in piecemeal fashion since the first match between Scotland and England in November 1872. Some competitions, like the Mitropa Cup, faded and disappeared. But the strongest, like the World Cup for nations and the Copa Libertadores and the European club cups, flourished as a world-wide competitive structure developed.

First there was the British Home Championship, the South American Championship and the Mitropa Cup for continental Europe's top clubs, then the World Cup itself . . . by the start of the 1930s the foundations of today's international competitive structure had been laid. The 1950s brought a further expansion, with the success of the European club cups and the launch of the European Championship. Each developing geographical region copied the competitive structures of Europe.

Now the sheer weight of the international fixture list has led soccer's world governing body, FIFA, into designing a worldwide fixture schedule around which the game can organize into the next century.

To qualify for the World Cup, many nations play around a dozen matches. When the various club competitions are added, top players can face around 70 games year with very little let-up.

THE WORLD CUP

The World Cup was conceived by FIFA's founders, but the driving force behind its launch was Frenchman Jules Rimet, the president of both FIFA and the French federation in the 1920s. The British had shunned FIFA's first meeting in Paris in 1904, and by the time the inaugural World Cup tournament was introduced in 1930 they had both joined and then withdrawn from the world governing body over the question of broken time payments for amateurs.

Italy, Holland, Spain, Sweden and Uruguay all applied to stage the tournament, but the European countries withdrew after an impassioned plea from the Latin Americans, who in 1930 would be celebrating one hundred years of independence.

Uruguay were to build a new stadium in Montevideo and would pay all travelling and hotel expenses for the competing nations. However, faced by a three-week boat trip each way, the Europeans were reluctant to participate, and two months before the competition not one European entry had been received. Meanwhile, Argentina, Brazil, Paraguay, Peru, Chile, Mexico and Bolivia had all accepted, as well as the United States.

The Latin American federations were bitter and threatened to withdraw from FIFA. Eventually France, Belgium, Yugoslavia and, under the influence of King Carol, Romania, all relented and travelled to Uruguay.

URUGUAY 1930
Triumph for ambitious party-throwers

Because of the limited response the 13 teams were split into four groups, with Uruguay, Argentina, Brazil and the USA the seeded nations.

On the afternoon of Sunday, July 13, France opened the tournament against Mexico, and in the 10th minute lost goalkeeper Alex Thepot, who was kicked on the jaw. Left-half Chantrel took over between the posts (there would be no substitutes

VIVE LA FRANCE *French coach Aime Jacquet shows off the World Cup trophy*

for another forty years), but even with 10 men the French proved too good. Goals by Laurent, Langiller and Maschinot gave them a 3–0 advantage before Carreno replied for Mexico. Maschinot then grabbed a second to complete a 4–1 victory for France.

Two days later France lost to Argentina through a goal scored by Monti, nine minutes from time. The game had finished in chaos when Brazilian referee Almeida Rego ended the game six minutes early just as Langiller raced through for a possible equalizer. In their next match, against Mexico, Argentina brought in young Guillermo Stabile, known as "El Infiltrador". He scored three goals in Argentina's 6–3 victory – in a game of five penalties – and finished as the top scorer of the tournament.

Argentina topped Group 1, while from Group 2 Yugoslavia qualified with victories over Brazil and Bolivia. The USA were most impressive in Group 4, reaching the semi-final without conceding a goal. However, their direct-play tactics were no match for Argentina, who cruised into the Final 6–1. In the other semi-final Uruguay dispatched Yugoslavia by the same margin to set up a repeat of the 1928 Olympic Final.

On this occasion Pablo Dorado shot Uruguay into a 12th-minute lead but Peucelle equalized and Argentina forged ahead in the 35th minute with a disputed goal by Stabile – who the Urugayans claimed was offside! Excitement grew when Pedro Cea made it 2–2 just after half time. In the 65th minute outside-left Santos Iriarte made it 3–2 for Uruguay, who underlined their victory with a fourth goal, smashed into the net by Castro in the closing seconds.

ITALY 1934
Tetchy Europeans battle it out

RESPITE *Italy prepare for extra time*

Uruguay are the only World Cup winners in history who did not defend their title. Upset by the Europeans' reluctance to participate in 1930, and plagued by players' strikes, they stayed at home.

No fewer than 32 countries – 22 from Europe, eight from the Americas and one each from Asia and Africa – played a qualifying series in which even hosts Italy had to take part, and before the competition proper got under way the USA beat Mexico in Rome, but then crashed 7–1 to Italy in Turin.

Of the 16 finalists, Italy and Hugo Meisl's "Wunderteam" were the clear favourites, though the Austrians, who were just past their peak, were taken to extra time by a spirited French side in the first knockout round. Belgium led Germany 2–1 at half-time, then crumbled as Conen, Germany's center-forward, completed a hat-trick in a 5–2 win.

Brazil, beaten 3–1 by Spain, and Argentina, defeated 3–2 by Sweden, had travelled 8,000 miles to play one solitary game.

Spain forced Italy to a replay in the second round after a physical 1–1 draw was not resolved by extra time. In the replay, the following day, Meazza's 12th-minute header put Italy into the semi-finals. Austria, who led Hungary 2–0 after 51 minutes through Horwarth and Zischek, then found themselves in what Meisl described as "a brawl, not an exhibition of football." Sarosi replied for Hungary from the penalty spot, but the Magyars' comeback was spoiled when Markos foolishly got himself sent off.

Italy and Austria now faced each other in the semi-finals. A muddy field was not conducive to good soccer and Italy won when right-winger Guaita capitalized on a brilliant set-play, following a corner, to score in the 18th minute. Czechoslovakia, the conquerers of Romania and Switzerland joined Italy in the Final after a 3–1 victory over Germany, with two goals by Nejedly.

In the Final, Puc shot the Czechs into a deserved 70th-minute lead, Italian keeper Combi reacting late to the shot from 20 yards. Sobotka then squandered a fine opportunity and Svoboda rattled a post as the Czechs impressed with their short-passing precision. With eight minutes left the Slavs were still 1–0 ahead. Then left-winger Raimondo Orsi left Czech defenders in his wake as he dribbled through on goal. He shaped to shoot with his left but hit the ball with his right foot. The ball spun crazily goal-wards, and though Planicka got his fingers to it, he could not prevent a goal. Schiavio grabbed the Italian winner seven minutes into extra time. Italy were World Champions.

FRANCE 1938
Italians make it two in a row

Europe was in turmoil, Argentina and Uruguay were absent but the tournament welcomed for the first time Cuba, Poland and Dutch East Indies.

1930

Pool 1									
France	4	Mexico	1
Argentina	1	France	0
Chile	3	Mexico	0
Chile	1	France	0
Argentina	6	Mexico	3
Argentina	3	Chile	1

	P	W	D	L	F	A	Pts
Argentina	3	3	0	0	10	4	6
Chile	3	2	0	1	5	3	4
France	3	1	0	2	4	3	2
Mexico	3	0	0	3	4	13	0

Pool 2				
Yugoslavia	2	Brazil	1
Yugoslavia	4	Bolivia	0
Brazil	4	Bolivia	0

	P	W	D	L	F	A	Pts
Yugoslavia	2	2	0	0	6	1	4
Brazil	2	1	0	1	5	2	2
Bolivia	2	0	0	2	0	8	0

Pool 3				
Romania	3	Peru	1
Uruguay	1	Peru	0
Uruguay	4	Romania	0

		P	W	D	L	F	A	Pts
Uruguay		2	2	0	0	5	0	4
Romania		2	1	0	1	3	5	2
Peru		2	0	0	2	1	4	0

Pool 4				
USA	3	Belgium	0
USA	3	Paraguay	0
Paraguay	1	Belgium	0

	P	W	D	L	F	A	Pts
USA	2	2	0	0	6	0	4
Paraguay	2	1	0	1	1	3	2
Belgium	2	0	0	2	0	4	0

Semi-finals			
Argentina	6	USA	1
Uruguay	6	Yugoslavia	1

Final

Uruguay (1) 4	Argentina (2) 2
Dorado, Cea,	*Peucelle,*
Iriarte, Castro	*Stabile*

ARGENTINA Botasso, Della Torre, Paternoster, Evaristo J., Monti, Suarez, Peucelle, Varallo, Stabile, Ferreira (capt.), Evaristo M.

Leading scorers:
8 Stabile (Argentina); 5 Cea (Uruguay).

URUGUAY Ballesteros, Nasazzi (capt.), Mascheroni, Andrade, Fernandez, Gestido, Dorado, Scarone, Castro, Cea, Iriarte.

1934

First round			
Italy	7	USA	1
Czech.	2	Romania	1
Germany	5	Belgium	2
Austria	3	France	2*
Spain	3	Brazil	1
Switzerland	3	Holland	2
Sweden	3	Argentina	2
Hungary	4	Egypt	2

Second round			
Germany	2	Sweden	1
Austria	2	Hungary	1
Italy	1	Spain	1*
Italy	1	Spain	0®
Czech.	3	Switzerland	2

Semi-finals			
Czech.	3	Germany	1
Italy	1	Austria	0

Third place match

Germany	3	Austria	2

Final

Italy	(0) 2	Czech.	(0) 1*
Orsi, Schiavio		*Puc*	

ITALY Combi (capt.), Monzeglio, Allemandi, Ferraris, Monti, Bertolini, Guaita, Meazza, Schiavio, Ferrari, Orsi.

CZECHOSLOVAKIA Planicka (capt.), Zenisek, Ctyroky, Kostalek, Cambal, Kreil, Junek, Svoboda, Sobotka, Nejedly, Puc.

Leading scorers:
4 Nejedly (Czechoslovakia), Schiavio (Italy), Conen (Germany).

*Notes: * After extra time ® Replay*

BACK TO BACK *Vittorio Pozzo brandishes the World Cup in Paris*

In the first round only Hungary, who eclipsed the Dutch East Indies 6–0, and France – 3–1 winners over Belgium – came through in 90 minutes, all the other ties going to extra time or replays. Defending champions Italy were saved by their goalkeeper Olivieri, who made a blinding save from Norwegian center-forward Brunyldsen in the last minute of the game to earn extra time, and Piola struck to see them through.

Brazil emerged from the mud of Strasbourg after an 11-goal thriller. A Leonidas hat-trick gave the South Americans a 3–1 half-time lead, but the Poles ran riot after the half to force extra time. Willimowski netted four times but by then Leonidas had grabbed his fourth to help Brazil to a 6–5 win! The second round provided no shocks, though Brazil needed two games to eliminate Czechoslovakia and earn a semi-final joust with Italy, whose captain, Meazza, converted the winning penalty. In the other semi-final, Hungary beat Sweden, 5–1.

When Italy met Hungary in the final, Colaussi drilled Italy ahead in the sixth minute after a scintillating run almost the length of the field from Biavati, but Titkos equalized from close range within a minute. Then, with inside-forwards Meazza and Ferrari in dazzling form, Italy asserted themselves. Piola scored in the 15th minute, and Colaussi made it 3–1 in the 35th. In the 65th minute Sarosi forced the ball over the Italian line, but a magnificent back-heeled pass from Biavati set up Piola to smash in the decisive goal.

BRAZIL 1950
Hosts upstaged in final act

The first tournament after the war – for what was now known as the Jules Rimet Trophy – was to prove a thriller. Argentina refused to play in Brazil, and the Czechs and Scots declined to take their places, but England were there for the first time.

The competition was arranged, as in 1930, on a pool basis. Brazil won Pool 1 despite a 2–2 draw with Switzerland, and Uruguay topped two-team Pool 4, where they thrashed Bolivia 8–0. The shocks came in Pools 2 and 3. Italy started well enough, Riccardo Carapellese shooting them into a seventh-minute lead against Sweden. But by half time they were 2–1 down to goals from Jeppson and Sune Andersson. Jeppson grabbed another midway through the second half and, though Muccinelli replied and Carapellese hit the crossbar, this was Sweden's day. It was a setback the Italians were unable to overcome.

The greatest shock of all time, however, was to beset England. After a 2–0 victory over Chile, the game against the USA in Belo Horizonte seemed a formality. Instead it became a fiasco. England hit the crossbar and found goalkeeper Borghi unbeatable. Then in the 37th minute the impossible happened. Bahr shot from the left and Gaetjens got a touch with his head to divert the ball into the net. 1–0 to the USA!

There was no final in this competition, Brazil, Uruguay, Sweden and Spain qualifying for the Final Pool. The hosts were favored as they faced Uruguay in the last game (a virtual final), a point ahead. A draw would make Brazil champions.

It proved a real thriller. Brazil's much-acclaimed inside-forward trio of Zizinho, Ademir and Jair, weaving gloriously through the Uruguayan defence, found goalkeeper Maspoli playing the game of his life. The giant Varela proved another stumbling block, as did Andrade. They cracked in the 47th minute, Friaca shooting past Maspoli. Uruguay's response was positive, and in the 65th minute Ghiggia's cross found Schiaffino unmarked – his thunderous shot gave Barbosa no hope. Brazil were shaken, the fizz went out of their game, and when Ghiggia ran in to score in the 79th minute they were beaten. After 20 years the World Cup returned to Uruguay.

1938

First round								
Switzerland	1	Germany	1*					
Switzerland	4	Germany	2®					
Cuba	3	Rumania	3*					
Cuba	2	Rumania	1®					
Hungary	6	Dutch E.Ind.	0					
France	3	Belgium	1					
Czech.	3	Holland	0*					

Brazil	6	Poland	5*
Italy	2	Norway	1*

Second round

Sweden	8	Cuba	0
Hungary	2	Switzerland	0
Italy	3	France	1
Brazil	1	Czech.	1*
Brazil	2	Czech.	1®

Semi-finals

Italy	2	Brazil	1
Hungary	5	Sweden	1

Third place match

Brazil	4	Sweden	2

Final

Italy	(3) 4	Hungary (1)	2

Colaussi (2),   *Titkos, Sarosi*
Piola (2)

ITALY Olivieri, Foni, Rava, Serantoni, Andreolo, Locatelli, Biavati, Meazza (capt.), Piola, Ferrari, Colaussi.

HUNGARY Szabo, Polgar, Biro, Szalay, Szucs, Lazar, Sas, Vincze, Sarosi (capt.), Szengeller, Titkos.

Leading scorers
8 Leonidas (Brazil); 7 Szengeller (Hungary); 5 Piola (Italy).

1950

First round Pool 1

Brazil	4	Mexico	0
Yugoslavia	3	Switzerland	0
Yugoslavia	4	Mexico	1
Brazil	2	Switzerland	2
Brazil	2	Yugoslavia	0
Switzerland	2	Mexico	1

	P	W	D	L	F	A	Pts
Brazil	3	2	1	0	8	2	5
Yugoslavia	3	2	0	1	7	3	4
Switzerland	3	1	1	1	4	6	3
Mexico	3	0	0	3	2	10	0

Pool 2

Spain	3	USA	1

England	2	Chile	0
USA	1	England	0
Spain	2	Chile	0
Spain	1	England	0
Chile	5	USA	2

	P	W	D	L	F	A	Pts
Spain	3	3	0	0	6	1	6
England	3	1	0	2	2	2	2
Chile	3	1	0	2	5	6	2
USA	3	1	0	2	4	8	2

Pool 3

Sweden	3	Italy	2
Sweden	2	Paraguay	2
Italy	2	Paraguay	0

	P	W	D	L	F	A	Pts
Sweden	2	1	1	0	5	4	3
Italy	2	1	0	1	4	3	2
Paraguay	2	0	1	1	2	4	1

Pool 4

Uruguay	8	Bolivia	0

	P	W	D	L	F	A	Pts
Uruguay	1	1	0	0	8	0	2
Bolivia	1	0	0	1	0	8	0

Final pool

Uruguay	2	Spain	2
Brazil	7	Sweden	1
Uruguay	3	Sweden	2
Brazil	6	Spain	1
Sweden	3	Spain	1
Uruguay	2	Brazil	1

	P	W	D	L	F	A	Pts
Uruguay	3	2	1	0	7	5	5
Brazil	3	2	0	1	14	4	4
Sweden	3	1	0	2	6	11	2
Spain	3	0	1	2	4	11	1

Deciding match

Uruguay	(0) 2	Brazil (0)	1

Schiaffino,   *Friaca*
Ghiggia

URUGUAY Maspoli, Gonzales, M., Tejera, Gambetta, Varela, Andrade, Ghiggia, Perez, Miguez, Schiaffino, Moran.

BRAZIL Barbosa, Augusto, Juvenal, Bauer, Danilo, Bigode, Friaca, Zizinho, Ademir, Jair, Chico.

Leading scorers:
9 Ademir (Brazil); 6 Schiaffino (Uruguay); 5 Zarra (Spain).

*Notes: * After extra time ® Replay*

SWITZERLAND 1954
'Magic Magyars' found out by astute Germans

Hungary arrived in Zurich as the hottest ever World Cup favorites. The magic of Puskas, Hidegkuti and Kocsis had added a new dimension to the beautiful game and, what is more, had proved an unbeatable combination in the 1952 Olympic tournament.

No one was really surprised when the Magyars rattled in 17 goals in their opening pool matches against Korea and Germany. Kocsis scored four against the Germans but Hungary were left a significant legacy by their opponents, center-half Werner Liebrich delivering a fateful kick on Puskas that caused him to retire from the match in the 30th minute. It was an injury from which he never fully recovered during the remainder

NOT SO FAST *Morlock gets one back*

of the tournament. Hungary of course cruised into the quarter-finals, where they dispatched Brazil 4–2, but Germany had to win a play-off with Turkey to earn the right to face Yugoslavia.

England began with a 4–4 draw with Belgium, yet secured a quarter-final place with a 2–0 win over Switzerland. The Scots were not so successful. They failed to score and were beaten by Austria and Uruguay,

neither of whom conceded a goal in their pool. Stanley Matthews and Schiaffino took the individual honors as Uruguay beat England 4–2, but the competition was sullied by a notorious clash between Brazil and Hungary, which was dubbed "The Battle of Berne". Three players were sent off, and a shameful fight ensued in the dressing-rooms afterwards. If that was infamous, then the Austria-Switzerland tie was incredible. The Swiss scored three in 20 minutes, and Austria replied with three in three minutes. In one seven-minute period, there were five goals! Eventually Austria came out 7–5 winners.

Puskas returned for the Final, but it was a mistake. Although he scored the opening goal in a devastating start which saw Hungary score twice in eight minutes, his ankle was not fully recovered. Morlock replied for Germany in the 11th minute and Rahn blasted in two fine goals – the last only seven minutes from time – to win it for Germany.

SWEDEN 1958
Brazil teach the world a soccer lesson

Brazil enthralled the world in this competition, which was notable for the emergence of 4–2–4 and the outstanding individual talents of stars such as Didi, Garrincha, Vava and the teenager Pele. France too were to perform with style, Just Fontaine and Raymond Kopa providing the magic, while hosts Sweden provided their share of surprises.

West Germany headed Pool 1, where Northern Ireland, who had eliminated Italy in the qualifying rounds, caused an upset by beating Czechoslovakia in a play-off to earn a quarter-final tie with France, who headed Pool 2 with Yugoslavia. Likewise Wales also made the quarter-finals, following a play-off with Hungary, and did themselves proud

1954

Pool 1

Yugoslavia	1	France	0
Brazil	5	Mexico	0
France	3	Mexico	2
Brazil	1	Yugoslavia	1

	P	W	D	L	F	A	Pts
Brazil	2	1	1	0	6	1	3
Yugoslavia	2	1	1	0	2	1	3
France	2	1	0	1	3	3	2
Mexico	2	0	0	2	2	8	0

Pool 2

Hungary	9	Korea	0
W. Germany	4	Turkey	1
Hungary	8	W. Germany	3
Turkey	7	Korea	0

Hungary	2	2	0	0	17	3	4
W. Germany	2	1	0	1	7	9	2
Turkey	2	1	0	1	8	4	2
Korea	2	0	0	2	0	16	0

(with headers P W D L F A Pts)

Play-off

W. Germany	7	Turkey	2

Pool 3

Austria	1	Scotland	0
Uruguay	2	Czech.	0
Austria	5	Czech.	0
Uruguay	7	Scotland	0

	P	W	D	L	F	A	Pts
Uruguay	2	2	0	0	9	0	4
Austria	2	2	0	0	6	0	4
Czech.	2	0	0	2	0	7	0
Scotland	2	0	0	2	0	8	0

Pool 4

England	4	Belgium	4
England	2	Switzerland	0
Switzerland	2	Italy	1
Italy	4	Belgium	1

	P	W	D	L	F	A	Pts
England	2	1	1	0	6	4	3
Italy	2	1	0	1	5	3	2
Switzerland	2	1	0	1	2	3	2
Belgium	2	0	1	1	5	8	1

Play-off

Switzerland	4	Italy	1

Quarter-finals

W. Germany	2	Yugoslavia	0
Hungary	4	Brazil	2
Austria	7	Switzerland	5
Uruguay	4	England	2

Semi-finals

W. Germany	6	Austria	1
Hungary	4	Uruguay	2

Third-place match

Austria	3	Uruguay	1

Final

W. Germany	(2)	3	Hungary	(2)	2
Morlock,			*Puskas, Czibor*		
Rahn (2)					

WEST GERMANY: Turek, Posipal, Kohlmeyer, Eckel, Liebrich, Mai, Rahn, Morlock, Walter O., Walter F (capt.), Schäfer.
HUNGARY: Grosics, Buzansky, Lantos, Bozsik, Lorant, Zakarias, Czibor, Kocsis, Hidegkuti, Puskas (capt.), Toth J.

Leading scorers

11 Kocsis (Hungary); 8 Morlock (W. Germany); 6 Probst (Austria), Hügi (Switzerland).

1958

Pool 1

W. Germany	3	Argentina	1
N. Ireland	1	Czech.	0
W.Germany	2	Czech.	2
Argentina	3	N. Ireland	1
W. Germany	2	N. Ireland	2
Czech.	6	Argentina	1

	P	W	D	L	F	A	Pts
W. Germany	3	1	2	0	7	5	4
Czech.	3	1	1	1	8	4	3
N. Ireland	3	1	1	1	4	5	3
Argentina	3	1	0	2	5	10	2

Play-off

N. Ireland	2	Czech.	1

Pool 2

France	7	Paraguay	3
Yugoslavia	1	Scotland	1
Yugoslavia	3	France	2
Paraguay	3	Scotland	2
France	2	Scotland	1
Yugoslavia	3	Paraguay	3

	P	W	D	L	F	A	Pts
France	3	2	0	1	11	7	4
Yugoslavia	3	1	2	0	7	6	4
Paraguay	3	1	1	1	9	12	3
Scotland	3	0	1	2	4	6	1

Pool 3

Sweden	3	Mexico	0
Hungary	1	Wales	1
Wales	1	Mexico	1
Sweden	2	Hungary	1
Sweden	0	Wales	0
Hungary	4	Mexico	0

	P	W	D	L	F	A	Pts
Sweden	3	2	1	0	5	1	5
Hungary	3	1	1	1	6	3	3
Wales	3	0	3	0	2	2	3
Mexico	3	0	1	2	1	8	1

Play-off

Wales	2	Hungary	1

Pool 4

England	2	Soviet Union	2
Brazil	3	Austria	0
England	0	Brazil	0
Soviet Union	2	Austria	0
Brazil	2	Soviet Union	0
England	2	Austria	2

	P	W	D	L	F	A	Pts
Brazil	3	2	1	0	5	0	5
England	3	0	3	0	4	4	3
Soviet Union	3	1	1	1	4	4	3
Austria	3	0	1	2	2	7	1

Play-off

Soviet Union	1	England	0

Quarter-finals

France	4	N. Ireland	0
W. Germany	1	Yugoslavia	0
Sweden	2	Soviet Union	0
Brazil	1	Wales	0

Semi-finals

Brazil	5	France	2
Sweden	3	W. Germany	1

Third place match

France	6	W. Germany	3

Final

Brazil		(2) 5	Sweden	(1)	2
Vava (2),			*Liedholm*		
Pele (2), Zagallo			*Simonsson*		

BRAZIL: Gilmar, Santos D., Santos N., Zito, Bellini (capt.), Orlando, Garrincha, Didi, Vava, Pele, Zagallo.

SWEDEN: Svensson, Bergmark, Axbom, Boerjesson, Gustavsson, Parling, Hamrin, Gren, Simonsson, Liedholm (capt.), Skoglund.

Leading scorers

13 Fontaine (France); 6 Pele (Brazil), Rahn (W. Germany); 5 Vava (Brazil), McParland (N. Ireland).

by limiting Brazil to one goal, inevitably scored by Pele. Brazil had comfortably emerged from Pool 4 without conceding a goal, but England were knocked out, when they lost 1–0 to Russia in another play-off.

The semi-finals pitted Sweden against West Germany and Brazil against France. Hans Schäfer blasted West Germany into the lead with a spectacular volley from 25 yards. Sweden's equalizer from Skoglund should not have been given – Liedholm blatantly controlling the ball with a hand before setting up the chance. Juskowiak was sent off in the 57th minute, and Sweden took full advantage to clinch their Final place with goals from Gren and Hamrin. Brazil took a second-minute lead against France thanks to a spectacular finish from Vava. Fontaine equalized within nine minutes, but Didi restored the lead for the South Americans, and in the second half young Pele ran riot with three more goals.

There was a sensational start to the Final, when Liedholm kept his poise and balance to shoot Sweden into a fourth-minute lead. It was the first time in the tournament that Brazil had been behind. Six minutes later it was 1–1. Garrincha exploded down the right, and cut the ball back for Vava to run on to and fire firmly past Svensson. This was proving a fascinating spectacle. Pele slammed a shot against a post, Zagallo headed out from beneath the bar. In the 32nd minute the Garrincha-Vava combination struck again, and when Pele made it 3–1 in the 55th minute with a touch of sheer magic, the game

LAP OF HONOUR *Brazil celebrate their first World Cup triumph in 1958*

was won. Bringing a dropping ball down on a thigh in a crowded penalty area, the youngster hooked it over his head, spun and volleyed thunderously into the net. Zagallo and Pele added further goals, either side of a dubious second Swedish goal from Agne Simonsson, who looked offside. There was no doubt that Brazil were the best in the world.

CHILE 1962
Brazil without Pele still can't be matched

Brazil retained their world crown as Garrincha took center stage and 4–3–3 became the subtle change. But this was a World Cup marred by violence.

The Soviet Union and Yugoslavia comfortably overcame the Uruguayan and Colombian challenge in Group 1, while in Group 3 Brazil's only hiccup was a goalless draw with Czechoslovakia, who were to prove the surprise package of this tournament.

England got off to a bad start. Unable to break down the massed Hungarian defense after Springett was beaten by a thunderous long-range effort from Tichy, they equalized from a Ron Flowers penalty, but the impressive Albert clinched it for Hungary 18 minutes from time with a glorious individual goal. England did find some form to beat Argentina 3–1. Another Flowers penalty, a Bobby Charlton special and Jimmy Greaves clinched their first World Cup finals victory since 1954.

The Chile-Italy tie turned into a violent confrontation, with spitting, fighting, and two-footed tackles

intended to maim. That referee Ken Aston sent only two players off was amazing in a game that sullied the name of soccer. Brazil, however, continued to thrill, even without the injured Pele, who was to take no further part after the group match against Mexico. Garrincha mesmerized England to defeat, then took Chile apart in the semi-final, only to be sent off for retaliation.

In Vina del Mar a mere 5,000 watched Czechoslovakia earn their Final place at the expense of Yugoslavia, and the Czechs threatened to upset all the odds when Masopust cleverly gave them the lead over Brazil in the 16th minute. The equalizer, from Amarildo – Pele's replacement – was quickly registered but it was not until the 69th minute that Zito headed them into the lead. Vava made it 3–1 when goalkeeper Schroiff fumbled a chip.

SIMPLY THE BEST *Pele bides his time*

ENGLAND 1966
Victory for Ramsey's wingless wonders

For the first time in 32 years the host nation was to win the title. This was a series that had everything – passion, controversy, some fine soccer, and one of the greatest upsets of all time when North Korea knocked Italy out at Ayresome Park!

The tournament got off to a slow start, with England held 0–0 by Uruguay, but in Group 2 West Germany quickly displayed their potential with a 5–0 win over Switzerland. Brazil, alas, disappointed. Having beaten Bulgaria 2–0, they lost a classic encounter with Hungary, for whom Albert was the dominating factor, then succumbed to Portugal, whose striker Eusebio was to be one of the stars of the competition. The Soviet Union, efficient and technically sound, cruised through to the quarter-finals without alarm. For Italy, however, there was a rude awakening. Having lost 1–0 to the Soviets, they had to beat North Korea to stay in the competition, but what seemed a formality turned into a nightmare. In the 42nd minute Pak Doo Ik dispossessed Rivera, advanced and crashed a searing shot past Albertosi. It was the only goal. Italy was eliminated.

At Goodison Park there was a sensational opening to Korea's quarter-final with Portugal. There was a goal in the opening minute, followed by a second and a third – and all for Korea. It was then that Eusebio

IT'S ALL OVER NOW *Bobby Moore celebrates with England their extra-time victory over West Germany at Wembley*

proved his genius and, thanks to him and the towering Torres, the Portuguese clawed back the deficit to win a sensational game 5–3.

The England–Portugal semi-final produced an emotional classic, Bobby Charlton upstaging the mercurial Eusebio with what many felt was his greatest game for England. This, unlike the bad-tempered quarter-final shambles with Argentina, when Rattin was sent off and Geoff Hurst arrived as a new shooting star, was a

wonderful advertisement for the game.

West Germany had edged out the Soviet Union, in a disappointing tie, to secure their place in the Final, and there they struck the first blow through Haller. Hurst equalized and his West Ham colleague Martin Peters gave England the lead. But a scrambled goal from Weber just before time forced the game into extra time. In the 100th minute controversy raged. Alan Ball crossed, and Hurst coming in on the near post, ham-

mered his shot goalwards. It thumped against the underside of the bar and dropped – but which side of the line? Swiss referee Dienst was not sure, but the Soviet linesman Bakhramov was. 3–2 England! Any feeling of injustice felt by the Germans was quickly irrelevant. Bobby Moore swept a long ball upfield for Hurst to chase, and the big striker slammed his shot into the roof of Tilkowski's net to become the first player ever to score a hat-trick in a World Cup Final.

1966

Group 1

England	0	Uruguay	0
France	1	Mexico	1
Uruguay	2	France	1
England	2	Mexico	0
Uruguay	0	Mexico	0
England	2	France	0

	P	W	D	L	F	A	Pts
England	3	2	1	0	4	0	5
Uruguay	3	1	2	0	2	1	4
Mexico	3	0	2	1	1	3	2
France	3	0	1	2	2	5	1

Group 2

W. Germany	5	Switzerland	0
Argentina	2	Spain	1
Spain	2	Switzerland	1
Argentina	0	W. Germany	0
Argentina	2	Switzerland	0
W. Germany	2	Spain	1

	P	W	D	L	F	A	Pts
W. Germany	3	2	1	0	7	1	5
Argentina	3	2	1	0	4	1	5
Spain	3	1	0	2	4	5	2
Switzerland	3	0	0	3	1	9	0

Group 3

Brazil	2	Bulgaria	0
Portugal	3	Hungary	1
Hungary	3	Brazil	1
Portugal	3	Bulgaria	0
Portugal	3	Brazil	1
Hungary	3	Bulgaria	1

	P	W	D	L	F	A	Pts
Portugal	3	3	0	0	9	2	6
Hungary	3	2	0	1	7	5	4
Brazil	3	1	0	2	4	6	2
Bulgaria	3	0	0	3	1	8	0

Group 4

Soviet Union	3	North Korea	0
Italy	2	Chile	0
Chile	1	North Korea	1
Soviet Union	1	Italy	0
North Korea	1	Italy	0
Soviet Union	2	Chile	1

	P	W	D	L	F	A	Pts
Soviet Union	3	3	0	0	6	1	6
North Korea	3	1	1	1	2	4	3
Italy	3	1	0	2	2	2	2
Chile	3	0	1	2	2	5	1

Quarter-finals

England	1	Argentina	0
W. Germany	4	Uruguay	0
Portugal	5	North Korea	3
Soviet Union	2	Hungary	1

Semi-finals

| W. Germany | 2 | Soviet Union | 1 |
| England | 2 | Portugal | 1 |

Third place match

| Portugal | 2 | Soviet Union | 1 |

Final

England (1) 4   W. Germany (1) 2*
Hurst (3), Peters   Haller, Weber

ENGLAND: Banks, Cohen, Wilson, Stiles, Charlton J., Moore (capt.), Ball, Hurst, Hunt, Charlton R., Peters.

WEST GERMANY: Tilkowski, Höttges, Schülz, Weber, Schnellinger, Haller, Beckenbauer, Overath, Seeler (capt.), Held, Emmerich.

Leading scorers
9 Eusebio (Portugal); 5 Haller (West Germany); 4 Beckenbauer (West Germany), Hurst (England), Bene (Hungary), Porkujan (USSR).

*Note: * After extra time*

MEXICO 1970
The beautiful game secures the Jules Rimet trophy

The beautiful game triumphed again in Mexico, where the colorful free-flowing Brazilians delighted, overcoming the heat, the altitude and, in a dramatic Final, Italy – the masters of defensive caution.

There were no surprises in Groups 1 and 2 where the Soviet Union and Mexico and Italy and Uruguay qualified comfortably. The fixture between Brazil and England in Group 3 provided the outstanding tie of the series. In the 10th minute Jairzinho, a wonderful player of power and pace, delivered the perfect cross from the line. Pele timed his run and jump to perfection, and his header was hard and true, angled to bounce before passing just inside the left post. The shout of "Goal!" was already in the air when Gordon Banks, who had anticipated the ball going the other way, twisted athletically to pounce and incredibly push the wickedly bouncing ball over the bar. It was one of the greatest saves ever seen.

The only goal was scored in the second half by Jairzinho, who was to score in all of Brazil's six matches. England faltered in the quarter-final. Without Banks, because of an upset stomach, they squandered a two-goal lead to lose to West Germany in extra time.

The semi-final between Italy and

TOTAL FOOTBALL *But Johan Cruyff could not overcome West Germany in '74*

West Germany was dramatic. Having taken the lead through Boninsegna, Italy withdrew in the second half to protect their advantage. Given control of midfield, Germany took the initiative but did not equalize until the third minute of injury time through Schnellinger. In extra time, the goals came thick and fast: Müller for Germany, 1–2, Burgnich, then Riva for Italy, 3–2. Müller again, 3–3, before Rivera clinched it for Italy.

The Final proved a marvellous affirmation of attacking soccer. Pele opened the scoring and made two more after Boninsegna had made it 1–1, capitalizing on a dreadful error by Clodoaldo. Gerson drove in a powerful cross-shot in the 66th minute, and the match was sewn up with goals from Jairzinho and Carlos Alberto.

WEST GERMANY 1974
Pyrrhic victory for 'Total Football'

European teams dominated this series in which West Germany regained the World Cup after 20 years. It was another triumph for positive tactics, as Holland and Poland – who had surprisingly eliminated England – demonstrated to the full the attributes of skill and technique. The term "Total Football" crept into the soccer vocabulary, with Cruyff, Neeskens and Rep leading the Dutch masters who abandoned the rigidity of 4–2–4 and 4–3–3 to introduce the concept of "rotation" play.

Half of the 16 competing nations had been eliminated after the first series of group matches. The two Germanys qualified for the second phase comfortably, as did Holland and Sweden, and Poland from Group 4, where Argentina just edged Italy on goal difference thanks to a 4–1 victory over Haiti, whom Italy had beaten 3–1.

Group 2 proved to be the most competitive. Brazil, now sadly without the retired Pele, could only draw 0–0 with Yugoslavia and Scotland. Zaïre were to be the key factor. Scotland defeated them 2–0, but Yugoslavia overwhelmed them 9–0 to clinch pole position on goal difference. As they went into the final round Scotland needed a victory over Yugoslavia to win the group. They could only draw 1–1, and Brazil squeezed through, by virtue of one goal, thanks to a 3–0 win over Zaïre.

Holland looked impressive. They topped Group A to qualify for the Final without conceding a goal. Brazil, a shadow of their former selves, bowed out leaving us with one magic memory, their winning goal against East Germany. Jairzinho, standing on the end of the German wall facing a free-kick, ducked as Rivelino crashed his shot towards him, the ball swerving past the bewildered goalkeeper Croy.

West Germany's passage was a little more uncertain. It hinged on their clash with the impressive Poles in the final game of Group B. On a waterlogged pitch they made their physical strength pay. Tomaszewski saved a Hoeness penalty, but the German atoned for his miss when his shot was deflected to "The Bomber,"

1970

Group 1				
Mexico	0	Soviet Union	0	
Belgium	3	El Salvador	0	
Soviet Union	4	Belgium	1	
Mexico	4	El Salvador	0	
Soviet Union	2	El Salvador	0	
Mexico	1	Belgium	0	

	P	W	D	L	F	A	Pts
Soviet Union	3	2	1	0	6	1	5
Mexico	3	2	1	0	5	0	5
Belgium	3	1	0	2	4	5	2
El Salvador	3	0	0	3	0	9	0

Group 2				
Uruguay	2	Israel	0	
Italy	1	Sweden	0	
Uruguay	0	Italy	0	
Sweden	1	Israel	1	
Sweden	1	Uruguay	0	
Italy	0	Israel	0	

	P	W	D	L	F	A	Pts
Italy	3	1	2	0	1	0	4
Uruguay	3	1	1	1	2	1	3
Sweden	3	1	1	1	2	2	3
Israel	3	0	2	1	1	3	2

Group 3				
England	1	Romania	0	
Brazil	4	Czech.	1	
Romania	2	Czech.	1	
Brazil	1	England	0	
Brazil	3	Romania	2	
England	1	Czech.	0	

	P	W	D	L	F	A	Pts
Brazil	3	3	0	0	8	3	6
England	3	2	0	1	2	1	4
Romania	3	1	0	2	4	5	2
Czech.	3	0	0	3	2	7	0

Group 4				
Peru	3	Bulgaria	2	
W. Germany	2	Morocco	1	
Peru	3	Morocco	0	
W. Germany	5	Bulgaria	2	
W. Germany	3	Peru	1	
Morocco	1	Bulgaria	1	

	P	W	D	L	F	A	Pts
W. Germany	3	3	0	0	10	4	6
Peru	3	2	0	1	7	5	4
Bulgaria	3	0	1	2	5	9	1
Morocco	3	0	1	2	2	6	1

Quarter-finals

W. Germany	3	England	2*
Brazil	4	Peru	2
Italy	4	Mexico	1
Uruguay	1	Soviet Union	0

Semi-finals

Italy	4	W. Germany	3*
Brazil	3	Uruguay	1

Third place match

W. Germany	1	Uruguay	0

Final

Brazil	4	Italy	1
Pele, Gerson,		Boninsegna	
Jairzinho,			
Carlos Alberto			

BRAZIL: Felix, Carlos Alberto (capt.), Brito, Piazza, Everaldo, Clodoaldo, Gerson, Jairzinho, Tostao, Pele, Rivelino.

ITALY: Albertosi, Cera, Burgnich, Bertini (Juliano), Rosato, Facchetti (capt.), Domenghini, Mazzola, De Sisti, Boninsegna (Rivera), Riva.

Leading scorers
9 Müller (West Germany); 7 Jairzinho (Brazil); 4 Pele (Brazil), Cubillas (Peru), Byscevietz (USSR), Seeler (West Germany).

1974

Group 1

W. Germany 1 Chile 0
E. Germany 2 Australia 0
W. Germany 3 Australia 0
E. Germany 1 Chile 1
E. Germany 1 W. Germany 0
Chile 0 Australia 0

	P	W	D	L	F	A	Pts
E. Germany	3	2	1	0	4	1	5
W. Germany	3	2	0	1	4	1	4
Chile	3	0	2	1	1	2	1
Australia	3	0	1	2	0	5	1

Group 2

Brazil 0 Yugoslavia 0
Scotland 2 Zaïre 0
Brazil 0 Scotland 0
Yugoslavia 9 Zaïre 0
Scotland 1 Yugoslavia 1
Brazil 3 Zaïre 0

	P	W	D	L	F	A	Pts
Yugoslavia	3	1	2	0	10	1	4
Brazil	3	1	2	0	3	0	4
Scotland	3	1	2	0	3	1	4
Zaïre	3	0	0	3	0	14	0

Group 3

Holland 2 Uruguay 0
Sweden 0 Bulgaria 0
Holland 0 Sweden 0
Bulgaria 1 Uruguay 1
Holland 4 Bulgaria 1
Sweden 3 Uruguay 0

	P	W	D	L	F	A	Pts
Holland	3	2	1	0	6	1	5
Sweden	3	1	2	0	3	0	4
Bulgaria	3	0	2	1	2	5	2
Uruguay	3	0	1	2	1	6	1

Group 4

Italy 3 Haiti 1
Poland 3 Argentina 2
Italy 1 Argentina 1
Poland 7 Haiti 0
Argentina 4 Haiti 1
Poland 2 Italy 1

	P	W	D	L	F	A	Pts
Poland	3	3	0	0	12	3	6
Argentina	3	1	1	1	7	5	3
Italy	3	1	1	1	5	4	3
Haiti	3	0	0	3	2	14	0

Group A

Brazil 1 E. Germany 0
Holland 4 Argentina 0
Holland 2 E. Germany 0
Brazil 2 Argentina 1
Holland 2 Brazil 0
Argentina 1 E. Germany 1

	P	W	D	L	F	A	Pts
Holland	3	3	0	0	8	0	6
Brazil	3	2	0	1	3	3	4
E. Germany	3	0	1	2	1	4	1
Argentina	3	0	1	2	2	7	1

Group B

Poland 1 Sweden 0
W. Germany 2 Yugoslavia 0
Poland 2 Yugoslavia 1
W. Germany 4 Sweden 2
Sweden 2 Yugoslavia 1
W. Germany 1 Poland 0

	P	W	D	L	F	A	Pts
W. Germany	3	3	0	0	7	2	6
Poland	3	2	0	1	3	2	4
Sweden	3	1	0	2	4	6	2
Yugoslavia	3	0	0	3	2	6	0

Third place match

Poland 1 Brazil 0

Final

W. Germany (2) 2 Holland (1) 1
Breitner (pen), Neeskens (pen)
Müller

WEST GERMANY: Maier, Beckenbauer (capt.), Vogts, Schwarzenbeck, Breitner, Bonhof, Hoeness, Overath, Grabowski, Müller, Hölzenbein.

HOLLAND: Jongbloed, Suurbier, Rijsbergen (De Jong), Haan, Krol, Jansen, Neeskens, Van Hanegem, Rep, Cruyff (capt.), Rensenbrink (Van de Kerkhof, R.).

Leading scorers 7 Lato (Poland); 5 Neeskens (Holland), Szarmach (Poland); 4 Müller (West Germany), Rep (Holland), Edstroem (Sweden).

Gerd Müller, who booked the date with Holland.

The Dutch produced the most dramatic opening to a Final in the history of the competition. Right from the kick-off the ball was fluently played into the German area, where Cruyff was brought down by Hoeness. Neeskens calmly converted the first penalty awarded in a World Cup Final to record the fastest Final goal ever. And the Germans had yet to play the ball.

After being outplayed, West Germany got off the hook. Hölzenbein was homing in on goal when he was tripped by Jansen, and Breitner duly rammed in the resultant penalty himself to make it 1–1. A 43rd-minute goal from Gerd Müller – his 68th, last and most important for his country – won the World Cup.

CLINCHER *Bertoni scores for Argentina*

ARGENTINA 1978
Tickertape triumph for hyper hosts

Ecstasy and euphoria greeted Argentina's eventual triumph on home soil, yet for neutral fans the failure of Holland, as in 1974, to claim their rightful crown as the best team in the world left a void.

The home nation, backed by fanatical support and animated tickertape adoration in the River Plate Stadium, staged a colorful and dramatic tournament. Yet their passage to the Final was not without controversy. Their opening game proved a torrid affair. Hungary took the lead in 12 minutes through Zombori only for Leopoldo Luque to equalize three minutes later. The Hungarians were to have two players sent off before Bertoni fired the winning goal. Italy and Argentina had already qualified for the second stage when they met to decide the final Group 1 places. The Italians played it tight and snatched the win through Bettega in the 67th minute.

In Group 2 Poland carried on where they left off in Germany, with slick precise play. The shock result featured Tunisia, who held West Germany to a goalless draw and could have won. Brazil once again failed to inspire, and only a fortunate 1–0 victory over Austria, who topped their group, squeezed them into the second phase. Scotland, the United Kingdom's only representatives, suffered humiliation. Rocked by a 3–1 defeat by Peru, they received a further blow to morale when Willie Johnston failed a drug test and was ordered home. A 1–1 draw with Iran added to the troubles, but they went out in style against Holland.

While Italy and West Germany played not to lose, Holland thrilled with their adventurous attitude. The "reprise" of the 1974 Final between them and Germany provided one of the best games of this series. The final score was 2–2 and Holland were back in the Final. Meanwhile Brazil's

1978

Group 1

Argentina 2 Hungary 1
Italy 2 France 1
Argentina 2 France 1
Italy 3 Hungary 1
Italy 1 Argentina 0
France 3 Hungary 1

	P	W	D	L	F	A	Pts
Italy	3	3	0	0	6	2	6
Argentina	3	2	0	1	4	3	4
France	3	1	0	2	5	5	2
Hungary	3	0	0	3	3	8	0

Group 2

W. Germany 0 Poland 0
Tunisia 3 Mexico 1
Poland 1 Tunisia 0
W. Germany 6 Mexico 0
Poland 3 Mexico 1
W. Germany 0 Tunisia 0

	P	W	D	L	F	A	Pts
Poland	3	2	1	0	4	1	5
W.Germany	3	1	2	0	6	0	4
Tunisia	3	1	1	1	3	2	3
Mexico	3	0	0	3	2	12	0

Group 3

Austria 2 Spain 1
Sweden 1 Brazil 1
Austria 1 Sweden 0
Brazil 0 Spain 0
Spain 1 Sweden 0
Brazil 1 Austria 0

	P	W	D	L	F	A	Pts
Austria	3	2	0	1	3	2	4
Brazil	3	1	2	0	2	1	4
Spain	3	1	1	1	2	2	3
Sweden	3	0	1	2	1	3	1

Group 4

Peru 3 Scotland 1
Holland 3 Iran 1
Scotland 1 Iran 1
Holland 0 Peru 0
Peru 4 Iran 1
Scotland 3 Holland 2

	P	W	D	L	F	A	Pts
Peru	3	2	1	0	7	2	5
Holland	3	1	1	1	5	3	3
Scotland	3	1	1	1	5	6	3
Iran	3	0	1	2	2	8	1

Group A

Italy 0 W. Germany 0
Holland 5 Austria 1
Italy 1 Austria 0
Austria 3 W.Germany 2
Holland 2 Italy 1
Holland 2 W. Germany 2

	P	W	D	L	F	A	Pts
Holland	3	2	1	0	9	4	5
Italy	3	1	1	1	2	2	3
W. Germany	3	0	2	1	4	5	2
Austria	3	1	0	2	4	8	2

Group B

Argentina 2 Poland 0
Brazil 3 Peru 0
Argentina 0 Brazil 0
Poland 1 Peru 0
Brazil 3 Poland 1
Argentina 6 Peru 0

	P	W	D	L	F	A	Pts
Argentina	3	2	1	0	8	0	5
Brazil	3	2	1	0	6	1	5
Poland	3	1	0	2	2	5	2
Peru	3	0	0	3	0	10	0

Third place match

Brazil 2 Italy 1

Final

Argentina (1)3 Holland (0)1*
Kempes (2), Nanninga
Bertoni

ARGENTINA: Fillol, Olguin, Galvan, Passarella (capt.), Tarantini, Ardiles (Larrosa), Gallego, Kempes, Bertoni, Luque, Ortiz (Houseman).
HOLLAND: Jongbloed, Krol (capt.), Poortvliet, Brandts, Jansen (Suurbier), Van de Kerkhof W., Neeskens, Haan, Rep (Nanninga), Rensenbrink, Van de Kerkhof R.

Leading scorers 6 Kempes (Argentina); 5 Rensenbrink (Holland), Cubillas (Peru).

*Note: * After extra time*

3–1 defeat of Poland left Argentina needing to beat Peru by at least four goals to make the Final. They beat them by six in a shambolic exercise that tarnished the image of the whole competition.

The Final, more dramatic than distinguished, saw Mario Kempes score twice as once more Holland fell at the final hurdle.

SPAIN 1982
Italy have the last laugh

Italy deservedly won the 1982 World Cup, after a slow start in which they drew all three games in Group 1 and qualified on the slenderest goal difference. West Germany, who were to finish runners-up, were on the wrong end of a shock 2–1 defeat in their opening tie against Algeria but, like Italy, got better as the tournament progressed.

England, in contrast, started with a bang then gradually eased up. Captain Bryan Robson got them off to a dream start against France with a goal in 27 seconds, but although Ron Greenwood's team proved hard to beat, without the injured Keegan

CIAO BELLA *Marco Tardelli kisses the cup alongside Dino Zoff after Italy's triumph over West Germany in 1982*

and Brooking they had little guile. The outstanding game was that between Italy and the favourites, Brazil. Three times Italy took the lead, twice Brazil came back to level the score in a classic that would not be matched for quality. Paolo Rossi, back after a two-year suspension, was the hero with a brilliant hat-trick.

In the semi-finals Rossi scored twice more to beat the impressive Poles, while West Germany and France, who had grown in stature and confidence following that initial setback against England, were involved in a pulsating thriller. With Platini, Tigana and Giresse at their teasing best, many fancied France as winners. In a tense 90 minutes they carved out the better chances but

failed to make them count, then in extra-time lost in a penalty-kick shoot-out after German keeper Toni Schumacher got away with an appalling foul on Battiston.

The less glamorous sides also had their moments. Algeria, Honduras and Kuwait caught the eye, and Northern Ireland – whose Norman Whiteside was, at 17, the youngest ever

1982

Group 1

Italy	0	Poland	0
Peru	0	Cameroon	0
Italy	1	Peru	1
Poland	0	Cameroon	0
Poland	5	Peru	1
Italy	1	Cameroon	1

	P	W	D	L	F	A	Pts
Poland	3	1	2	0	5	1	4
Italy	3	0	3	0	2	2	3
Cameroon	3	0	3	0	1	1	3
Peru	3	0	2	1	2	6	2

Group 2

Algeria	2	W. Germany	1
Austria	1	Chile	0
W. Germany	4	Chile	1
Austria	2	Algeria	1
Algeria	3	Chile	2
W. Germany	1	Austria	0

	P	W	D	L	F	A	Pts
W. Germany	3	2	0	1	6	3	4
Austria	3	2	0	1	3	1	4
Algeria	3	2	0	1	5	5	4
Chile	3	0	0	3	3	8	0

Group 3

Belgium	1	Argentina	0
Hungary	10	El Salvador	1
Argentina	4	Hungary	1
Belgium	1	El Salvador	0
Belgium	1	Hungary	1
Argentina	2	El Salvador	0

	P	W	D	L	F	A	Pts
Belgium	3	2	1	0	3	1	5
Argentina	3	2	0	1	6	2	4
Hungary	3	1	1	1	12	6	3
El Salvador	3	0	0	3	1	13	0

Group 4

England	3	France	1
Czech.	1	Kuwait	1
England	2	Czech.	0
France	4	Kuwait	1
France	1	Czech.	1
England	1	Kuwait	0

	P	W	D	L	F	A	Pts
England	3	3	0	0	6	1	6
France	3	1	1	1	6	5	3
Czech.	3	0	2	1	2	4	2
Kuwait	3	0	1	2	2	6	1

Group 5

Spain	1	Honduras	1
N. Ireland	0	Yugoslavia	0
Spain	2	Yugoslavia	1
N. Ireland	1	Honduras	1
Yugoslavia	1	Honduras	0
N. Ireland	1	Spain	0

	P	W	D	L	F	A	Pts
N. Ireland	3	1	2	0	2	1	4
Spain	3	1	1	1	3	3	3
Yugoslavia	3	1	1	1	2	2	3
Honduras	3	0	2	1	2	3	2

Group 6

Brazil	2	Soviet Union	1
Scotland	5	New Zealand	2
Brazil	4	Scotland	1
Soviet Union	3	New Zealand	0
Scotland	2	Soviet Union	2
Brazil	4	New Zealand	0

	P	W	D	L	F	A	Pts
Brazil	3	3	0	0	10	2	6
Soviet Union	3	1	1	1	6	4	3
Scotland	3	1	1	1	8	8	3
New Zealand	3	0	0	3	2	12	0

Group A

Poland	3	Belgium	0
Soviet Union	1	Belgium	0
Soviet Union	0	Poland	0

	P	W	D	L	F	A	Pts
Poland	2	1	1	0	3	0	3
Soviet Union	2	1	1	0	1	0	3
Belgium	2	0	0	2	0	4	0

Group B

W. Germany	0	England	0
W. Germany	2	Spain	1
England	0	Spain	0

	P	W	D	L	F	A	Pts
W. Germany	2	1	1	0	2	1	3
England	2	0	2	0	0	0	2
Spain	2	0	1	1	1	2	1

Group C

Italy	2	Argentina	1
Brazil	3	Argentina	1
Italy	3	Brazil	2

	P	W	D	L	F	A	Pts
Italy	2	2	0	0	5	3	4
Brazil	2	1	0	1	5	4	2
Argentina	2	0	0	2	2	5	0

Group D

France	1	Austria	0
N. Ireland	2	Austria	2
France	4	N. Ireland	1

	P	W	D	L	F	A	Pts
France	2	2	0	0	5	1	4
Austria	2	0	1	1	2	3	1
N. Ireland	2	0	1	1	3	6	1

Semi-finals

Italy	2	Poland	0
W. Germany	3	France	3*

(West Germany won 5–4 on pens)

Third place match

Poland	3	France	2

Final

Italy	(0) 3	W. Germany	(0) 1

Rossi, Tardelli   *Breitner*
Altobelli

ITALY: Zoff (capt.), Bergomi, Cabrini, Collovati, Scirea, Gentile, Oriale, Tardelli, Conti, Graziani (Altobelli)(Causio), Rossi.

WEST GERMANY: Schumacher, Kaltz, Förster K., Stielike, Förster B., Breitner, Dremmler (Hrubesch), Littbarski, Briegel, Fischer (Müller, H.), Rummenigge (capt.).

Leading scorers
6 Rossi (Italy); 5 Rummenigge (West Germany); 4 Zico (Brazil), Boniek (Poland).

*Notes: * After extra time*

to play in the finals – distinguished themselves in a win over Spain.

The Final did not live up to its billing. There was not a shot on target in the opening 45 minutes including Cabrini's effort from a penalty. But in the second half the Germans paid, in fatigue, the price of their extra-time victory over France. Italy, inspired by the effort of Marco Tardelli and counter-attacking pace of Bruno Conti, were deserving winners – thus sealing a World Cup hat-trick.

MEXICO 1986
Divine intervention determines destiny of Cup

Mexico staged its second World Cup finals in the wake of a tragic earthquake, and set records all round with 52 matches played before 2,406,511 spectators.

West Germany continued their impressive World Cup record by reaching their fifth Final, once again eliminating France at the semi-final stage, while Argentina overcame the impressive Belgiums to make a third Final appearance. However, their 2-1 quarter-final victory over England had been soured by the infamous "hand of God" incident,

THEY SHALL NOT PASS *Karl-Heinz Rummenigge is stopped by Argentina's Oscar Ruggeri during the Final in 1986*

when Maradona knocked the ball past goalkeeper Peter Shilton with his hand to score the opening goal. There was no argument about Argentina's second goal, a brilliant solo run by the Argentinian ace taking him past three England defenders before he dispatched the ball into the back of the net.

Of the earlier games, the Soviet Union's 6–0 demolition of Hungary and Belgium's thrilling 4–3 victory over the Soviets in the second round were the most memorable. England muddled through after a desperate start, Carlos Manuel's lone strike giving Portugal a 1–0 win. Bobby Robson's team were then held 0–0 by Morocco. A Gary Lineker hat-trick against Poland revived England's flagging fortunes and earned them a place in the second round.

In a dramatic Final Argentina led 2–0 through Brown and Valdano before West Germany launched a remarkable recovery to equalize through Karl-Heinz Rummenigge and Völler. Burruchaga snatched the winner for Argentina's second World Cup title.

1986

Group A
Bulgaria	1	Italy	1
Argentina	3	South Korea	1
Italy	1	Argentina	1
Bulgaria	1	South Korea	1
Argentina	2	Bulgaria	0
Italy	3	South Korea	2

	P	W	D	L	F	A	Pts
Argentina	3	2	1	0	6	2	5
Italy	3	1	2	0	5	4	4
Bulgaria	3	0	2	1	2	4	2
South Korea	3	0	1	2	4	7	1

Group B
Mexico	2	Belgium	1
Paraguay	1	Iraq	0
Mexico	1	Paraguay	1
Belgium	2	Iraq	1
Paraguay	2	Belgium	2
Mexico	1	Iraq	0

	P	W	D	L	F	A	Pts
Mexico	3	2	1	0	4	2	5
Paraguay	3	1	2	0	4	3	4
Belgium	3	1	1	1	5	5	4
Iraq	3	0	0	3	1	4	0

Group C
Soviet Union	6	Hungary	0
France	1	Canada	0
Soviet Union	1	France	1
Hungary	2	Canada	0
France	3	Hungary	0
Soviet Union	2	Canada	0

	P	W	D	L	F	A	Pts
Soviet Union	3	2	1	0	9	1	5
France	3	2	1	0	5	1	5
Hungary	3	1	0	2	2	9	2
Canada	3	0	0	3	0	5	0

Group D
Brazil	1	Spain	0
N. Ireland	1	Algeria	1
Spain	2	N. Ireland	1
Brazil	1	Algeria	0
Spain	3	Algeria	0
Brazil	3	N. Ireland	0

	P	W	D	L	F	A	Pts
Brazil	3	3	0	0	5	0	6
Spain	3	2	0	1	5	2	4
N. Ireland	3	0	1	2	2	6	1
Algeria	3	0	1	2	1	5	1

Group E
W. Germany	1	Uruguay	1
Denmark	1	Scotland	0
Denmark	6	Uruguay	1
W. Germany	2	Scotland	1
Scotland	0	Uruguay	0
Denmark	2	W.Germany	0

	P	W	D	L	F	A	Pts
Denmark	3	3	0	0	9	1	6
W. Germany	3	1	1	1	3	4	3
Uruguay	3	0	2	1	2	7	2
Scotland	3	0	1	2	1	3	1

Group F
Morocco	0	Poland	0
Portugal	1	England	0
England	0	Morocco	0
Poland	1	Portugal	0
England	3	Poland	0
Morocco	3	Portugal	1

	P	W	D	L	F	A	Pts
Morocco	3	1	2	0	3	1	4
England	3	1	1	1	3	1	3
Poland	3	1	1	1	1	3	3
Portugal	3	1	0	2	2	4	2

Second round
Knock-out phase comprising the top two teams from each group plus the four best third-placed teams.

Mexico	2	Bulgaria	0
Belgium	4	Soviet Union	3*
Brazil	4	Poland	0
Argentina	1	Uruguay	0
France	2	Italy	0
W.Germany	1	Morocco	0
England	3	Paraguay	0
Spain	5	Denmark	1

Quarter-finals
France	1	Brazil	1*
(France won 4–3 on pens)
| W.Germany | 0 | Mexico | 0* |
(W Germany won 4–1 on pens)
| Argentina | 2 | England | 1 |
| Spain | 1 | Belgium | 1* |
(Belgium won 5–4 on pens)

Semi-finals
Argentina	2	Belgium	0
W.Germany	2	France	0

Third place match
France	4	Belgium	2

Final
Argentina (1) 3   W.Germany (0) 2
Brown, Valdano,   Rummenigge,
Burruchaga   Völler

ARGENTINA: Pumpido, Cuciuffo, Olarticoechea, Ruggeri, Brown, Giusti, Burruchaga (Trobbiani), Batista, Valdano, Maradona (capt.), Enrique.

WEST GERMANY: Schumacher, Berthold, Briegel, Jakobs, Förster, Eder, Brehme, Matthäus, Allofs (Völler), Magath (Hoeness, D.), Rummenigge (capt.).

Leading scorers
6 Lineker (England); 5 Butragueño (Spain), Careca (Brazil), Maradona (Argentina); 4 Altobelli (Italy), Belanov (USSR), Elkjaer (Denmark), Valdano (Argentina).

*Note: * After extra time*

TOP OF THE WORLD *West German captain Lothar Matthäus celebrates a victory over Argentina after the Final in Rome*

ITALY 1990

Penalties decide in a tear-jerking anti-climax

The 14th World Cup finals did not live up to the setting. There was a miserly shortage of goals, but perhaps the saddest failure of all was on the part of the established stars who failed to enhance their reputations. The occasion was saved by the Italians themselves, for this was the People's World Cup.

It started dramatically with Cameroon beating the champions Argentina – Omam Biyik scoring the only goal. The Africans topped their group, with Argentina trailing in third place, and were later to frighten the life out of England when they took a 2–1 lead over them in the quarter-finals. "Toto" Schillaci's tense expressions were to reflect the Italian mood. He scored the winner against Austria and the first against the Czechs as Italy comfortably headed Group A. Scotland were humiliated by Costa Rica, bounced back against Sweden, then crashed out to Brazil after taking them all the way. Scotland's gloom contrasted with the Republic of Ireland's popular success, their shoot-out win over Romania earning them a match against Italy in the quarter-finals. Belgium emerged as an impressive combination, but their journey ended when David Platt thumped home a brilliant volley to see England to the elite eight.

The highlights included the drama in Milan, when Littbarski's goal seemed to have ended Colombia's dream before one of the great characters of the tournament, Carlos Valderrama, who had been carried off, returned to lay on an equalizer for Freddy Rincon. There was the reckless stupidity of Colombian goalkeeper René Higuita, the grace of Tomas Skuhravy, the Czech striker and the magic of Yugoslavia's Dragan Stojkovic. There was also the sheer theatre of West Germany blasting England in a penalty shoot-out, with Gascoigne sobbing.

But the lasting impression of Italia '90 was the villain of the tournament, Argentina, who ousted Brazil, and spoiled the script by beating Italy on penalties to reach a Final they tarnished with dour tactics and flagrant abuse of the rules. Two Argentines were sent off, before, ironically, they were beaten by a penalty.

1990

Group A

Italy	1	Austria	0
Czech.	5	USA	1
Italy	1	USA	0
Czech.	1	Austria	0
Italy	2	Czech.	0
Austria	2	USA	1

	P	W	D	L	F	A	Pts
Italy	3	3	0	0	4	0	6
Czech.	3	2	0	1	6	3	4
Austria	3	1	0	2	2	3	2
USA	3	0	0	3	2	8	0

Group B

Cameroon	1	Argentina	0
Romania	2	Soviet Union	0
Argentina	2	Soviet Union	0
Cameroon	2	Romania	1
Argentina	1	Romania	1
Soviet Union	4	Cameroon	0

	P	W	D	L	F	A	Pts
Cameroon	3	2	0	1	3	5	4
Romania	3	1	1	1	4	3	3
Argentina	3	1	1	1	3	2	3
Soviet Union	3	1	0	2	4	4	2

Group C

Brazil	2	Sweden	1
Costa Rica	1	Scotland	0
Brazil	1	Costa Rica	0
Scotland	2	Sweden	1
Brazil	1	Scotland	0
Costa Rica	2	Sweden	1

	P	W	D	L	F	A	Pts
Brazil	3	3	0	0	4	1	6
Costa Rica	3	2	0	1	3	2	4
Scotland	3	1	0	2	2	3	2
Sweden	3	0	0	3	3	6	0

Group D

Colombia	2	UAE	0
W. Germany	4	Yugoslavia	1
Yugoslavia	1	Colombia	0
W. Germany	5	UAE	1
W. Germany	1	Colombia	1
Yugoslavia	4	UAE	1

	P	W	D	L	F	A	Pts
W. Germany	3	2	1	0	10	3	5
Yugoslavia	3	2	0	1	6	5	4
Colombia	3	1	1	1	3	2	3
UAE	3	0	0	3	2	11	0

Group E

Belgium	2	South Korea	0
Uruguay	0	Spain	0
Belgium	3	Uruguay	1
Spain	3	South Korea	1
Spain	2	Belgium	1
Uruguay	1	South Korea	0

	P	W	D	L	F	A	Pts
Spain	3	2	1	0	5	2	5
Belgium	3	2	0	1	6	3	4
Uruguay	3	1	1	1	2	3	3
South Korea	3	0	0	3	1	6	0

Group F

England	1	Rep of Ireland	1
Holland	1	Egypt	1
England	0	Holland	0
Egypt	0	Rep of Ireland	0
England	1	Egypt	0
Holland	1	Rep of Ireland	1

	P	W	D	L	F	A	Pts
England	3	1	2	0	2	1	4
Rep of Ireland	3	0	3	0	2	2	3
Holland	3	0	3	0	2	2	3
Egypt	3	0	2	1	1	2	2

Second phase

Knock-out phase comprising the top two teams from each group plus the four best third-placed teams

Cameroon	2	Colombia	1*
Czech.	4	Costa Rica	1
Argentina	1	Brazil	0
W. Germany	2	Holland	1
Rep of Ireland	0	Romania	0*

(Rep. of Ireland won 5–4 on pens)

Italy	2	Uruguay	0
Yugoslavia	2	Spain	1*
England	1	Belgium	0*

Quarter-finals

Argentina	0	Yugoslavia	0*

(Argentina won 3–2 on pens)

Italy	1	Rep of Ireland	0
W. Germany	1	Czech.	0
England	3	Cameroon	2*

Semi-finals

Argentina	1	Italy	1*

(Argentina won 4–3 on pens)

W. Germany	1	England	1*

(West Germany won 4–3 on pens)

Third place match

Italy	2	England	1

Final

W.Germany (0) 1 Argentina (0) 0
Brehme (pen)

WEST GERMANY: Illgner, Berthold (Reuter), Kohler, Augenthaler, Buchwald, Brehme, Littbarski, Hässler, Matthäus (capt.), Völler, Klinsmann.

ARGENTINA: Goycochea, Lorenzo, Serrizuela, Sensini, Ruggeri (Monzon), Simon, Basualdo, Burruchaga (Calderon), Maradona (capt.), Troglio, Dezotti.

Leading scorers

6 Schillaci (Italy); 5 Skuhravy (Czechoslovakia); 4 Michel (Spain), Milla (Cameroon), Matthäus (West Germany), Lineker (England).

*Note: * After extra time*

USA 1994
Brazil's glory in Final shoot-out

History was made twice over at the 1994 World Cup finals. Brazil secured a fourth title to add to their triumphs in 1958, 1962 and 1970. But to do so they needed to win the first-ever penalty shoot-out at the end of extra time after a goalless Final against Italy in the Rose Bowl in Pasadena.

FIFA introduced four radical measures in an attempt to improve the quality of the action: three points for a win instead of two in the first round group matches; a relaxation over the offside law by which play was to be stopped only if an attacking player was interfering with play; a crackdown on the tackle from behind in particular – for which a red card would be automatic – and violent conduct in general; and finally, injured players would be taken off the field immediately for treatment.

In simple statistical terms these changes added up to 15 ejections and a record 235 yellow cards. But, on the positive side, they also computed to 141 goals in 52 matches, a match average of 2.71 and an improvement on Italia '90.

More Than a Game

The biggest shadow over the finals was cast by the death of Andres Escobar, the Colombian defender, who was shot dead a few days after returning back home to Medellin. The exact reason for his murder is not known – gambling losses, probably involving drug barons, is thought to be the cause – but what was certain was that the center-back had, inadvertently, scored an own goal against the United States in Colombia's 2–1 defeat.

That victory for the US was probably the most significant single result in the finals because it virtually ensured the hosts a place in the second round. This success struck a chord with the domestic audience which helped carry the World Cup along on a wave of excitement and enthusiasm which surprised even the most optimistic of American soccer people.

However, the team of Group A

were undoubtedly Romania, inspired by their attacking general Gheorghe Hagi. The well-organized Swiss team qualified in second place, but Colombia – among the pre-tournament favorites – played without conviction or pattern and were eliminated.

Group B offered clear favourites in Brazil and they did not disappoint their colorful, noisy and musical supporters. Brazil's strength was the striking partnership of Romario and Bebeto. Romario either scored or had a creative hand in 10 of Brazil's 11 goals. Brazil topped the group with Sweden second.

FIVE GOALS IN ONE MATCH *Russia's Oleg Salenko set an individual goalscoring record for the World Cup finals*

Group C included the formal Opening Match in which holders Germany beat Bolivia 1–0. The Germans appeared sluggish, and Stefan Effenberg was expelled from the squad at the end of the first round for making a rude gesture towards jeering German fans in the narrow 3–2 win over South Korea. This was the other group which provided only two, rather than three, second round qualifiers. Germany finished top followed by Spain.

Maradona's Misery

In Group D Argentina's Diego Maradona was his team's attacking inspiration in the opening 4–0 win over Greece and in the 2–1 follow-up defeat of Nigeria, but it was after this game that he failed a drug test which showed traces of the banned stimulant ephedrine. The tourna-

ment was over for Maradona and Argentina lost their next game, without him, 2–0 to Bulgaria. The Bulgarians thus qualified for the second round despite having fallen 3–0 to the entertaining World Cup newcomers Nigeria in the group's opening match.

Ten Men Fight Back

The tightest division was Group E, featuring Italy, the Republic of Ireland, Mexico and Norway, and the six matches produced only eight goals.

Ireland shocked Italy with a 1–0 victory in their opening match, and Norway appeared on the verge of inflicting a second defeat on the group favorites when goalkeeper Gianluca Pagliuca was sent off. Remarkably, however, Italy fought back to win, 1–0, when defeat would have resulted in almost certain elimination. Wasting that numerical superiority cost Norway dear. All four teams ended up on four points and zero goal difference, but Norway finished last in the group on goals scored and were thus eliminated.

Another favored team who struggled in the first round were Holland. They beat Saudi Arabia only 2–1 in their first match then lost an exciting duel 1–0 to Belgium next time out and escaped early elimination by defeating Morocco 2–1 in their final match, to qualify along with Belgium and World Cup newcomers Saudi Arabia – who beat Belgium 1–0 along the way.

The opening match of the second round saw Germany, as on the opening day, playing in Chicago. This time they defeated Belgium 3–2 in an exciting game which marked the successful two-goal return of veteran World Cup-winner Rudi Völler.

The Republic of Ireland committed defensive suicide against Holland, losing 2–0 on mistakes by full-back Terry Phelan and goalkeeper Packie Bonner. Spain had an easy time in beating Switzerland 3–0 and Sweden defeated Saudi Arabia 3–1. Brazil also spoiled the Americans' Independence Day holiday by defeating the hosts more easily than the 1–0 scoreline suggests. The other three second-round games were even more dramatic. Bulgaria defeated Mexico 3–1 on penalties – the first shoot-out of the finals – after an entertaining 1–1 draw, marred by two contentious ejections.

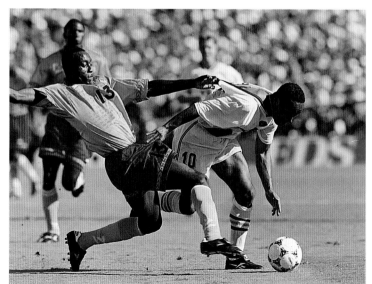

AFRICAN CHALLENGE *Kalla Nkongo of Cameroon tussles with Dahlin of Sweden*

A TANGO NOT A SAMBA *Romario and Baresi battle for supremacy in the Final at the Rose Bowl*

Hagi's Army March On

In Pasadena, Romania's Ilie Dumitrescu played the game of his life scoring twice and creating a third for Hagi in a 3–2 defeat of Argentina. Italy dramatically defeated Nigeria; with two minutes remaining the Italians were 1–0 down and had again been reduced to ten men by the dis-

missal, this time, of midfield substitute Gianfranco Zola. Roberto Baggio snatched an equalizer and as the Nigerians sagged in extra time, he scored again, from the penalty spot.

In the quarter-finals, Sweden, themselves down to 10 men after Stefan Schwarz was sent off, defeated Romania on penalties after a 2–2 draw.

Roberto Baggio confirmed his star rating with Italy's late second goal in their 2–1 victory over Spain. Another tight game saw Brazil defeat Holland 3–2, the first time an opposing team had put Brazil's defense under serious sustained pressure.

Completing the semi-final line-up were rank outsiders Bulgaria. Germany went ahead through a Lothar Matthäus penalty. But the holders conceded two last-gasp goals, from Hristo Stoichkov and Iordan Lechkov. It was Germany's earliest elimination since their quarter-final failure in 1962 and Bulgaria, who had played 16 matches at the finals without winning one before this tournament, were into the semi-finals.

That was to prove the end of the road. The two-goal brilliance of Roberto Baggio lifted Italy into their fifth Final while, in the other semi-final, Brazil encountered few difficulties in defeating a lackluster and leg-weary Sweden 1-0.

Penalties in Pasadena

Italy gambled twice over, in playing superstar striker Roberto Baggio despite a hamstring strain and in recalling veteran sweeper Franco Baresi for his first appearance after a cartilage operation following his injury against Norway in the first round.

In fact, Baresi was Italy's man of the match. The game saw Brazil employing their technical brilliance to try to outflank Italy's defensive discipline while the Italians sat back and waited for the right moment to unleash their rapid counter-attacks.

It was a game of few chances, most of which fell to Brazil. Romario misplaced a first-half header and Mazinho couldn't quite capitalize on a half-chance when Pagliuca dropped a Branco free-kick. In the 75th minute Pagliuca also allowed a long-range Mauro Silva effort to slip through his hands, but the ball bounced off the post and back into his arms. Pagliuca kissed the post in gratitude. Italy's best chance ended with Taffarel saving from Massaro.

Roberto Baggio went close with one effort in each half of extra time while Brazil should again have taken the lead in the 109th minute when the industrious Cafu crossed to the far post and Romario put the ball fractionally wide from four yards out from just

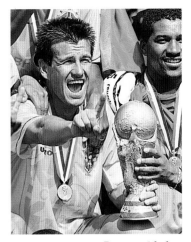

WE ARE THE CHAMPIONS *Dunga with the World Cup trophy*

beyond the far post.

In the penalty shoot-out, Taffarel benefited immediately when Baresi shot over. Baresi sank to his knees in despair. Pagliuca then stopped Marcio Santos and Italy went briefly ahead as Albertini scored from kick No 2. Romario squared for Brazil, Evani netted for Italy and Branco for Brazil. This was the point at which it fell apart for Italy as Taffarel saved from Massaro and Dunga scored what proved the vital Brazilian kick. Roberto Baggio needed to score with Italy's last kick of the five to keep his country alive. Instead, he scooped the ball over the bar. Brazil were back on top of the world.

1994

Group A

USA	1	Switzerland	1
Colombia	1	Romania	3
USA	2	Colombia	1
Romania	1	Switzerland	4
USA	0	Romania	1
Switzerland	0	Colombia	2

	P	W	D	L	F	A	Pts
Romania	3	2	0	1	5	5	6
Switzerland	3	1	1	1	5	4	4
USA	3	1	1	1	3	3	4
Colombia	3	1	0	2	4	5	3

Group B

Cameroon	2	Sweden	2
Brazil	2	Russia	0
Brazil	3	Cameroon	0
Sweden	3	Russia	1
Russia	6	Cameroon	1
Brazil	1	Sweden	1

	P	W	D	L	F	A	Pts
Brazil	3	2	1	0	6	1	7
Sweden	3	1	2	0	6	4	5
Russia	3	1	0	2	7	6	3
Cameroon	3	0	1	2	3	11	1

Group C

Germany	1	Bolivia	0
Spain	2	South Korea	2
Germany	1	Spain	1
South Korea	0	Bolivia	0
Bolivia	1	Spain	3
Germany	3	South Korea	2

	P	W	D	L	F	A	Pts
Germany	3	2	1	0	5	3	7
Spain	3	1	2	0	6	4	5
South Korea	3	0	2	1	4	5	2
Bolivia	3	0	1	2	1	4	1

Group D

Argentina	4	Greece	0
Nigeria	3	Bulgaria	0
Argentina	2	Nigeria	1
Bulgaria	4	Greece	0
Greece	0	Nigeria	2
Argentina	0	Bulgaria	2

	P	W	D	L	F	A	Pts
Nigeria	3	2	0	1	6	2	6
Bulgaria	3	2	0	1	6	3	6
Argentina	3	2	0	1	6	3	6
Greece	3	0	0	3	0	10	1

Group E

Italy	0	Rep of Ireland	1
Norway	1	Mexico	0
Italy	1	Norway	0
Mexico	2	Rep of Ireland	1
Rep of Ireland	0	Norway	0
Italy	1	Mexico	1

	P	W	D	L	F	A	Pts
Mexico	3	1	1	1	3	3	4
Rep of Ireland	3	1	1	1	2	2	4
Italy	3	1	1	1	2	2	4
Norway	3	1	1	1	1	1	4

Group F

Belgium	1	Morocco	0
Holland	2	Saudi Arabia	1
Belgium	1	Holland	0
Saudi Arabia	2	Morocco	1
Morocco	1	Holland	2
Belgium	0	Saudi Arabia	1

	P	W	D	L	F	A	Pts
Holland	3	2	0	1	4	3	6
Saudi Arabia	3	2	0	1	4	3	6
Belgium	3	2	0	1	2	1	6
Morocco	3	0	0	3	2	5	0

Second phase

Germany	3	Belgium	2
Spain	3	Switzerland	0
Saudi Arabia	1	Sweden	3
Romania	3	Argentina	2
Holland	2	Rep of Ireland	0
Brazil	1	USA	0
Nigeria	1	Italy	2*
Mexico	1	Bulgaria	1*

(*Bulgaria won 3–1 on pens*)

Quarter-finals

Italy	2	Spain	1
Holland	2	Brazil	3
Germany	1	Bulgaria	2
Sweden	2	Romania	2*

(*Sweden won 5–4 on pens*)

Semi-finals

Brazil	1	Sweden	0
Italy	2	Bulgaria	1

Third place match

Sweden	4	Bulgaria	0

Final

Brazil	0	Italy	0*

(*Brazil won 3–2 on pens*)

BRAZIL: Taffarel, Jorginho (Cafu 20), Aldair, Marcio Santos, Branco, Mazinho (Viola 106), Dunga (capt.), Mauro Silva, Zinho, Romario, Bebeto.

ITALY: Pagliuca, Mussi (Apolloni 34), Maldini, Baresi (capt.), Benarrivo, Berti, Albertini, Baggio D. (Evani 94), Donadoni, Baggio R., Massaro.

Leading scorers

6 Salenko (Russia), Stoichkov (Bulgaria);
5 K. Andersson (Sweden), R. Baggio (Italy), Klinsmann (Germany), Romario (Brazil)
4 Batistuta (Argentina), Dahlin (Sweden), Raducioiu (Romania)

*Note: * After extra time*

FRANCE 1998
After 68 years, the French triumph

FRANCE, the nation which invented the World Cup, finally won it in 1998 with a spectacular 3–0 victory over Brazil on home soil.

It was Frenchman Jules Rimet who first introduced the idea of a worldwide tournament of nations in 1930. And he would no doubt have been delighted that 68 years later, France should host the finals and be crowned world champions.

Even before it began, France '98 was billed as the biggest and most glamorous World Cup of all time – not least because it featured 32 teams instead of the usual 24. And due to the ever-increasing popularity of soccer, and the ever-expanding sponsorship and media circus which surrounds it, it was virtually impossible to escape the tournament wherever you lived in the world.

The line-up included four nations, Jamaica, Japan, South Africa and Croatia, making their debut in a World Cup finals – and that only served to add to the anticipation – with many pundits predicting upsets.

In fact, although Croatia proved to be the fairytale side of the finals, France '98 really only confirmed the status quo, with European and South American countries dominating as usual and the African and Asian nations failing to make an impact.

Brazil get off to a flyer

The opening game saw champions Brazil win 2–1 against the Tartan Army of Scotland, thanks to an unfortunate own goal from Tom Boyd. And when the Samba stars went on to crush Morocco 3–0, they became the first team to qualify for round two.

But there was still plenty of drama to come in the group. Scotland (having held Norway to a draw) faced Morocco in the final fixture, with each team believing that the winner would go through – providing Norway didn't do the unthinkable and beat Brazil.

The Moroccans were already partying after they went 3–0 up – only to find that Norway had turned the

tables by winning 2–1. The pictures of Moroccan celebrations turning to tears were some of the most haunting of the World Cup.

In Group B, Italy came back to draw 2–2 with Chile when Roberto Baggio, who missed a penalty in the 1994 World Cup final shoot-out, bravely volunteered to take a spot-kick when his side were 2–1 down – and duly converted.

The Azzuri went on to crush Cameroon and beat Austria to reach the second round, with striker Christian Vieri helping himself to four goals. Chile, led by three-goal striker Marcelo Salas, were second.

French prove they can score goals

Hosts France defied criticism that they would struggle to hit the net by beating South Africa 3–0, Saudi Arabia 4–0 (despite Zinedine Zidane being sent off) and Denmark 2–1 in Group C. And the Danes, with the inspirational Laudrup brothers Michael and Brian, also qualified.

Nigeria won Group D by winning their opening two games, and ended up as the only African nation in the second round. The key to their progress was a stunning 3–2 victory over Spain, in which they twice came from behind. But it was an awful mistake from experienced Spanish keeper Zubizarreta, credited as an own goal, which turned the game.

There was more misery to come for Spain, who had to beat Bulgaria to go through in the final group game. They romped to a thrilling 6–1 victory – only to find that Paraguay (without a goal up to that point) had unexpectedly beaten a weakened Nigeria side 3–1 to snatch second place.

In Group E, Holland posted a fine 5–0 win against South Korea and drew 2–2 with Mexico in a thriller.

The Mexicans won many fans with their never-say-die attitude, twice coming from 2–0 down to secure draws. Striker Cuauhtemoc Blanco also provided one of the light-hearted moments of the tournament with his 'bunny-hop' trick that bamboozled opposition defenders!

Group F saw German captain Jürgen Klinsmann, playing his farewell tournament, turn back the years by firing goals against the

United States and Iran to send his side comfortably into round two.

Peace breaks out at Iran vs USA

Perhaps the most memorable match of Group F, and the first round, was the politically sensitive clash between the USA and Iran. Both sets of players exchanged gifts before the kick-off and posed for a joint team picture, arms around each other, to prove that politics has no place on a soccer field. Iran won the battle, 2–1.

Group G saw England, tipped to be one of the big guns of France '98, open with a comfortable 2–0 win over Tunisia. But they then crashed to a 2–1 defeat against Romania when Dan Petrescu, based in England with Chelsea, rolled home the winner.

The one consolation for England was that teenage substitute Michael Owen looked lively, scoring once and hitting a post in the last minute. Not surprisingly, he started England's crucial third game against Colombia, and helped them to a comfortable 2–0 victory, sealed by a stunning David Beckham free-kick.

Group H was more clear-cut. Argentina dominated, winning all three of their games including a 5–0 thrashing of Jamaica in which Gabriel Batistuta hit a hat-trick. Croatia took second place and Jamaica scored their first victory in a World Cup finals, beating a disappointing Japan side 2–1.

The tension increased in round two, where Vieri handed Italy a narrow win over Norway and the Klinsmann-Bierhoff combination sent

Germany through against Mexico.

A Davor Suker penalty saw Croatia scrape past Romania; Brazil cruised home against South American rivals Chile with Ronaldo and Cesar Sempaio scoring twice each in a 4–1 win, and Denmark easily disposed of Nigeria by the same score.

The Dutch, though, needed a dramatic 90th minute strike from Edgar Davids to beat Yugoslavia, while France relied on a "Golden Goal" from defender Laurent Blanc to see off a stoic challenge from Paraguay.

The England vs Argentina clash, as expected, proved to be the tie of the round. A penalty for each side, both converted, made for an exciting opening and then Owen ran all the way from the half-way line to score the goal of the tournament.

The Argentinians hit back with a cleverly-worked free-kick and must have expected to win after England's Beckham was controversially sent off for petulantly kicking out at Diego

BRAZILIAN DESPAIR *Inconsolable Brazil players after their 3-0 final defeat*

blemish was a red card for Laurent Blanc (the 15th of the finals) after some terrible play-acting from Bilic.

Suker, of course, scored for Croatia and he did so again in a 2–1 third-place play-off win against Holland to clinch the Golden Boot with six goals.

Ronaldo drama in final

The final, between hosts France and champions Brazil, proved to be dramatic, controversial and disappointing all at the same time.

The drama began when Brazil handed in their teamsheet – with Ronaldo left out of the side. But 15 minutes later they sent out a correction – with the striker back in.

It later transpired that Ronaldo had suffered a convulsive fit on the morning of the match, and was only cleared to play at the last minute.

The whole affair clearly affected Brazil, who looked deflated right from the start. But in contrast, France were magnificent. Two headed goals from the inspirational Zinedine Zidane, both from corners, put them in control and then Emmanuel Petit rounded things off in a 3–0 win.

The celebrations in Paris were remarkable, with millions packing the streets for three days.

ZIDANE THE HERO *French star Zinedine Zidane thunders home a header from a corner in the 3–0 win over Brazil*

Simeone. But the English showed their bulldog spirit by surviving with 10 men all the way to the end of extra-time, before losing 4–3 on penalties (David Batty missing the last one).

Surprise package Croatia

In the quarter-finals, Croatia confirmed their reputation as the surprise of the tournament by crushing Germany (who had defender Christian Wörns sent off) 3–0 with goals from Jarni, Vlaovic and that man Suker. Holland beat Argentina 2–1 thanks to a glorious goal from Dennis Bergkamp in the very last minute, while France needed a penalty shoot-out to beat Italy following a 0–0 draw.

The match of the round was undoubtedly Brazil's exciting 3–2 win over Denmark, with two-goal Rivaldo breaking Danish hearts.

In the semi-finals, Holland more than matched Brazil and Patrick Kluivert sent the game into extra-time by equalizing a Ronaldo strike in the 87th minute. But the Dutch cruelly lost on penalties. In contrast, France, cannily coached by Aime Jacquet, sent the home fans wild with a 2–1 victory over Croatia.

As usual, the French struggled up front but found an unexpected hero in the shape of right-back Lilian Thuram, who scored twice. The only

---

1998

Round 1 Group A						
Brazil	2	Scotland	1			
Morocco	2	Norway	2			
Brazil	3	Morocco	0			
Scotland	1	Norway	1			
Brazil	1	Norway	2			
Scotland	0	Morocco	3			

	P	W	D	L	F	A	Pts
Brazil	3	2	0	1	6	3	6
Norway	3	1	2	0	5	4	5
Morocco	3	1	1	1	5	5	4
Scotland	3	0	1	2	2	6	1

Group B

Italy	2	Chile	2
Austria	1	Cameroon	1
Chile	1	Austria	1
Italy	3	Cameroon	0
Chile	1	Cameroon	1
Italy	2	Austria	1

	P	W	D	L	F	A	Pts
Italy	3	2	1	0	7	3	7
Chile	3	0	3	0	4	4	3
Austria	3	0	2	1	3	4	2
Cameroon	3	0	2	1	2	5	2

Group C

Saudi Arabia	0	Denmark	1
France	3	South Africa	0
France	4	Saudi Arabia	0
South Africa	1	Denmark	1
France	2	Denmark	1
South Africa	2	Saudi Arabia	2

	P	W	D	L	F	A	Pts
France	3	3	0	0	9	1	9
Denmark	3	1	1	1	3	3	4
S Africa	3	0	2	1	3	6	2
S Arabia	3	0	1	2	2	7	1

Group D

Paraguay	0	Bulgaria	0
Spain	2	Nigeria	3
Nigeria	1	Bulgaria	0
Spain	0	Paraguay	0
Nigeria	1	Paraguay	3
Spain	6	Bulgaria	1

	P	W	D	L	F	A	Pts
Nigeria	3	2	0	1	5	5	6
Paraguay	3	1	2	0	3	1	5
Spain	3	1	1	1	8	4	4
Bulgaria	3	0	1	2	1	7	1

Group E

South Korea	1	Mexico	3
Holland	0	Belgium	0
Belgium	2	Mexico	2
Holland	5	South Korea	0
Belgium	1	South Korea	1
Holland	2	Mexico	2

	P	W	D	L	F	A	Pts
Holland	3	1	2	0	7	2	5
Mexico	3	1	2	0	7	5	5
Belgium	3	0	3	0	3	3	3
S Korea	3	0	1	2	2	9	1

Group F

Germany	2	USA	0
Yugoslavia	1	Iran	0
Germany	2	Yugoslavia	2
USA	1	Iran	2
Germany	2	Iran	0
USA	0	Yugoslavia	1

	P	W	D	L	F	A	Pts
Germany	3	2	1	0	6	2	7
Yugoslavia	3	2	1	0	4	2	7
Iran	3	1	0	2	2	4	3
USA	3	0	0	3	1	5	0

Group G

England	2	Tunisia	0
Romania	1	Colombia	0
Colombia	1	Tunisia	0
Romania	2	England	1
Romania	1	Tunisia	1
Colombia	0	England	2

	P	W	D	L	F	A	Pts
Romania	3	2	1	0	4	2	7
England	3	2	0	1	5	2	6
Colombia	3	1	0	2	1	3	3
Tunisia	3	0	1	2	1	4	1

Group H

Argentina	1	Japan	0
Jamaica	1	Croatia	3
Japan	0	Croatia	1
Argentina	5	Jamaica	0
Argentina	1	Croatia	0
Japan	1	Jamaica	2

	P	W	D	L	F	A	Pts
Argentina	3	3	0	0	7	0	9
Croatia	3	2	0	1	4	2	6
Jamaica	3	1	0	2	3	9	3
Japan	3	0	0	3	1	5	0

Second phase

Italy	1	Norway	0
Brazil	4	Chile	1
France	1	Paraguay	0
(golden goal, after extra time)			
Nigeria	1	Denmark	4
Germany	2	Mexico	1
Holland	2	Yugoslavia	1
Romania	0	Croatia	1
Argentina	2	England	2
(Argentina won 4–3 on pens)			

Quarter-finals

Italy	0	France	0
(France won 4–3 on pens)			
Brazil	3	Denmark	2
Holland	2	Argentina	1
Germany	0	Croatia	3

Semi-finals

Brazil	1	Holland	1
(Brazil won 4–2 on pens)			
France	2	Croatia	1

Third place match

Holland	1	Croatia	2

Final

Brazil	0	France	3

BRAZIL: Taffarel, Cafu, Junior Baiano, Aldair, Roberto Carlos, Dunga, Cesar Sempaio (Edmundo 75), Leonardo (Denilson 45), Rivaldo, Bebeto, Ronaldo

FRANCE: Barthez, Thuram, Leboeuf, Desailly, Lizarazu, Petit, Deschamps, Karembeu (Boghossian 58), Zidane, Guivarc'h (Dugarry 66), Djorkaeff (Viera 76)

Leading scorers
6 Suker (Croatia)
5 Vieri (Italy), Batistuta (Argentina)
4 Salas (Chile), Hernandez (Mexico), Ronaldo (Brazil)
3 Sampaio, Rivaldo (both Brazil), Henry (France), Klinsmann, Bierhoff (Germany), Bergkamp (Holland)

COPA AMERICA (SOUTH AMERICAN CHAMPIONSHIP)

The South American Championship is the oldest running international competition in the world. The Copa America, as the competition has been known since 1975, is contested by the 10 members of CONMEBOL, the South American Confederation, and is 50 years older than its European equivalent.

The first tournament, in 1910, was not an official championship ("extra-ordinario."). Argentinia decided to arrange a tournament involving themselves, Uruguay, Brazil and Chile. Brazil withdrew before the tournament began, but on May 29, 1910, Uruguay and Chile contested the very first South American Championship match at in Buenos Aires.

Penarol's José Piendibene scored the first goal in the Copa America as Uruguay ran out 3–0 winners. Seven days later Argentina had an even easier 5–1 victory over Chile.

Almost 40,000 crowded into the Gimnasia ground to see the great rivals, Argentina and Uruguay, battle it out for the inaugural title, but they were to be disappointed. The fans burned one stand and the match was abandoned before it started. A day later a rearranged match was staged at Racing Club's ground, where only 8,000 saw Argentina win 4–1. The second tournament, in 1916, was also unofficial, organized to celebrate

NO PLACE LIKE HOME *When Uruguay host the Copa America they usually win it*

Argentina's centenary as an independent country. Argentina and Uruguay again clashed in the "decider," with Uruguay avenging their defeat of six years previously.

Between 1916 and 1959 the tournament was held, on average, every two years in one country. Uruguay won six of the first 11 tournaments.

Argentina then gained the upper hand winning 11 of the 18 tournaments from the 1920s to the 1950s. Brazil's four victories have all been on home soil but it was unlucky that, when they were at their peak, in the 1960s, only two tournaments were staged. Successes for the rest of the South American nations have

been few and far between. Peru won their titles in 1939 and 1975, Paraguay triumphed in 1953 and 1979. Most remarkably of all, Bolivia won in 1963 when they were hosts.

There is credence to the belief that the tournament had been held in disdain by some countries. Some countries entered weak or "B" teams or even youth sides. Indeed, 1975 was the first occasion on which all 10 CONMEBOL countries played.

Argentina has played host nine times, Chile seven, Uruguay six, Peru five and the indifferent Brazilians only four. The 1987 tournament was played in Argentina and won by Uruguay, repeating their 1983 triumph. Brazil hosted the 1989 event and won their first title in 40 years, while Argentina won in 1991.

In 1993, in Ecuador, the tournament underwent another face-lift. Mexico and the United States were invited to take part as guests, and three first round groups produced eight quarter-finalists. One of the invited guests, Mexico, almost spoiled the party by reaching the Final, where they lost 2–1 to Argentina. Mexico and the USA were invited again in 1995 in Uruguay and this time it was the US turn to embarrass their hosts, reaching the semi-finals before losing 1–0 to Brazil. But Brazil lost in the Final to hosts Uruguay, 5–3 in a penalty shoot-out, after a 1–1 draw.

Brazil made up for lost time in 1997, beating Bolivia at altitude by 3–1 in the final at La Paz with a new hero, Ronaldo, among the goals.

Winners: South American Championship

1910 *Buenos Aires*: 1st Argentina, 2nd Uruguay*
1916 *Buenos Aires*: 1st Uruguay, 2nd Argentina*
1917 *Montevideo*: 1st Uruguay, 2nd Argentina
1919 *Rio de Janeiro* (play-off): Brazil 1 (Friedenreich), Uruguay 0. Att: 28,000
1920 *Vina del Mar*: 1st Uruguay, 2nd Argentina
1921 *Buenos Aires*: 1st Argentina, 2nd Brazil
1922 *Rio de Janeiro* (play-off): Brazil 3 (Formiga 2, Neco), Paraguay 1 (Rivas G.). Att: 20,000
1923 *Montevideo*: 1st Uruguay, 2nd Argentina
1924 *Montevideo*: 1st Uruguay, 2nd Argentina
1925 *Buenos Aires*: 1st Argentina, 2nd Brazil
1926 *Santiago*: 1st Uruguay, 2nd Argentina
1927 *Lima*: 1st Argentina, 2nd Uruguay
1929 *Buenos Aires*: 1st Argentina, 2nd Paraguay
1935 *Lima*: 1st Uruguay, 2nd Argentina*
1937 *Buenos Aires* (play-off): Argentina 2 (De la Mata 2), Brazil 0. Att: 80,000
1939 *Lima*: 1st Peru, 2nd Uruguay.
1941 *Santiago*: 1st Argentina, 2nd Uruguay*
1942 *Montevideo*: 1st Uruguay, 2nd Argentina
1945 *Santiago*: 1st Argentina, 2nd Brazil*
1946 *Buenos Aires*: 1st Argentina, 2nd Brazil*
1947 *Guayaquil*: 1st Argentina, 2nd Paraguay

1949 *Rio de Janeiro* (play-off): Brazil 7 (Ademir Menezes 3, Tesourinha 2, Jair R. Pinto 2), Paraguay 0. Att: 55,000
1953 *Lima* (play-off): Paraguay 3 (Lopez A., Gavilan, Fernandez R.), Brazil 2 (Baltazar 2). Att: 35,000
1955 *Santiago*: 1st Argentina, 2nd Chile
1956 *Montevideo*: 1st Uruguay, 2nd Chile*
1957 *Lima*: 1st Argentina, 2nd Brazil
1959 *Buenos Aires*: 1st Argentina, 2nd Brazil*
1959 *Guayaquil*: 1st Uruguay, 2nd Argentina
1963 *Bolivia*: 1st Bolivia, 2nd Paraguay
1967 *Montevideo*: 1st Uruguay, 2nd Argentina
1975 *Bogota* (1st leg): Colombia 1 (Castro P.), Peru 0. Att: 50,000

Lima (2nd leg): Peru 2 (Oblitas, Ramirez O.), Colombia 0. Att: 50,000
Caracas (play-off): Peru 1 (Sotil), Colombia 0. Att: 30,000
1979 *Asuncion* (1st leg): Paraguay 3 (Romero C. 2, Morel M.), Chile 0.
Santiago (2nd leg): Chile 1 (Rivas), Paraguay 0. Att: 55,000
Buenos Aires (play-off): Paraguay 0, Chile 0. Att: 6,000 (*Paraguay won on goal difference*)
1983 *Montevideo* (1st leg): Uruguay 2 (Francescoli, Diogo), Brazil 0. Att: 65,000
Salvador (2nd leg): Brazil 1 (Jorginho), Uruguay 1 (Aguilera). Att: 95,000
1987 *Buenos Aires*: Uruguay 1 (Bengochea), Chile 0. Att: 35,000
1989 *Brazil*: 1st Brazil, 2nd Uruguay
1991 *Chile*: 1st Argentina, 2nd Brazil

1993 *Guayaquil*: Argentina 2 (Batistuta 2), Mexico 1 (Galindo pen.). Att: 40,000
1995 *Montevideo*: Uruguay 1 (Bengoechea 48), Brazil 1 (Tulio 30). (*Uruguay 5-3 on pens*). Att: 58,000
1997 *La Paz*: Brazil 3 (Edmundo 37, Ronaldo 79, Ze Roberto 90), Bolivia 1 (Irwin Sanchez 45). Att: 45,000
1999 *Asuncion*: Brazil 3 (Rivaldo 21, 27, Ronaldo 47), Uruguay 0. Att: 36,000

Notes: Details of finals or championship play-offs have been given where applicable. For all other tournaments, played on a league basis, only the first and second have been listed
* unofficial "extraordinarios" tournaments

EUROPEAN CHAMPIONSHIP

The European Championship, surprisingly, was the last of the continental tournaments to get under way, and was yet another French innovation. Proposed in the mid-1950s by Henri Delaunay, secretary of the French soccer federation, the European Nations Cup, as the event was previously known, was designed to bring together the various regional tournaments such as the British Home International Championship, the Nordic Cup and the Central European Championship for the Dr Gero Cup.

Delaunay, sadly, died before the tournament got under way, but the trophy still bears his name, and his idea has grown into the second most important international competition after the World Cup.

The first tournament was held in 1959–60, and was played on a straightforward home and away knock-out basis. A four-team final series followed, though the hosts for the final matches were not decided until the semi-finalists were known. The very first European Championship match took place in Moscow on September 28, 1958, when the Soviet Union beat Hungary 3–1 in a first round, first leg tie. Soviet winger Anatoly Ilyin scored the first ever European Championship goal after four minutes. There were many absentees from the tournament, including Sweden, Italy, West Germany, Switzerland, Holland and the four British nations.

The Eastern Bloc occupied three of the four semi-final slots in the 1960 finals, which France hosted. In the Final, Yugoslavia's all-out attack threatened to overrun the Soviets, but Lev Yashin responded with a string of fine saves. The Yugoslavs did take the lead, but the Soviets equalized almost immediately and made their superior physical strength count in

extra time to win 2–1.

The 1964 finals tournament took place in Spain, where the hosts made good use of home advantage to win the trophy beating the Soviet Union in Madrid, 2–1.

The qualifying tournament was expanded to eight groups for the 1968 event. Hosts Italy beat the Soviet Union in the first semi-final, but only by the rather dubious method of tossing a coin. World champions England also reached the semi-finals, but were beaten 1–0 by Yugoslavia. The final went to a replay, where goals by Riva and Anastasi were too much for the exhausted Yugoslav players, who again had to be content with runners-up medals.

The Soviets reached their third final out of four in 1972, but were no match for the West Germans. The incomparable Gerd Müller was at his peak, and two goals by him in the Final set up a 3–0 victory, and confirmed the Germans as favorites for the World Cup to be held two years later on their home soil.

The 1976 tournament threw up surprises from start to finish. England, Italy and France were eliminated in the qualifying round, and the semi-final line-up comprised surprising Czechoslovakia, 1974 World Cup winners West Germany and runners-up Holland and hosts Yugoslavia. Both semi-finals went to extra-time, the Czechs beating the Dutch 3–1 and the West Germans defeating the Yugoslavs 4–2, with a hat-trick from substitute Dieter Müller.

The Germans were clear favorites, but the Czechs had other ideas. Goals by Svehlik and Dobias gave them a 2–0 lead inside half an hour, but West Germany fought back, Holzenbein snatching an equalizer in the 89th minute. Extra time failed to separate the teams, and in the penalty shoot-out, Antonin Panenka chipped his penalty past Sepp Maier to win the trophy.

In 1980 the format for the final stages of the competition changed. The quarter-finals were abolished and the seven qualifying group winners proceeded straight to the finals along with the hosts, Italy, who received a bye direct to the final stage. The eight teams were divided into two groups of four, with the winners meeting in the final.

The Soviets failed to qualify for their "favorite" tournament, and the Yugoslavs also missed out, but there was a first-ever finals appearance for Greece. Belgium proved the surprise package of the tournament, reaching the final after conquering England, Spain and Italy in the group matches. West Germany won the other group with a little to spare and became the only nation to win the trophy twice when they beat the Belgians 2–1 with two goals from Horst Hrubesch – one early in the game, the other in the 88th minute.

The 1984 tournament was the best to date, with the flamboyant French hosts in unstoppable form. They had Michel Platini to thank for their success. His nine goals in five games was a superb achievement as the French swept aside Denmark, Belgium and Yugoslavia in the group matches. Unfancied Spain clinched the other group and then squeezed past the impressive Danes on penalties after a 1–1 draw in the re-introduced semi-finals. The Final was more conclusive. Platini and Bellone scored the goals as the host country won for the third time in seven events.

The 1988 finals in West Germany included all Europe's big names, except the French, plus one new one: the Republic of Ireland. The Irish shocked lackluster England in their first game and almost qualified for the semi-finals, but lost 1–0 to a late Dutch goal from Wim Kieft, a miscued header which spun past Pat Bonner into the Irish net.

The Soviet Union qualified with Holland to reach the semi-finals, where they met – and beat – Italy and West Germany respectively. With Rinus Michels in charge, the Dutch played irresistible soccer, beating the hosts 2–1 in the semi-final with a splendidly taken goal by Marco Van Basten with two minutes left in the match. Van Basten did even better in the Final against the Soviet Union, crashing home a volley from an almost impossible angle to seal a 2–0 victory following Ruud Gullit's goal in the first half.

Sweden hosted the 1992 finals. They and Scotland were making their debut in the finals and the now former Soviet Union played under the banner of Commonwealth of Independent States, but the biggest surprises were Denmark, last-minute replacements for the suspended Yugoslavia. They arrived with little time to prepare and walked off with the trophy after beating Holland in penalties in the semi-finals and then a shocked Germany by 2–0 in the final in Gothenburg. Midfielders John Jensen and Kim Vilfort were their goal-scoring heroes with Peter Schmeichel a rock in goal.

The 1996 finals took the European Championship to a new plane. Entry doubled to 16 finalists in four groups in the most exciting soccer extravanza in England since the 1966 World Cup. England started slowly with a 1–1 draw against Switzerland and steadily improved. Alan Shearer was the tournament's top scorer with an impressive five goals. But in the semi-finals Germany once again proved the masters of the penalty shoot-out at the hosts expense. Despite a horrendous injury list, Berti Vogt's men went on to beat the Czech Republic 2–1 in the final. Substitute Oliver Bierhoff made history, scoring both German goals including the first top-level golden goal decider.

Finals

European Championship Finals

1960 *Paris:* Soviet Union 2 (Metreveli, Ponedelnik), Yugoslavia 1 (Galic). Att: 18,000
1964 *Madrid:* Spain 2 (Pereda, Marcelino), Soviet Union 1

(Khusainov). Att: 105,000
1968 *Rome:* Italy 1 (Domenghini), Yugoslavia 1 (Dzajic). Att: 85,000.
Replay – *Rome:* Italy 2 (Riva, Anastasi), Yugoslavia 0. Att: 85,000
1972 *Brussels:* West Germany 3 (Müller G. 2, Wimmer), Soviet

Union 0. Att: 65,000
1976 *Belgrade:* Czechoslovakia 2 (Svehlik, Dobias), West Germany 2 (Müller D., Holzenbein) (aet). Czechoslovakia won 5–4 on penalties. Att: 45,000
1980 *Rome:* West Germany 2

(Hrubesch 2), Belgium 1 (Vandereycken). Att: 48,000
1984 *Paris:* France 2 (Platini, Bellone), Spain 0. Att: 47,000
1988 *Munich:* Holland 2 (Gullit, Van Basten), Soviet Union 0. Att: 72,000

1992 *Stockholm:* Denmark 2 (Jensen, Vilfort), Germany 0. Att: 37,000
1996 *Wembley:* Germany 2 (Bierhoff 72, 94 golden goal), Czech Republic 1 (Berger 59pen). Att: 73,611

WOMEN'S WORLD CUP

WOMEN'S WORLD CUP HISTORY

Throughout its history and for the first seven decades of the twentieth century, soccer had been almost exclusively a man's sport. But emancipation gave women more opportunity to express themselves on the soccer field, as in other walks of life, and as the century moved into its final quarter, women's soccer began to become more and more established.

It was inevitable when, 60 years after the men's World Cup was launched, the women were finally given their own version by FIFA, fulfilling a pledge made at the world governing body's 1986 Congress in Mexico by the then FIFA president Joao Havelange.

The inaugural 1991 Women's World Cup was held in China, a country that, despite its developing status in the men's game and its male-dominated society, held the women's game in high esteem. The quality of soccer, understandably, was not as sophisticated as the men's game but the enthusiasm with which the tournament was greeted vindicated FIFA's decision.

The favorites were the United States, another country which, paradoxically, had a women's team of which to be proud, but was still learning to come to grips with the highly competitive professional men's side of the game.

The American team in 1991 was led by a dominating forward line dubbed "the triple-edged sword" by the Chinese media, and tore through the tournament to win the trophy.

In the final, the Americans defeated Norway, who had recovered from a stunning 4–0 defeat by the host nation in their opening match. The Chinese, disappointingly, failed to make it past the quarterfinals where they were beaten 1–0 by Sweden, who in turn lost 4–1 to the Norwegians in the semis, setting up the final against the United States.

A crowd of 65,000 packed into the Guangzhou's Tianhe Stadium as Michelle Akers – the darling of the American team – scored both goals in a narrow 2–1 win and simultaneously set new standards for her female colleagues around the world.

The Norwegians waited four years to gain their revenge at the second Women's World Cup held in Sweden.

The tournament opened with a shock as Brazil downed the host nation 1-0 but the South Americans, not as powerful a force as their male counterparts, lost their next two matches to go out of the competition. Sweden, meantime, rallied with an emotional come-from-behind 3–2 win over Germany, scoring twice in the last 10 minutes, then cruised past Japan to reach the last eight where they were cruelly knocked out by China on penalties.

All the while, however, Norway were banging in the goals, scoring 17 in their group games and conceding none, waiting for the opportunity to play the United States in the semifinals.

When it came, the Norwegians, who have always been Europe's most advanced women's soccer nation, edged home 1–0 to play Germany in an all-European final. In steady rain, a crowd of over 17,000 saw the Scandinavians triumph 2–0 with goals from Hege Riise and Marianne Pettersen.

By now, the reservations of yesteryear concerning physical risks to women players had become a thing of the past.

Today some 30 million females are members of clubs while more than 100 of FIFA's national associations regularly organize women's competitions. In the United States, it is estimated that some 40 percent of regular players are women.

THE 1999 PHENOMENON

No one, not even America's most loyal soccer aficionados, expected the remarkable turn of events at the third Women's World Cup, held in the United States in the summer of 1999.

LADIES IN WAITING *The U.S. Women's squad before they won the inaugural Women's World Cup in China in 1991.*

If ever the phrase "the future is feminine," first used by FIFA president Sepp Blatter, was justified, Team America, as they were dubbed, proved it in one of the most remarkable roller-coaster team triumphs ever witnessed in world soccer.

Five years previously, America had hosted the men's World Cup. Stadiums were full, organization impeccable and much of the action a joy to watch. But in the back of many soccer experts' minds was the nagging feeling that when it was all over, American fans would go back to the sports they felt most comfortable with – baseball, hockey, basketball and football – once the novelty had worn off.

Many observers felt that was sadly true, despite the launch of the men's Major League Soccer. But, then along came the women.

Doubts that America could not embrace another major soccer tournament were shattered in three euphoric weeks. Soccer became front-page as well as back-page news, as multi-national sponsors rushed to seize maximum publicity from the fanatically followed American team. The incredible success, both on and off the field, of USA 99 assured the Women's World Cup as a genuine social phenomenon as well as a landmark in the history of the sport.

The players, for almost a month, became national icons as traditional sports were pushed into the background.

Once again, of course, there were the sceptics who found the whole thing somewhat tedious in comparison to the men's game. But the positive aspect was proof that women play to win rather than not to lose. The boundless enthusiasm of the fans and the impeccable behavior of the players contributed to a tournament that, until the final itself, was full of goals and attacking endeavor.

The competition began as it was destined to continue – a sunny day at Meadowlands Stadium and some dynamic soccer from the Americans that proved too hot for Denmark. The next day, America woke up to a new set of sporting heroes and watched as the team racked up 13 goals in the group stage, conceding only one. Players such as striker Mia Hamm, with rock-star status and a Nike sponsorship many male players would die for, burst into the spotlight.

Just as in the two previous tournaments, China and Norway were the Americans' two biggest rivals and, as expected, also cruised through their groups. The Chinese, in particular, had considerable individual skills and electric pace and were considered by many to be the best overall team. The game of the first round, however, was the 3–3 draw between Brazil and Germany that saw the South Americans score an injury-time equalizer to win their group.

The first quarter-final in San Jose saw China beat Russia 2–0 in one of the few sterile matches of the competition. Norway then beat Sweden 3–1 but everyone was waiting for the third quarter-final between the host nation and Germany. A crowd of more than 55,000, including President Bill Clinton, groaned as the Germans twice took the lead but ended up in raptures after a stirring 3–2 victory by the host nation.

The fourth quarterfinal was just as exciting as Brazil let slip a three-goal lead against Nigeria before scoring a golden goal in extra time.

Perhaps the best tribute to the women's game was that the semifinal line-up featured countries from four different continents, reflecting its development around the world.

Exactly five years after the USA played Brazil at Stanford in the men's World Cup, so the two nations met again in the same stadium. Only Briana Scurry's athleticism in the U.S. goal prevented the American dream being shattered. In the end, inspired by

1991

Winners

GROUP A				GROUP B				GROUP C				QUARTERFINALS				FINAL
China PR	4	Norway	0	Brazil	1	Japan	0	Germany	4	Nigeria	0	Germany	2	Denmark	1*	United States (1) 2 Norway (1) 1
Denmark	3	New Zealand	0	USA	3	Sweden	2	Italy	5	Chinese Taipei	0	Sweden	1	China PR	0	*Akers-Stahl 2 Medalen*
Norway	4	New Zealand	0	Sweden	8	Japan	0	Italy	1	Nigeria	0	Norway	3	Italy	2*	
China PR	2	Denmark	2	USA	5	Brazil	0	Germany	3	Chinese Taipei	0	USA	7	Chinese Taipei	0	U.S.: Harvey, Heinrichs, Higgins,
China PR	4	New Zealand	1	USA	3	Japan	0	Chinese Taipei	2	Nigeria	0					Werden, Hamilton, Hamm, Akers-
Norway	2	Denmark	1	Sweden	2	Brazil	0	Germany	2	Italy	0					Stahl, Foudy, Jennings, Lilly, Biefeld.

	G	W	D	L	F	A	P		G	W	D	L	F	A	P		G	W	D	L	F	A	P	SEMIFINALS
China PR	3	2	1	0	10	3	5	United States	3	3	0	0	11	2	6	Germany	3	3	0	0	9	0	6	Norway 4 Sweden 1
Norway	3	2	0	1	6	5	4	Sweden	3	2	0	1	12	3	4	Italy	3	2	0	1	6	2	4	USA 5 Germany 2
Denmark	3	1	1	1	6	4	3	Brazil	3	1	0	2	1	7	2	Chinese Taipei	3	1	0	2	2	8	2	THIRD PLACE
New Zealand	3	0	0	3	1	11	0	Japan	3	0	0	3	0	12	0	Nigeria	3	0	0	3	0	7	0	Germany 4 Sweden 0

Leading scorer:
10 Michelle Akers-Stahl (U.S.)

NORWAY: Seth, Zaborowski, Espeseth, Nyborg, Carlsen, Haugen, Stoere, Riise, Medalen, Hedstad, Svensson.

1995

GROUP A				GROUP B				GROUP C				QUARTERFINALS				FINAL
Germany	1	Japan	0	Norway	8	Nigeria	0	USA	3	China PR	3	USA	4	Japan	0	Norway (2) 2 Germany (0) 0
Brazil	1	Sweden	0	England	3	Canada	2	Denmark	5	Australia	0	Norway	3	Denmark	1	*Riise, Pettersen*
Sweden	3	Germany	2	Norway	2	England	0	USA	2	Denmark	0	Germany	3	England	0	
Japan	2	Brazil	1	Nigeria	3	Canada	3	China PR	4	Australia	2	China PR	1	Sweden	1*	NORWAY: Norbdy, Svensson, Nymark
Sweden	2	Japan	0	Norway	7	Canada	0	USA	4	Australia	1	*(China PR wins 4–3 on pens)*				Andersen, N., Espeseth, Myklebust,
Germany	6	Brazil	1	England	3	Nigeria	2	China PR	3	Denmark	1					Pettersen, Riise, Haugen, Nymark

	G	W	D	L	F	A	P		G	W	D	L	F	A	P		G	W	D	L	F	A	P	SEMIFINALS
Germany	3	2	0	1	9	4	6	Norway	3	3	0	0	17	0	9	United States	3	2	1	0	9	4	7	Norway 1 USA 0
Sweden	3	2	0	1	5	3	6	England	3	2	0	1	6	6	6	China PR	3	2	1	0	10	6	7	Germany 1 China PR 0
Japan	3	1	0	2	2	4	3	Canada	3	0	1	2	5	13	1	Denmark	3	1	0	2	6	5	3	THIRD PLACE
Brazil	3	1	0	2	3	8	3	Nigeria	3	0	1	2	5	14	1	Australia	3	0	0	3	3	13	0	USA 2 China PR 0

Andersen, A., Medalen, Aarones.
GERMANY: Goller, Lohn, Austermühl, Bernhard, Neid, Mohr, Wiegmann, Voss, Pohlmann (Wunderlich), Meinert (Smisek), Prinz (Brocker).

Leading scorer:
6 Ann Kristin Aarones (Norway)

* = After extra time

TIFFANY MILBRETT *The striker shoots in the 1999 World Cup quarter-final. The U.S. defeated Germany 3–2.*

BRANDI CHASTAIN *World cup winner*

BRIANA SCURRY *Goalkeeping heroine.*

Scurry and the veteran Akers, a 2–0 victory sent the host nation into the final against China.

The Chinese performance in the semi-finals, a 5–0 hammering of Norway full of guile and speed, was arguably the most complete 90 minutes of the tournament.

Many experts in the build-up to the final did not see how the American defense could hold out against the penetrative Asian attack. But what they lacked in individual technique, the Americans made up for in power, team spirit and the biggest crowd ever to witness a single women's sporting event anywhere in the world.

At the same Pasadena Rose Bowl where Brazil had beaten Italy in the men's final five years previously, a remarkable 90,185 spectators took their seats on a baking afternoon in suburban Los Angeles.

After a goalless 90 minutes, the hosts survived a mighty scare when a goal-bound Chinese effort in extra time was cleared off the line by Kristine Lilly. Both teams had cancelled each other out and in the ensuing penalty shoot-out, the whole of America from coast to coast counted on Briana Scurry to pull off more heroics.

She duly obliged, diving low to palm away Liu Yang's spot-kick. Now it was up to fullback Brandi Chastain to seal a 5–4 penalty shootout victory and she did so with an unstoppable drive into the top corner.

Chastain's reaction, ripping off her shirt in the same fashion as the men to reveal her sports bra before being submerged by ecstatic teammates, made front pages across the world.

The 13.3 rating at ABC Television for the final was the highest ever for a soccer game in the United States and, indeed, for any domestic sporting event that summer.

As the women's game was taken to unprecedented heights of popularity, at least in the United States, several of the players had emerged as instant role-models in the tide of soccer fever that had swept across the country, none more so than Akers, head and shoulders above anyone else in the tournament with her tiger-ish midfield displays.

Battered and bruised, she sadly missed the final due to exhaustion but joined her teammates on the field to soak up the celebrations and adulation.

In one sense, it was the ultimate soccer paradox: the whole of

America gripped by a soccer match in which much of the western world took only a passing interest.

Normally, of course, it is the other way around.

The women's game, mocked to the point of derision by a macho section of European soccer society, has become decidedly a la mode in the United States. Packed press conference, individual interviews with the American players, platform speeches by prominent officials and even a two-day symposium covering every aspect of the women's game.

In other words, blanket cover-age. In all, 658,000 tickets were sold for 32 matches.

How did it happen? Part of the reason is a landmark law passed in 1972 and known as Title IX. This required schools and universities to treat men and women equally when it came to sports scholarships. As a result, more than nine million American women now play soccer.

"Title IX made an enormous difference," said Donna de Varona, chairwoman of the World Cup organizing committee. "It's true we have had a problem embracing the men's game because we don't have the best players. In 1994 the stadia were packed but the best were not from America."

She added: "In some countries, like in England, the women are always compared to the best male soccer players. We don't have those comparisons. Here, by the age of 10, you have a generation of kids who relate to the game. Our best women athletes have chosen to play soccer in a sophisticated program that caters for the grass-roots, then picks off the best."

Yet even de Varona, a former Olympic swimming champion, admitted that the outburst of interest took her by surprise, saying: "I thought we'd be successful, but it exceeded my expectations."

There were those, of course, who wondered whether it will all be a passing phase. There remains, in many countries, a huge barrier of prejudice to break down. But the Americans look well capable of staying ahead of the pack.

"Our men's professional league is only four years old," said U.S. Soccer Federation boss Bob Contiguglia. "With the women we are ahead of the rest because we started earlier."

Winners

1999

GROUP A

United States	3	Denmark	0
Nigeria	2	PR Korea	1
United States	7	Nigeria	1
PR Korea	3	Denmark	1
United States	3	PR Korea	0
Nigeria	2	Denmark	0

	G	W	D	L	F	A	P
United States	3	3	0	0	13	1	9
Nigeria	3	2	0	1	5	8	6
PR Korea	3	1	0	2	4	6	3
Denmark	3	0	0	3	1	8	0

GROUP B

Germany	1	Italy	1
Brazil	7	Mexico	1
Germany	6	Mexico	0
Brazil	2	Italy	0
Germany	3	Brazil	3
Italy	2	Mexico	0

	G	W	D	L	F	A	P
Brazil	3	2	1	0	12	4	7
Germany	3	1	2	0	10	5	5
Italy	3	1	1	1	3	3	3
Mexico	3	0	0	3	1	15	0

GROUP C

Norway	2	Russia	1
Japan	1	Canada	1
Norway	7	Canada	1
Russia	5	Japan	0
Norway	4	Japan	0
Russia	4	Canada	1

	G	W	D	L	F	A	P
Norway	3	3	0	0	13	2	9
Russia	3	2	0	1	10	3	6
Canada	3	0	1	2	3	12	1
Japan	3	0	1	2	1	10	1

GROUP D

China	2	Sweden	1
Australia	1	Ghana	1
China	7	Ghana	0
Sweden	3	Australia	1
China	3	Australia	1
Sweden	2	Ghana	0

	G	W	D	L	F	A	P
China	3	3	0	0	12	2	9
Sweden	3	2	0	1	6	3	6
Australia	3	0	1	2	3	7	1
Ghana	3	0	1	2	1	10	1

QUARTERFINALS

United States	3	Germany	2
Brazil	4	Nigeria	3
Norway	3	Sweden	1
China	2	Russia	1

SEMIFINALS

United States	2	Brazil	0
China	5	Norway	0

THIRD PLACE

Brazil	0	Norway	0*

(Brazil wins 5–4 on penalties)

FINAL

United States (0) 0 China (0) 0*

(U.S. wins 5–4 on penalties)

U.S.: Scurry, Overbeck, Chastain, Hamm, Akers (Whalen), Foudy, Parlow (Macmillan), Lilly, Fawcett, Milbrett (Venturini), Sobrero.

CHINA: Gao, Wang, Fan, Zhao (Qiu), Jin (Xie), Sun, Liu, A., Pu (Zhang), Wen, Liu, Y., Bai.

Leading scorers:
7 Wen Sun (China), Sissi (Brazil)

* = After extra time

JULIE FOUDY *The U.S. midfielder forces her way past a couple of Nigerian defenders in her team's 7–1 victory in Group A of the 1999 Women's World Cup.*

CLUB COMPETITIONS

WORLD CLUB CUP

The World Club Cup is not, as its name suggests, open to every side in the world. In reality it is a challenge match between the champions of Europe and the champions of South America. Asia, Africa and the rest of the world do not get an opportunity … yet. FIFA is now considering plans to expand the tournament to include the best sides from each of the continental confederations in an end-of-season event in years in between World Cups and European Championships. The idea is still in its infancy and may never come to fruition.

Henri Delaunay, UEFA general secretary, first suggested the idea of a challenge match between the champions of Europe and South America in a letter to CONMEBOL, the South American Confederation, in 1958. His idea provided the impetus for them to get the Copa Libertadores (the South American Club Cup) up and running because, at that stage, South America had no continental championship for its clubs, even though an event for national sides had been taking place since 1910.

Before 1980, matches in the World Club Cup, or Intercontinental Cup as it is sometimes known, were played on a home and away basis, and up until 1968 the result was decided by points, not the aggregate score. This meant that if the clubs won one match each or both were drawn, a deciding match would take place. Until 1964 this replay had, for reasons never fully explained, to take place on the ground of the team who played at home in the second leg, giving them a massive advantage. Then for another four years the decider at least had to be played on that club's continent.

Despite these tortuous rules, the competition got off to a flying start in 1960, when Real Madrid met Penarol of Uruguay. Madrid had just won their fifth European Cup in a row, with a 7–3 demolition of Ein-

tracht Frankfurt, while Penarol had become the first winners of the Copa Libertadores. The first leg, in Montevideo, produced a 0–0 draw, but in the return two months later Real Madrid pounded the Uruguayans 5–1. The Real forward line was one of the best ever, and contained Del Sol, Di Stefano, Gento and Puskas, who scored twice. A combined attendance of 200,000 saw the matches.

In 1961 it was Penarol's turn to chalk up five goals, this time against the emerging Portuguese eagles, Benfica. However, a solitary Coluna goal in the first leg meant a decider was necessary, and Penarol only just managed to win 2–1 at home against a Benfica side bolstered by a young Eusebio, who was specially flown in.

Benfica represented Europe again in 1962, but this time they ran head-long into Brazil's Santos… and Pele. The "Black Pearl" scored twice in Rio as Santos narrowly won 3–2, and

then scored a breathtaking hat-trick in Lisbon as Benfica crashed to a 5–2 home defeat. Santos became one of only four sides to retain the trophy when they beat Milan in 1963. Both teams won 4–2 at home, but the decider provided a nasty taste of things to come, with a player from each side sent off and a penalty deciding the outcome, in favor of the Brazilians, who were without Pele for the second and third games.

The next two editions were contested by Internazionale of Italy and Independiente of Argentina, with Inter winning on both occasions. A goal by Corso in a decider in Madrid was enough in 1964, and the following year Inter drew 0–0 away and won the home leg 3–0 to retain the trophy. Among the famous names in the Inter line-up were Suarez, Mazzola and Fachetti.

In 1966 Penarol returned to win for the third time, beating Real

Madrid 2–0 in both legs, with Spencer scoring three of the Uruguayans' goals. From this encouraging start, the World Club Cup ran into severe problems in the late 1960s and early 1970s, largely owing to different styles of play and behavior.

The 1967 series paired Argentina's Racing Club with Scotland's Celtic. Feelings in Argentina were still running high over their 1966 World Cup quarter-final elimination by England, and the matches degenerated into a bad-tempered farce. After a 1–0 Celtic win in Glasgow, the return in Buenos Aires was chaotic. Celtic goalkeeper Ronnie Simpson was struck by a missile from the crowd before the kick-off, and could not play. Racing won 2–1 to set up a decider, in Montevideo, which was doomed before it began. Celtic lost their composure under extreme provocation and had four men sent off after Basile had spat at Lennox. Racing also had

WORLD'S BEST *Barcelona's Dane Michael Laudrup takes the ball away from São Paulo's Rai in Tokyo in 1992*

two men sent off but won 1–0.

It was extremely unfortunate, therefore, that the next team to represent South America – for three years running – were Estudiantes de la Plata of Argentina, a team who were solely interested in winning, and would stop at nothing to do it. At home in 1968 they battered Manchester United, who had Nobby Stiles sent off for a gesture to a linesman and Bobby Charlton taken off with a shin injury caused by a kick from Pachame. In the return at Old Trafford, Medina and Best were ejected for fighting as, under the competition's revised rules, the Argentinians completed a 2–1 aggregate win.

The following year, 1969, Milan came off even worse than United. After winning 3–0 at home, Milan were savaged in Buenos Aires, where Combin had his nose broken and Prati was kicked in the back while receiving treatment, but managed to hold on for a 4–2 aggregate victory. Three Estudiantes players were imprisoned after the game for their outrageous behavior and were given severe suspensions at the request of the Argentinian president.

Sadly, Estudiantes did not learn their lesson, and things were as bad in 1970 when they played Feyenoord, who came out on top after drawing the drawing the first leg in Buenos Aires. In the return in Rotterdam, Feyenoord's bespectacled Van Deale had his glasses smashed early in the game but still scored the winner. Feyenoord made it known that they would not have taken part in a decider if it had been needed, and the following year their countrymen, Ajax, went a step further by refusing to play against Nacional of Uruguay. Panathinaikos, beaten finalists in the European Cup, were appointed by UEFA to replace Ajax, and put up a brave performance before losing 3–2 on aggregate.

After such violent clashes, the value of the competition came into question, and it looked as if the World Club Cup would fade into history. Ajax did restore some credibility with a fine 4–1 aggregate win over Independiente in 1972, despite some rough treatment for Johan Cruyff, but the trend they started the year before continued throughout the 1970s.

Rather than risk their valuable players being mangled by the South Americans, Ajax, Liverpool, Bayern Munich and Nottingham Forest refused to take part, reducing the competition to a side-show. On all but two occasions, 1975 and 1978 (when the competition was not held), the beaten European Cup finalists substituted for the real champions – Atletico Madrid even managing a victory in 1974 against Independiente, who were making the fourth of their six appearances in the event. Clearly this situation could not continue and it is, ironically, Japan we have to thank for the event's survival.

In 1980 the format of the World Club Cup was changed. The two-legged tie was replaced by a single game at the National Stadium in Tokyo. The car manufacturer Toyota sponsored the competition.

The tournament has now regained much of its credibility, and since 1980 the European and South American champions have consistently taken part. The South Americans won the first five matches played in Tokyo, with the Europeans enjoying more success in the second half of the decade. In 1991 Red Star Belgrade became the first Eastern European side to win when they beat Chile's Colo Colo 3–0, with two goals from midfielder Vladimir Jugovic – whose European Cup-winning penalty in 1996 would earn Juventus another crack at the crown.

In the meantime, Barcelona and Milan (twice), however highly-rated in Europe, were successively dismissed by São Paulo (twice) and Argentina's Velez Sarsfield. While European commentators called Milan the world's best, their duel with São Paulo suggested otherwise.

Not until 1995 did Europe regain the trophy and then they clung on to it. First Ajax needed a penalty shoot-out to defeat yet another contestant from Brazil in Gremio. Then Juventus, having succeeded the Dutch as European champions, took over their world mantle with a 1–0 win over River Plate.

Further Brazilian failures were

Winners

World Club Cup Finals

1960 *Montevideo*: Penarol 0, Real Madrid 0. Att: 75,000
Madrid: Real Madrid 5 (Puskas 2, Di Stefano, Herrera, Gento), Penarol 1 (Borges). Att: 125,000
1961 *Lisbon*: Benfica 1 (Coluna), Penarol 0. Att: 50,000
Montevideo: Penarol 5 (Sasia, Joya 2, Spencer 2), Benfica 0. Att: 56,000
Montevideo (play-off): Penarol 2 (Sasia 2), Benfica 1 (Eusebio). Att: 62,000
1962 *Rio de Janeiro*: Santos 3 (Pele 2, Coutinho), Benfica 2 (Santana 2). Att: 90,000
Lisbon: Benfica 2 (Eusebio, Santana), Santos 5 (Pele 3, Coutinho, Pepe). Att: 75,000
1963 *Milan*: Milan 4 (Trapattoni, Amarildo 2, Mora), Santos 2 (Pele 2). Att: 80,000
Rio de Janeiro: Santos 4 (Pepe 2, Almir, Lima), Milan 2 (Altafini, Mora). Att: 150,000
Rio de Janeiro (play-off): Santos 1 (Dalmo), Milan 0. Att: 121,000
1964 *Avellanada*: Independiente 1 (Rodriguez), Internazionale 0. Att: 70,000
Milan: Internazionale 2 (Mazzola, Corso), Independiente 0. Att: 70,000
Milan (play-off): Internazionale 1

(Corso), Independiente 0 (aet). Att: 45,000
1965 *Milan*: Internazionale 3 (Peiro, Mazzola 2), Independiente 0. Att: 70,000
Avellanada: Independiente 0, Internazionale 0. Att: 70,000
1966 *Montevideo*: Penarol 2 (Spencer 2), Real Madrid 0. Att: 70,000
Madrid: Real Madrid 0, Penarol 2 (Rocha, Spencer). Att: 70,000
1967 *Glasgow*: Celtic 1 (McNeill), Racing Club 0. Att: 103,000
Avellanada: Racing Club 2 (Raffo, Cardenas), Celtic 1 (Gemmell). Att: 80,000
Montevideo (play-off): Racing Club 1 (Cardenas), Celtic 0. Att: 65,000
1968 *Buenos Aires*: Estudiantes 1 (Conigliaro), Manchester United 0. Att: 65,000
Manchester: Manchester United 1 (Morgan), Estudiantes 1 (Veron). Att: 60,000
1969 *Milan*: Milan 3 (Sormani 2, Combin), Estudiantes 0. Att: 80,000
Buenos Aires: Estudiantes 2 (Conigliaro, Aguirre-Suarez), Milan 1 (Rivera). Att: 65,000. Milan won 4–2 on aggregate
1970 *Buenos Aires*: Estudiantes 2 (Echecopar, Veron), Feyenoord 2 (Kindvall, Van Hanegem).

Rotterdam: Feyenoord 1 (Van Deale), Estudiantes 0. Att: 70,000. Feyenoord won 3–2 on aggregate.
1971 *Athens*: Panathinaikos 1 (Filakouris), Nacional (Uru) 1 (Artime). Att: 60,000
Montevideo: Nacional 2 (Artime 2), Panathinaikos 1 (Filakouris). Att: 70,000. Nacional won 3–2 on aggregate
1972 *Avellanada*: Independiente 1 (Sa), Ajax 1 (Cruyff). Att: 65,000.
Amsterdam: Ajax 3 (Neeskens, Rep 2), Independiente 0. Att: 60,000. Ajax won 4–1 on aggregate
1973 *Rome* (single match): Independiente 1 (Bochini 40), Juventus 0. Att: 35,000
1974 *Buenos Aires*: Independiente 1 (Balbuena 33), Atletico Madrid 0. Att: 60,000
Madrid: Atletico Madrid 2 (Irureta 21, Ayala 86), Independiente 0. Att: 45,000. Atletico won 2–1 on aggregate
1975 not played.
1976 *Munich*: Bayern Munich 2 (Müller, Kapellmann), Cruzeiro 0. Att: 22,000
Belo Horizonte: Cruzeiro 0, Bayern Munich 0. Att: 114,000. Bayern won 2–0 on aggregate
1977 *Buenos Aires*: Boca Juniors 2 (Mastrangelo, Ribolzi), Borussia Monchengladbach 2 (Hannes,

Bonhof). Att: 50,000
Karlsruhe: Borussia Mönchengladbach 0, Boca Juniors 3 (Zanabria, Mastrangelo, Salinas). Att: 21,000. Boca Juniors won 5–2 on aggregate
1978 not played.
1979 *Malmö*: Malmö 0, Olimpia 1 (Isasi). Att: 4,000
Asuncion: Olimpia 2 (Solalinde, Michelagnoli), Malmö 1 (Earlandsson). Att: 35,000. Olimpia won 3–1 on aggregate
1980 *Tokyo*: Nacional (Uru) 1 (Victorino), Nottingham Forest 0. Att: 62,000
1981 *Tokyo*: Flamengo 3 (Nunes 2, Adilio), Liverpool 0. Att: 62,000
1982 *Tokyo*: Penarol 2 (Jair, Charrua), Aston Villa 0. Att: 62,000
1983 *Tokyo*: Gremio 2 (Renato 2), Hamburg SV 1 (Schroder). Att: 62,000
1984 *Tokyo*: Independiente 1 (Percudiani), Liverpool 0. Att: 62,000
1985 *Tokyo*: Juventus 2 (Platini, Laudrup M.), Argentinos Juniors 2 (Ereros, Castro) (aet). Att: 62,000 (*Juventus won 4–2 on penalties*)
1986 *Tokyo*: River Plate 1 (Alzamendi), Steaua Bucharest 0. Att: 62,000
1987 *Tokyo*: FC Porto 2 (Gomes, Madjer), Penarol 1 (Viera) (aet). Att: 45,000
1988 *Tokyo*: Nacional (Uru) 2

(Ostolaza 2), PSV Eindhoven 2 (Romario, Koeman R.) (aet). Att: 62,000
(*Nacional won 7–6 on penalties*)
1989 *Tokyo*: Milan 1 (Evani), Nacional (Col) 0 (aet). Att: 62,000
1990 *Tokyo*: Milan 3 (Rijkaard 2, Stroppa), Olimpia 0. Att: 60,000
1991 *Tokyo*: Red Star Belgrade 3 (Jugovic 2, Pancev), Colo Colo 0. Att: 60,000
1992 *Tokyo*: São Paulo 2 (Rai 2), Barcelona 1 (Stoichkov). Att: 80,000
1993 *Tokyo*: São Paulo 3 (Palinha, Cerezo, Müller), Milan 2 (Massaro, Papin). Att: 52,000
1994 *Tokyo*: Velez Sarsfield 2 (Trott, Abad), Milan 0. Att: 65,000
1995 *Tokyo*: Ajax 0, Gremio 0 (aet). Att: 62,000 (*Ajax won 4–3 on penalties*)
1996 *Tokyo*: Juventus 1 (Del Piero), River Place 0. Att: 55,000
1997 *Tokyo*: Borussia Dortmund 2 (Zorc, Herrlich), Cruzeiro 0. Att: 60,000
1998 *Tokyo*: Real Madrid 2 (Naza og, Raul), Vasco da Gama 1 (Juninho). Att: 51,514
Notes:
From 1960 to 1979 the World Club Cup was decided on points, not goal difference. Since 1980 it has been a one-off match in Tokyo.

WORLD'S SECOND BEST *Liverpool lost to Independiente in 1984*

recorded in 1997 and 1998 when Cruzeiro and then Vasco da Gama fell to Borussia Dortmund and Real Madrid – the original winners of an increasingly questionable event, whose survival is threatened by FIFA's own plan for a world club championship.

COPA LIBERTADORES (SOUTH AMERICAN CLUB CUP)

The Copa Libertadores is undoubtedly South America's premier club event, but has had a long history of problems both on and off the field.

The competition was started in 1960 after a proposition from UEFA that the champions of South America should play against the European champions for the world title. A South American Champion Clubs Cup had been organized by Chile's Colo Colo as early as 1948, but the competition, won by Brazil's Vasco da Gama, was a financial disaster and was not staged again. But UEFA's success with the European Cup prompted CONMEBOL to consider giving the competition another chance, and the lucrative carrot of the World Club Cup swayed the balance in favor of trying again.

The first series was held in 1960, with seven of the continent's champions playing home and away matches on a knock-out basis, including the Final. This has always been played over two legs, with games won, not goal difference, deciding the winners. Goal difference only came into the equation if the play-off failed to produce a win-

ner, and is no longer relevant, since recently the penalty-kick shoot-out has replaced the play-off.

The first two competitions were won by Penarol, and almost passed unnoticed. Alberto Spencer scored in both those victories, against Olimpia and Palmeiras, and he remains top scorer in the Copa Libertadores with over 50 goals.

In the following year, 1962, the format of the competition changed as more teams entered. The home-and-away knock-out method was replaced by groups, played for points, up until the Final. Penarol again appeared in the Final, against Santos, and the first of many unsavory incidents which have scarred the Copa Libertadores occurred.

The first leg, in Montevideo, passed peacefully with a 2–1 win for Santos, but the second leg took three and a half hours to complete! The game was suspended shortly after half-time, with Penarol leading 3–2, because the Chilean referee, Carlos Robles, had been hit by a stone and knocked unconscious. After discussions lasting 80 minutes he agreed to continue the game, but there was more trouble to follow.

Santos equalized just as a linesman, raising his flag, was knocked out by another stone from the terraces, prompting Robles to suspend the game once more. At a disciplinary hearing later, Robles claimed that the match had officially been suspended when Penarol were 3–2 up, and that he had only concluded the match to ensure his own safety! So, the game was duly logged as a 3–2 win for

Penarol, forcing a play-off which Santos won easily, 3–0.

Santos retained their trophy a year later, beating Boca Juniors home and away, but had been helped by the rule which gave the holders a bye into the semi-finals. With Pele in the Santos side, the Copa Libertadores received the image boost it needed. Interest in the competition increased dramatically, and by 1964 every CONMEBOL country entered.

Boca's run to the Final was another important factor, as it encouraged the other Argentinian clubs to take the competition more seriously. Independiente became champions in 1964, and retained the trophy in 1965. That year, a Uruguayan proposal to include league runners-up almost killed the tournament. The Brazilians refused to enter in 1966, as more matches would make it even less financially rewarding.

The 1966 tournament involved no fewer than 95 games – without the Brazilians – Penarol, the winners, playing 17 games to win the title. Here again, controversy occurred. A play-off with River Plate was needed in the Final, and, having led 2–0 at half-time, River Plate eventually lost 4–2 after extra time. River had two former Penarol players in their side, Matosas and Cubilla, who both played badly and were accused of "selling" the game.

The 1967 Final, between Argentina's Racing Club and Uruguay's Nacional, witnessed the birth of the South American clubs' win-at-all-costs approach to the competition, especially the Argentinians. The three-game final series was peppered with gamesmanship and rough play, a familiar sight in Copa Libertadores and World Club Cup finals to come.

Racing's win marked the beginning of a period of Argentinian dominance, especially by the small-town club Estudiantes de La Plata, who won the Copa Libertadores three years running (1968–70) on the back of a single Argentine championship in 1967. Estudiantes were the worst offenders when it came to gamesmanship. Every conceivable method was employed to distract opponents, from verbal harassment and time-wasting to spitting and even pricking opponents with pins when out of the

referee's view! Estudiantes made few friends and very little money. Indeed, their hat-trick of titles earned them a net loss of $1,600,000. As a result, their president committed suicide, the board resigned and their replacements were forced to sell the players at knock-down prices.

The second leg of their third Final, against Penarol, ended in a free-for-all between both sets of players and reserves in the middle of the pitch. The disciplinary committee were extremely lenient, and then came down heavily on Boca Juniors a year later, after a battle between the players in a first-round tie against Peru's Sporting Cristal in Buenos Aires, which resulted in all of them being locked up in prison!

Top-level diplomatic negotiations earned the players' release the following day, and they were all promptly suspended by the clubs. Then, inexplicably, CONMEBOL punished Boca by closing their stadium for cup games, a strange move given that the fans were generally well-behaved on the day. Boca refused to accept this and duly turned up at their stadium for their next match, against Universitario of Peru, who did not – on the express orders of CONMEBOL's Peruvian president Salinas Fuller. Universitario were awarded the points and Boca were expelled from the competition… just another strange tale in the history of the Copa Libertadores.

With the ever-increasing disruption caused to domestic championships, Argentina joined Brazil in a boycott in 1969, prompting CONMEBOL to streamline the competition slightly by reducing the number of group matches. Argentina's Independiente then embarked on an unprecedented sequence of victories, winning the trophy four times in succession from 1972 to 1975.

The Brazilians, who returned in 1970, also began to enjoy some success, with Cruzeiro, Flamengo and Gremio winning between 1976 and 1983. Overall, however, Brazil's record in the tournament was disappointing until the 1990s.

Boca Juniors won the trophy for Argentina in 1977 and again in 1978, but in 1979 Olimpia of Paraguay broke the Argentina-Uruguay-Brazil domination of the competition. Olimpia's breakthrough marked a new era for the competition, which became more even and more open. Argentinian clubs still enjoyed success – Independiente, Argentinos Juniors and River Plate all tasted victory – but the "smaller" nations were starting to make an impression. Chilean champions Cobreloa reached two successive finals in 1981 and 1982, and were followed by Colombia's America Cali, who lost three successive finals from 1985.

Uruguay came back into contention with wins by Nacional (1980 and 1988) and by Penarol (1982 and 1987), but no Argentinian or Uruguayan club has won the Copa Libertadores since 1988.

In 1989 Nacional of Medellin won the trophy for Colombia for the first time, beating Olimpia 5–4 on penalties after a 2–2 aggregate draw. Olimpia returned the following year to win for the second time, beating Barcelona of Ecuador in the Final, and made it a hat-trick of Final appearances in 1991 when they lost to Chile's Colo Colo.

In 1992 São Paulo beat Newell's Old Boys, of Argentina, to win Brazil's first Copa Libertadores for almost a decade. The São Paulo side, containing many Brazil internationals such as Rai, Cafu, Palinha and Muller, won again in 1993, beating Chile's Universidad Catolica 5–3 on aggregate, to become the first club to retain the trophy since 1978.

The Copa Libertadores is now a respectable, clean competition which attracts all the continent's leading clubs. There are still moments of controversy and high drama, but that is all part and parcel of South American soccer. Such is the excitement generated that it is worth putting up with the constantly changing format which, at present, involves five first-round groups, playing 60 matches to eliminate just five teams! The holders still receive a bye into the second round, which is a huge help, because any team progressing from the first round to ultimate victory will have to play a gruelling 14 games on the way.

São Paulo almost made it a hat-trick in 1994 – reaching the Final for a third straight year – but lost on penalty kicks to Velez Sarsfield. A year later, Gremio took Brazilian revenge, beating Nacional of Colombia in the Final. The 1996 Final saw a repeat of 1986, with River Plate again beating America. Cruzeiro, Vasco da Gama and Palmeiras then re-emphasised the Brazilian club revival by winning in 1997, 1998 and 1999, respectively.

Copa Libertadores Finals
Winners

1960 *Montevideo*: Penarol 1 (Spencer), Olimpia 0. *Asuncion:* Olimpia 1 (Recalde), Penarol 1 (Cubilla).

1961 *Montevideo*: Penarol 1 (Spencer), Palmeiras 0. *São Paulo:* Palmeiras 1 (Nardo), Penarol 1 (Sasia).

1962 *Montevideo*: Penarol 1 (Spencer), Santos 2 (Coutinho 2). *Santos* Santos 2 (Dorval, Mengalvio), Penarol 3 (Spencer, Sasia 2) *Buenos Aires* (play-off): Santos 3 (Coutinho, Pele 2), Penarol 0.

1963 *Rio de Janeiro*: Santos 3 (Coutinho 2, Lima), Boca Juniors 2 (Sanfilippo 2). *Buenos Aires*: Boca Juniors 1 (Sanfilippo), Santos 2 (Coutinho, Pele).

1964 *Montevideo:* Nacional (Uru) 0, Independiente 0 *Avellaneda:* Independiente 1 (Rodriguez), Nacional (Uru) 0

1965 *Avellaneda:* Independiente 1 (Bernao), Penarol 0 *Montevideo:* Penarol 3 (Goncalvez, Reznik, Rocha), Independiente 1 (De la Mata) *Santiago* (play-off): Independiente 4 (Acevedo, Bernao, Avallay, Mura), Penarol 1 (Joya).

1966 *Montevideo*: Penarol 2 (Abbadie, Joya), River Plate 0. *Buenos Aires*: River Plate 3 (Onega E., Onega D., Sarnari), Penarol 2 (Rocha, Spencer). *Santiago* (play-off): Penarol 4 (Spencer 2, Rocha, Abbadie), River Plate 2 (Onega D., Solari).

1967 *Avellaneda*: Racing Club 0, Nacional (Uru) 0. *Montevideo*: Nacional (Uru) 0,

Racing Club 0. *Santiago* (play-off): Racing Club 2 (Cardozo, Raffo), Nacional (Uru) 1 (Esparrago).

1968 *La Plata*: Estudiantes 2 (Veron, Flores), Palmeiras 1 (Servillio) *São Paulo*: Palmeiras 3 (Tupazinho 2, Reinaldo), Estudiantes 1 (Veron) *Montevideo* (play-off): Estudiantes 2 (Ribaudo, Veron), Palmeiras 0

1969 *Montevideo*: Nacional (Uru) 0, Estudiantes 1 (Flores). *La Plata:* Estudiantes 2 (Flores, Conigliaro), Nacional (Uru) 0.

1970 *La Plata*: Estudiantes 1 (Togneri), Penarol 0. *Montevideo*: Penarol 0, Estudiantes 0.

1971 *La Plata*: Estudiantes 1 (Romeo), Nacional (Uru) 0. *Montevideo*: Nacional (Uru) 1 (Masnik), Estudiantes 0. *Lima* (play-off): Nacional (Uru) 2 (Esparrago, Artime), Estudiantes 0.

1972 *Lima*: Universitario 0, Independiente 0. *Avellaneda*: Independiente 2 (Maglioni 2), Universitario 1 (Rojas).

1973 *Avellaneda*: Independiente 1 (Mendoza), Colo Colo 1 (o.g.). *Santiago*: Colo Colo 0, Independiente 0. *Montevideo* (play-off): Independiente 2 (Mendoza, Giachello), Colo Colo 1 (Caszely).

1974 *São Paulo*: São Paulo 2 (Rocha, Mirandinha), Independiente 1 (Saggioratto). *Avellaneda*: Independiente 2 (Bochini, Balbuena), São Paulo 0. *Santiago* (play-off): Independiente 1 (Pavoni), São Paulo 0.

1975 *Santiago:* Union Espanola 1 (Ahumada), Independiente 0. *Avellaneda*: Independiente 3 (Rojas, Pavoni, Bertoni), Union Espanola 1

(Las Heras). *Asuncion* (play-off): Independiente 2 (Ruiz Moreno, Bertoni), Union Espanola 0.

1976 *Belo Horizonte*: Cruzeiro 4 (Nelinho, Palinha 2, Waldo), River Plate 1 (Mas). *Buenos Aires*: River Plate 2 (Lopez, J., Gonzalez), Cruzeiro 1 (Palinha). *Santiago* (play-off): Cruzeiro 3 (Nelinho, Ronaldo, Joazinho), River Plate 2 (Mas, Urquiza).

1977 *Buenos Aires*: Boca Juniors 1 (Veglio), Cruzeiro 0. *Belo Horizonte*: Cruzeiro 1 (Nelinho), Boca Juniors 0. *Montevideo* (play-off): Boca Juniors 0, Cruzeiro 0.

1978 *Cali*: Deportivo Cali 0, Boca Juniors 0 *Buenos Aires*: Boca Juniors 4 (Perotti 2, Mastrangelo, Salinas), Deportivo Cali 0

1979 *Asuncion:* Olimpia 2 (Aquino, Piazza), Boca Juniors 0. *Buenos Aires*: Boca Juniors 0, Olimpia 0.

1980 *Porto Alegre*: Internacional PA 0, Nacional (Uru) 0. *Montevideo*: Nacional (Uru) 1 (Victorino), Internacional PA 0.

1981 *Rio de Janeiro*: Flamengo 2 (Zico 2), Cobreloa 1 (Merello). *Santiago*: Cobreloa 1 (Merello), Flamengo 0. *Montevideo* (play-off): Flamengo 2 (Zico 2), Cobreloa 0.

1982 *Montevideo*: Penarol 0, Cobreloa 0. *Santiago*: Cobreloa 0, Penarol 1 (Morena).

1983 *Montevideo*: Penarol 1 (Morena), Gremio 1 (Tita). *Porto Alegre*: Gremio 2 (Caio, Cesar), Penarol 1 (Morena).

1984 *Porto Alegre*: Gremio 0, Independiente 1 (Burruchaga). *Avellaneda*: Independiente 0, Gremio 0.

1985 *Buenos Aires*: Argentinos Juniors 1 (Comisso), America Cali 0. *Cali*: America Cali 1 (Ortiz), Argentinos Juniors 0. *Asuncion* (play-off): Argentinos Juniors 1 (Comizzo), America Cali 1 (Gareca). (*Argentinos Juniors won 5–4 on penalties*).

1986 *Cali*: America Cali 1 (Cabanas), River Plate 2 (Funes, Alonso). *Buenos Aires*: River Plate 1 (Funes), America Cali 0.

1987 *Cali*: America Cali 2 (Bataglia, Cabanas), Penarol 0. *Montevideo*: Penarol 2 (Aguirre, Villar), America Cali 1 (Cabanas). *Santiago* (play-off): Penarol 1 (Aguirre), America Cali 0.

1988 *Rosario*: Newell's Old Boys 1 (Gabrich), Nacional (Uru) 0. *Montevideo*: Nacional (Uru) 3 (Vargas, Ostolaza , De Leon), Newell's Old Boys 0.

1989 *Asuncion:* Olimpia 2 (Bobadilla, Sanabria), Atletico Nacional 0. *Bogota*: Atletico Nacional 2 (o.g., Usurriaga), Olimpia 0. (*Atletico Nacional won 5–4 on penalties*).

1990 *Asuncion:* Olimpia 2 (Amarilla, Samaniego), Barcelona 0. *Guayaquil:* Barcelona 1 (Trobbiani), Olimpia 1 (Amarilla).

1991 *Asuncion:* Olimpia 0, Colo Colo 0. *Santiago*: Colo Colo 3 (Perez 2, Herrera), Olimpia 0.

1992 *Rosario*: Newell's Old Boys 1 (Berizzo), São Paulo 0. *São Paulo:* São Paulo 1 (Rai), Newell's Old Boys 0. (*São Paulo*

won 3–2 on penalties).

1993 *São Paulo*: São Paulo 5 (o.g., Dinho, Gilmar, Rai, Muller), Universidad Catolica 1 (Almada). *Santiago*: Universidad Catolica 2 (Lunari, Almada), São Paulo 0. São Paulo won 5–3 on aggregate.

1994 *Buenos Aires*: Velez Sarsfield 1 (Asad), São Paulo 0 Att:48,000 *São Paulo:* São Paulo 1 (Muller), Velez Sarsfield 0. (*Velez Sarsfield won 5–3 on penalties*)

1995 *Porto Alegre:* Gremio 3 (Marulanda og, Jardel, Paulo Nunes), Nacional Medellin 0 (Angel). *Medellin:* Nacional 1 (Aristizabal), Gremio 1 (Dinho pen). Gremio won 4–2 on agg.

1996 *Cali:* America 1 (De Avila), River Plate 0. *Buenos Aires:* River Plate 2 (Crespo 2), America 0. River Plate won 2–1 on agg.

1997 *Lima:* Sporting Cristal 0, Cruzeiro 0. *Belo Horizonte:* Cruzeiro 1 (Elivelton), Sporting Cristal 0. Cruzeiro won 1–0 on agg.

1998 *Rio de Janeiro:* Vasco da Gama 2 (Donizette. Luizao), Barcelona Guayaquil 0. *Guayaquil:* Barcelona Guayaquil 1 (De Avila), Vasco da Gama 2 (Donizette. Luizao). Vasco da Gama won 4–1 on agg.

1999 *Cali:* Deportivo Cali 1 (Bonilla), Palmeiras 0 *São Paulo:* Palmeiras 2 (Evair, Oseas), Deportivo Cali 1 (Zapata). (*Palmeiras won 4–3 on penalties*)

EUROPEAN CUP

Originally the European Champion Clubs Cup, what is now the UEFA Champions League is not only the most lucrative club event in the world but has become, since its inception in 1956, also the most prized trophy in world club soccer.

The idea for the competition came, typically, from the French. Gabriel Hanot, a former international and then editor of the French daily sports paper *L'Equipe*, was angered by English newspaper claims that Wolverhampton Wanderers were the champions of Europe because they had beaten Honved and Moscow Spartak in friendlies.

Hanot decided to launch a competition to find the real champions of Europe and, in 1955, invited representatives of 20 leading clubs to Paris to discuss the idea. The meeting was attended by 15 clubs and it was agreed that the competition should begin in the 1955–56 season.

The clubs, restricted to the champions of each country plus the holders after the first series, play home and away on a knock-out basis, and the result is decided by the aggregate score – except in the Final, which has always been one match played at a neutral venue. Drawn ties used a number of systems to produce a winner. Now it is away goals counting double, followed by a penalty shoot-out.

Sixteen teams entered the first tournament, though several were not really champions, merely replacements for teams who could not, or would not, take part. English champions Chelsea stayed away on the advice of the Football League, while Hibernian, who had finished fifth, represented Scotland.

By a fortunate coincidence, just as the competition was launched, Real Madrid were blossoming into one of the greatest club sides ever seen. In the Final, played in Paris, Real faced Stade de Reims, containing Raymond Kopa, who joined Real the following season. Reims could not cope with Real's deadly forwards, Alfredo Di Stefano, Hector Rial and Paco Gento, and lost 4–3.

Real went on to win the Cup for the next four years running, a feat which is unlikely to be matched in the modern game. Fiorentina (1957), Milan (1958), Reims again (1959) and Eintracht Frankfurt (1960) were all beaten in successive finals, with the match against Frankfurt being arguably the best final ever. In front of 135,000 fans at Hampden Park in Glasgow, Real thrashed the West German champions 7–3, with Ferenc Puskas, the "galloping major" of the great Hungarian team of the 1950s, scoring four goals and Di Stefano getting a hat-trick.

Real's run came to an end the following season in the second round, beaten by deadly rivals Barcelona, who went on to contest the Final with Portugal's Benfica – the newly emerging kings of Europe. Benfica contained the bulk of the Portuguese national side and would go on to play in five Finals during the 1960s, winning two of them. The first was won without their Mozambique-born striker Eusebio.

Eusebio was in the line-up the following year, though, when Benfica faced Real Madrid, and he scored twice as Benfica won 5–3 despite Puskas scoring another hat-trick for Real. In 1963, the Lisbon Eagles appeared in their third consecutive Final, but lost 2–1 to Italy's Milan.

Milan's victory was the first of three for the city in the mid-1960s, as Internazionale emerged to win the trophy in 1964 and 1965. Coached by the legendary Helenio Herrera, Inter fielded a host of international stars including Sarti, Burgnich, Facchetti, Jair from Brazil, Mazzola and the Spaniard Suarez. Their Final victims were Real Madrid and Benfica.

Real returned to claim "their" crown in 1966 with a 2–1 win over Partizan Belgrade in Brussels. Of the 1950s attack all bar Gento had gone, but Amancio and Serena proved worthy successors as both scored in the Final. Real's sixth triumph marked the end of an era in the European Cup. For the first 11 years of its existence, the Cup had only been won by clubs from Spain, Portugal and Italy – and of the first 22 finalists, 18 were from these three countries. Now the power-base of European club soccer shifted from the Mediterranean to northern Europe – Britain, Holland and Germany to be precise. The 1967 Final paired Inter with Scotland's Celtic. The Scots, under the guiding hand of the great Jock Stein, won every competition open to them that season, rounding off with a fine 2–1 win over the Italians in Lisbon. The breakthrough had been made, and Manchester United consolidated the position by becoming England's first winners the following season. Benfica again lost in the Final, where Matt Busby's side won 4–1 after extra time.

Milan regained the trophy in 1969, with a 4–1 demolition of Ajax in Madrid, but it was the last Latin success in the Cup for 17 years as Holland, Germany and then England dominated the trophy during the 1970s and early 1980s.

Feyenoord of Rotterdam were the first Dutch winners, in 1970, when they narrowly defeated Celtic 2–1 after extra time in Milan. Feyenoord's great rivals, Ajax, maintained Holland's position the following season when they beat Panathinaikos of Greece 2–0 at Wembley. It was the first of three consecutive titles for the Amsterdam club, which contained the bulk of the thrilling Dutch "total football" side of the 1970s. Johan Cruyff was the star of the show, scoring both goals in the 2–0 1972 Final win over Inter in Rotterdam. In 1973, Ajax beat Juventus in Belgrade with a solitary goal by the mercurial Johnny Rep.

Coach Udo Lattek molded Bayern Munich into a highly effective unit, winning three times. Players such as Franz Beckenbauer, Sepp Maier, Gerd Müller and Paul Breitner, formed the core of the dominant West German side. Bayern beat Atletico Madrid in a replay for the first of their wins, Uli Hoeness and Müller scoring two each in a 4–0 win after a 1–1 draw in Brussels. In 1975 they beat Leeds United 2–0 in a hotly-disputed match and their hat-trick came with a 1–0 win over France's Saint-Etienne.

Then, in 1977, Liverpool clinched the first of six consecutive English victories with a 3–1 win over Borussia Mönchengladbach. Liverpool held onto the trophy at Wembley the following year by beating Club Brugge. Kenny Dalglish scored the only goal.

In 1979 a cruel twist of fate drew Liverpool with Nottingham Forest in the first round. Forest had risen from the Second Division to win the title in successive seasons, and they outfought Liverpool to win 2–0 on aggregate. In the Final, against Swedish outsiders Malmö, Britain's first $1.5 million player, Trevor Francis, scored the only goal. Forest retained the Cup in 1980, against Hamburg. Kevin Keegan was completely shackled by Forest's Scottish center-back Kenny Burns, and a single goal by John Robertson was enough for victory.

Liverpool returned for their third triumph the following season with a 1–0 win over Real Madrid in Paris, and Aston Villa became the fourth English winners in 1982, when they beat Bayern Munich 1–0. Hamburg broke the English monopoly in 1983 by beating Juventus 1–0, but it was only a brief respite. Liverpool, the most successful side in the history of English soccer, returned for the 1984 Final and beat AS Roma in Rome, 4–2 on penalties after a 1–1 draw.

The period of English dominance was about to end, however, and the 1985 Final at the Heysel Stadium in Brussels will never be remembered for its soccer. Before the game, a group of English hooligans charged at Juventus fans behind one of the goals. A safety wall collapsed and 39 people, mostly Italian, lost their lives in the crush. Juventus won a meaningless game 1–0. Liverpool were banned from European competitions indefinitely, while all English clubs were banned for five years.

In 1986 Romania's Steaua Bucharest became the first Eastern European side to win the Cup, beating Barcelona. The Final was possibly the worst in the tournament's history; still goalless after extra time, the penalty shoot-out produced only two successful kicks – both for the Romanians. Portugal's FC Porto won in 1987 in Vienna with a fine 2–1 win over Bayern Munich, having been a goal down. PSV Eindhoven became Holland's third European champions when they beat Benfica in 1988, 6–5 on penalties, after a dull 0–0 draw after 120 minutes.

Milan then returned to reclaim the trophy. Free from the restrictions on importing foreign players, and backed by media magnate Silvio Berlusconi's money, Milan bought the best and beat the rest. Their Dutch axis of Frank Rijkaard, Ruud Gullit and Marco Van Basten steered them to a crushing 4–0 victory over Steaua in 1989, Gullit and Van Basten both scoring twice, while a single goal from Rijkaard was enough to beat the perennial bridesmaids Benfica in 1990.

English clubs returned for the 1991 tournament, but Yugoslavia's Red Star Belgrade met Marseille in the Final. France, originators of the European Cup, were still looking for a first ever victory … but the wait had to go on. Red Star abandoned their free-flowing, attacking style of play in favour of a blanket defence approach designed to stifle president Bernard Tapie's expensively assembled French champions. The plan worked. Red Star took the game to penalties and won the shoot-out 5–3, to become the second Eastern side to become European champions.

The format of the competition was radically changed in 1992, after pressure from Europe's bigger clubs who wanted to form a European Super League. The quarter-finals and semi-finals were replaced with

BACK ON TOP *Karlheinz Riedle celebrates his second goal in the 1997 Cup Final*

two groups of four, playing home and away, to produce the two finalists. Johan Cruyff's Barcelona took the Cup for the first time – completing a hat-trick of European trophies – by beating Sampdoria 1–0.

Then, in 1993, came the biggest scandal the competition has ever witnessed. After 37 years, the French drought in the European Cup ended. Marseille beat Milan 1–0 in Munich, with a goal by Basile Boli. The celebrations were cut short, however, when a bribery scandal came to light. Tapie was eventually jailed for his part in the affair, but Marseille were

stripped of both French and European titles and denied a lucrative World Club Cup match too.

The format changed slightly again for the 1994 tournament, with the re-introduction of semi-finals for the winners and runners-up of the two Champions League groups. But nothing could stop Milan, their 4–0 defeat of Barcleona was a stunning display. Yet more tinkering with the format followed for 1995 as UEFA sought a compromise with the bigger clubs. The holders and top seven seeded teams went through directly to the Champions League, which was

expanded to 16 teams in four groups of four; the eight other teams came from a preliminary round involving the teams ranked eight to 23 in the seeding list. All the other "minnow" national champions were off-loaded into an expanded UEFA Cup.

The first redeveloped Champions League Cup Final – as it was clumsily repackaged – was won by Ajax, who defeated wealthy Milan, 1–0. But big money spoke louder in 1996 when Ajax lost in a penalty shoot-out to Juventus. The Italian club, just for good measure, thrashed them in the 1997 semi-finals too, but were then themselves beaten, 3–1, by Germany's Borussia Dortmund, the first German victory for 14 years. History repeated itself in 1998, when Juventus returned to the Final as favorites but lost again. The underdogs were Real Madrid, but the Spaniards claimed a record seventh Cup, 1–0.

As if to prove the staying power of traditional giants, Manchester United succeded Madrid in 1999 with an appropriately sensational victory to end the century. Two injury-time goals turned an apparent 1–0 defeat by Bayern Munich into a win. United became the first English club to achieve a treble of European Cup, plus the league championship and national Cup.

Winners

Champions Cup Finals

1956 *Paris*: Real Madrid 4 (Di Stefano, Rial 2, Marquitos), Stade de Reims 3 (Leblond, Templin, Hidalgo). Att: 38,000

1957 *Madrid*: Real Madrid 2 (Di Stefano, Gento), Fiorentina 0. Att: 124,000

1958 *Brussels*: Real Madrid 3 (Di Stefano, Rial, Gento), Milan 2 (Schiaffino, Grillo) (aet). Att: 67,000

1959 *Stuttgart*: Real Madrid 2 (Mateos, Di Stefano), Stade de Reims 0. Att: 80,000

1960 *Glasgow*: Real Madrid 7 (Di Stefano 3, Puskas 4), Eintracht Frankfurt 3 (Kress, Stein 2). Att: 127,621

1961 *Berne*: Benfica 3 (Aguas, o.g., Coluna), Barcelona 2 (Kocsis, Czibor). Att: 33,000

1962 *Amsterdam*: Benfica 5 (Aguas, Cavem, Coluna, Eusebio 2), Real Madrid 3 (Puskas 3). Att: 68,000

1963 *Wembley*: Milan 2 (Altafini 2), Benfica 1 (Eusebio). Att: 45,000

1964 *Vienna*: Internazionale 3 (Mazzola 2, Milani), Real Madrid 1 (Felo). Att: 72,000

1965 *Milan*: Internazionale 1 (Jair), Benfica 0. Att: 80,000

1966 *Brussels*: Real Madrid 2 (Amancio, Serena), Partizan Belgrade 1 (Vasovic). Att: 55,000

1967 *Lisbon*: Celtic 2 (Gemmell, Chalmers), Internazionale 1 (Mazzola). Att: 55,000

1968 *Wembley*: Manchester United 4 (Charlton 2, Best, Kidd), Benfica 1 (Graca) (aet). Att: 100,000

1969 *Madrid*: Milan 4 (Prati 3, Sormani), Ajax 1 (Vasovic). Att: 50,000

1970 *Milan*: Feyenoord 2 (Israel, Kindvall), Celtic 1 (Gemmell) (aet). Att: 53,187

1971 *Wembley*: Ajax 2 (Van Dijk, o.g.), Panathinaikos 0. Att: 90,000

1972 *Rotterdam*: Ajax 2 (Cruyff 2), Internazionale 0. Att: 61,000

1973 *Belgrade*: Ajax 1 (Rep), Juventus 0. Att: 93,500

1974 *Brussels*: Bayern Munich 1 (Schwartzbeck), Atletico Madrid 1 (Luis) (aet). Att: 65,000
Brussels (replay): Bayern Munich 4 (Hoeness 2, Müller 2), Atletico Madrid 0. Att: 23,000

1975 *Paris*: Bayern Munich 2 (Roth, Müller), Leeds United 0. Att: 48,000

1976 *Glasgow*: Bayern Munich 1 (Roth), St Etienne 0. Att: 54,684

1977 *Rome*: Liverpool 3 (McDermott, Smith, Neal), Borussia Mönchengladbach 1 (Simonsen). Att: 57,000

1978 *Wembley*: Liverpool 1 (Dalglish), Club Brugge 0. Att: 92,000

1979 *Munich*: Nottingham Forest 1 (Francis), Malmö 0. Att: 57,500

1980 *Madrid*: Nottingham Forest 1 (Robertson), Hamburg 0. Att: 51,000

1981 *Paris*: Liverpool 1 (Kennedy A.), Real Madrid 0. Att: 48,360

1982 *Rotterdam*: Aston Villa 1 (Withe), Bayern Munich 0. Att: 46,000

1983 *Athens*: Hamburg 1 (Magath), Juventus 0. Att: 80,000

1984 *Rome*: Liverpool 1 (Neal), AS Roma 1 (Pruzzo) (aet). (*Liverpool won 4–2 on penalties*). Att: 69,693

1985 *Brussels*: Juventus 1 (Platini), Liverpool 0. Att: 58,000

1986 *Seville*: Steaua Bucharest 0, Barcelona 0 (aet). (*Steaua won 2–0 on penalties*). Att: 70,000

1987 *Vienna*: FC Porto 2 (Madjer, Juary), Bayern Munich 1 (Kogl). Att: 56,000

1988 *Stuttgart*: PSV Eindhoven 0, Benfica 0 (aet). (*PSV won 6–5 on penalties*). Att: 55,000

1989 *Barcelona*: Milan 4 (Gullit 2, Van Basten 2), Steaua Bucharest 0. Att: 97,000

1990 *Vienna*: Milan 1 (Rijkaard), Benfica 0. Att: 56,000

1991 *Bari*: Red Star Belgrade 0, Marseille 0 (aet). (*Red Star won 5–3 on penalties*). Att: 50,000

1992 *Wembley*: Barcelona 1 (Koeman R.), Sampdoria 0 (aet). Att: 74,000

1993 *Munich*: Marseille 1 (Boli), Milan 0. Att: 72,300 (*Marseille were later stripped of their title for alleged match fixing*)

1994 *Athens*: Milan 4 (Massaro 2, Savicevic, Desailly), Barcelona 0. Att: 76,000

1995 *Vienna*: Ajax 1 (Kluivert), Milan 0. Att 49,000

1996 *Rome*: Juventus 1 (Ravanelli), Ajax 1 (Litmanen) (aet). (*Juventus won 4–2 on penalties*). Att: 67,000.

1997 *Munich*: Borussia Dortmund 3 (Riedle 2, Ricken), Juventus 1 (Del Piero). Att: 55,000

1998 *Amsterdam:* Real Madrid 1 (Mijatovic), Juventus 0. Att: 47,000

1999 *Barcelona:* Manchester United 2 (Sheringham, Solskjaer), Bayern Munich 1 (Basler). Att: 85,000

EUROPEAN CUP-WINNERS' CUP

When Lazio held aloft the Cup-Winners' Cup after beating Mallorca at Villa Park, Birmingham in May 1999 they were also celebrating the end of an era – UEFA having decided that the tournament should be scrapped to make way for its expansion of the Champions League and the UEFA Cup. Yet the Cup-Winners' Cup had earned a distinguished place in the history of the game since its launch in the 1960–61 season.

The Final, played over two legs for the first and only time, saw Fiorentina at their best. In the first leg, in Glasgow, they frustrated the Rangers forwards, while winger Kurt Hamrin twice led the charge for Milani to score. In the return Hamrin again proved the match-winner, setting up Milani for the first and scoring the winner after Scott had equalized.

The success of the first tournament encouraged more clubs to get involved, and 23 entered the second in 1961–62. Fiorentina's impressive defense took them all the way again

in 1962, where they met Atletico Madrid in the Final, now played as a single match. The match, in Glasgow, produced a disappointing 1–1 draw, and when the replay took place – four months later – Atletico won the Cup with a straightforward 3–0 win.

In the 1963 competition the holders again reached the Final, and again they lost. Atletico faced Tottenham in Rotterdam and could not contain Bill Nicholson's international-packed side, who had won the FA Cup in successive seasons. Jimmy Greaves and Terry Dyson both scored twice as Tottenham won 5–1 to become the first English winners of a European trophy.

Tottenham's reign ended in the second round in 1964, when they were unfortunate to be drawn against Manchester United, who won 4–2 on aggregate. United fell in the quarter-finals to Portugal's Sporting Lisbon, who went on to win the Cup against MTK Budapest, although they needed a 1–0 replay win after a 3–3 draw in Belgium.

The Cup-winners' Cup had now established itself on the European scene, and 30 clubs entered the 1965

tournament. West Ham United, essentially novices at the European game, emulated Tottenham's success by beating TSV Munich 1860 in front of a full house at Wembley. The match was fast and open, but two goals in two minutes by reserve winger Tony Sealey won the Cup for the Londoners.

The following year, 1966, featured another England-West Germany Final, this time involving Liverpool and Borussia Dortmund. On a rain-lashed night in Glasgow, the Germans were slightly fortunate to win in extra time when a mis-hit cross by Libuda was deflected in by Yeats. Rangers returned for the 1967 Final, also against a German club, Bayern Munich – and were strangely out of sorts. Gerd Müller was well shackled but in the 18th minute of extra time Roth fired home the winner to keep the Cup in Germany. Another German club, Hamburg, contested the 1968 Final, but were no match for Milan, for whom Hamrin scored twice to win his second medal.

In 1969 the original draw was abandoned after Soviet troops entered Czechoslovakia, and a new

draw, keeping East and West apart, was made. Most Eastern countries were against the idea and withdrew, but the Czechs remained … and with sweet irony Slovan Bratislava collected the trophy, beating the favorites Barcelona 3–2 in Basle.

For the following three years the Cup stayed in Britain as Manchester City, Chelsea and, at the third attempt, Rangers all won. Manchester City beat Poland's Gornik Zabrze 2–1 in front of a poor crowd of 8,000 in Vienna in 1970; Chelsea needed a replay the next year in Athens to overcome Real Madrid, and Rangers finally won the trophy with a 3–2 victory over Moscow Dynamo in 1972.

The Rangers victory, however, was marred by ugly scenes in and around the Nou Camp stadium in Barcelona. The lunatic fringe of their supporters invaded the pitch before, during and after the match, and charged riot police outside the stadium, leaving one dead and scores injured. Rangers, having done so well to hang on for their victory, were banned for a year and were consequently unable to defend their title.

Leeds United almost made it four

MARKED MAN *Manchester United's Hughes in action during the 1991 final. The Welsh international scored both of United's goals.*

in a row for Britain in 1973 when they faced Milan in the Final in Salonika. Milan scored after five minutes through Chiarugi and promptly began using spoiling tactics, which were not appreciated by the Greek crowd. Leeds' frustration finally boiled over two minutes from the end, when Hunter and Sogliano were sent off for fighting.

Milan reached the Final again the following year, but lost to FC Magdeburg, who became the only East German winners of a European trophy. A paltry crowd of 4,000 in Rotterdam, the smallest for a Final in the competition's history, saw an own goal by Lanzi just before half-time set the East Germans on their way to a 2–0 victory

Kiev Dynamo kept the trophy behind the Iron Curtain with their first win, by beating Ferencvaros 3–0 in Basle in 1975. Belgium's Anderlecht then emerged as the competition's specialists with three successive appearances in the Final – of which they won the first and the third. In 1976 they beat West Ham 4–2 in Brussels, then lost 2–0 to Hamburg in 1977, before beating FK Austria 4–0 in Paris. Dutch striker Rob Rensenbrink scored two in each of the wins.

The 1979 tournament produced the highest-scoring Final in the competition's history as Barcelona beat Fortuna Düsseldorf 4–3 in Basle. Level at 2–2 after 90 minutes, Austrian striker Hans Krankl scored the clincher for the Spanish in extra time – after Rexach had made it 3–2 and Seel had equalized. Valencia retained the Cup for Spain the following season in the first European Final to be decided on penalties. A disappointing 0–0 draw in Brussels was decided when Graham Rix missed Arsenal's fifth penalty in the shoot-out, giving Valencia a 5–4 victory.

In the 1981 competition, Welsh Cup winners Newport County, then in the English Fourth Division, caused a sensation by knocking out the holders Valencia in the second round. Newport then narrowly lost in the quarter-finals to East Germany's Carl Zeiss Jena, who went on to contest an all-Eastern Final with Dynamo Tbilisi, who had destroyed West Ham in the quarter-finals. Tbilisi, with several internationals in the side, won 2–1 to clinch the Soviet Union's second Cup.

Barcelona won for the second time in four years in 1982, when they beat Belgium's Standard Liège 2–1 at the Nou Camp. Real Madrid spurned the chance to match their Catalan rivals the next year, when they lost to Aberdeen. . Juventus became the third Italian side to win the Cup when they beat FC Porto 2–1 in 1984. Everton won it for England the following season by outplaying Rapid Vienna in Rotterdam to complete a League Championship and Cup-winners' Cup double.

In1986 Kiev Dynamo won their second title with an outstanding 3–0 win over Atletico Madrid. Kiev, at the time, were one of the top clubs in Europe and supplied the bulk of the Soviet Union's national squad, including the great Oleg Blokhin, who scored in Kiev's 1975 triumph and again against Atletico.

Ajax of Amsterdam appeared in the next two finals. In 1987 they beat Lokomotive Leipzig 1–0 in Lyon, with Marco Van Basten scoring the winner in his last game for the club before his move to Milan. The following season Ajax were expected to retain the trophy against European debutants Mechelen, but the Belgians pulled off a shocking 1–0 win.

Barcelona collected their third Cup-winners' Cup in 1989, beating Italy's emerging Sampdoria 2–0 in Bern. The Italians, though, made amends the following year, beating Anderlecht 2–0, with Gianluca Vialli scoring twice in extra time.

Barcelona were back for 1991, and so were the English clubs. Manchester United went all the way to the Final and then won 2–1. The match provided Welsh striker Mark Hughes – dumped by Barcelona three years before – with sweet revenge as he scored both United's goals.

In 1992 Werder Bremen beat Monaco, veteran striker Klaus Allofs putting the German club on the way with the opening goal in a 2–0 win. Then Parma completed a remarkable 10-year transition from the Italian Third Division to European trophy-winners in 1993, when they beat Antwerp 3–1 at Wembley.

In both 1994 and 1995 the defending champions lost in the Final to extend the record of no holder retaining the Cup. Arsenal beat Parma 1–0 in 1994, but lost 2–1 to a freak 120th minute goal to Spain's Zaragoza.

Zarargoza's attempt to become the first club to retain the cup faltered in their 1996 quarter-finals against compatriots La Coruña, who fell to Paris Saint-Germain at the next stage. PSG became only the second French club to win a European trophy when they beat Rapid Vienna 1–0 in the final – the first in Brussels since 1985. The unwritten law which prevents holders from retaining the cup was again evident in 1997, when PSG fell 1–0 to Barcelona in Rotterdam. A penalty kick from Ronaldo was all that separated the teams on paper though Barcelona were far superior on the day. The same could not be said of Chelsea when they beat Stuttgart the following year in Stockholm. Vialli was back in his new role as Chelsea player-manager, but it was Gianfranco Zola who scored a superb winner.

Chelsea continued the odd tradition of failing to defend the trophy, defeated by European newcomers Mallorca who were themselves duly despatched, 2–1, by Lazio, winning their first European trophy.

Winners

European Cup-winners' Cup Finals

1961 *Glasgow.* Rangers 0, Fiorentina 2 (Milani 2).
Florence. Fiorentina 2 (Milani, Hamrin), Rangers 1 (Scott). Fiorentina won 4–1 on aggregate.

1962 *Glasgow.* Atletico Madrid 1 (Peiro), Fiorentina 1 (Hamrin) (aet).
Stuttgart: Atletico Madrid 3 (Jones, Mendonca, Peiro), Fiorentina 0.

1963 *Rotterdam:* Tottenham Hotspur 5 (Greaves 2, White, Dyson 2), Atletico Madrid 1 (Collar).

1964 *Brussels:* Sporting Lisbon 3 (Mascaranha, Figueiredo), MTK Budapest 3 (Sandor 2, Kuti) (aet).
Antwerp (replay): Sporting Lisbon 1 (Morais), MTK Budapest 0.

1965 *Wembley.* West Ham United 2 (Sealey 2), TSV Munich 1860 0.

1966 *Glasgow.* Borussia Dortmund 2 (Held, Libuda), Liverpool 1 (Hunt) (aet).

1967 *Nuremberg:* Bayern Munich 1 (Roth), Rangers 0 (aet).

1968 *Rotterdam:* Milan 2 (Hamrin 2), Hamburg SV 0.

1969 *Basle:* Slovan Bratislava 3 (Cvetler, Hrivnak, Jan Capkovic), Barcelona 2 (Zaldua, Rexach).

1970 *Vienna:* Manchester City 2 (Young, Lee), Gornik Zabrze 1 (Oslizlo).

1971 *Athens:* Chelsea 1 (Osgood), Real Madrid 1 (Zoco) (aet).
Athens (replay): Chelsea 2 (Dempsey, Osgood), Real Madrid 1 (Fleitas).

1972 *Barcelona:* Rangers 3 (Stein, Johnston 2), Moscow Dynamo 2 (Estrekov, Makovikov).

1973 *Salonika:* Milan 1 (Chiarugi), Leeds United 0.

1974 *Rotterdam:* FC Magdeburg 2 (o.g., Seguin), Milan 0.

1975 *Basle:* Kiev Dynamo 3 (Onischenko 2, Blokhin), Ferencvaros 0.

1976 *Brussels:* Anderlecht 4 (Rensenbrink 2, Van der Elst 2), West Ham United 2 (Holland, Robson).

1977 *Amsterdam:* Hamburg SV 2 (Volkert, Magath), Anderlecht 0.

1978 *Paris:* Anderlecht 4 (Rensenbrink 2, Van Binst 2), FK Austria 0.

1979 *Basle:* Barcelona 4 (Sanchez, Asensi, Rexach, Krankl), Fortuna Düsseldorf 3 (Allofs K., Seel 2) (aet).

1980 *Brussels:* Valencia 0, Arsenal 0 (aet). (*Valencia won 5–4 on pens.*)

1981 *Düsseldorf:* Dynamo Tbilisi 2 (Gutsayev, Daraselia), Carl Zeiss Jena 1 (Hoppe).

1982 *Barcelona:* Barcelona 2 (Simonsen, Quini), Standard Liège 1 (Vandermissen).

1983 *Gothenburg:* Aberdeen 2 (Black , Hewitt), Real Madrid 1 (Juanito) (aet).

1984 *Basle:* Juventus 2 (Vignola, Boniek), FC Porto 1 (Sousa).

1985 *Rotterdam:* Everton 3 (Gray, Steven, Sheedy), Rapid Vienna 1 (Krankl).

1986 *Lyons:* Kiev Dynamo 3 (Zavarov, Blokhin, Yevtushenko), Atletico Madrid 0.

1987 *Athens:* Ajax 1 (Van Basten), Lokomotive Leipzig 0.

1988 *Strasbourg:* Mechelen 1 (De Boer), Ajax 0.

1989 *Berne:* Barcelona 2 (Salinas, Recarte), Sampdoria 0.

1990 *Gothenburg:* Sampdoria 2 (Vialli 2), Anderlecht 0 (aet).

1991 *Rotterdam:* Manchester United 2 (Hughes 2), Barcelona 1 (Koeman).

1992 *Lisbon:* Werder Bremen 2 (Allofs K., Rufer), Monaco 0.

1993 *Wembley.* Parma 3 (Minotti, Melli, Cuoghi), Antwerp 1 (Severeyns).

1994 *Copenhagen:* Arsenal 1 (Smith), Parma 0.

1995 *Paris:* Real Zaragoza 2 (Esnaider, Nayim), Arsenal 1 (Hartson).

1996 *Brussels:* Paris St Germain 1 (N'Gotty), Rapid Vienna 0.

1997 *Rotterdam:* Barcelona 1 (Ronaldo), Paris St Germain 0.

1998 *Stockholm:* Chelsea 1 (Zola), Stuttgart 0.

1999 *Birmingham:* Lazio 2 (Vieri, Nedved), Mallorca 1 (Dani).

UEFA CUP

The UEFA Cup started life in 1955, and, unusually, was not a French idea. When UEFA was formed in 1954, FIFA vice-president Ernst Thommen, of Switzerland, thought up the idea of a European competition to give a competitive edge to friendly matches between cities holding trade fairs.

This rather dubious reason for a competition was no deterrent, as officials from 12 cities holding trade fairs approved Thommen's plans in April 1955, and the International Inter-Cities Fairs Cup, as it was originally named, was under way. The competition was to be held over two seasons to avoid disrupting domestic fixtures, but because the original entrants represented cities holding trade fairs, and wherever possible fixtures were designed to coincide with

the fairs, the first tournament overran into a third year.

The Fairs Cup, as it was commonly known, was designed for representative sides, but it soon became clear that it was a competition that the clubs would dominate. In the first tournament, which ran from 1955 to 1958, 12 cities were represented by select teams. But the composition of the sides was a matter of individual choice. Thus while London chose its team from the 11 professional sides in the city, Barcelona was represented by CF Barcelona, with one token Español player, and Birmingham was represented by the entire Birmingham City side. This discrepancy clearly favored the more coherent clubs, and it was almost inevitable that two would meet in the Final.

Almost three years after the first ball had been kicked in the tournament, London and Barcelona fought out a

2–2 draw at Stamford Bridge in the first leg of the Final, only for the Spaniards to win the return 6–0 – Suarez and Evaristo each scoring twice. Barcelona's win was the first of six in a row by Latin clubs in the competition, in keeping with the European Cup, which was also dominated by Latin sides in the early years of its existence.

The second tournament, 1958–60, drew 16 entrants, mostly club sides, and was played on a straight home-and-away knock-out basis. Barcelona, strengthened by the arrivals of Hungary's Sandor Kocsis and Zoltan Czibor, retained the trophy without losing a match. Their opponents were again English, but this time it was Birmingham City and not London who made it to the Final. A 0–0 draw on a terrible field in Birmingham set Barcelona up for the 4–1 return win, with goals by Martinez, Czibor (two) and Coll.

Barcelona's attempt to win a hat-trick of Fairs Cups ended in the second round of the 1960–61 tournament, at the unlikely hands of Scotland's Hibernian. The Edinburgh side only took part because Chelsea withdrew, but, having beaten Lausanne in the first round, they surprised everybody by beating the holders in the next round. Birmingham again made it the Final, where they faced Italy's Roma, who needed a third match to beat Hibs in the semi-finals. This extended semi-final meant that the Final itself was held over until the following season, by which time Roma had added to an already impressive line-up. Birmingham did well to force a 2–2 draw at home, but were beaten 2–0 in Rome in the return … their second successive defeat in the Final.

The organizers had decided to allow three teams per country to enter

Winners

Fairs Cup Finals

1958 *London*: London Select XI 2 (Greaves, Langley), Barcelona 2 (Tejada, Martinez). Att: 45,000
Barcelona: Barcelona 6 (Suarez 2, Evaristo 2, Martinez, Verges), London Select XI 0. Att: 62,000
1960 *Birmingham*: Birmingham City 0, Barcelona 0. Att: 40,000
Barcelona: Barcelona 4 (Martinez, Czibor 2, Coll), Birmingham City 1 (Hooper). Att: 70,000
1961 *Birmingham*: Birmingham City 2 (Hellawell, Orritt), Roma 2 (Manfredini 2). Att:21,000
Rome: Roma 2 (o.g., Pestrin), Birmingham City 0. Att: 60,000
1962 *Valencia*: Valencia 6 (Yosu 2, Guillot 3, Nunez), Barcelona 2 (Kocsis 2). Att: 65,000
Barcelona: Barcelona 1 (Kocsis), Valencia 1 (Guillot). Att: 60,000
1963 *Zagreb*: Dinamo Zagreb 1 (Zambata), Valencia 2 (Waldo, Urtiaga). Att: 40,000
Valencia: Valencia 2 (Manio, Nunez), Dinamo Zagreb 0. Att: 55,000
1964 *Barcelona*: Real Zaragoza 2 (Villa , Marcelino), Valencia 1 (Urtiaga). Att: 50,000
1965 *Turin*: Ferencvaros 1 (Fenyvesi), Juventus 0. Att: 25,000.
1966 *Barcelona*: Barcelona 0, Real Zaragoza 1 (Canario). Att: 35,000
Zaragoza: Real Zaragoza 2, (Marcellino 2), Barcelona 4 (Pujol 3, Zaballa) . Att: 29,000
1967 *Zagreb*: Dinamo Zagreb 2 (Cercek 2), Leeds 0. Att: 40,000.
Leeds: Leeds 0, Dinamo Zagreb 0. Att: 35,000
1968 *Leeds*: Leeds 1 (Jones), Ferencvaros 0. Att: 25,000

Budapest: Ferencvaros 0, Leeds 0. Att: 76,000
1969 *Newcastle*: Newcastle 3 (Moncur 2, Scott), Ujpest Dozsa 0. Att: 60,000
Budapest: Ujpest Dozsa 2 (Bene, Gorocs), Newcastle 3 (Moncur, Arentoft, Foggon). Att: 37,000
1970 *Brussels*: Anderlecht 3 (Devrindt, Mulder 2), Arsenal 1 (Kennedy). Att: 37,000
London: Arsenal 3 (Kelly, Radford, Sammels), Anderlecht 0. Att: 51,000
1971 *Turin*: Juventus 2 (Bettega, Capello), Leeds 2 (Madeley, Bates). Att: 65,000
Leeds: Leeds 1 (Clarke), Juventus 1 (Anastasi). Att: 42,000. (*Leeds won on away goals*)

UEFA Cup Finals

1972 *Wolverhampton*: Wolverhampton 1 (McCalliog), Tottenham Hotspur 2 (Chivers 2). Att: 38,000
London: Tottenham Hotspur 1 (Mullery), Wolverhampton 1 (Wagstaffe). Att: 54,000
1973 *Liverpool*: Liverpool 3 (Keegan 2, Lloyd), Borussia Mönchengladbach 0. Att: 41,000
Mönchengladbach: Borussia Mönchengladbach 2 (Heynckes 2), Liverpool 0. Att: 35,000
1974 *London*: Tottenham Hotspur 2 (England, o.g.), Feyenoord 2 (Van Hanegem, De Jong). Att: 46,000.
Rotterdam: Feyenoord 2 (Rijsbergen, Ressel), Tottenham Hotspur 0. Att: 59,000
1975 *Düsseldorf*: Borussia Mönchengladbach 0, Twente Enschede 0. Att: 42,000
Enschede: Twente Enschede 1

(Drost), Borussia Mönchengladbach 5 (Simonsen 2, Heynckes 3). Att: 21,000
1976 *Liverpool*: Liverpool 3 (Kennedy, Case, Keegan), Club Brugge 2 (Lambert, Cools). Att: 49,000
Bruges: Club Brugge 1 (Lambert), Liverpool 1 (Keegan). Att: 32,000
1977 *Turin*: Juventus 1 (Tardelli), Athletic Bilbao 0. Att: 75,000
Bilbao: Athletic Bilbao 2 (Churruca, Carlos), Juventus 1 (Bettega). Att: 43,000. (*Juventus won on away goals*.)
1978 *Corsica*: Bastia 0, PSV Eindhoven 0. Att: 15,000
Eindhoven: PSV Eindhoven 3 (Van der Kerkhof W., Deijkers, Van der Kuijlen), Bastia 0. Att: 27,000
1979 *Belgrade*: Red Star Belgrade 1 (Sestic), Borussia Mönchengladbach 1 (o.g.). Att: 87,000
Düsseldorf: Borussia Mönchengladbach 1 (Simonsen), Red Star Belgrade 0. Att: 45,000
1980 *Mönchengladbach*: Borussia Mönchengladbach 2 (Kulik 2, Matthäus), Eintracht Frankfurt 2 (Karger, Holzenbein). Att: 25,000
Frankfurt: Eintracht Frankfurt 1 (Schaub), Borussia Mönchengladbach 0. Att: 59,000. (*Eintracht won on away goals*.)
1981 *Ipswich*: Ipswich 3 (Wark, Thijssen, Mariner), AZ 67 Alkmaar 0. Att: 27,000
Amsterdam: AZ 67 Alkmaar 4 (Welzl, Metgod, Tol, Jonker), Ipswich 2 (Thijssen, Wark). Att: 28,000
1982 *Gothenburg*: IFK Gothenburg 1 (Tord Holmgren), Hamburg SV 0. Att: 42,000
Hamburg: Hamburg SV 0, IFK Gothenburg 3 (Corneliusson,

Nilsson, Fredriksson). Att: 60,000
1983 *Brussels*: Anderlecht 1 (Brylle), Benfica 0. Att: 55,000
Lisbon: Benfica 1 (Sheu), Anderlecht 1 (Lozano). Att: 80,000
1984 *Brussels*: Anderlecht 1 (Olsen), Tottenham Hotspur 1 (Miller). Att: 35,000
London: Tottenham Hotspur 1 (Roberts), Anderlecht 1 (Czerniatynski) (aet). (*Tottenham won 4–3 on penalties*). Att: 46,000
1985 *Szekesfehervar*: Videoton 0, Real Madrid 3 (Michel, Santilana, Valdano). Att: 30,000
Madrid: Real Madrid 0, Videoton 1 (Majer). Att: 90,000
1986 *Madrid*: Real Madrid 5 (Sanchez, Gordillo, Valdano 2, Santilana), Köln 1 (Allofs). Att: t: 85,000
Berlin: Köln 2 (Bein, Geilenkirchen), Real Madrid 0. Att: 15,000
1987 *Gothenburg*: IFK Gothenburg 1 (Pettersson), Dundee United 0. Att: 50,000
Dundee: Dundee United 1 (Clark), IFK Gothenburg 1 (Nilsson L.). Att: 21,000
1988 *Barcelona*: Español 3 (Losada 2, Soler), Bayer Leverkusen 0. Att: 42,000
Leverkusen: Bayer Leverkusen 3 (Tita, Gotz, Cha-Bum-Kun), Español 0 (aet). (*Leverkusen won 3–2 on penalties*). Att: 22,000
1989 *Naples*: Napoli 2 (Maradona, Careca), Stuttgart 1 (Gaudino). Att: 83,000
Stuttgart: Stuttgart 3 (Klinsmann, o.g., Schmaler O.), Napoli 3 (Alemao, Ferrera, Careca). Att: 67,000
1990 *Turin*: Juventus 3 (Galia, Casiraghi, De Agostini), Fiorentina

1 (Buso). Att: 45,000
Avellino: Fiorentina 0, Juventus 0. Att: 32,000
1991 *Milan*: Internazionale 2 (Matthäus, Berti), Roma 0. Att: 75,000
Rome: Roma 1 (Rizzitelli), Internazionale 0. Att: 71,000
1992 *Turin*: Torino 2 (Casagrande 2), Ajax 2 (Jonk, Pettersson). Att: 65,000
Amsterdam: Ajax 0, Torino 0. Att: 42,000. (*Ajax won on away goals*)
1993 *Dortmund*: Borussia Dortmund 1 (Rummenigge), Juventus 3 (Baggio D., Baggio R. 2). Att: 37,000
Turin: Juventus 3 (Baggio D. 2, Möller), Borussia Dortmund 0. Att: 60,000
1994 *Vienna*: Salzburg 0, Internazionale 1 (Berti). Att: 43,500
Milan: Internazionale 1 (Vonk), Salzburg 0. Att: 80,326
1995 *Parma*: Parma 1(D. Baggio), Juventus 0, Att: 26,350
Milan: Juventus 1 (Vialli) , Parma 1 (D. Baggio). Att: 80.750
1996 *Munich*: Bayern Munich 2 (Helmer, Scholl), Bordeaux 0. Att: 62,500
Bordeaux: Bordeaux 1 (Dutuel), Bayern Munich 3 (Scholl, Kostadinov, Klinsmann). Att: 36,000
1997 *Gelsenkirchen*: Schalke 1 (Wilmots), Internazionale 0. Att: 56,824
Milan: Internazionale 1 (Zamorano), Schalke 0 (Schalke won 4–1 on penalties). Att: 81,675
1998 *Paris*: Internazionale 3 (Zamorano, Zanetti, Ronaldo), Lazio 0. Att: 45,000
1999 *Moscow*: Parma 3, (Crespo, Vanoli, Chiesa), Marseille 0.

the 1961–62 tournament, which had an entry of 28, and now the Spanish showed their dominance. Barcelona and Valencia reached the Final, with Valencia powering to a 7–3 aggregate victory over their countrymen. Valencia held on to the trophy the following season, beating Dinamo Zagreb 4–1 on aggregate in the Final, but were thwarted in their hat-trick bid by another Spanish side, Real Zaragoza. The 1964 Final was played as a single match in Barcelona, where goals by Villa and Marcelino secured a 2–1 win for Zaragoza.

The 1965 competition attracted 48 entries, and for the first time the Cup left Latin Europe, and headed east. Hungary's Ferencvaros fought their way through from the first round, with victories over Spartak Brno, Wiener Sport-Club, Roma, Athletic Bilbao and Manchester United, to face Juventus in the Final. The Italians, having safely negotiated the two opening rounds, were given a bye in the quarter-finals as the organizers sought to balance the numbers. This, coupled with the fact that the Final (again a single match) was in Turin, seemed to give Juve a definite advantage. But Ferencvaros produced a defensive formation that surpassed even the Italians' catenaccio, and a single goal by Fenyvesi after 74 minutes was enough.

The 1966 tournament returned to the two-game format for the Final, but the earlier rounds were marked by violence. Chelsea were pelted with rubbish in Rome, Leeds and Valencia fought a battle which resulted in three expulsions, and Leeds then had Johnny Giles expelled in the semi-final against Real Zaragoza. Spain again emerged triumphant, with Barcelona and Real Zaragoza meeting in the Final. The Catalans won the trophy for the third time, 4–3 on aggregate.

The tournament was now moving into an era of English dominance. Leeds reached the 1967 Final, where they lost to Dinamo Zagreb, but they made amends the following season by beating Ferencvaros 1–0 on aggregate in the Final, after going unbeaten in previous rounds. This was the first of six consecutive victories by English clubs during the late 1960s and early 1970s.

In 1971 the Cup returned to Leeds, who beat Juventus. The first leg of the Final, in Turin, was abandoned at 0–0 because of rain, and in the rearranged fixture Leeds forced an excellent 2–2 draw. Juve were more threatening in the return, but could only manage a 1–1 draw, which meant Leeds won on away goals. Amazingly neither finalist had lost en route to the Final so the unfortunate Italians had only runners-up medals to show for 12 unbeaten matches.

The competition name changed in 1972, and the first UEFA Cup Final was between two English clubs – Tottenham and Wolverhampton Wanderers. Tottenham won 3–2 on aggregate, and Liverpool won the next tournament, beating Borussia Mönchengladbach in the Final, to complete a double hat-trick for English clubs in the tournament. Tottenham returned for the 1974 Final, but could not cope with Holland's Feyenoord – European champions in 1970 – who won 4–2 on aggregate. The Final, however, was marred by violence as both sets of supporters fought running battles with each other and the police.

Another Dutch club, Twente Enschede, reached the Final in 1975, but they were outclassed by Borussia Mönchengladbach of West Germany. After a surprising 0–0 draw, Borussia turned on the power in the return to win 5–1, with Jupp Heynckes scoring a hat-trick, and Allan Simonsen two. Liverpool won again in 1976, beating Club Brugge 4–3 on aggregate in the Final. It was ironic, therefore, that this emerging Liverpool side should then go on to win two successive European Cups, 1977 and 1978, beating Borussia and Brugge respectively in the Finals.

Italy and Spain contested the 1977 UEFA Cup Final, represented by Juventus and Athletic Bilbao, with the Italians winning on away goals after a 2–2 aggregate draw. In 1978 PSV Eindhoven won the Cup for Holland again, beating France's Bastia 3–0 at home after a 0–0 draw in Corsica – the only time a European Final has been played on an island outside the British Isles.

Borussia Mönchengladbach got to their third Final in 1979, and made it two wins out of three by beating Red Star Belgrade 2–1 on aggregate, although they needed an own goal and a Simonsen penalty to do it. Borussia reached the Final again the following year, and faced fellow West Germans Eintracht Frankfurt in the Final. Eintracht won the trophy on the away goals rule. In 1981 Ipswich Town brought the Cup back to England with a 5–4 aggregate victory over Dutch side AZ 67 Alkmaar. Ipswich's John Wark scored in both legs of the Final to bring his total in that season's competition to 14 – equalling the all-time record set by Milan's José Altafini in the 1963 European Cup.

IFK Gothenburg became the first Swedish winners of a European trophy when they beat Hamburg in 1982, and they went on to win again in 1987, beating Dundee United. Between those two victories, Anderlecht and Real Madrid dominated the competition. Anderlecht beat Benfica 2–1 on aggregate to win the 1983 competition, and they returned to the Final the following year against Tottenham. Both legs produced 1–1 draws, and after extra time produced no winner, Tottenham took the Cup on penalties, reserve goalkeeper Tony Parks saving the decisive kick.

Tottenham's defence of the trophy in 1985 ended in the quarter-finals, where they were narrowly and unluckily beaten 1–0 on aggregate by Real Madrid. The Spaniards, aided by the German Uli Stielike and the Argentinian Jorge Valdano, went on to beat Hungary's Videoton 3–1 in the Final. Real retained the trophy the following season with an demolition of West Germany's Köln. A 5–1 win in Madrid was followed by a 2–0 defeat, but Real kept the trophy with a 5–3 aggregate margin.

Following Gothenburg's second success in 1987, the Cup was won on penalties for the second time when Bayer Leverkusen and Español contested the Final. Español won the first leg 3–0 at home and looked all set for Spain's ninth victory, but Bayer levelled the aggregate score in the second leg, and then won 3–2 on penalties.

Since then the UEFA Cup has been dominated by Italian clubs. In the seven Finals up to 1995, 10 finalists have been Italian, three have been all-Italian affairs, and Serie A clubs have won six. In 1989 Napoli, led by Diego Maradona, beat VfB Stuttgart; Juventus and Fiorentina contested an all-Italian Final in 1990, with Juventus winning 3–1 at home and on aggregate; in 1991 Internazionale narrowly beat Roma 2–1; in 1992 Torino lost to Ajax – who were completing a hat-trick of European trophy wins – but only on away goals after 2–2 and 0–0 draws; and in 1993 Juventus won the Cup again, proving themselves to be far too good for Borussia Dortmund.

Internazionale overcame Austrians Salzburg to win in 1994, 1–0 in both games. In 1994–95, Juventus and Parma were first and second for most of the Serie A season, and reached both the UEFA and domestic Cup finals. In the UEFA Cup it was the newcomers who prevailed 2–1 on aggregate, with ex-Juventus player Dino Baggio scoring both goals.

The system of entry into the UEFA Cup, based on past performances, ensures that the more successful countries, such as Italy, Spain, Germany and England, get four entrants. However, as more countries enter UEFA, more clubs are entering the tournament, and UEFA had to expand the tournament with a preliminary round in mid-July.

The rebuilt UEFA-Intertoto Cup was used as a qualifying event for 1995–96. French club Bordeaux entered through that route went all the way to the final – beating Milan in a shock quarter-final, reversing a 2–0 first leg deficit – before losing to Bayern Munich. Jürgen Klinsmann scored a European club record 15 goals in the tournament,

The Cup stayed in Germany in 1997 when historic Schalke from the Ruhr, appearing in a European final for the first time, defeated Internazionale on penalties in Milan.

Inter bounced back a year later to beat their fellow Italians of Lazio 3–0 in the Parc des Princes in Paris. UEFA's decision to abandon the two-leg format in favor of a single-match final was vindicated by a superb display from Inter while Parma maintained Italy's pre-eminence in 1999.

THE GREAT CLUBS

Professional soccer swept through Britain in the 1880s and western Europe in the late 1920s. The big clubs of Spain, Italy, France and Portugal were importing star foreigners by the turn of the 1930s, but it was not until the mid-1950s that Belgium, Holland and then Germany caught up with full-time professional clubs. When they did, the balance of the European game changed yet again.

The great traditions of soccer are kept alive, week in, week out, by the clubs. From Ajax in Holland to Vasco da Gama in Brazil, from Barcelona in Spain to Liverpool in England, they provide the first call of loyalty on the public. People who may never have attended a match in years still look out for the result of "their" club each week. Evidence of the depths of loyalty which certain clubs can inspire is widely available – from the way Real Madrid's fans came up with the money to fund the building of the Estadio Bernabeu in the 1940s to the proud boast from Portugal's Benfica of 122,000 members. Every club has its tales of the great days and great players, great managers and great victories. Some, like Manchester United, have been touched by tragedy, others, like Marseille, with controversy. The greatest, clearly, are those who have repeatedly proved their power and strength by lifting the continental club competitions in Europe and South America. Some of them are described here.

AJAX AMSTERDAM
HOLLAND

Founded: 1900
Stadium: Arena (50,000)
Colors: Red and white broad stripes/white
League: 26
Cup: 12
World Club Cup: 1972, 1995
European Cup: 1971, 1972, 1973, 1995
European Cup-winners' Cup: 1987
UEFA Cup: 1992
Supercup: 1972, 1973, 1995

Ajax, on beating Torino in the 1992 UEFA Cup Final, became only the second team after Italy's Juventus to have won all three European trophies and a full house of all seven titles on offer to clubs. The achievement was a popular one, bearing in mind the entertainment and style the Amsterdam club had consistently provided. The first hints of glory to come were in evidence in 1966–67 when, under former Dutch international Rinus Michels, Ajax thrashed Liverpool 5–1 in a European Cup tie. Two years later Ajax became the first Dutch side to reach the European Cup Final, though they lost 4–1 to Milan. In 1971 Ajax were back as winners, beating Panathinaikos 2–0 at Wembley. In the next two Finals, they beat Internazionale 2–0, then Juventus 1–0. Johan Cruyff was their inspiration.

Ajax's trademark was the "total football" system, which involved taking full advantage of a generation of skilled well-rounded players whose versatility and intelligence allowed bewildering changes of position. It was "The Whirl," as envisaged early in the 1950s by that soccer prophet, Willi Meisl. After the sale of Cruyff to Barcelona in 1973, Ajax fell away and it took his return, a decade later, as technical director, to propel them back to the peaks of the European game. Under Cruyff, the new Ajax generation won the

FINNISHED ARTICLE *Ajax's Jari Litmanen*

Cup-winners' Cup in 1987 – his friend and pupil Marco Van Basten scoring the goal which beat Lokomotive Leipzig in the Final in Athens. Cruyff's successor Louis Van Gaal then secured the UEFA Cup five years later. Despite continuing to sell many of their best players, Ajax's 1994–95 squad was statistically their best ever; the team won the League championship without losing a game, and the European Cup for the fourth time. Injury problems foiled their bid for a fifth Cup the following season when Ajax lost on penalties to Juventus after a 1–1 draw in Rome.

ANDERLECHT
BRUSSELS, BELGIUM

Founded: 1908
Stadium: Constant Vanden Stock/Parc Astrid (28,063)
Colors: White with mauve/white
League: 23
Cup: 7
European Cup-winners' Cup: 1976, 1978
UEFA Cup: 1983
Supercup: 1976, 1978

Anderlecht's international debut was not a happy one: they crashed 10–0 and 12–0 on aggregate to Manchester United in an early European Cup. Since then, however, the Royal Sporting Club have earned respect far and wide for their domestic domination and an international outlook which has brought success in both the European Cup-winners' Cup and the UEFA Cup. Much credit reflects on the coaching work of Englishman Bill Gormlie, a former Blackburn goalkeeper, who helped lay the foundations for success in the late 1940s and early 1950s. Equally important was the financial power of the millionaire brewer, Constant Vanden Stock. Before his take-over Anderlecht relied mainly on homegrown talent like Paul Van Himst, the greatest Belgian player of all time. As Anderlecht's prestige grew, particularly thanks to the European Cup competitions, they were able to compete in the international transfer market. A significant coaching influence, in the early 1960s, was Frenchman Pierre Sinibaldi, who perfected a tactical formation which relied on a flat back four, the offside trap, and possession in midfield. It worked well against almost all opposition except British clubs, whose more direct style constantly caught the defenders on the turn. Thus, the first time Anderlecht reached a European final – in the Fairs Cup in 1970 – they were beaten by Arsenal. European success, in the Cup-winners' Cup in 1976 and 1978, had to await the more pragmatic coaching approach of Dutchman Wiel Corver and Belgian Raymond Goethals. Later, with Van Himst having returned as coach, Anderlecht won the UEFA Cup and in Enzo Scifo produced the finest Belgian player since Van Himst himself.

ENZO SCIFO *Anderlecht discovery, and the finest Belgian player of recent years*

GLORY GOAL *Arsenal's 1989 title-clincher*

ARSENAL
LONDON, ENGLAND

Founded: 1886
Stadium: Highbury (38,500)
Colors: Red/white
League: 10
Cup: 6
European Cup-winners's Cup: 1994
Fairs Cup: 1970

Arsenal, today a North London club, had their origins south of the Thames, at the Woolwich Arsenal. The club turned professional in 1891 and entered the Football League a year later, reaching the First Division in 1904 and the FA Cup semi-finals in 1906. After the First World War they moved to Highbury, and appointed the legendary Herbert Chapman as manager in 1925.

Chapman had a flair for publicity, an innovative approach to tactics and a talent for motivation. He spent heavily but wisely on the likes of first Charlie Buchan and Alex James, introduced the stopper center-half and created the all-conquering outfit which won the League five times in the 1930s and the FA Cup twice. Arsenal won the League twice more and the FA Cup once in the eight years after the war. A 17-year hiatus then followed before the Gunners ended their longest trophy drought by winning the Fairs Cup.

A year later, manager Bertie Mee celebrated a historic league and cup "double." Classy midfielder George Graham later returned as manager, master-minding a string of successes in the League, FA Cup, League Cup and Cup-winners' Cup, but his reign ended abruptly in 1995 amid controversy over transfer "bungs."

French manager Arsene Wenger arrived from Japan and turned the Gunners into a multi-national attacking side with flair, winning the "double" in his first full season.

ATLETICO MADRID
SPAIN

Founded: 1903
Stadium: Vicente Calderon/Manzanares
(62,000)
Colors: Red and white stripes/blue
League: 9
Cup: 9
World Club Cup: 1974
European Cup-winners' Cup: 1962

Atletico Madrid have always existed in the shadow of neighbors Real, but they still rank among the Big Three of Spanish soccer and boast a proud record at international level. Not that life has always been easy. In the late 1930s, after the Spanish Civil War, it took a merger with the Air Force club to keep Atletico in business; in 1959, they just failed to reach the European Cup Final when Real beat them in a semi-final play-off; in the early 1960s they had to share Real's Estadio Bernabeu, because Atletico's Metropolitano had been sold to developers before the club's new stadium could be completed. European glory did come to Atletico in the shape of the Cup-winners' Cup in 1962 and was a well-deserved prize for players such as inside-left Joaquin Peiro and his wing partner Enrique Collar. But it was not until the early 1970s that Atletico put together a comparable team, thanks to the purchases of Argentines Ruben Hugo Ayala and Ramon Heredia. In 1974, Atletico secured that elusive place in the European Cup Final. But, after taking the lead against Bayern Munich in extra time, Atletico conceded a late equalizer.

Consolation for their 4–0 defeat in the replay came with the opportunity to substitute for reluctant Bayern in the World Club Cup against Independiente of Argentina. By the time the tie came around Atletico had appointed as coach Luis Aragones, the midfielder who had scored their goal in the European Cup Final against Bayern. Atletico duly beat Independiente 1–0 and were, for a year at least, on top of the world. In the late 1980s the club was taken over by the extrovert builder Jesus Gil. He pumped millions of dollars into the club but generated more bad publicity than good, hiring and

KINGMAKER *Atletico Madrid's president Jesus Gil finally enjoyed success in 1996*

firing coaches at a breathtaking rate. It all came together in dramatic fashion when Atletico won the league and cup "double" in the spring of 1996.

ATLETICO NACIONAL
MEDELLIN, COLOMBIA

Founded: 1938
Stadium: Atanasio Giradot (35,000)
Colors: Green and white stripes/white
League: 5
South American Club Cup: 1989
Inter-American Cup: 1989

Atletico Nacional of Medellin are not the most famous club to come out of Colombia. That honor will always belong to Millonarios, who led the professional, pirate revolution in the early 1950s. But Nacional earned a

place in history by becoming the first club to take the Copa Libertadores, the South American Club Cup, across the Andes to the western side of the continent. Nacional, who provided the base of the Colombian World Cup team in 1990, were in 1954 the first champions of Colombia after the rapprochement with FIFA. Yet it was not until 1971 that they made their debut in the South American Club Cup under Argentine coach Osvaldo Zubeldia. He had earned a fearsome reputation as boss of the rugged Estudiantes de La Plata team which had dominated Argentine and South American club soccer in the late 1960s. However, without resorting to the cynicism which made Estudiantes hated, he turned Nacional into Colombian champions three times in the mid-1970s and early 1980s. Zubeldia was followed by Luis Cubilla, at

whose suggestion, in 1986, Nacional appointed a former stalwart central defender, Francisco Maturana, as boss. In 1987 and 1988 they finished championship runners-up and then, in 1989, seized the South American club crown. Unfortunately, their preparations for the world club showdown with Milan were wrecked when the government halted the league season because of the increasing violence being engendered on the fringes of the game by the drug and betting cartels. Nacional did not emerge with their reputation unscathed. It was not only that Medellin was the center of the drug trade; several Nacional players were friends of the notorious drugs baron Pablo Escobar. Indeed, when Escobar was eventually killed in 1993 by security forces, at his funeral the coffin was draped in a Nacional flag.

BARCELONA
SPAIN

Founded: 1899
Stadium: Nou Camp (115,000)
Colors: Blue and red stripes/blue
League: 16
Cup: 24
European Cup: 1992
European Cup-winners' Cup: 1979, 1982, 1989, 1997
Fairs Cup: 1958, 1960, 1966
Supercup: 1992

Barcelona finally ended a duel with destiny when, in 1992, they beat Sampdoria 1–0 at Wembley to win the European Cup. It was a case of third time lucky, for the greatest prize in the European club game had twice eluded them at the final hurdle. Barcelona had been the first winners of the Inter-Cities Fairs Cup and had won the Cup-winners' Cup three times. But their European Cup campaigns seemed to have been jinxed. First, in 1961, when Barcelona had apparently achieved the hard part by eliminating the title-holders and their bitter rivals Real Madrid, they lost to Benfica in the Final in Berne. Barcelona hit the woodwork three times, yet lost 3–2 against the run of play. Great players such as Luis Suarez, Ladislav Kubala, Sandor Kocsis and Zoltan Czibor had everything on their side except luck.

HELENIO HERRERA

Coach of Red Star Paris, Stade Francais (France), Atletico Madrid, Valladolid, Sevilla (Spain), Belenenses (Portugal), Barcelona (Spain), Internazionale and Roma (Italy); also Spanish and Italian national teams (born April 17, 1916)

One of the world's most innovative and single-minded coaches. Herrera, born in Argentina, brought up in Morocco and a player in France, experimented at Barcelona in the 1950s by using inside-forwards at wing-half to turn "easy" matches into goal sprees. His attacking tactics proved ineffective at Inter so Herrera developed, instead, the most ruthlessly disciplined catenaccio. Herrera demanded total obedience, insisting that his players place their hands on the ball and swear loyalty to each other before going out for a match. Stars who balked at such rituals were sold, however popular or successful. Inter won the World and European Cups twice each before Herrera's career went into decline at Roma.

NO LOVE LOST *Jürgen Klinsmann (right) shoots for goal in Bayern Munich's UEFA Cup semi-final victory over Spain's Barcelona – one year earlier, the beaten defender, Gica Popescu, had been Klinsmann's teammate at Tottenham*

IMPORT DUTY *Portugal's Luis Figo was one of the more recent of Barcelona's foreign acquisitions*

History repeated itself in even more galling circumstances in 1986. Barcelona, coached by Terry Venables and gambling on the fitness of long-time injured Steve Archibald, faced Steaua Bucharest in Seville. Barcelona lost in a penalty shoot-out after a goal-less draw.

It took the return of 1970s inspiration Johan Cruyff, this time as coach, to steer a new generation of international stars – including Ronald Koeman, Hristo Stoichkov and Michael Laudrup – to victory long overdue for one of the world's biggest clubs. Barcelona's 1994 league title was their fourth in a row, the last three of them achieved in the closing moments of the final day, twice at the expense of great rivals Real Madrid.

Failure to win a trophy in 1995 or 1996, however, resulted in Cruyff's dismissal after eight years in charge. He was replaced by Bobby Robson.

BAYERN MUNICH
GERMANY

Founded: 1900
Stadium: Olimpiastadion (69,261)
Colors: All red
League: 15
Cup: 8
World Club Cup: 1976
European Cup: 1974, 1975, 1976
European Cup-winners' Cup: 1967
UEFA Cup: 1996

Bayern are Germany's most glamorous club, even though high tax rates mean they have never been able to hold stars tempted by the rich pickings of Italy. In the 1980s Bayern became almost an Italian nursery as they lost Karl-Heinz Rummenigge, Andy Brehme and Lothar Matthäus to Internazionale and Stefan Reuter and Jurgen Kohler to Juventus. All this transfer activity underlined the fact that the Bayern success story is – with the exception of one championship in 1932 and one cup in 1957 – a relatively recent affair. The identities of the men who secured all the glittering titles read like a Who's Who of the world game: Franz Beckenbauer, Gerd Müller, Sepp Maier, Paul Breitner, Rummenigge and Matthäus. The German championship was originally organized in regional leagues, with the winners playing off at the end of each season for the title: only once in the pre-war years did Bayern win all the way through. That was in 1932, when they defeated Eintracht Frankfurt 2–0. Not until 1957, and a 1–0 win over Fortuna Düsseldorf in the cup final, did Bayern have anything more to celebrate. Indeed their record was so mediocre that they were not included in the inaugural Bundesliga in 1963–64. But, a year later, Bayern won promotion; in 1966 they won the cup, and in 1967 they secured the European Cup-winners' Cup, thanks to an extra-time victory over Rangers. That was the team led and inspired by Beckenbauer in the role of attacking sweeper, with Maier in goal and Müller up front. All three stars shone even more brightly as Bayern landed a European Cup hat-trick in the mid-1970s. In the 1980s Bayern were twice European Cup runners-up, but complacency set in and it was not until Beckenbauer returned – first as vice-president, then coach, then president – that Bayern regained their pre-eminence. Their 1996 UEFA Cup triumph made Bayern the fourth club to win all three European trophies.

BENFICA
LISBON, PORTUGAL

Founded: 1904
Stadium: Estadio do Benfica/Da Luz (92,385)
Colors: Red/white
League: 29
Cup: 26
European Cup: 1961, 1962

Benfica are a national institution with their huge stadium – rated as 130,000 before recent security constraints – and 122,000 membership. Living up to the standards of history is what Benfica believe they owe Cosme Damiao who, on February 28, 1904, organized the first recorded local game of "futebol" on a patch of Lisbon wasteland. The next day he formed his "team" into a club named Sport Lisboa and, two years later was instrumental in arranging a merger with neighbors Sport Clube de Benfica. In the early years it was cycling which brought the club its first prizes. From the launch of a unified Portuguese championship in the late 1920s, Benfica lorded it over Portuguese sport. In due course, Benfica set their sights on international glory and, in 1950, won the Latin Cup – a forerunner of the European Cup. English manager Ted Smith laid the foundations of a team which would dominate not only Portugal but then Europe.

In 1954 Benfica followed the example being set in Spain and built a vast new stadium. An exiled Hungarian named Bela Guttman became coach, and his team filled the new stadium as Benfica twice swept to success in the European Cup in 1961 and 1962. First they beat Barcelona, amid intense drama, by 3–2 in Berne, then Real Madrid 5–3 in Amsterdam. On both occasions Benfica were captained by their veteran center-forward, José Aguas. They also introduced one of the most famous Portuguese soccer players of all time in Eusebio, greatest of the many fine players Benfica had discovered in the Portuguese colonies of Angola and Mozambique. Benfica's boast of only "Portuguese" (including colonial) players was scrapped in the mid-1970s, when the African colonies were cast adrift. Now they hunt Brazilians, Slavs and Danes with the rest.

BOCA JUNIORS
BUENOS AIRES, ARGENTINA

Founded: 1905
Stadium: Bombonera (58,740)
Colors: Blue with yellow hoop/blue
League: 19
World Club Cup: 1977
South American Club Cup: 1977, 1978
South American Supercup: 1989
Inter-American Cup: 1989

Boca are one of the two great clubs in the Argentine capital of Buenos Aires, along with old rivals River Plate. They were founded by an Irishman named Patrick MacCarthy and a group of newly-arrived Italian immigrants. They joined the league in 1913 and were immediately caught up in a domestic soccer "war" which saw two championships being organized for most of the 1920s and early 1930s. Boca bestrode the two eras. They won the last Argentine amateur championship in 1930 and the first unified professional one the following year. Two more titles followed in the next four years, thanks to some fine players, including the great Brazilian defender, Domingos da Guia. In the 1940s and 1950s Boca slipped into River Plate's shadow, re-emerging in 1963 when a team fired by the goals of José Sanfilippo reached the Final of the South American Club Cup.

Winning the title, however, would have to wait until the late 1970s. Then they reached the Final three years in a row – beating Brazil's Cruzeiro in 1977 and Deportivo Cali of Colombia in 1978 before losing to Olimpia of Paraguay in 1979. Boca's rugged style, under Juan Carlos Lorenzo, proved controversial. Not one Boca player figured in the squad which won the 1978 World Cup. But Boca had already secured their own world crown, beating West Germany's Borussia Mönchengladbach in the World Club Cup in 1977. Boca rebuilt their team around Diego Maradona in 1981, but had added few prizes to their trophy room when he rejoined them in 1995.

CELTIC
GLASGOW, SCOTLAND

Founded: 1888
Stadium: Celtic Park (51,709)
Colors: Green and white hoops/white
League: 35
Cup: 30
European Cup: 1967

SCANDINAVIAN STYLE *Henrik Larsson has brought a touch of flair to Celtic Park*

Celtic and old rivals Rangers are Scottish soccer's greatest clubs, but it was Celtic who first extended that hunger for success into Europe when, in 1967, they became the first British club to win the European Cup. It was a measure of the way they swept all before them that season that they won every domestic competition as well: the League, the Cup and League Cup. No other team in Europe had, until then, ended the season with a 100 per cent record in four major competitions. In winning the European Cup Celtic refuted accusations – mostly from England – that their Scottish honors owed more to a lack of solid opposition than their own abilities. Celtic's 1967 team was shrewdly put together by manager Jock

Stein, a former Celtic player. As well as new Scottish stars he included veterans such as goalkeeper Ronnie Simpson and scheming inside-left Bertie Auld. In the Lisbon Final they beat former holders Internazionale 2–1 with goals from full-back Tommy Gemmell and center-forward Steve Chalmers.

Sadly, Celtic's golden touch did not survive long. A few months later they were beaten by Kiev Dynamo right at the start of their European Cup defence, and were then dragged down to defeat and fisticuffs in the infamous World Club Cup battle with Racing of Argentina. In 1970 Celtic returned to the European Cup Final, only to lose to Feyenoord in Milan; and, two years later, they lost only on penalties after two goal-less draws in the semi-finals against Inter. More trouble lay ahead as Celtic proved unable to match Rangers' commercial and playing example in the late 1980s and slipped to the brink of bankruptcy before turning the corner after a boardroom revolution.

COLO COLO
SANTIAGO, CHILE

Founded: 1925
Stadium: Colo Colo (50,000)
Colors: White/black
League: 19
South American Recopa: 1991

Colo Colo, Chilean nickname for a wildcat, were founded by five angry members of the old Magallanes FC. Even though Chilean soccer is generally held to lag far behind that of traditional giants Brazil, Argentina and Uruguay, Colo Colo have an enviable reputation throughout the continent. The club's vision has always stretched beyond the Andes. Such a tradition was laid down by David Orellano. He was a founder member of Colo Colo and one of the five Magallanes rebels who disagreed over the choice of a new club captain. The choice of the five fell upon Orellano and, within two years of Colo Colo's foundation, they had sent a team off to tour Spain and Portugal. In 1933 Colo Colo were among the founders of a professional league; in 1941 they set another pioneering trend by introducing a for-

eign coach in the Hungarian, Ferenc Platko; and in 1948 they organized a South American club tournament which can now be seen as a forerunner of the Copa Libertadores, the official South American Club Cup launched in 1960. Record league winners in Chile and the supreme transfer destination for most domestic players, Colo Colo's greatest achievement was in reaching the 1973 South American Club Cup Final. The teams drew 1–1 in Avellaneda and 0–0 in Santiago, and thus went on to a play-off in Montevideo, which Independiente won 2–1 in extra time. Colo Colo's consolation goal was scored by their most famous and popular player of the modern era, Carlos Caszely.

EINTRACHT FRANKFURT
GERMANY

Founded: 1899
Stadium: Waldstadion (61,146)
Colors: Black and red stripes/black
League: 1
Cup: 4
UEFA Cup: 1980

Eintracht Frankfurt occupy a very special place in soccer legend as the team Real Madrid beat in the European Cup Final at Hampden back in 1960. The score was 7–3 to Madrid, but Frankfurt were far from crushed and had proved their class by putting six goals past Glasgow Rangers – both home and away – in the semi-finals. Frankfurt's team was built on the midfield strength of Dieter Stinka and Jurgen Lindner, plus the creative talents of veteran inside-left Alfred Pfaff and right-winger Richard Kress. It may sound odd to suggest that everything after a defeat was an anti-climax, but though Frankfurt were founder members of the West German Bundesliga in 1963, they

have achieved comparatively little.

Boardroom problems in the mid-1980s dogged the club until the businessman Matthias Ohms took over and appointed Bernd Holzenbein, a World Cup winner in 1974 and an old Frankfurt favorite, as his executive vice-president. Holzenbein put Frankfurt back on a sound financial footing and bought stars such as midfielder Andy Möller (later sold to Juventus) and the brilliant Ghanaian striker, Anthony Yeboah. In 1992–93 they were denied for the league title after the controversial mid-season departure of charismatic Yugoslav coach, Dragoslav Stepanovic. His successor Jupp Heynckes did not last long either, after falling out with Yeboah who was allowed to depart for English club Leeds, leaving Frankfurt to sink towards a first-ever relegation.

Frankfurt's one European success over the years was in winning the UEFA Cup in 1980. Frankfurt beat their fellow Germans, Borussia Mönchengladbach, on the away goals rule in the Final, losing 3–2 away and then winning 1–0 back in the Waldstadion. Holzenbein had himself scored the all-important second away goal in the first leg.

FEYENOORD
ROTTERDAM, HOLLAND

Founded: 1908
Stadium: De Kuyp (52,000)
Colors: Red and white halves/black
League: 14
Cup: 10
World Club Cup: 1970
European Cup: 1970
UEFA Cup: 1974

Feyenoord were founded by mining entrepreneur C. R. J. Kieboom. Their star player in the successful pre-war years was left-half Puck Van Heel, who appeared in the final tournaments of both the 1934 and 1938 World Cups and set what was for many years a Dutch record of 64 international appearances. The postwar years were bleak until after the introduction of professionalism in the late 1950s. Then Feyenoord entered their most glorious domestic era, winning the league title six times in 13 years. Indeed, their 1965 and 1969 successes brought them league and cup "doubles." Stars included goalkeeper Eddie Pieters-Graafland, a then record £20,000 signing from Ajax, half-backs Reinier Kreyermaat, Hans Kraay and Jan Klaasens and, above all, outside-left Coen Moulijn. He was still a key figure when they won the European Cup in 1970, along with Swedish striker Ove Kindvall and burly midfield general Wim Van Hanegem. Feyenoord's coach, for their extra time victory over Celtic in Milan, was Ernst Happel, the former Austrian international. Feyenoord – and not Ajax – were thus the first Dutch club to break through to European success, and they went on to defeat Estudiantes de La Plata of Argentina in the World Club Cup Final.

In 1974, with Van Hanegem pulling the strings in midfield, Feyenoord added the UEFA Cup to their trophy room. But, as time went on, they lost their grip on the Dutch game. Star players had to be sold to balance the books, among them Ruud Gullit, whom Feyenoord had discovered with Haarlem. He was sold to PSV Eindhoven and, later, of course, moved on to Milan. Not until the arrival as general manager of

GIVING CHASE *Gaston Taument (right, behind Vitesse Arnhem's Philip Cocu) is one of Feyenoord's rising young stars*

Wim Jansen, a former Feyenoord star who starred with Holland at the 1974 World Cup, did Feyenoord pull themselves back together and regain the league title in 1993.

FK AUSTRIA
VIENNA, AUSTRIA

Founded: 1911
Stadium: Horr (10,500) / Prater (62,270)
Colors: White with mauve/white
League: 21
Cup: 21

The history of the Fussball Klub Austria-Memphis began with a game of cricket. Just as the English exported their industrial know-how and educational skills around the world in the latter half of the nineteenth century, they also took with them their newly codified games and sports. Thus the Vienna Cricket and Football Club was founded by the expatriate community in the 1890s. Cricket did not gain universal acceptance, but soccer was another matter, and November 15, 1894 saw the first proper soccer match ever staged in Austria. The Vienna Cricket and Football Club beat 1st Vienna FC by 4–0 – and they have been winning matches and titles ever since.

Changing their name in 1925, FKA notched up many domestic honors in a list which includes runners-up spot in the European Cup-winners' Cup in 1978, when a team inspired by midfield general Herbert Prohaska became the first Austrian side to reach a modern-day European final. That was long overdue since, in the late 1920s, FK Austria were one of the pioneers of European international club soccer when the Mitropa Cup drew clubs from Austria, Czechoslovakia, Hungary, Yugoslavia, Switzerland and Italy. FK Austria were triumphant in 1933 and 1936, inspired by the legendary center-forward Matthias Sindelar. Their delicate style of play, known as the "Vienna School," was modelled on the old Scottish close-passing game and had been taught them by Englishman Jimmy Hogan. His coaching genius contributed mightily to the development of the so-called "Wunderteam" which lost unluckily to England, by 4–3, at

61

Stamford Bridge in 1932 and then reached the semi-finals of the 1934 World Cup. The backbone of the Wunderteam was provided by FK Austria. That tradition has been maintained ever since. Thus no fewer than six FKA stars travelled with the national squad to the 1990 World Cup Finals in Italy.

FLAMENGO
RIO DE JANEIRO, BRAZIL

Founded: 1895 as sailing club; 1911 as soccer club
Stadium: Gavea (20,000) and Maracana (130,000)
Colors: Black and red hoops/white
Rio state league: 22
Brazil championship (incl. Torneo Rio-São Paulo): 5
World Club Cup: 1981
South American Club Cup: 1981

Flamengo are the most popular club in Brazil, having been formed by dissident members of the Fluminense club but under the umbrella of the Flamengo sailing club – which now boasts more than 70,000 members. They first competed in the Rio league in 1912, winning the title two years later. In 1915 they regained the crown without having lost a game. A string of great names have graced the red-and-black hoops over the years, among them defenders Domingos Da Guia and the legendary center-forward Leonidas da Silva. Known as the "Black Diamond," Leonidas played for Flamengo from 1936 to 1942, inspiring two state championship triumphs and earning a worldwide reputation through his brilliance in the 1938 World Cup finals in France.

Flamengo ran up a Rio state hat-trick in the mid-1950s with their team nicknamed the "Steamroller," but had to wait until 1981 for their greatest success. Then, riding high on the goals of a new hero, Zico – the so-called "White Pele" – they won both the South American and World Club Cups. The South American Club Cup campaign was one of the most hostile in memory. Flamengo won a first round play-off against Atletico Mineiro after their rival Brazilians had five players sent off, provoking referee José Roberto Wright to aban-

don the game. In the Final, Flamengo beat Cobreloa of Chile in a play-off in Montevideo which saw the expulsion of five players. Fears about the outcome of Flamengo's world showdown against Liverpool proved unfounded. Zico was in a class of his own. Liverpool could not touch him as he created all of Flamengo's goals in a 3–0 win. The players dedicated the success to the memory of Claudio Coutinho, a former coach who had died in a skin-diving accident. In the mid-1990s, Flamengo sought to revive the glory days by signing World Cup-winning striker Romario from Spain's Barcelona.

FLUMINENSE
RIO DE JANEIRO, BRAZIL

Founded: 1902
Stadium: Laranjeira (20,000) and Maracana (130,000)
Colors: Red, green and white stripes/white
Rio state league: 27
Brazil championship (incl. Torneo Rio-São Paulo): 4

Fluminense have yet to win an international trophy, but that does not alter their status as one of South America's great clubs. "Flu" were founded in 1902 by an Englishman named

Arthur Cox, and many of their first players were British residents. The club's wealth and upper-class clientele resulted in the nickname "Po de Arroz" ("Face Powder," after the fashion of the time at the turn of the century). Today the club's fans wear white powder on their faces as a sign of loyalty. In 1905 Flu were founder members of the Rio de Janeiro league and of the Brazilian confederation; they won the first four Rio (Carioca) championships in 1906–09; and, in 1932, Flu became the first Brazilian club to go professional.

By this time the "Flu-Fla" derby (against Flamengo) had been flourishing for 20 years, the first meeting between the clubs having taken place in 1912. In 1963 their clash drew an official crowd of 177,656 to the Maracana stadium in Rio, which remains a world record for a club game. By 1930 Flu's stadium was the home of the national team and the club had launched a weekly newspaper, among other schemes. A few years later and Flu were ruling the roost with five Rio titles between 1936 and 1941. Star players were forwards Romeu, Carreiro and Tim – who coached Peru at the 1978 World Cup finals. In the early 1950s Fluminense's star was the World Cup winning midfield general Didi.

In the late 1960s and early 1970s the key player was another World Cup winner, Brazil's 1970 captain and right-back, Carlos Alberto Torres. In the 1980s the mantle of inspiration-in-chief passed to the Paraguayan Romerito (Julio César Romero). Fluminense won a hat-trick of Rio titles in 1983, 1984 and 1985 with Romero their guiding light. He was rewarded by being nominated as South American Footballer of the Year in 1985 and later starred at the 1986 World Cup finals.

HAMBURG
GERMANY

Founded: 1887
Stadium: Volksparkstadion (61,234)
Colors: White/red
League: 6
Cup: 3
European Cup: 1983
European Cup-winners' Cup: 1977

Hamburg can be considered by many to be the oldest league club in Germany, if one takes as their foundation date that of SC Germania, the oldest of three clubs which later amalgamated. The other two were Hamburger FC (1888) and FC Falke (1905). Hamburg's tradition, from that day to this, has been one of attacking soccer. The first major trophy

ROMERITO *Fluminense's midfield general scoring for Paraguay against Chile in a World Cup qualifying tie in Santiago*

KEVIN KEEGAN *European Footballer of the Year with Hamburg in 1978 and 1979*

could have been theirs in 1922. But when the championship play-off was abandoned because injury-hit Nürnberg had only seven men left on the field, Hamburg sportingly declined to accept the title. A year later Hamburg did win the championship, and again in 1928.

They did not win it again until 1960, by which time they were being led by the greatest player in the club's history. Center-forward Uwe Seeler, son of a former Hamburg player, was four times Hamburg's top scorer in the old regional league system, and after the creation of the Bundesliga was on one occasion the country's leading marksman. He also spearheaded Hamburg's thrilling 1960–61 European Cup campaign, in which they lost to Barcelona only in a play-off in the semi-finals. Seeler went on to captain West Germany in their brave World Cup efforts of 1966 and 1970, but he had retired by the time Hamburg achieved a European breakthrough and won the Cup-winners' Cup in 1977. Hamburg beat defending cup-holders Anderlecht of Belgium 2–0 in a final which was the big-occasion debuts of two long-serving internationals, defender Manni Kaltz and midfield general Felix Magath.

Both were stalwarts of the side beaten by Nottingham Forest in the 1980 European Cup Final, when Englishman Kevin Keegan tried in vain to stimulate the Hamburg attack. Keegan had returned to England by the time Hamburg beat Juventus in Athens three years later.

After a decade in the doldrums Uwe Seeler returned as president and Hamburg ended the 1995–96 German season in fifth place, their best finish in six years.

INDEPENDIENTE
AVELLANEDA, ARGENTINA

Founded: 1904
Stadium: Cordero (55,000)
Colors: Red/blue
League: 11
World Club Cup: 1973, 1984
South American Club Cup: 1964, 1965, 1972, 1973, 1974, 1975, 1984
Inter-American Cup: 1973, 1974, 1976

Independiente are perhaps the least familiar of international club soccer's great achievers, outside Argentina at least. This is because, despite two lengthy periods of command in South American club soccer, they won the world title only twice in five attempts, and that at a time when the competition's image was tarnished.

Also, Independiente have always relied on team play rather than superstar inspiration. One outstanding player who made his name with the club, however, was Raimundo Orsi. He was the left-winger who played for Argentina in the 1928 Olympics, signed for Juventus, and then scored Italy's vital equalizer on their way to victory over Czechoslovakia in the 1934 World Cup Final. Later, the Independiente fans had the great Paraguayan center-forward, Arsenio Erico, to idolize. Erico had been the boyhood hero of Alfredo Di Stefano and, in 1937, set an Argentine First Division goalscoring record of 37 in

a season.

Independiente did not regain prominence until the early 1960s, when coach Manuel Giudice imported an Italian-style catenaccio defense which secured the South American Club Cup in both 1964 and 1965. Independiente were the first Argentine team to win the continent's top club prize. But in the World Club Cup Final they fell both years to the high priests of catenaccio, Internazionale of Italy.

In the 1970s Independiente's Red Devils won the South American Club Cup four times in a row and collected the World Club Cup. It was an odd victory: European champions Hamburg declined to compete, so runners-up Juventus took their place – on condition that the Final was a single match in Italy. Independiente not only agreed, they won it with a single goal from midfield general Ricardo Bochini.

INTERNAZIONALE
MILAN, ITALY

Founded: 1908
Stadium: Meazza (85,443)
Colors: Blue and black stripes/black
League: 13
Cup: 3
World Club Cup: 1964, 1965
European Cup: 1964, 1965
UEFA Cup: 1991, 1994

Internazionale were founded out of an argument within the Milan club in the early years of the century. Some 45 members, led by committee man Giovanni Paramithiotti, broke away in protest at the authoritarian way the powerful Camperio brothers were running the club. That was not the end of the politics, however. In the 1930s, fascist laws forced Internazionale into a name change to rid the club of the foreign associations of their title. So they took the name of the city of Milan's patron saint and became Ambrosiana. Under this title they led the way in continental club competition – being one of the leading lights in the pre-war Mitropa Cup.

After the war, the club reverted to the Internazionale name and pioneered a tactical revolution. First manager Alfredo Foni, who had been a World Cup-winning full-back before the war, won the league title twice by withdrawing outside-right Gino Armani into midfield; then Helenio Herrera conquered Italy, Europe and the world with catenaccio. Goalkeeper Giuliano Sarti, sweeper Armando Picchi and man-marking backs Tarcisio Burgnich, Aristide Guarneri and Giacinto Facchetti were as near watertight as possible. They were

MATTHÄUS
Internazionale's driving force and Germany's World Cup captain in 1990

the foundation on which Spanish general Luis Suarez constructed the counter-attacking raids carried forward by Brazil's Jair da Costa, Spain's Joaquim Peiro and Italy's own Sandro Mazzola. Inter won the European and World Club Cups in both 1964 and 1965 – beating Real Madrid and Benfica in Europe, and Argentina's Independiente twice for the world crown. But even they could not soak up pressure indefinitely. In 1966 Real Madrid toppled Inter in the European Cup semi-finals, Celtic repeated the trick a year later in a memorable Lisbon final, and Herrera was lured away to Roma. Not until the late 1980s could Inter recapture their international and domestic allure, when West German midfielder Lothar Matthäus drove them to the 1989 league title, following up with success in the 1991 UEFA Cup.

JUVENTUS
TURIN, ITALY

Founded: 1897
Stadium: Delle Alpi (71,012)
Colors: Black and white stripes/white
League: 24
Cup: 10
World Club Cup: 1985, 1996
European Cup: 1985, 1996
European Cup-winners' Cup: 1984
UEFA Cup: 1977, 1990, 1993
Supercup: 1984, 1996

Juventus were founded by a group of Italian students who decided to adopt red as the color for their shirts. In 1903, however, when the club was six years old, one of the committee members was so impressed on a trip to England by Notts County's black-and-white stripes that he bought a set of shirts to take home to Turin. In the 1930s Juventus laid the foundations for their legend, winning the Italian league championship five times in a row. Simultaneously they also reached the semi-finals of the Mitropa Cup on four occasions and supplied Italy's World Cup-winning teams with five players in 1934 and three in 1938. Goalkeeper Gianpiero Combi, from Juventus, was Italy's victorious captain in 1934, just as another Juventus goalkeeper, Dino Zoff, would be in 1982.

After the war, the Zebras (after

Great Managers

GIOVANNI TRAPATTONI

Coach of Milan, Juventus, Internazionale, Bayern Munich, Cagliari, Bayern Munich (born March 17, 1939)

Trapattoni was a sure tackling wing-half in the 1950s and 1960s. He earned a reputation as the only man who could play Pele out of a game fairly. After winning two European Cups with Milan, Trapattoni retired and joined the coaching staff. He became first-team caretaker before moving to Juventus where he became the most successful club coach of all time. In eight years, Trapattoni took Juve to the World Club Cup, European Cup, European Cup-winners' Cup, UEFA Cup, European Supercup, seven Italian championships and two national cups. Nothing in his career, either at Internazionale or after returning to Juventus, matched that spell. But he proved that his coaching talent could transcend cultural and linguistic obstacles when he guided Bayern Munich to the 1997 German league title.

the colors of their shirts) scoured the world for talent to match their import-led rivals. First came the Danes, John and Karl Hansen, then the Argentine favourite Omar Sivori and the Gentle Giant from Wales, John Charles, followed by Spanish inside-forward Luis Del Sol and French inspiration Michel Platini. In 1971 they lost the Fairs Cup Final to Leeds on the away goals rule but in 1977 they beat Bilbao in the UEFA Cup Final on the same regulation.

In 1982 no fewer than six Juventus players featured in Italy's World Cup winning line-up, and Cabrini, Tardelli, Scirea, Gentile and Paolo Rossi helped Juve win the 1984 European Cup-winners' Cup and the 1985 European Cup. Seeking new magic in the 1990s, Juventus paid huge fees for Gianluca Vialli and Roberto Baggio. Both shared in the 1995 league and cup double triumph but Baggio then left for Milan on the eve of a season which saw Vialli captain Juventus to victory in the European Cup Final over Ajax. The 1996 Final was to be the first of three consecutive trips to the Final for Juventus, but their only victory.

IGOR BELANOV *Kiev's European Footballer of the Year in 1986*

KIEV DYNAMO
UKRAINE

Founded: 1927
Stadium: Republic (100,100)
Colors: White/blue
League: 7 Ukraine, 13 Soviet
Cup: 3 Ukraine, 9 Soviet
European Cup-winners' Cup: 1975, 1986
Supercup: 1975

Kiev were founder members of the Soviet top division, yet had to wait until 1961 before they became the first club outside Moscow to land the title. Soon they were dominating the Soviet scene. They achieved the league and cup "double" five years later and went on to a record-equalling hat-trick of league titles. Key players were midfielders Iosif Sabo and Viktor Serebryanikov and forwards Valeri Porkuyan and Anatoli Bishovets. Porkuyan starred at the 1966 World Cup finals in England, and Bishovets four years later in Mexico.

In 1975 Kiev became the first Soviet team to win a European trophy when they beat Ferencvaros of Hungary by 3–0 in the Cup-winners' Cup. Later that year they clinched the league title for the seventh time in 14 seasons. It was then that the Soviet federation grew too demanding, saddling the Ukraine club with all the national team fixtures and, when the Olympic qualifying team began to falter, with their schedule as well. It all proved too much. But that did not deter Kiev coach Valeri Lobanovsky from going back to square one and painstakingly developing another formidable team around record goal-scorer Oleg Blokhin. In 1985, the renewed Kiev stormed to another league and cup "double." A year later, Kiev charmed their way to the European Cup-winners' Cup as well, defeating Atletico Madrid 3–0 in the Final. Igor Belanov was named European Footballer of the Year. Kiev were the richest and most powerful club in the Ukraine upon the collapse of the Soviet Union, but they failed to achieve European success and were expelled from the 1995–96 Champions League after club officials were accused of trying to bribe a referee. A three-year ban was quashed by UEFA on compassionate grounds.

LIVERPOOL
ENGLAND

Founded: 1892
Stadium: Anfield (41,000)
Colors: All red
League: 18
FA Cup: 5
League Cup: 4
European Cup: 1977, 1978, 1981, 1984
UEFA Cup: 1973, 1976
Supercup: 1977

Liverpool: a name which says so much, in pop music, in sport – specifically, in soccer. The Beatles may have moved on, split up, become part of the memorabilia of a major industrial center in the north-west of England. But the club goes on, purveyor of dreams not only for the thousands who fill the seats and the condemned terracing but for the millions on Merseyside who achieved international acclaim through their players.

For years the proud boast of English soccer's hierarchy had been that such was the depth of talent that no one club would ever dominate the championship in the manner of Juventus in Italy, Real Madrid in Spain or Benfica in Portugal. Then, along came Bill Shankly. He was appointed manager of shabby, run-down, half-forgotten Liverpool FC in December, 1959. In two-and-a-half years he won promotion; a pair of low-cost trades for left-half Billy Stevenson and outside-left Peter Thompson helped to secure the League Championship in 1964; and a year later they had won the FA Cup. Those years and the succeeding 20 brought success on the greatest scale at home and abroad.

The secret was continuity. Shankly was succeeded in the manager's tracksuit by two of his former assistant coaches, Bob Paisley and Joe Fagan. A new player would be bought young and cheap, consigned to the reserves for a year to learn "the Liverpool way," then slotted in to replace one of the fading heroes whose game had lost its edge. Thus the generation of Emlyn Hughes, Ian St John, Roger Hunt and Ron Yeats gave way to the likes of Kevin Keegan and John Toshack, who were followed in turn by Alan Hansen, Kenny Dalglish and Graeme Souness, the last two of whom also later succeeded to Anfield managership. Under Dalglish Liverpool became in 1986 only the third English club to achieve the League and Cup "double" this century – a wonderful achievement on the field which was tarnished by the disasters off it, first at the Heysel stadium in 1985 and then at Hillsborough in 1989.

MANCHESTER UNITED
ENGLAND

Founded: 1878
Stadium: Old Trafford (55,000)
Colors: Red/white
League: 12
FA Cup: 10
League Cup: 1
European Cup: 1968, 1999
European Cup-winners' Cup: 1991
Supercup: 1991

Manchester United were appropriate leaders of English re-entry into Europe in 1990, after the five-year Heysel disaster ban, since United had been the first English club to play in Europe in the mid-1950s when they reached the semi-finals of the European Cup in both 1957 (losing to eventual winners Real Madrid) and in 1958. On the latter occasion they lost to Milan with a somewhat makeshift side which had been hastily pulled together in the wake of the Munich air disaster in which eight players, including captain Roger Byrne and the inspirational young Duncan Edwards, had been killed.

It took United ten years to recover, in international terms. Thus it was in May 1968 that manager Matt Busby's European quest was rewarded as United defeated Benfica 4–1 in extra time at Wembley. Bobby Charlton, a Munich survivor along with defender Bill Foulkes and manager Busby, scored twice to secure the club's most emotional triumph. Busby had been a Scotland international wing-half with Manchester City in the 1930s and took over United when war damage to Old Trafford meant playing home games at Maine Road. Yet within three years Busby had constructed a side who scored a superb FA Cup Final victory over Blackpool and created the entertaining, attacking style which has been mandatory for the club ever since. In the 1960s United boasted not only Charlton but great crowd-pullers such as Scotland's Denis Law and Northern Ireland's George Best. Later came England's long-serving captain Bryan Robson, who was still in harness in the 1990s when United, under Alex Ferguson, regained the English League title for the first time in 26 years and made history by winning the domestic double three times. Over and above all that, United wrote their name deeper into soccer legend by becoming, in 1999, the first English club to achieve the fabulous treble – adding the Champions League, in sensational style, to their domestic crown.

TREBLE CLINCHER *Ole Gunnar Solskjaer secures United's historic treble*

Great Managers
Bill Shankly

Manager of Carlisle, Grimsby, Workington, Huddersfield and Liverpool (born September 2, 1913; died September 29, 1981)

Shankly played for Carlisle, Preston and Scotland in the 1930s and returned to Carlisle to begin his managerial career. He took over a faded Liverpool in the Second Division in December, 1959, and there was no stopping either him or the club once promotion had been achieved in 1962. Shankly's dry humour struck a chord with Anfield fans. He brought them League, FA Cup and League successes in consecutive seasons, signed some of the club's greatest servants and laid foundations for further success both on and off the field. Shankly had an eye for youthful talent — which he squirreled away in the reserves until they were ready — and for managerial expertise. Later managers Bob Paisley, Joe Fagan and Roy Evans came out of Shankly's fabled "boot room."

Great Managers
Matt Busby

Manager of Manchester United (born May 26, 1909; died January 20, 1994)

Busby was a Scottish international wing-half who played before the Second World War for Liverpool and Manchester City and took over as manager at Manchester United in 1945 when air raid damage had reduced Old Trafford to near-rubble. Such was his gift for management that, within three years, he had created the first of three memorable teams. His 1948 side won the FA Cup, his Busby Babes of the mid-1950s went twice to the European Cup semi-finals before being wrecked by the Munich air disaster, and his third team completed the European quest with victory over Benfica in 1968's European Cup Final. Busby's love of entertaining soccer inspired some of the greatest British players and set a standard which was emulated by his protege, Alex Ferguson.

DOOMED *Marseille's Basile Boli, scorer of the only goal, robs Milan's Marco Van Basten in the French club's ill-fated 1993 European Cup Final triumph*

MARSEILLE
FRANCE

Founded: 1898
Stadium: Vélodrome (46,000)
Colors: All white
League: 9 (1993 title revoked)
Cup: 10
European Cup: 1993

No French club had ever won the European Cup before Marseille; and no one will ever forget what happened when they did. Millionaire entrepreneur Bernard Tapie, the club's high-profile president, had invested millions of dollars in pursuit of European glory. Unfortunately, some of the money had been used to try to fix matches along the road – if not in Europe then in the French championship. Barely had Marseille finished celebrating their Cup-winning 1–0 victory over Milan in Munich in May, 1993, than it emerged that midfielder Jean-Jacques Eydelie had passed cash to three players from

Valenciennes to "go easy" on Marseille in a league match a week earlier. Marseille were duly banned from their European title defense in 1993–94, the French federation revoked their league championship title and they were subsequently further penalized with enforced relegation. Bankruptcy, inevitably, followed.

Marseille's first championship had been celebrated back in 1929. Personalities in those days included Emmanuel Aznar (scorer of eight goals in a 20–2 league win over Avignon) and three English managers in Peter Farmer, Victor Gibson and Charlie Bell. After the war Marseille soon won the championship in 1948, but heavy expenditure on big-name foreigners such as Yugoslavia's Josip Skoblar, Sweden's Roger Magnusson and Brazil's Jairzinho and Paulo César drew only sporadic rewards, and Marseille had slipped into the Second Division by the time

ambitious businessman-turned-politician Tapie took over the helm in 1985. Marseille immediately gained promotion and then, thanks to the attacking genius of Jean-Pierre Papin and Chris Waddle, swept to four league titles in a row. They also suffered a penalty shoot-out defeat by Red Star Belgrade in the 1991 European Cup Final.

MILAN
ITALY

Founded: 1899
Stadium: Meazza (85,443)
Colors: Red and black stripes/white
League: 16
Cup: 4
World Club Cup: 1969, 1989, 1990
European Cup: 1963, 1969, 1989, 1990, 1994
European Cup-winners' Cup: 1968, 1973
Supercup: 1989, 1990

Milan's domination of the European club game in the late 1980s and the early 1990s was achieved on a unique stage

which would appear to represent the pattern of the future for a sport increasingly controlled by the intertwined commercial interests and demands of big business and television. In Milan's case, all these strands were in the hands of a puppet-master supreme in media magnate and then Prime Minister of Italy, Silvio Berlusconi. He had come to the rescue in 1986, investing $30 million to save Milan from bankruptcy and turn the club into a key player in his commercial empire. Milan had been one of the founders of the Italian championship back in 1898, but until the Second World War they tended to be in the shadow of neighbors Inter. After the war Milan achieved spectacular success, largely thanks to the Swedish inside-forward trio of Gunnar Gren, Gunnar Nordahl and Nils Liedholm. They also paid a then world record fee of $100,000 for Uruguay's Juan Schiaffino. They were dangerous rivals to Real Madrid in the new European Cup – losing narrowly to the

SAFETY FIRST *Milan's Alessandro Costacurta (right) clears his lines in the 1993 European Cup Final*

Spanish club in the semi-finals in 1956 and then only in extra time in the Final of 1958. That was the year Milan's scouts first saw the teenage "Golden Boy" Gianni Rivera, whose cultured inside-forward play and partnership with José Altafini inspired Milan to a European Cup victory in 1963 over Benfica. Rivera was Milan's figurehead as they won the European Cup again in 1969 and the European Cup-winners' Cup in 1968 and 1973. But even his charisma could not save the club from the scandals and financial disasters inflicted by a string of disastrous presidents. That was where Berlusconi came in, providing the money and the men – among them Holland's Ruud Gullit and Marco Van Basten, Liberia's George Weah and Yugoslavia's Dejan Savicevic – who turned Milan into a millionaires' club.

MILLONARIOS
BOGOTA, COLOMBIA

Founded: 1938
Stadium: El Campin – Estadio Distrital Nemesio Camacho (57,000)
Colors: Blue/white
League: 13

Millonarios remain a legendary

name, if only because of the manner in which they led Colombia's fledgeling professional clubs into the El Dorado rebellion which lured star players from all over the world in the late 1940s and the early 1950s. Many famous names in the game made their reputations there. The then club president, Alfonso Senior, later became president of the Colombian federation and a highly-respected FIFA delegate. Star player Alfredo Di Stefano used Millonarios as a springboard to greatness with Real Madrid.

Taking massive advantage of an Argentine players' strike, Millonarios led the flight from FIFA and the chase for great players – not only Di Stefano but the acrobatic goalkeeper Julio Cozzi, attacking center-half Nestor Rossi and attacking general Adolfo Pedernera. Nicknamed the "Blue Ballet," they dominated the pirate league and, when an amnesty was negotiated with FIFA, made lucrative "farewell" tours in Europe. Credit for the club's name goes to a journalist, Camacho Montayo. The club had been founded as an amateur side, Deportivo Municipal, in 1938. But as they pushed for a professional league, so Montayo wrote: "The

Municipalistas have become the Millonarios." The name stuck. Millonarios remain a leading club but, despite appearing frequently in the South American Club Cup, the glory days have never been repeated.

MOSCOW DYNAMO
RUSSIA

Founded: 1923
Stadium: Dynamo (51,000)
Colors: White/blue
League: 11 Soviet
Cup: 6 Soviet

Dynamo are probably the most famous of all Russian clubs, having been the first Soviet side to venture out beyond the Iron Curtain in the 1940s and 1950s. Also, they were fortunate enough to possess, in goalkeeper Lev Yashin, one of the greatest personalities in the modern game – a show-stopper wherever he went.

Dynamo's origins go back to the start of soccer in Russia, introduced by the Charnock brothers at their cotton mills towards the end of the last century. The team won successive Moscow championships under the name Morozovsti and, after the Russian Revolution, were taken over first by the electrical trades union

and then by the police. Thus the 1923 date marks the formal setting-up of Moscow Dynamo rather than the foundation of the original club. Immediately after the end of the Second World War, Dynamo became a legend as a result of a four-match British tour in the winter of 1945. They drew 3–3 with Chelsea and 2–2 with Rangers, thrashed Cardiff 10–1 and beat a reinforced Arsenal 4–3 in thick fog. Inside-forward Constantin Beskov later became national manager, but it was goalkeeper Alexei "Tiger" Khomich whose reputation lasted long after he had retired to become a sports press photographer. He was succeeded in the team by an even greater goalkeeper in Yashin, who was to become the first Soviet player to be nominated as European Footballer of the Year. Given Dynamo's leadership, it was appropriate that, in 1972, they became the first Soviet side to reach a European final. But their 3–2 defeat by Rangers in Barcelona also stands as the high point of their modern achievement. Back home, Dynamo were pushed back down the ranks by neighburs Moscow Spartak.

MOSCOW SPARTAK
RUSSIA

Founded: 1922
Stadium: Olympic-Lenin/Luzhniki (102,000)
Colors: Red and white/white
League: 5 Russia; 12 Soviet
Cup: 10 Soviet

Moscow Spartak, champions of Russia for both the first two seasons after the collapse of the Soviet Union, face an enormous challenge in the years ahead. Spartak were a power in the land under the old system, but those were the days when players were not allowed to move abroad. Now Spartak must maintain their domestic command and compete effectively in Europe in an "open" transfer society. This is all the more challenging because Spartak had, for years, represented the Party line. They play their home matches in what was known as the Lenin stadium in the Luzhniki suburb, and their past heroes included such officially-approved characters as 1950s' top scorer Nikita Simonian (a club record-holder with 133 goals) and left-half Igor Netto (another club record-holder with 367 appearances). Spartak's best season in European competitions was 1990–91, when they beat both Napoli and Real Madrid to reach the semi-finals of the European Cup, before falling 5–1 on aggregate to Marseille.

For years the club had been ruled by the most respected members of the managerial old guard in veteran administrator Nikolai Starostin and former national coach Constantin Beskov. Starostin, a Spartak player in the club's early days, stayed on after the political upheaval, but Beskov handed over the coaching mantle to his former pupil and international full-back, Oleg Romantsev. Despite the loss of sweeper Vasili Kulkov and midfielders Igor Shalimov and Alexander Mostovoi, Romantsev kept Spartak on top of the table. New heroes were left-back and captain Viktor Onopko, versatile Igor Lediakhov and the young forward Mikhail Beschastnikh. Not only did Spartak win the 1992, 1993, 1994 and 1996 Russian league titles; they also won – in both 1993 and 1994 – the pre-season CIS Cup, contested by the champions of all the former Soviet states.

NACIONAL
MONTEVIDEO, URUGUAY

Founded: 1899
Stadium: Parque Central (20,000) and Centenario (73,609)
Colors: White/blue
League: 36
World Club Cup: 1971, 1980, 1988
South American Club Cup: 1971, 1980, 1988
South American Recopa: 1988
Inter-American Cup: 1971

Nacional and Penarol are the two great clubs of Uruguay and bitter rivals on both the domestic and international stages. Nacional were formed from a merger of the Montevideo Football Club and the Uruguay Athletic Club, and in 1903 were chosen to line up as Uruguay's national team against Argentina in Buenos Aires. Nacional won 3–2

VICTOR ONOPKO *New hero of Moscow Spartak in the post-Communist era*

and have enjoyed the international limelight ever since.

Penarol won the first South American Club Cup in 1960, but Nacional soon set about catching up: runners-up three times in the 1960s, they first won the cup by defeating Estudiantes de La Plata in 1971. That led Nacional on to the World Club Cup, where they beat Panathinaikos of Greece (European title-holders Ajax having refused to compete). The two decisive goals in Montevideo were scored by Nacional's former Argentine World Cup spearhead, Luis Artime. It was nine years before Nacional regained those crowds. This time they had a new center-forward in Waldemar Victorino, who scored the only goal in the 1980 South

American Club Cup triumph over Internacional of Brazil, and then the lone strike which decided the world final against Nottingham Forest in Tokyo. By the time Nacional regained the crown in 1988 Victorino had left for Italy, just as so many Uruguayan stars before and since.

Back in the 1930s Nacional sold center-half Michele Andreolo to Italy, with whom he won the 1938 World Cup. But Nacional quickly replaced him and, from 1939 to 1943, achieved what is nostalgically recalled as their Quinquenio de Oro: their golden five years. Nacional won the league in each of those seasons with a legendary forward line built around the prolific Argentine marksman Atilio Garcia. He was Uruguay's top scorer eight times and ended his career with a record of 464 goals in 435 games. Under Scottish manager William Reasdale, Nacional also celebrated an 8–0 thrashing of the old enemy from Penarol.

PENAROL
MONTEVIDEO, URUGUAY

Founded: 1891
Stadium: Las Acacias (15,000) and Centenario (73,609)
Colors: Black and yellow stripes/black
League: 43
World Club Cup: 1961, 1966, 1982
South American Club Cup: 1960, 1961, 1966, 1982, 1987
Inter-American Cup: 1969

Penarol were the first club to win the World Club Cup three times, but their success is no modern phenomenon. Penarol have been the pre-eminent power in Uruguayan soccer since its earliest days, providing a host of outstanding players for Uruguay's 1930 and 1950 World Cup-winning teams. Their own international awakening came in 1960, when Penarol won the inaugural South American Club Cup (the Copa Libertadores). They were thrashed by Real Madrid in the World Club Cup, but made amends the next year with victory over Benfica. It was no less than the talents of players such as William Martinez, center-half Nestor Goncalves and striker Alberto Spencer deserved.

Penarol regained the world club crown in 1966, at the expense of Real Madrid, and then again in 1982 when they beat Aston Villa in Tokyo. By now Penarol had unearthed an other superstar in center-forward Fernando Morena. He was the latest in a long line of great players, which included the nucleus of the Uruguayan national team who shocked Brazil by winning the 1950 World Cup. Goalkeeper Roque Maspoli – later World Club Cup-winning coach in 1966 – captain and center-half Obdulio Varela, right-winger Alcide Ghiggia, center-forward Oscar Miguez, right-half Rodriguez Andrade and inside-right Juan Schiaffino all came from Penarol. Schiaffino was the greatest of all.

Penarol had been founded as the Central Uruguayan Railway Cricket Club in 1891, and changed their name in 1913 as the British influence waned. The railways sidings and offices were near the Italian Pignarolo district – named after the landowner Pedro Pignarolo – and so the Spanish style of the name was adopted for the club.

FC PORTO
OPORTO, PORTUGAL

Founded: 1893
Stadium: Das Antas (76,000)
Colors: Blue and white stripes/white
League: 17
Cup: 11
World Club Cup: 1987
European Cup: 1987
Supercup: 1987

Porto were always considered to be No. 3 in the Portuguese soccer hierarchy until their thrilling European Cup victory over Bayern Munich in Vienna in 1987. Events then and since have ensured that, while their trophy count may not yet match those of Benfica and Sporting, Porto are clearly seen as an alternative center of power in the domestic game. Porto beat Bayern with the Polish goalkeeper Mlynarczyk, Brazil-

EX COACH *Porto's Bobby Robson*

ians Celso and Juary, and Algerian winger Rabah Madjer supporting Portugal's own wonderboy, Paulo Futre. But that was entirely appropriate since, in the early 1930s, Porto had been pioneers in the international transfer market.

They began by bringing in two Yugoslavs, and that ambition was reflected in Porto's initial championship successes in 1938 and 1939. In those days Porto's home was the old, rundown Campo da Constituciao. Now, as befits a club with European Cup-winning pedigree, home is the impressive, 76,000-capacity Estadio das Antas.

Not only have Porto won the Champions' Cup; they also finished runners-up to Juventus in the European Cup-winners' Cup in 1984. The creative force behind the club's progress in the 1980s was the late José Maria Pedroto. He led Porto to the cup in 1977 and league title in 1978 and 1979.

His work would be carried on by his pupil, former national team center-forward Artur Jorge, who coached Porto to their 1987 European title and later took over the national side. Later, under Brazilian Carlos Alberto da Silva, duly succeeded by Bobby Robson, Porto enhanced their standing as members of the European establishment when they reached the semi-finals of the Champions League in 1994 and the quarter-finals in 1997. Robson left Porto in 1996 after building a team which won a hat-trick of league titles.

PHILIPS SV
EINDHOVEN, HOLLAND

Founded: 1913
Stadium: Philips (30,000)
Colors: Red and white stripes/white
League: 14
Cup: 7
European Cup: 1988
UEFA Cup: 1978

PSV equalled the achievements of Celtic (in 1967) and Ajax Amsterdam (in 1972) when they defeated Benfica in a penalty shoot-out to win the 1988 European Cup. Only those other two clubs had previously secured the treble of European Cup and domestic league and cup all in the same season. Remarkably, PSV achieved all they did despite having sold their finest player, Ruud Gullit, to Milan at the start of the season for a world record $9 million. The money was, however, invested wisely to secure the best players from Holland, Denmark and Belgium.

Such success was the reward for a long wait since PSV had been one of the invited entrants in the inaugural European Cup in 1955–56, when they crashed 1–0, 1–6 to Rapid Vienna in the first round. Surprisingly, considering PSV's position as the sports club of the giant Philips electrics corporation, they were long outshone by Ajax and Feyenoord. For years the Philips company took comparatively little interest in PSV, even though an estimated 40,000 of the 200,000 urban population of Eindhoven work directly or indirectly for Philips. Only in the past decade have Philips become seriously involved with club policy and finance.

PSV had won the 1976 UEFA Cup without much fanfare. But ten years later, realising the potential to be reaped from soccer sponsorship, the company came up with the funds, and were duly rewarded two years later with the European Cup. In 1992, taking the process a stage further, the club changed its name in order to promote itself outside Holland as Philips SV (while domestic sponsorship regulations required it to stick with the PSV abbreviation in Holland).

RANGERS
GLASGOW, SCOTLAND

Founded: 1873
Stadium: Ibrox Park (50,471)
Colors: Blue/white
League: 48
Cup: 28
League cup: 19
European Cup-winners' Cup: 1972

Rangers are one half of the "Old Firm" – their rivalry with Celtic having dominated Scottish soccer for a century. Yet Rangers have never extended that power into Europe, their only prize from virtual non-stop international competition being the 1972 Cup-winners' Cup Final win over Moscow Dynamo. Not that Rangers' history is short on proud moments. One particularly glorious era was the 1920s, when Rangers' heroes included the legendary "Wee Blue Devil," Alan Morton. In the 1960s, Rangers endured heavy European defeats at the hands of Eintracht Frankfurt, Tottenham and Real Madrid. The start of the 1970s was a time of mixed emotions: 1971 saw the Ibrox disaster, when 66 fans died in a stairway crush at the end of a game against Celtic. Then, a year later, Rangers' European Cup-winners' Cup triumph was immediately followed by a European ban because of the way their celebrating fans ran amok in Barcelona. The upturn began in November, 1985, when Lawrence Marlboro bought control of the club. He brought in Graeme Souness as player-manager. In 1988 David Murray bought Rangers, and Souness revolutionized their image by buying 18 English players and smashing the club's Protestants-only ethic with his $2.25 million capture of Catholic Mo Johnston. Subsequent signings such as Brian Laudrup and Paul Gascoigne enabled Rangers to maintain their league title dominance for a remarkable nine years in a row. Striker Ally McCoist smashed the club record of 233 goals set 60 years earlier by legendary Bob McPhail. Rangers failed to make it a record 10 straight championships in 1998, so they hired Dick Advocat, a Dutch coach. He won the domestic treble in his first season.

mered a free-kick through the defensive wall. Binder ended a great career with 1,006 goals and later became club coach.

Many of Rapid's old heroes returned as coaches, among them Karl Rappan (who developed the Swiss Bolt system), Edi Fruhwirth and Karl Decker. Great players in the post-war years included wing-half Gerhard Hanappi – an architect by profession, who laid out the designs for the club stadium – tough-tackling defender Ernst Happel and another prolific goal-scoring center-forward in Hans Krankl. He led Rapid's attack in 1985 in the first of their two defeats in the European Cup-winners' Cup Final, but had long retired when they fell to Paris Saint-Germain in 1996.

CROWN PRINCE *Raul Gonzalez is the latest sensation to grace the Bernabeu Stadium at "royal" Real Madrid*

RAPID VIENNA
AUSTRIA

Founded: 1899
Stadium: Hanappi (19,600)
Colors: Green and white/green
League: 29
Cup: 13

Rapid were founded as the 1st Arbeiter-Fussballklub (First Workers Football Club) but, on changing their name, also set about refining the short-passing style of the "Vienna School" to such good effect that they won the championship eight times between 1912 and 1923. The success story did not end there. In 1930 Rapid became the first Austrian club to win the Mitropa Cup, defeating powerful Sparta Prague 2–0, 2–3 in the Final. Several of Rapid's key players were members of the "Wunderteam," the national side who finished fourth in the 1934 World Cup under the captaincy of Rapid center-half Pepe Smistik.

Four years later Austria was swallowed up into Greater Germany, and the Austrian league was incorporated into the Greater German championship. To the mischievous delight of their fans, Rapid not only won the German Cup in 1938 (3–2 against FSV Frankfurt in the Final) but also the German championship in 1941. On a day which has entered soccer legend, Rapid hit back from 3–0 down to defeat an outstanding Schalke side 4–3 before a 90,000 crowd in the Olympic stadium in Berlin. Their hero was center-forward Franz "Bimbo" Binder, whose hat-trick was crowned by the winning goal when he ham-

REAL MADRID
SPAIN

Founded: 1902
Stadium: Santiago Bernabeu (105,000)
Colors: All white
League: 28
Cup: 17
World Club Cup: 1966, 1998
European Cup: 1956, 1957, 1958, 1959, 1960, 1966, 1998
UEFA Cup: 1985, 1986

What else is there left to say about Real Madrid? Six times champions of Europe, 27 times champions of Spain – both record achievements. They have also won the World Club Cup, two UEFA Cups and 16 Spanish cups, which add up to an honors degree for the club founded by students as Madrid FC. (The Real prefix, meaning Royal, was a title bestowed on the club later by King Alfonso XIII.) Madrid were not only among the founders of the Spanish cup and league competitions: it was also the Madrid president, Carlos Padros, who attended on Spain's behalf the inaugural meeting of FIFA in Paris in 1904. In the late 1920s Madrid launched a policy of buying big. They paid a then Spanish record fee for Ricardo Zamora, still revered as the greatest Spanish goalkeeper of all time.

The Spanish Civil War left Madrid's Chamartin stadium in ruins. At the time the club had no money, but boasted one of the greatest visionaries in European soccer history. He was Santiago Bernabeu, a lawyer who had been, in turn, player, team manager and secretary, and was now club president. Bernabeu launched an audacious public appeal which raised the cash to build the wonderful stadium which now bears his name. The huge crowds which flocked in provided the cash to build the team who dominated the first five years of the European Cup. Argentine-born center-forward Alfredo Di Stefano was the star of stars, though Bernabeu surrounded him with illustrious teammates such as Hungary's Ferenc Puskas, France's Ramond Kopa, Uruguay's José Santamaria and Brazil's Didi. They set impossibly high standards for all the players and teams who followed. Madrid won the European Cup again in 1966 and the UEFA Cup twice in the 1980s, but even later superstars such as Pirri, Santillana, Juanito, Hugo Sanchez and Emilio Butragueño would occasionally complain that nothing they achieved would ever be quite enough. The 1960 team had been, if anything, too good.

RED STAR BELGRADE
YUGOSLAVIA

Founded: 1945
Stadium: Crvena Zvezda (Red Star) (97,422)
Colors: Red and white stripes/white
League: 20
Cup: 15
World Club Cup: 1991
European Cup: 1991

This may be the most schizophrenic club in the world. In Germany they are known as Roter Stern; in France as Etoile Rouge; in Spain as Estrella Roja; in Italy as Stella Rossa; in Serbo-Croat it's Fudbalski Klub Crvena Zvezda; in English, of course, Red Star Belgrade. Under whichever name, the 1991 European and world club champions stood revered as one of the pillars of the worldwide establishment until civil strife in the former Yugoslavia led to international suspension for both country and clubs. The consequences for Red Star were almost disastrous, since millions of dollars paid in trans-

fer fees for their star players were suddenly frozen in banks around Europe.

But Red Star are no strangers to disaster, having been the last team to play Manchester United's "Busby Babes" before the Munich air disaster. Red Star fought back from 3–0 down to draw 3–3, but lost on aggregate despite all the efforts of balletic goalkeeper Vladimir Beara, gypsy midfielder Dragoslav Sekularac and dynamic striker Bora Kostic (scorer of a club record 157 goals in 256 league games). All three men later moved abroad, members of an ongoing exodus of more than 40 players including stars like Dragan Dzajic (to Bastia), Dragan Stojkovic (to

Marseille), Robert Prosinecki (to Real Madrid) and Darko Pancev (to Internazionale). This explains, perhaps, why Red Star, for all their talent, boast only one victory in the European Cup (the 1991 penalty shoot-out victory over Marseille in Bari) and one runners-up spot in the UEFA Cup (beaten on away goals by Borussia Mönchengladbach in 1979).

Red Star were formally set up by students of Belgrade University after the war. They play their home matches in the so-called "Marakana," which was the first stadium in eastern Europe to host a mainstream European final, when Ajax beat Juventus in the 1973 European Cup.

ROBERT PROSINECKI *Outstanding graduate of the Red Star soccer "university"*

RIVER PLATE
BUENOS AIRES, ARGENTINA

Founded: 1901
Stadium: Antonio Liberti/Monumental (76,000)
Colors: White with red sash/black
League: 24
World Club Cup: 1986
South American Club Cup: 1986, 1996
Inter-American Cup: 1986

River Plate are one of the two giants of Argentine soccer, Boca Juniors being the other. Traditionally the club from the rich side of Buenos Aires, River were founder members of the first division in 1908, then took a leading role in the "war" which accompanied the introduction of professional soccer in the 1920s. Over the years River have fielded some wonderful teams. In the 1930s they boasted Bernabe Ferreyra, a legendary figure in Argentine soccer; in the late 1940s their high-scoring forward line was so feared and admired they were nicknamed "La Maquina" (The Machine). The names of Muñoz, Moreno, Pedernera, Labruna and Loustau mean little outside Argentina today, but there they inspire awe like Real Madrid in Europe.

Later River produced more great players: Alfredo Di Stefano, who would one day turn Real Madrid into possibly the greatest team of all time; Omar Sivori, who would form a wonderful partnership with John Charles after joining Juventus; and then 1978 World Cup winners Ubaldo Fillol, Daniel Passarella, Leopoldo Luque and Mario Kempes. In 1986 they were joined in River's Hall of Fame by the likes of goalkeeper Nery Pumpido, center-back Oscar Ruggeri and schemer Norberto Alonso, after victory in the South American Club Cup provided River with formal confirmation of their lofty status. River really should have succeeded to the crown years earlier, but were unlucky runners-up in 1966 to Penarol of Uruguay and in 1976 to Cruzeiro of Brazil. In 1986 they made no mistake, beating America of Colombia, then adding the World Club Cup by defeating Steaua of Romania 1–0 in Tokyo.

SANTOS
SÃO PAULO, BRAZIL

Founded: 1912
Stadium: Vila Belmiro (20,000)
Colors: All white
São Paulo state league: 15
Brazil championship (incl. Torneo Rio-São Paulo): 5
World Club Cup: 1962, 1963
South American Club Cup: 1962, 1963

The name of Santos will always be synonymous with that of Pele, who played all his mainstream career with the club and returned as a director at the end of 1993 to try to help lift his old club out of the depths of a severe financial and administrative crisis.

Santos had been founded by three members of the Americano club, who stayed home in the port of Santos when their club moved to São Paulo. Santos joined the São Paulo state championship in 1916, became only the second Brazilian club to embrace professionalism in 1933, but did not hit the headlines until the mid-1950s. Then, to organize a host of talented youngsters, they signed the 1950 World Cup veteran, Jair da Rosa Pinto, and discovered the 15-year-old Pele.

To say that Santos were a one-man team, as it often appeared from the publicity, would be unfair. Santos harvested millions of dollars from whistle-stop friendly match tours around the world and reinvested heavily in surrounding Pele with fine players: World Cup winners in goalkeeper Gilmar, center-back Mauro and wing-half Zito; an outside-left with a ferocious shot in Pepe; and the precocious young talents of right-winger Dorval, schemer Mengalvio and center-forward Coutinho, Pele's so-called "twin" with whom he established an almost telepathic relationship on the field. Santos were more than a soccer team; they were a touring circus.

Sadly, the constant touring and playing burned out many young players before they had a chance to establish their talent. But not before Santos had scaled the competitive heights as

PELE *The man who "made" Santos*

Pele inspired their victories in the South American Club Cup and the World Club Cup in both 1962 and 1963.

One more year and it was all over. Independiente beat Santos in the 1964 South American Club Cup semi-finals, and the spell had been broken. Santos went on touring and raking in cash, capitalizing on Pele's name, for as long as they could. Pele returned, briefly, as a director in the 1990s, but without inspiring the sort of success Santos had achieved when he was a player.

SÃO PAULO
BRAZIL

Founded: 1935
Stadium: Morumbi (150,000)
Colors: White with a red and black hoop/white
São Paulo state league: 17
Brazil championship (incl. Torneo Rio-São Paulo): 4
World Club Cup: 1992, 1993
South American Club Cup: 1992, 1993

São Paulo's victories over Barcelona and Milan in the 1992 and 1993 World Club Cups in Tokyo left no doubt about which was the finest club side in the world – for all the European hype which had surrounded the Italian champions. Those victories also underlined the depth of talent available to São Paulo, since their key midfielder, Rai (younger brother of 1986 World Cup star Socrates), had been sold to French club Paris Saint-Germain in the summer of 1993. Dual success also enhanced the reputation of coach Tele Santana, Brazil's World Cup manager in 1982 and 1986 and one of the most eloquent

and down-to-earth of soccer coaches and analysts.

São Paulo are, even so, comparative newcomers – having been founded in 1935, at a time when the likes of River Plate, Penarol and the rest were already well-established powers in their own lands. The club was formed from a merger between CA Paulistano and AA Palmeiras. A leading light was Paulo Machado de Carvalho, who would later, as a senior administrator, contribute behind the scenes to Brazil's World Cup hat-trick.

Within a decade of being founded, São Paulo developed into the strongest team in the country, winning the state title five times in the 1940s. They imported Argentine inside-forward Antonio Sastre, and the continuing pressure of success led to the construction of the 150,000-capacity Morumbi stadium – the world's largest club-owned sports arena.

In the 1960s São Paulo had to take a back seat to Santos. In 1974 they reached their first South American Club Cup Final (losing to Argentina's Independiente), but it was not until the arrival of Santana, in the late 1980s, that São Paulo emerged from the doldrums. Despite the continuing sale of star players – key defender Ricardo Rocha went to Real Madrid – São Paulo secured three state league titles in four years, used the cash to strengthen their squad and were duly rewarded at the highest level.

São Paulo's World Club Cup victory over the highly rated European giants Milan in Tokyo in 1993 was very impressive, with Cafu and Massaro the outstanding players. São Paulo became the first side to register consecutive wins in the Tokyo final.

JAN STEJSKAL *Maintaining Sparta's great traditions*

SPARTA PRAGUE
CZECH REPUBLIC

Founded: 1893
Stadium: Letna (36,000)
Colors: All red
League: 23
Cup: 9

Sparta are the most popular club in what is now the Czech Republic, as well as one of the oldest. They were founded as King's Vineyard in 1893, and took the name of Sparta, from one of the states of Ancient Greece, a year later. They were one Europe's great sides preceding the Second World War, winning the Mitropa Cup in the inaugural final in 1927 against Rapid Vienna. Victory over Ferencvaros of Hungary followed in 1935, and they were runners-up in 1936. Sparta's team then included the great inside-left, Oldrich Nejedly.

He was a star in the 1934 World Cup, when Czechoslovakia finished runners-up. Again in 1962, when the Czechs next reached the World Cup Final, there were key places in the team for Sparta men such as right-winger Tomas Pospichal and schemer Andrzej Kvasnak.

Sparta suffered after the last war, and were forced to alter their name to Sparta Bratrstvi and then Spartak Sokolovo. But their loyal fans never called them anything but Sparta, and reality was recognized when the club's present title was adopted in 1965. That same year they celebrated their first league title in more than a decade. Memories of the glory days of the Mitropa Cup were revived by the club's run to the European Cup-winners' Cup semi-finals in 1973 and by the impressive 1983–84 UEFA Cup campaign, during which they

TELE SANTANA

Coach of Atletico Mineiro, Gremio, Flamengo, Fluminense, Palmeiras (Brazil), Al Ahly (Saudi Arabia), São Paulo FC (Brazil); also Brazil national team (born July 26, 1933)

Santana was an outside-right with Fluminense in the early 1950s but never good enough to challenge Julinho or Garrincha in Brazil's World Cup teams. Instead, he reached the World Cup finals in both 1982 and 1986 as manager of Brazil. Santana's insistence on attacking soccer was criticized as naive after Brazil's failures in, respectively, the second round and quarter-finals. But Santana had the last laugh when he won the World Club Cup twice as boss of São Paulo in 1992 and 1993. Simultaneously, Santana was not afraid to pinpoint high levels of corruption in the Brazilian game as well as poor refereeing for the failure to regain World Cup primacy in the 1980s and early 1990s.

scored notable victories over Real Madrid and Widzew Lodz. Sparta's continuing domination of the domestic game in the early 1990s was remarkable because, immediately after the World Cup finals, they lost a string of senior internationals, such as goalkeeper Jan Stejskal, defenders Julius Bielik and Michal Bilek, midfield general Ivan Hasek and striker Tomas Skuhravy, the second-top scorer at Italia '90 with five goals.

SPORTING CLUBE
LISBON, PORTUGAL

Founded: 1906
Stadium: José Alvalade (70,000)
Colors: Green and white hoops/white
League: 16
Cup: 16
European Cup-winners' Cup: 1964

Sporting Clube do Portugal last reached a European final back in 1964, when they won the Cup-winners' Cup. Now Benfica's deadly rivals – the grounds are barely a mile apart – dream of the day when they can bring those old heroes out of retirement obscurity to celebrate a European revival. The late 1980s and early 1990s brought Sporting the worst era in their history, an empty decade following the heady 1981–82 season in which they won the league and cup "double" under Englishman Malcolm Allison.

In 1992 the new president, José Sousa Cintra, brought in ex-England manager Bobby Robson to try to recapture the Allison magic. Robson was given only 18 months, however, before former Portugal national coach Carlos Queiros, instead, was given the task of reviving the glories of the 1950s, when Sporting rivalled Benfica as the country's top club and took the championship seven times in eight years.

En route to Sporting's sole European trophy, they beat APOEL Nicosia in the second round first leg by a European record 16–1.In the Final against MTK Budapest, an entertaining match saw Sporting go 1–0 down, recover to lead 2–1 then go 3–2 behind before securing a 3–3 draw and a replay. In Antwerp a single 20th-minute goal from winger Morais, direct from a corner, was enough to win the cup. Their back four

of Morais, Batista, José Carlos and Hilario starred in the Portugal team which finished third in the 1966 World Cup finals in England.

The nearest Sporting have since gone to European success was in 1990–91,when they reached the UEFA Cup semi-final before falling 0–0, 0–2 to eventual winners Internazionale.

STEAUA
BUCHAREST, ROMANIA

Founded: 1947
Stadium: Steaua (30,000)
Colors: Red/blue
League: 18
Cup: 17
European Cup: 1986

Steaua – the word means 'Star' – were one of the army clubs created in eastern Europe after the Communist takeovers of political power. Originally Steaua were known as CCA Bucharest, under which title they won the championship three times in a row in the early 1950s. Later, renamed Steaua, they won the cup five times in six seasons in the late 1960s and early 1970s.

In 1986 Steaua became the first eastern European team to win the European Cup when the beat Barcelona on penalties in Seville. Their penalty stopping hero in the climactic minutes was Helmut Ducadam, whose career ended prematurely by illness soon after. Steaua's power – including the right to sign any player they liked from

any other Romanian club – was significantly reduced after the overthrow of the Communist dicatorship of the Ceausescu family.

VASCO DA GAMA
RIO DE JANEIRO, BRAZIL

Founded: 1898 as sailing club, 1915 as soccer club
Stadium: São Januario (50,000) and Maracana (130,000)
Colors: All white with black sash
South American Cup: 1
Brazil championship (incl. Torneo Rio-São Paulo): 4

Like Flamengo, one of their long-time Rio de Janeiro rivals, Vasco grew from a sailing club – the impetus for soccer coming from former members of a club called Luzitania FC, who had been refused entry to the early Rio de Janeiro state championship because of their "Portuguese-only" policy. Transformed into Vasco da Gama, however, they were elected to the championship in 1915 and had progressed to the top flight by 1923. Support, both vocal and financial, has come to the club over the years from the city's Portuguese community. In spite of their original policies, Vasco quickly became noted for their inclusion of mixed-race players at a time, early in Brazilian soccer's development, when the game was riven by race and class divisions. Vasco led the way, too, by creating the São Januario stadium, which was the first national stadium in Brazil and hosted all major club and national team matches before the building of the Maracana in 1950.

In 1958 Vasco supplied Brazil's World Cup-winning team with center-back Luiz Bellini, the captain, and center-forward Vava. They earned a long-awaited consolation for events eight years earlier when no fewer than eight Vasco players had figured in the Brazilian squad which was pipped to the World Cup by Uruguay. In the 1960s and 1970s Vasco figured, as ever, among the most powerful of challengers to Fluminense and Flamengo – from whom they controversially signed the popular striker, Bebeto.

LEGENDS

In soccer, as in other sports, the word "great" is over-used and devalued, having been applied to almost any and every fleeting moment of drama or high skill. Thousands of players have been described in terms of ultimate praise. But at the highest echelon of the game there is a small elite group acknowledged by millions of fans as the truly great.

BECKENBAUER
WEST GERMANY

"Kaiser Franz" can boast that he has lifted the World Cup as both captain, in 1974, and manager, in 1990. But his achievements are not the only measure of his true greatness. Beckenbauer's innovative strength was through the revolutionary role of attacking sweeper which, with majestic calm and precision, he introduced in the late 1960s.

CHARLTON
ENGLAND

Bobby Charlton, throughout the world, is probably the most famous English player who has ever thrilled a crowd. He won 106 caps, and his name is synonymous with some of the greatest moments of the modern English game, but also with the highest traditions of sportsmanship, modesty and integrity.

CRUYFF
HOLLAND

Johan Cruyff stands out as not merely the greatest Dutch player but one of the greatest players of all time.

He made his first-team debut at 17, his goal-scoring international debut at 19 and went on to inspire Ajax and Holland through most of their golden 1970s.

DI STEFANO
SPAIN

Alfredo Di Stefano is reckoned by many to be the greatest soccer player of all. Although Pele's admirers may consider that sacrilege, the millions who wondered at Di Stefano's awesome majesty as he dominated European soccer in the 1950s and early 1960s will happily concur.

EUSEBIO
PORTUGAL

Eusebio, the greatest Portuguese player in history, did not come from Portugal at all. Born and brought up in Mozambique, then still one of Portugal's African colonies, Eusebio was the first African soccer player to earn a worldwide reputation. Fans around the world took Eusebio to their hearts not only for his ability but for the sportsmanlike way he played.

MARADONA
ARGENTINA

Diego Maradona was not only the world's greatest soccer player throughout the 1980s and early 1990s. He was also the most controversial and the most enigmatic player, unable to appear in public or on a soccer field without arousing the most contrasting of emotions.

MATTHEWS
ENGLAND

Stanley Matthews was the first great soccer player of the modern era. There will be cases made for Billy Wright, Bobby Charlton, Bobby Moore and others but none dominated his particular era as long as the barber's son from Hanley in the Potteries area of the English Midlands.

PELE
BRAZIL

Pele remains one of those great examples and inspirations of world sport: a poor boy taking the world stage at 17, whose talent lifted him to the peaks of achievement, fame and fortune ... yet who, amidst all

that, retained his innate sense of sportsmanship, his love of his calling, the desire to entertain fans and the respect of fellow players.

PUSKAS
HUNGARY

Ferenc Puskas remains one of the greatest players of all time – a symbol of the legendary "Magical Magyars" who dominated European soccer in the early 1950s and stand as perhaps the greatest team never to have won the World Cup. He very rarely used his right foot (except to stand on, as they say) but his left was so lethal that he hardly ever needed it.

YASHIN
USSR

In South America they called Lev Yashin the "Black Spider;" in Europe the "Black Panther." Eusebio described him as "the peerless goalkeeper of the century." Yashin's fame spread throughout the world, not merely for his ability as a goalkeeper to stop shots that no one else could reach, but as a great sportsman and ambassador for the game.

"KAISER FRANZ" AND A UNIQUE DOUBLE

Franz Beckenbauer has always been accompanied by the sort of luck which only a player of his genius deserves.

The smile of fate was on him through an illustrious playing career and on into management when – in his first appointment at any level – he took West Germany to the Final of the World Cup in Mexico in 1986 and four years later went one better with victory in Italy.

Thus only "Kaiser Franz" can boast that he has lifted the World Cup as both captain, in 1974, and manager, in 1990.

No other player has ever had a career which reached such tangible heights. He was the first German to reach a century of international appearances before leaving Bayern Munich for spells with New York Cosmos and then with Hamburg, where he wound down his playing career.

His honours include the World Cup in 1974 (runner-up in 1966), the European Championship in 1972 (runner-up 1976), the World Club Cup (1976), the European Cup (1974, 1975, 1976), the European Cup-winners' Cup (1967), as well as the West German league and cup. He was also a runner-up in the UEFA Cup with Hamburg and a runner-up in the SuperCup with Bayern. With New York Cosmos, Beckenbauer also won the NASL Soccer Bowl in 1977, 1978 and 1980.

But achievement is not the only measure of true greatness. Beckenbauer's innovative strength was through the revolutionary role of attacking sweeper which, with the encouragement of Bayern Munich coach Tschik Cajkovski, he introduced in the late 1960s.

The boy Beckenbauer took his first steps on the soccer ladder with local club Munich 1906, before he

BECKENBAUER *Attacking sweeper*

switched to Bayern and was first recognized by West Germany at youth level. Within a year of making his league debut with Bayern, as an outside-left, Beckenbauer was promoted into the senior national team.

The occasion was one to test the nerve of the most experienced player, never mind a fledgeling newcomer: West Germany were away to Sweden in a decisive qualifier for the 1966 World Cup. The odds were against them. Yet they won 2–1. West Germany's place in the World Cup finals was all but secured as was Beckenbauer's place in the national team for almost a decade.

In due course he was voted German Footballer of the Year and European Footballer of the Year. Out on the field he was grace and elegance personified, combining an athlete's physique with a computer-like brain for the game which saw

> **❝ He's converted football into an art form. ❞**
>
> *Willi Schulz, 1966 World Cup team-mate*

gaps before they had opened and goal opportunities – for himself and his team-mates – for which the opposing defense had not prepared.

The Elegant Manipulator

Beckenbauer spent almost all his senior career with Bayern Munich as attacking sweeper. Many critics said he was wasting his talent. But Beckenbauer, in an increasingly crowded modern game, found that the sweeper role provided him with time and space in which to work his magical influence on a match. He was the puppet master, standing back and pulling the strings which earned West Germany and Bayern Munich every major prize.

Not that Beckenbauer shied away from the attacking opportunity when it presented itself. He scored the goal which inspired West Germany's revival against England in the 1970 World Cup quarter-final.

During his four years with Cosmos Beckenbauer made many friends and admirers in the United States and was expected to take a central role in their 1994 World Cup build-up before other interests distracted him.

On retiring, Beckenbauer was much in demand as a newspaper and television columnist. Then he was invited to put his words into deeds when offered the post of national manager in succession to Jupp Derwall after the disappointing 1984 European Championship.

The Germans had always promoted managers from within their system. Beckenbauer was an outsider with no coaching experience: his appointment represented a huge gamble. It paid off. Such was Beckenbauer's Midas touch that "his" West Germany were crowned world champions in Rome and he earned his unique place in history.

Career facts

1945 Born on September 11 in Munich

1955 Began playing for the schoolboy team, FC 1906 Munich

1959 Joined Bayern Munich youth section

1962 Gave up a job as a trainee insurance salesman to sign full-time with Bayern

1964 Made his Bayern debut in a 4–0 win away to St Pauli in Hamburg

1965 Made his national team debut in a 2–1 World Cup qualifying win in Sweden

1966 Starred in midfield, on the losing side, for West Germany in the 4–2 World Cup Final defeat by England at Wembley

1967 Captained Bayern Munich, from sweeper, to victory over Rangers in the European Cup-winners' Cup Final

1972 Captained West Germany to European Championship victory over the Soviet Union in Brussels

1974 Captained Bayern Munich to victory in the European Cup Final and then West Germany to victory in the World Cup Final against Holland

1976 Completed a record 103 appearances for West Germany before transferring to the New York Cosmos in the North American Soccer League

1984 Appointed national manager of West Germany in succession to Jupp Derwall

1986 Guided an average side to the World Cup Final, where they lost 3–2 to Argentina

1990 Became the first man to captain and then manage a World Cup-winning team when West Germany beat Argentina 1–0 in Rome

1993 After a short spell as coach of Olympique Marseille, Beckenbauer returned to Bayern as executive vice-president

1994 Took over as coach, guiding Bayern to the league title first as team manager then as club president

ENGLAND'S AMBASSADOR

THUNDERBOLT SHOOTING *Charlton on target against West Ham*

Bobby Charlton, throughout the world, is probably the most famous English player who has ever thrilled a crowd. His name is synonymous with some of the greatest moments of the English game, but also with the highest traditions of sportsmanship and integrity.

Long after he had finished playing Charlton's reputation worked wonders in breaking down the tightest security at World Cups and European Championships. It only needed a player or manager to glance out and see Charlton arriving for barred doors and gates to be flung open. Today's heroes may

> **❝It's difficult enough replacing him as a monument in the team without having to replace him as a person as well.❞**
>
> *Tommy Docherty, then Manchester United manager, after Charlton's retirement*

possess a string of fan clubs and millions in Swiss banks, but they still recognize magic.

The delight which much of the English public took in Manchester United's success in the inaugural Premier League in 1992–93 may be partly explained by the respect in which Bobby Charlton is held for reasons which transcend "mere" soccer.

Soccer was always in the blood. The Charltons – Bobby and World Cup-winning brother Jackie – were nephews of that great Newcastle United hero of the 1950s, Jackie Mil-

burn. They began in the back streets of Ashington in the north-east of England, and Charlton fulfilled every schoolboy's dream when, at 17, he was signed by Manchester United.

Busby Babe and United Captain

Matt Busby had invested more time and determination than any other manager in seeking out the finest young talents in the country. Not only Charlton, but Duncan Edwards, Eddie Colman, David Pegg and many more had been singled out for the Old Trafford treatment: turned from boys into young men under the tutelage of assistant Jimmy Murphy, and then released to explode into the League.

This was the philosophy behind the Busby Babes, the team of youngsters who took the League by storm in the mid-1950s and brought a breath of optimistic fresh air into an austere post-war England. The sense of that spirit of a new generation being lost added to the nation's grief when United's plane crashed in the snow and ice at the end of a runway in Munich on their way home from a European Cup quarter-final in Belgrade in February 1958.

Career facts

1937 *Born on October 11 in Ashington, County Durham*

1957 *Played in the FA Cup Final at 19*

1958 *Survived the Munich air crash to play in another FA Cup Final*

1963 *Played in his third FA Cup Final, and was at last on the winning side as United beat Leicester City 3–1*

1966 *Starred for England in the World Cup victory, scoring goals against Mexico and Portugal along the way to help earn him the European Footballer of the Year award*

1968 *Scored two of the goals as Manchester United finally won the European Cup, defeating Benfica 4–1 after extra time at Wembley*

1970 *Played his record 106th and last international for England in the 3–2 defeat by West Germany at the World Cup finals in Mexico*

1973 *Moved to Preston for two years as player-manager before becoming a director back at Old Trafford*

1994 *Received a knighthood*

Charlton had established his first-team potential the previous season. He was initially an inside-right, later switched to outside-left with England, and finally settled as a deep-lying center-forward, using his pace out of midfield and thunderous shot to score some of the most spectacular goals English soccer has ever seen. One such goal marked his England debut against Scotland, another broke the deadlock against Mexico in the 1966 World Cup finals, and dozens of them inspired Manchester United's post-Munich revival.

The European Cup victory at Wembley in 1968, when he captained United and scored twice, was a highly emotional moment.

Then, as now, the newly-ennobled Sir Bobby has been a perfect ambassador for the game.

TOTAL SOCCER PLAYER

> **❝Johan's secret is that he loves football, seeking out new ways of trying to achieve perfection.❞**
>
> *Stefan Kovacs, former Ajax coach*

FINAL SHOWDOWN *Cruyff's face-to-face with Berti Vogts*

Johan Cruyff stands out as not merely the greatest Dutch player but one of the greatest players of all time, a status which owes much to the persistence of his mother.

She worked as a cleaner in the offices of the Ajax club and persuaded the club coaching staff to take Johan into their youth sections when he was still only 12 years old. The rest is history and a virtually unbroken 25-year succession of trophies and awards on the highest plane as first player and then coach.

Cruyff made his first-team debut at 17, his goal-scoring international debut at 19 and went on to inspire Ajax and Holland through most of their golden 1970s. This was the era of "total football," a concept of the game first described as "The Whirl" in the early 1950s by the Austrian expert Willy Meisl. He saw the day when every player in a team would possess comparable technical and physical ability and would be able to interchange roles at will.

Cruyff was The Whirl in action. Nominally he played centre-forward. But Cruyff's perception of centre-forward was as orthodox as the squad No. 14 he wore on his back for most of his career with Ajax. Cruyff did turn up at the apex of the attack: but he was also to be found meandering through midfield and out on the wings, using his nimble, coltish pace to unhinge defenses from a variety of angles and positions.

Single-handed he not only pulled Internazionale of Italy apart in the 1972 European Cup final but scored both goals in Ajax's 2–0 win. The next year, in Belgrade, he inspired one of the greatest 20-minute spells of soccer ever seen as Ajax overcame another strong Italian outfit, Juventus.

Already the vultures were gathering. Spain had reopened their borders to foreign players and Cruyff was an obvious target. Eventually Barcelona won the transfer race – but after the close of the Spanish federation's autumn deadline. However, such was the magnitude of the transfer that the federation bent their own regulations so that Cruyff could play immediately.

When Cruyff arrived in Barcelona, the Catalans were struggling down the table. By the season's end they were champions, Cruyff's triumphant progress having included a spectacular 5–0 victory away to deadly rivals Real Madrid. Surprisingly, apart from that league title, Barcelona won little else, though Cruyff himself completed the first ever hat-trick of European Footballer of the Year awards.

It was at the end of his first season with Barcelona that Cruyff's career reached its international zenith. At the 1974 World Cup finals Holland took their total soccer through round after round. No one could withstand them. Above all, no

one could handle the mercurial Cruyff, who inspired victories over Uruguay and Bulgaria in the first round, then provided two goals to lead the way against Argentina in the second. The last group match – in effect the semi-final – was against Brazil: the old masters against the new. Cruyff scored Holland's decisive second goal in a 2–0 victory which signalled a new era.

The Final, of course, ended in defeat at the hands of West Germany and, though Holland reached the Final again in 1978, Cruyff, by then, had retired from the national team and was about to head west.

First he joined the Los Angeles Aztecs in the NASL. He won the Most Valuable Player award that year, moved to the Washington Diplomats in 1980 and, late in 1981, returned to Holland to win the Championship twice more with Ajax and once, mischievously, with old rivals Feyenoord.

Retracing his steps as a Manager

Cruyff's move into management, typically, aroused new controversy as he had never obtained the necessary examination qualifications. Not that it mattered. He guided Ajax to the European Cup-winners' Cup in 1987, and repeated the trick in 1989 after retracing his steps to Barcelona. His innovations now cause as much fuss as the total soccer of his playing days.

Career facts

1947 Born on April 25 in Amsterdam

1959 Enrolled by his mother in the Ajax youth section

1963 Signed his first Ajax contract at 16 on the recommendation of English coach Vic Buckingham, then marked his debut with a goal

1966 Made his debut for Holland in a 2–2 draw against Hungary and scored a last-minute equalizer in the first of his 48 internationals

1969 Made his first European Cup final appearance with Ajax, but Milan won 4–1 in Madrid

1971 Won the first of three successive European Cups, helping Ajax defeat Panathinaikos of Greece at Wembley. He was also voted European Footballer of the Year, the first of three such accolades

1973 Sold by Ajax to Barcelona for a world record transfer fee of $1.85 million

1974 Captained and inspired Holland to reach the 1974 World Cup Final in Munich, where they lost 2–1 to hosts West Germany

1978 Retired from the national team before the World Cup finals in Argentina, and left Barcelona to play in America with Los Angeles Aztecs and Washington Diplomats

1981 Returned to Europe to play for minor club Levante in Spain, then to Holland with Ajax and, finally, Feyenoord

1984 Went back to Ajax, this time as technical director

1987 Guided Ajax to victory in the European Cup-winners' Cup as a parting gift before being appointed coach to Barcelona

1992 Managed Barcelona to their long awaited victory in the European Cup Final, where they beat Sampdoria 1–0 at Wembley

1996 Left Barcelona after a record seven years in charge including four consecutive league championships

WORLD-CLASS PLAYER

Alfredo Di Stefano is reckoned by many to be the greatest soccer player of all. While Pele's admirers consider it sacrilege, the millions who wondered at Di Stefano's majestic domination of European soccer in the 1950s and early 1960s may concur.

Di Stefano's greatness lay not only in his achievement in leading Madrid to victory in the first five consecutive European Cup Finals – and inspiring a great breakthrough in international soccer – but also because no other player so effectively combined individual expertise with an all-embracing ability to organize a team to play to his command.

Today he is a wealthy elder statesman of soccer. Yet he was born in Barracas, a poor suburb of the Argentine capital of Buenos Aires, and learned his soccer in the tough streets of the city, then out on the family farm, where he built up the stamina which would become legendary across the world in later years.

Di Stefano's grandfather had emigrated to Argentina from Capri. His father had played for the leading Buenos Aires club, River Plate, but ended his career when professionalism was introduced. He felt soccer was a recreation, not an occupation. Thus he was not particularly pleased when his sons Alfredo and Tulio launched their own teenage careers with local teams.

Eventually, he relented and young Alfredo – nicknamed "El Aleman" (the German), because of his blond hair – made his River Plate debut on August 18, 1944, at outside-right.

Plate left on Shelf

Di Stefano wanted to be a center-forward himself. He learned his trade while on loan to Huracan, then returned to River Plate to replace the great Adolfo Pedernera. River's forward line was nicknamed *La Maquina* (the Machine), for the remorseless consistency with which they took opposing defenses apart. Di Stefano transferred his attacking prowess into the Argentine national team with equal success when they won the 1947 South American Championship.

In 1949 Argentine players went on strike and the star players were lured away to play in a pirate league which had been set up, outside FIFA's jurisdiction, in Colombia. Di Stefano was the star of stars there, playing for Millonarios of Bogota, the so-called "Blue Ballet." Di Stefano was spotted by Real Madrid after starring in the Spanish club's fiftieth anniversary tournament.

Madrid agreed a fee with Millonarios and thus nearly outflanked rivals Barcelona, who had sealed a deal with Di Stefano's old club, River Plate. A Spanish soccer court ruled that Di Stefano should play one season for Madrid, one season for Barcelona. But after he made a quiet start to the season, Barcelona sold out their share in Di Stefano to Madrid. Four days later he scored a hat-trick in a 5–0 win against … Barcelona. A legend had been born.

"Two Players in every Position"

Madrid were Spanish champions in Di Stefano's first two seasons and European Cup winners in his next five. He scored in each of Madrid's European Cup Finals, including a hat-trick against Frankfurt in 1960 in a 90-minute spectacular which has become one of the most-admired soccer matches of all time.

Di Stefano was "total football" personified before the term had been invented. One moment he was defending in his own penalty area, the next organizing his midfield, the next scoring from the edge of the opponents' six-yard box. As Miguel Muñoz, long-time Madrid colleague as player and then coach, once said: "The greatness of Di Stefano was that, with him in your side, you had two players in every position."

THE BLOND ARROW
of Real Madrid and Spain

"Di Stefano is the greatest player I have ever seen."
Luis Del Sol, 1960 European Cup-winning team-mate

Career facts

1926 Born Alfredo Stefano Di Stefano Lauhle on July 4 in Barracas, a poor suburb of Buenos Aires, Argentina

1940 Hinted at things to come by scoring a hat-trick in 20 minutes for his first youth team, Los Cardales

1942 Left Los Cardales after a row with the coach, to join his father's old club, River Plate

1943 Made his debut for River Plate, playing as a right-winger, aged 17, against Buenos Aires rivals San Lorenzo

1944 Transferred on loan to Huracan, for whom he scored the winner in a league game against River Plate

1946 Returned to River Plate to succeed the great Adolfo Pedernera at center-forward in an attack nicknamed La Maquina (the Machine)

1947 Already an international, won the South American Championship with Argentina

1949 Lured away, during the famous Argentine players' strike, to play in a pirate league outside of FIFA's jurisdiction in Colombia for Millonarios of Bogota

1953 Moved to Spain where he joined Real Madrid

1956 Inspired Madrid to the first of five successive European Cup victories and made his national team debut for Spain

1960 Scored a hat-trick in Real's legendary 7–3 victory over Eintracht Frankfurt in the European Cup final at Hampden Park, Glasgow

1963 Kidnapped – and later released unharmed – by urban guerrillas while on tour with Real Madrid in Venezuela

1964 Left Madrid for one last season as a player with Espanol of Barcelona, before becoming a coach in both Argentina and Spain

HIS MAJESTY KING SOCCER

Eusebio, the greatest Portuguese player in history, did not, in fact, come from Portugal at all. Born and brought up in Mozambique, then still one of Portugal's African colonies, Eusebio was the first African soccer player to earn a worldwide reputation.

The big Portuguese clubs such as Benfica, Sporting and Porto financed nursery teams in Mozambique and Angola and unearthed a wealth of talent which they then transported into not only Portuguese soccer but the Portuguese national team.

The young Eusebio, ironically, was a nursery product not of Benfica but of their great Lisbon rivals, Sporting. But when Sporting summoned him to Lisbon for a trial in 1961, he was virtually kidnapped off the aeroplane by Benfica officials and hidden away until the fuss had died down and Sporting, having all but forgotten about him, lost interest.

Hijacked by Benfica

Bela Guttmann, a veteran Hungarian, was coach of Benfica at the time. He had a high regard for the potential offered by Mozambique and Angola. The nucleus of the Benfica team which Guttmann had guided to European Cup victory over Barcelona that year came from Africa: goalkeeper Costa Pereira, center-forward and captain Jose Aguas, and the two inside-forwards Joaquim Santana and Mario Coluna. But Eusebio would prove the greatest of all.

Guttmann introduced him to the first team at the end of the 1960–61 season. He was a reserve when Benfica went to France to face Santos of Brazil – inspired by Pele – in the famous Paris Tournament. At half-time Benfica were losing 3–0.

Guttmann, with nothing to lose, sent on Eusebio. Benfica still lost, but Eusebio scored a spectacular hat-trick and outshone even Pele. He was still only 19.

A year later Eusebio scored two cannonball goals in the 5–3 victory Benfica ran up against Real Madrid in the European Cup Final in Amsterdam. In 13 seasons he helped Benfica win the League seven times and the Cup twice; he was European Footballer of the Year in 1965; top scorer with nine goals in the 1966 World Cup finals; scorer of 38 goals in 46 internationals and the league's leading scorer seven times before knee trouble forced a halt at 32.

But soccer was Eusebio's life. When the fledgeling North American Soccer League offered him the chance of a lucrative extension to his career, he flew west to play for the Boston Minutemen (alongside old Benfica team-mate Antonio Simoes), then for the Toronto Metros-Croatia, and then for the Las Vegas Quicksilver.

Benfica's faithful had mixed feelings about his self-imposed exile in North America. But controversy was soon forgotten when he returned to Lisbon to take up various appointments as television analyst, as assistant coach and as the most honored public face of Benfica.

> **"Everywhere I go, Eusebio is the name people mention."**
>
> *Mario Soares,*
> *President of Portugal*

A Majestic Sportsman

Fans around the world took Eusebio to their hearts not only because of his ability but because of the sportsmanlike way he played the game. At Wembley in 1968 Eusebio very nearly won the European Cup Final for Benfica against Manchester United in the closing minutes of the match, being foiled only by the intuition of Alex Stepney. Eusebio's reaction? He patted Stepney on the back, applauding a worthy opponent.

Wembley Stadium played a major role in Eusebio's career. It was at Wembley, in a 2–0 World Cup qualifying defeat by England in 1961, that his youthful power first made the international game sit up; it was at Wembley, in 1963, that he scored one of his finest individual goals as consolation in a 2–1 European Cup Final defeat by Milan; and it was at Wembley again, in 1966, that Eusebio led Portugal to their best-ever third place in the World Cup. The semi-final, in which Portugal lost 2–1 to England, will long be remembered as as exemplary exhibition of sportsmanship under pressure.

Appropriately, a statue of Eusebio in action now dominates the entrance to the Estadio da Luz. Appropriately, also, a film made about his life was subtitled *Sua Majestade o Rei ... His Majesty the King.*

He remained an ambassador for Portugal, helping them to secure the hosting rights to the 2004 UEFA European Championships.

Career facts

1942 *Born Eusebio Da Silva Ferreira on January 25 in Lourenço Marques, Mozambique*

1952 *Joined the youth teams of Sporting (Lourenço Marques), a nursery team for the Portuguese giants of the same name*

1961 *Sporting tried to bring Eusebio to Lisbon, but he was "kidnapped" on arrival by Benfica. In the autumn, with barely a dozen league games to his name, he made his debut for Portugal*

1962 *Scored two thundering goals as Benfica beat Real Madrid 5–3 in a classic European Cup Final in Amsterdam*

1965 *Voted European Footballer of the Year*

1966 *Crowned top scorer with nine goals as Portugal finished third in the World Cup finals in England, where he was nicknamed the "new Pele" and the "Black Panther"*

1969 *Won Portuguese championship medal for the seventh and last time with Benfica before winding down his career in Mexico and Canada*

1992 *A statue in his honor was unveiled at the entrance to Benfica's Estadio da Luz in Lisbon*

HOLD-UP *Yashin foils Eusebio in the 1966 World Cup third place game*

IDOL OF TWO CONTINENTS

CROWD-PULLER, CROWD-PLEASER *Maradona, the inspiration of Napoli*

Diego Maradona was not only the world's greatest soccer player throughout the 1980s and early 1990s. He was also the most controversial and the most enigmatic.

His admirers in Argentina, where he knew the early glory days with Argentinos Juniors and Boca Juniors, considered him little less than a god, and the *tifosi* in Italy, where he triumphed with Napoli, worshipped his shoe laces. So did all of Argentina after Maradona reached the zenith of his career, captaining his country to victory in the 1986 World Cup finals in Mexico.

English fans still rage over his "Hand of God" goal in the quarter-final in Mexico City. But Argentine fans remember most clearly his other goal in that game when he collected the ball inside his own half and out-witted five defenders and goalkeeper Peter Shilton before gliding home one of the greatest goals in the history of the World Cup. Maradona provided a repeat against Belgium in the semi-finals: another brilliant slalom through the defence but from the left, not the right. Then, in the Final against West Germany, his slide-rule pass sent Jorge Burruchaga away to score the dramatic winner.

Maradona's great ability made his subsequent fall all the greater. His love affair with Italian soccer went sour after the 1990 World Cup, when Maradona's Argentina defeated their hosts on penalties in the semi-final in Maradona's adopted home of Naples. The following spring a drug test showed cocaine traces. He was banned from Italian and then world soccer for 15 months, returned to Argentina and was arrested there for cocaine possession.

Released on probation, he sought to revive his playing career in Spain, but half a season at Sevilla proved a

> **❝Pele was the supreme player of his era; Maradona is the pre-eminent player of his time. You cannot compare them. Such greatness does not submit to comparison.❞**
> *Cesar Luis Menotti, former manager of Argentina*

disaster. Even his 1994 World Cup comeback ended in the shameful ignominy of drug-test failure and a new 15-month international playing ban. He turned briefly to coaching with Deportivo Mandiyu, then with Racing Avellaneda before undertaking yet another playing comeback with his old love, Boca Juniors.

A Roller-Coaster Career

It all began in the working-class Fiorito suburb of Lanus in the province of Buenos Aires where Maradona began playing for a kids' team named Estrella Roja (Red Star) at the age of nine. Later he and his friends founded a team known as Los Cebollitas (The Little Onions) who were so promising that the entire team was signed up by Argentinos Juniors as one of the club's youth sides.

On October 20, 1976, Maradona (wearing No. 16) made his league debut as a 15-year-old substitute against Talleres of Cordoba, and a week later he played his first full match against Newells Old Boys from Rosario. In February 1977 he made his international debut. It appeared odds-on that Maradona would be a member of the squad with which manager Cesar Luis Menotti planned to win the World Cup for Argentina for the first time in front of their own fanatical fans in 1978, but he was one of the three players dropped on the eve of the finals. It was months before he would speak to Menotti again, but their eventual peace talk paved the way for the first international success of Maradona's career at the 1979 World Youth Cup in Japan.

Boca Juniors bought him for a world record $1.5 million and resold him two years later to Barcelona for $4.5 million, another record. Before joining the Catalans he succumbed to the pressures of the World Cup, in Spain in 1982, where he was sent off for an awful lunge at Batista of Brazil. It was the recurring theme of his career: a unique talent for the game shadowed by a similarly unique aptitude for arousing controversy.

It says much for the magical technique of his left foot that, despite all the negative vibes, Maradona continued to entrance the game. In 1984 Napoli paid another world record, this time

$7.5 million, to end Maradona's injury-battered two-year stay with Barcelona. Within weeks Napoli sold a staggering 70,000 season tickets. Two Italian League championships and one UEFA Cup success were the reward for the fans.

Seven glorious, roller-coaster years went by before the partnership was dissolved. Soccer in Naples will never be the same again.

A LEFT-BACK'S NIGHTMARE

CHEERS! *Matthews is carried off by his Cup-winning team-mates in 1953*

Stanley Matthews was the first great soccer player of the modern era. There will be cases made for Billy Wright, Bobby Charlton, Bobby Moore and others but none dominated his particular era as long as the barber's son from Hanley in the Potteries area of the English Midlands.

Matthews was nicknamed the Wizard of Dribble and the magic of his talent and reputation survived right through to the closing days of his career when he returned to his original club, Stoke City, and inspired them to win promotion out of the Second Division doldrums. That achieved, at the climax of the longest first-class career of any player, he decided to retire, at the age of 50. Later, however, Matthews insisted that he could – and should – have played for several more years.

Matthews went out in a style befitting one of the legends of the game. Among the other great players who turned out for his testimonial match at Stoke were Di Stefano, Puskas and Yashin. Always keen to put back into soccer as much, if not more, than he had taken out in terms of fame and glory, Matthews became general manager of another Potteries club,

> ❝ **The greatest tribute to Stanley Matthews is that he can go to any ground and make a monkey of a full-back and still be loved by the crowd.** ❞
>
> *Leslie Edwards,*
> Liverpool Echo

Port Vale. But the role was too restrictive for a man who had painted his soccer on a grand canvas, and Matthews left after 18 months to take coaching and exhibition courses around the world, in particular to Africa. Later he lived for many years in Malta before returning to settle again in England.

In the 1930s and 1940s Matthews was without rival as the greatest outside-right in the world. Opposing left-backs feared their duels with him as Matthews brought the ball towards them, feinted one way and accelerated away in another. His adoring public desperately wanted to see him crown his career with an FA Cup winners' medal. That dream was denied by Manchester United in 1948 and Newcastle in 1951. But in 1953 – a remarkable year for English sport with England reclaiming cricket's "Ashes" trophy from Australia and the veteran jockey Sir Gordon Richards winning the Epsom Derby – the 38-year-old Matthews tried again.

When Blackpool were 3–1 down to Bolton with time running out, it seemed Matthews was destined never to claim that elusive prize. But Matthews took over, ripping the Bolton defense to shreds and providing not only the inspiration for Blackpool's climb back to equality, but also the cross from which Bill Perry shot the winning goal. Blackpool scored twice in the last three minutes.

An Artist and a Gentleman

Like any player, Matthews knew his share of defeats. One of the most remarkable was England's 1–0 upset by the United States at the 1950 World Cup finals in Belo Horizonte, Brazil, when he had to watch in embarrassment after being omitted from the team. But England might have found more consistency if controversy had not been raised now and again over whether Matthews or Preston's Tom Finney was the more effective right-winger. Eventually the problem was solved by switching the versatile Finney to outside-left.

Matthews, by contrast, was always and only an outside-right, demonstrating supreme artistry in a posi-

tion which was later declared redundant when work-rate mechanics took over the game in the mid-1960s. Only much later, when coaches suddenly understood the value of breaking down massed defenses by going down the wings, was old-fashioned wing play revived.

But Matthews was, like many of the game's greatest players, a personality and an inspiring example for all youngsters. His knighthood was appropriate recognition for a 33-year career, completed without a single yellow card, in which he had graced the game as the First Gentleman of Football.

Career facts

1915 Born on February 1 in Hanley, Stoke-on-Trent.

1932 Turned professional with local club Stoke City

1934 Made his debut for England in a 4–0 win over Wales in Cardiff

1946 Traded to Blackpool in a headline-making move

1948 Played a key role in one of England's greatest victories, by 4–0 over Italy in Turin, and was voted Footballer of the Year

1953 Sealed his place among soccer's legends by inspiring Blackpool's FA Cup Final comeback against Bolton

1955 One of his many summer exhibition tours took him to Mozambique, where among the ball boys mesmerized at a match in Lourenço Marques was Eusebio

1957 Played the last of 84 games for England (including wartime internationals) in a 4–1 World Cup qualifying victory over Denmark in Copenhagen

1961 Returned to Stoke for a modest fee and, despite his 46 years, inspired their successful campaign to get back into the First Division

1965 Retired after a star-spangled Farewell Match at Stoke's Victoria Ground featuring the likes of Di Stefano, Puskas and Yashin

THE MASTER SHOWMAN

Pele remains one of those great examples and inspirations of world sport: a poor boy whose talent lifted him to the peaks of achievement, fame and fortune … yet who, amidst all that, retained his innate sense of sportsmanship, his love of his calling and the respect of team-mates and opponents alike.

His father Dondinho had been a talented player in the 1940s, but his career had been ended prematurely by injury. He was his son's first coach and his first supporter.

Most Brazilian players are known by nicknames. Pele does not know the origin of his own tag. He recalled only that he did not like it and was in trouble at school for fighting with class-mates who called him Pele. Later, of course, it became the most familiar name in world sport.

World Cup Triumph

Pele's teenage exploits as a player with his local club, Bauru, earned him a transfer to Santos at the age of 15. Rapidly he earned national and then international recognition. At 16 he was playing for Brazil; at 17 he was winning the World Cup. Yet it took pressure from his teammates to persuade national manager Vicente Feola to throw him into the action in Sweden in 1958.

Santos were not slow to recognize the potential offered their club by Pele. The directors created a sort of circus, touring the world, playing two and three times a week for lucrative

> **❝ Pele is to Brazilian football what Shakespeare is to English literature. ❞**
>
> *Joao Saldanha, former manager of Brazil*

match fees. The income from this gave the club the financial leverage to buy a supporting cast which helped turn Santos into World Club Champions in 1962 and 1963.

Mexico Makes up for Everything

The pressure on Pele was reflected in injuries, one of which restricted him to only a peripheral role at the 1962 World Cup finals. He scored a marvellous solo goal against Mexico in the first round, but pulled a muscle and missed the rest of the tournament. Brazil, even without him, went on to retain the Jules Rimet Trophy.

In 1966 Pele led Brazil in England. But referees were unprepared to give players of skill and creativity the necessary protection. One of the saddest images of the tournament was Pele, a raincoat around his shoulders, leaving the field after being forced out of the tournament with injuries by Portugal. Brazil, this time, did not possess the same strength in depth as in 1962, and crashed out.

Four years later Pele took his revenge in the most glorious way. As long as the game is played, the 1970 World Cup finals will be revered as the apotheosis of a great player, not only at his very best, but achieving the rewards his talent deserved.

As a 17-year-old Pele had scored one of the unforgettable World Cup goals in the Final against Sweden – in 1970 he

MUTUAL RESPECT *With Bobby Moore*

O REI *Pele, king of Brazilian soccer from the late 1950s to the early 1970s*

twice nearly surpassed it. First, against Czechoslovakia, he just missed scoring with a shot from his own half of the field, and against Uruguay he sold an outrageous dummy to the goalkeeper and just missed again.

It says everything about Pele's transcending genius that he was the one man able to set light to soccer in the United States in the 1970s. Although the North American Soccer League eventually collapsed amid financial confusion, soccer was by that stage firmly established as a grass-roots American sport. Without Pele's original allure that could never have happened and the capture of host rights for the 1994 finals would never have been possible.

Career facts

1940 Born Edson Arantes do Nascimento on October 21 in Tres Coracoes

1950 Began playing with local club Bauru, where his father was a coach

1956 Transferred to big-city club Santos and made his league debut at 15

1957 Made his debut for Brazil, at 16, against Argentina

1958 Became the youngest-ever World Cup winner, scoring two goals in the Final as Brazil beat Sweden 5–2

1962 Missed the 1962 World Cup win because of injury in the first round … but compensated by winning the World Club Cup with Santos

1970 Inspired Brazil to complete their historic World Cup hat-trick in Mexico

1975 Ended an 18-month retirement to play for Cosmos of New York in the dramatic, short-lived North American Soccer League

1977 Retired again after lifting Cosmos to their third NASL championship

1982 Presented with FIFA's Gold Medal Award for outstanding service to the world-wide game

1994 Appointed Brazil's Minister for Sport

THE MAGICAL LEFT FOOT

Ferenc Puskas remains one of the greatest players of all time – a symbol of the legendary "Magic Magyars" who dominated European soccer in the early 1950s and stand as perhaps the greatest team never to have won the World Cup.

Puskas's father was a player and later coach with the local club, Kispest. At 16 Ferenc was a regular at inside-left, terrorizing opposing goalkeepers with the power of his shooting. He rarely used his right foot but then his left was so lethal that he seldom needed it.

At 18 he was in the national team, too. His brilliance had much to do with the decision to convert Kispest into a new army sports club named Honved, that formed the basis of the national side.

For four years Hungary, built around goalkeeper Gyula Grosics, right-half Jozsef Bozsik and the inside-forward trio of Sandor Kocsis, Nandor Hidegkuti and Puskas, crushed all opposition. They also introduced a new tactical concept. The inside-forwards, Kocsis and Puskas, formed the spearhead of the attack, with Hidegkuti a revolutionary deep-lying center-forward. Hungary won the 1952 Olympic title before ending England's record of invincibility against continental opposition with a stunning 6–3 triumph at Wembley.

Early the following year,

> **❝ His was a name fit for any sporting hall of fame, worthy of any and every superlative. ❞**
> *Billy Wright,*
> *England captain against*
> *Hungary in 1953*

Hungary thrashed England again, 7–1 in Budapest. No wonder they were overwhelming favorites to win the 1954 World Cup in Switzerland. But Puskas presented a problem. He had been injured in an early round game against West Germany and was a hobbling spectator at training before the Final, against these same West Germans, in Berne. Could his great left foot withstand the strain? Puskas thought so and decided to play, thus taking one of the most controversial gambles in the game's history. After only 12 minutes the gamble appeared to be paying off when Hungary led 2–0. However, they lost 3–2, their dominance finally ended in the one match which mattered most.

The Toast of Spain

It was eight long years before Puskas would return to the World Cup finals. Then, in Chile in 1962, his trusty left foot was doing duty for Spain, because Puskas had, in the meantime, defected to the West, joining

Real Madrid. Honved had been abroad when the Hungarian Revolution of 1956 erupted. Puskas and several teammates decided to stay in the West. He made an attempt to sign for several Italian clubs, but they thought him too old. Just how wrong they were was underlined when Puskas developed, at Madrid, a new career to emulate his first in brilliance.

Four times Puskas was the Spanish league's top scorer and his partnership with the Argentine center-forward, Alfredo Di Stefano, was one of the greatest of all time. They hit perfection together on the famous night when Madrid thrashed Eintracht Frankfurt 7–3 in the European Cup Final before a record 135,000 crowd at Hampden.

Di Stefano scored three goals, Puskas four. The Spanish fans loved him. In his Hungarian army club days at Honved, Puskas had been known as the Galloping Major. Now they called him *Cañoncito* – the little cannon.

In 1966 he finally retired. His future was secure, thanks to business investments which included a sausage factory near Madrid. He tried his hand at coaching without a great deal of success – save for the remarkable 1970–71 season when he took Panathinaikos of Athens to the European Cup Final.

In the course of time he was able to visit his native Hungary, where he was celebrated once more as a national hero. Hardly surprising. After all, how many can boast 83 goals in 84 games for their country?

"BLACK PANTHER" WAS THE SUPREME SOVIET

Career facts

1929 Born Lev Ivanovich Yashin on October 22 in Moscow

1946 Joined Moscow Dynamo as an ice hockey goaltender

1951 Made his first-team debut for Moscow Dynamo

1953 Finally took over as Dynamo's first-choice keeper

1954 Made his debut for the Soviet Union in a 3–2 win over Sweden

1956 Won Olympic gold with the Soviet Union at the Melbourne Games

1958 Appeared in his first World Cup and helped the Soviet Union reach the quarter-finals

1960 Won the first European Championship with the Soviet Union against Yugoslavia in Paris

1963 Voted European Footballer of the Year and played for FIFA's World XI at Wembley in a match to mark the centenary of the Football Association

1968 Awarded the Order of Lenin by the Soviet government

Lev Yashin was called the "Black Spider" in South America; the "Black Panther" in Europe. Portugal's Eusebio described him as "the peerless goalkeeper of the century." It says everything about his ability and his personality that the likes of Pele, Eusebio and Franz Beckenbauer made the journey to Moscow for his farewell match.

Yet Yashin very nearly gave up soccer altogether in favor of ice hockey. That was in 1953. He was tiring of standing in as reserve at Moscow Dynamo to the legendary Alexei "Tiger" Khomich. He was 23, after all, and Dynamo's ice hockey coaches were begging him to commit himself to their cause.

Then Khomich was injured. Dynamo coach Arkady Cherenyshev called on the impatient reserve, and Yashin took over to such outstanding effect that, a year later, he was making his debut for the Soviet Union in a 3–2 win over Sweden. Two years later, in 1956, Yashin kept goal for the Soviet side who won the Olympic title in Melbourne, Australia. In 1960 he was goalkeeper for the Soviet side who won the inaugural European Championship, then called the Nations Cup.

After that first summons in 1953, Yashin had never looked back. In the first seven years after his debut for the Soviet Union he missed only two internationals, ending his career with a then Soviet record 78 caps to his name. For Dynamo, Yashin played 326 Supreme League matches and won the league title six times and the Soviet cup twice. On his death in 1990, the official news agency, Tass, described him as, "the most famous Soviet sportsman ever."

First Goalkeeper and First Soviet

Yashin's fame had quickly spread throughout the world, not merely for his ability as a goalkeeper, to stop shots that no-one else could reach, but as an outstanding sportsman and ambassador for the game. Appropriately, in 1963 he became the first Soviet player to be nominated as European Footballer of the Year by the French magazine, *France Football*. To this day, he remains the only goalkeeper to have received the award. In South America, when the magazine *El Grafico* ran a readers' poll to determine the Greatest Team of All Time, Yashin was virtually unchallenged as goalkeeper.

The World Cups of 1958, 1962 and 1966 saw Yashin at work, and he was also in Mexico in 1970 though only as a reserve because of the value of his experience behind the scenes and in the dressing-rooms. In 1965, Yashin was outstanding in the Stanley Matthews Retirement Match at Stoke when a British XI lost narrowly to a World XI featuring not only Yashin but Di Stefano, Puskas, the other great exiled Hungarian Ladislav Kubala, and Yashin's immediate predecessor as European Footballer of the Year, Czechoslovakia's Josef Masopust.

One of Yashin's saves that night – diving full length across the face of his goal to grip a shot from Jimmy Greaves which few goalkeepers would even have got a finger to – will live for ever in the memory of those who were present.

Yashin was said to have saved more than 150 penalties during his career. One of the few which got past him was struck by Eusebio in the third place play-off at the 1966 World Cup finals at Wembley. The Soviets finished fourth, but that remains their best finish in the game's greatest competition.

Grand Testimonial

When Yashin retired in 1970, a testimonial match was arranged and stars from all over the world turned out in honor of the great sportsman. The match at Lenin stadium, before 100,000 fans, was an unforgettable event in Soviet soccer history.

Yashin remained in sport after his retirement, not as a coach or trainer but as head of the Ministry of Sport's soccer department and then as a vice-president of the national association. His film archive, compiled from shots he had taken all round the world, was an object of admiration, as was his modern jazz record collection. Towards the end of his career, Yashin was honoured by the Soviet government with its ultimate honour, the Order of Lenin. Lenin's reputation has gone into steep decline: something that could never be said of Lev Yashin.

> **Yashin was the peerless goalkeeper of the century.**
> *Eusebio*

SEMI-FINALISTS *The Soviet Union's 1966 World Cup side*

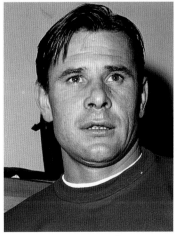

YASHIN *The "Black Panther"*

THE GREAT PLAYERS

Every country produces great players. These are the men who have delighted fans over the years not merely with their achievements but with their personalities. They drew spectators who may have had no previous attachment to their clubs but who were simply attracted by their skills. The advent of TV has widened their fame.

A

Andre "Trello" Abegglen

Born: March 7, 1909, Switzerland.
Clubs: Etoile Rouge, Cantonal, Grasshoppers (Swz), Sochaux (Fr), Servette, La Chaux-de-Fonds (Swz).

Abegglen was the first great Swiss player to make his mark on the world stage. He and brother Max, nicknamed Xam, were inside-forward stalwarts together at the Grasshoppers club of Zurich. Trello scored 30 goals in 52 internationals for Switzerland between 1927 and 1943. He starred at the 1934 and 1938 World Cup finals and won three Swiss championships, two while with Grasshoppers and one after moving on to Servette of Geneva. Brother Max played 68 times for Switzerland and was top scorer at the 1924 Olympic Games .

Ademir Marques de Menezes

Born: November 8, 1922, Brazil.
Clubs: FC Recife, Vasco da Gama, Fluminense, Vasco da Gama.

Ademir was the seven-goal leading scorer at the 1950 World Cup finals when he played center-forward for Brazil. The inside-forward trio of Ademir, Zizinho and Jair da Rosa was considered one of the greatest in Brazil's history. Ademir scored 32 goals in 37 internationals after beginning his career as an outside-left. He had a powerful shot in both feet and was six times a Rio state league champion, five times with Vasco da Gama and once with Fluminense. It was said that Brazilian coaches created 4–2–4 because Ademir's ability forced opposing teams to play with an extra central defender.

José Pinto Carvalho dos Santos Aguas

Born: c. 1930, Portugal.
Clubs: Benfica (Port), FK Austria.

Aguas was captain and center-forward of the Benfica side which succeeded Real Madrid as European champions in 1961. In his native Angola, legend has it, he was a famed local lion-hunter when Benfica persuaded him he could enjoy a more lucrative existence hunting goals. He flew to Portugal in 1950 and scored more than 250 goals for Benfica as well as finishing top league scorer five times. In 1960–61 he was also top scorer, with 11 goals, in the European Cup and collected the trophy as captain after the final victory over Barcelona. In 1963 he transferred to FK Austria but later returned to Portugal to work as a coach.

Florian Albert

Born: September 15, 1941, Hungary.
Club: Ferencvaros.

Albert was the first outstanding player to emerge in Hungary after the dissolution of the great team of the early 1950s. Albert was a farmer's son whose family moved to Budapest while he was still a boy. His talent was quickly recognized by the youth coaches of Ferencvaros, and he made his international debut at 17, in a 3–2 win over Sweden in Budapest, a few days after passing his major school examinations. Center-forward Albert was three times the leading scorer in the Hungarian league and four times a league championship winner with Ferencvaros. His most memorable display was as the inspiration of Hungary's 3–1 win over Brazil at the 1966 World Cup finals, and he was voted European Footballer of the Year the following year.

Ivor Allchurch

Born: October 16, 1919, Wales.
Clubs: Swansea (Wales), Newcastle (Eng), Cardiff, Swansea (Wales).

Slim, elegant, creative and a natural scorer: Ivor the Golden Boy had just about everything an inside-forward needed in the first quarter-century after the Second World War, except luck. He was fated to play in mediocre club teams throughout his long career, and even his excellent work for his country went largely to waste, except in the 1958 World Cup. He won 68 caps, spread over 16 years, and scored 23 goals – records which stood until the 1990s. His 251 League goals in nearly 700 appearances emphasized his excellent finishing.

Luigi Allemandi

Born: November 18, 1903, Italy.
Clubs: Juventus, Internazionale, Roma.

Allemandi was a left-back and one of the outstanding personalities in *Calcio* in the inter-war years. He played 25 times for his country and would have made more appearances but for a match-fixing scandal. Allemandi was accused of having accepted a bribe from a director of Torino to fix a match while playing for Juventus in 1927. The matter did not emerge until a year later when Allemandi, despite reports identifying him as one of the best players on the field, was found guilty and suspended for life. By now he was playing for

Internazionale, who challenged the ban on his behalf and had it quashed. In 1929 Allemandi returned to Italy's team for a match against Czechoslovakia, and he went on to win a World Cup medal in 1934.

José Altafini

Born: August 27, 1938, Brazil.
Clubs: Palmeiras, São Paulo FC (Br), Milan, Napoli, Juventus (It), Chiasso (Swz).

Altafini was a subject of both confusion and admiration throughout his career. A direct, aggressive center-forward, he began with Palmeiras of São Paulo, where he was known by the nickname of Mazzola because of his resemblance to the Italian star of the late 1940s. He played at the 1958 World Cup and was immediately signed by Milan. The Italians insisted on reverting to Altafini's own name and he played for his "new" country at the 1962 World Cup finals. A year later Altafini scored a record 14 goals in Milan's European Cup success, including two goals in the final victory over Benfica at Wembley. After falling out with Milan he joined Omar Sivori in inspiring a Napoli revival, then became a "super substitute" with Juventus. Altafini is now a TV soccer analyst in Italy.

AMANCIO *10 times a champion*

Amancio Amaro Varela

Born: October 12, 1939, Spain.
Clubs: La Coruña, Real Madrid.

In 1962 Real Madrid, seeking a replacement for Italy-bound Luis Del Sol, bought outside-right Amancio from his home town club, Real Deportivo de La Coruña. Coach Miguel Muñoz switched him to inside-right, playing him first in midfield and then as a striker. His outstanding technique and acceleration brought him a string of honors. He played 42 times for Spain between 1964 and 1971, was 10 times a Spanish league champion with Madrid

and four times a cup-winner. In 1968 he was honored with selection for a World XI against Brazil, but the highlight of his career was winning the European Nations Championship with Spain in 1964 on his home ground, the Estadio Bernabeu in Madrid.

Amarildo Tavares Silveira

Born: June 29, 1939, Brazil.
Clubs: Botafogo (Br), Milan, Fiorentina (It).

Amarildo, an attacking inside-left whose slight appearance disguised a wiry frame, burst on to the international scene at the 1962 World Cup finals after Pele was injured. He had not expected to play when he was called in to deputize for O Rei in a decisive group match against Spain. Brazil recovered from a goal down to win 2–1 thanks to two late strikes from Amarildo, and in the Final against Czechoslovakia he proved decisive once more – scoring with a snapshot which deceived the goalkeeper on the near post. A year later Amarildo was bought by Milan, and he enjoyed a successful career in Italy with Milan and Fiorentina, with whom he won the championship in 1969. Amarildo stayed in Italy after retiring and joined Fiorentina's youth coaching staff.

Manuel Amoros

Born: February 1, 1961, France.
Clubs: Monaco, Marseille, Lyon.

Amoros played both right- and left-back in the outstanding French national team of the 1980s. Born in Nimes of Spanish parents, Amoros was an outstanding teenage exponent of both soccer and rugby. Monaco persuaded him to concentrate on soccer, and he played for France at youth and Under-21 levels before a surprise, and highly successful, promotion to the senior national team at the 1982 World Cup finals, in which France finished fourth. Amoros won a European Championship medal in 1984, despite missing most of the tournament after being sent off in the opening match against Denmark. During his career, most of which he spent with Monaco before joining Marseille, then Lyon, he set a French record of 82 caps.

(LEFT) ALBERT *National debut at 17*

AMOROS *Set a French record of 82 international caps*

José Leandro Andrade

Born: November 20, 1898, Uruguay.
Clubs: Bella Vista, Nacional.

Andrade was an old-fashioned wing-half in the 2–3–5 tactical system which served much of the world for the first half of the century. He was a stalwart of the great Uruguayan teams of the 1920s and 1930s, winning gold medals at the Olympic Games soccer tournaments of both 1924 and 1928. Injury then threatened to end his career but Andrade was recalled, because of his vast experience, for the inaugural World Cup finals which Uruguay won on home ground in 1930. He played 41 times for his country before retiring in 1933. Andrade's nephew, Victor Rodriguez Andrade, won the World Cup in 1950 and was never once yellow-carded or ejected.

Giancarlo Antognoni

Born: April 1, 1954, Italy.
Club: Fiorentina.

In the 1970s and early 1980s Antognoni was considered by Italian fans to be the successor to Milan's Gianni Rivera as their Golden Boy of Italian soccer. A graceful, wonderfully intuitive midfield general, Antognoni cost Fiorentina a huge sum as a teenager from Fourth Division Astimacombi in 1972. He went straight into the Fiorentina team and made the first of his 73 appearances for Italy in the autumn of 1974. Antognoni was a regular transfer target for Italy's richest clubs but remained faithful to Fiorentina until he eventually wound down his career in Switzerland. Sadly, Antognoni missed Italy's victory over West Germany in the 1982 World Cup Final after suffering a gashed ankle in the semi-final defeat of Poland.

Osvaldo Ardiles

Born: August 3, 1952, Argentina.
Clubs: Huracan (Arg), Tottenham (Eng), Paris S-G (Fr), Tottenham, Queen's Park Rangers (Eng).

Ardiles combined legal and soccer studies in the mid-1970s when he earned his initial reputation as midfield general of Argentina under manager Cesar Luis Menotti. Hardly had Ardiles collected his winners'

ANTOGNONI *Italian soccer's golden boy of the 1970s*

medal at the 1978 World Cup when he and national teammate Ricardo Villa were together subjects of a remarkable transfer to Tottenham Hotspur. Ardiles cost Spurs $500,000, which made him one of the greatest bargains of modern soccer history. He completed his outstanding playing career which included Tottenham's FA Cup success of 1981 and their UEFA Cup triumph of 1984. He returned to White Hart Lane as manager in the summer of 1993, but lasted little more than a year.

ARDILES *success on two continents*

Luis Artime

Born: 1939, Argentina.
Clubs: Atlanta, River Plate, Independiente (Arg), Palmeiras (Br), Nacional (Uru), Fluminense (Br).

Artime was a center-forward in the traditional Argentine mould: powerful, aggressive and prolific. He scored 47 goals in two teenage seasons with minor Buenos Aires club Atlanta to earn a move in 1961 to River Plate, with whom he will always be most closely linked. He climaxed

a three-year spell, including 66 league goals, by leading Argentina's attack at the 1966 World Cup finals. Artime then joined Independiente, scoring 44 goals in 18 months before moving on to Palmeiras and then to Nacional of Montevideo, with whom he was top Uruguayan league marksman three years in a row. He also scored 24 goals for Argentina.

Georgi Asparoukhov

Born: May 4, 1943, Bulgaria.
Clubs: Botev Plovdiv, Spartak Sofia, Levski Sofia.

"Gundi" Asparoukhov remains one of the most outstanding yet tragic players in Bulgaria's history. A tall, direct center-forward, he had scored 19 goals in 49 internationals when he died in a car crash, aged 28, in 1971. Asparoukhov led Bulgaria's attack in the World Cup finals of 1962, 1966 and 1970 and scored 150 goals in 245 league games for his only senior club, Levski Sofia. Portuguese club Benfica tried to sign him in 1966 after he impressed in a European Cup tie. But Asparoukhov did not want to move because he had all he wanted in Bulgaria … including his favorite Alfa Romeo sports car which, ultimately, proved the death of him.

José Augusto

Born: April 13, 1937, Portugal.
Clubs: Barreirense, Benfica.

Augusto was originally a center-forward, and had already made his debut for Portugal in this position when Benfica bought him from local club Barreirense in 1959 on coach Bela Guttmann's recommendation. He

then succesfully converted him into an outside-right. Augusto was considered, after Frenchman Raymond Kopa, as the best "thinking" player in Europe and appeared in five European Cup finals. He was a winner in 1961 and 1962 and a loser in 1963, 1965 and finally in 1968 against Manchester United, by which time he was an attacking midfield player. Augusto was a key member of the Portugal side which finished third at the 1966 World Cup, and later coached both Benfica and Portugal.

Roberto Baggio

Born: February 18, 1967, Italy.
Clubs: Fiorentina, Juventus, Milan, Bologna, Internazionale.

Roberto Baggio became the world's most expensive soccer player when Juventus bought him from Fiorentina on the eve of the 1990 World Cup finals for $13m. His transfer provoked three days of riots by angry fans in the streets of Florence but he proved his worth by scoring a glorious World Cup goal against Czechoslovakia. He then helped Juventus win the 1993 UEFA Cup and was voted World Player of the Year in 1994, despite missing a penalty in the World Cup final shoot-out against Brazil. He made up for that error in the 1998 finals, bravely volunteering to take a penalty against Chile and also scoring in a shoot-out against France. He won the league with Juventus in 1995 and with Milan in 1996 before moving to Bologna, where he rediscovered his best form.

Gordon Banks

Born: December 20, 1937, England.
Clubs: Leicester, Stoke.

A product of the prolific Chesterfield "goalkeeper academy," Banks went on to undying fame with England. Against Brazil in 1970, he pulled off maybe the best ever World Cup save, flying across his goal to palm away a close-range header from Pele. He

BANKS *Saving England in the 1966 World Cup Final*

set all kinds of goalkeeping records, including 73 caps, 23 consecutive internationals, and seven consecutive shut-outs, a run eventually ended by Eusebio's penalty kick in the 1966 World Cup semi-final. His late withdrawal from the 1970 quarter-final probably cost England the match from 2–0 up; he was a loser in two FA Cup finals with Leicester (at fault with two goals in the second); and, unluckiest of all, he lost an eye in a car crash when he still had years left to play. Only Shilton, perhaps, has equalled him as a goalkeeper for England.

Franceschino "Franco" Baresi

Born: May 8, 1960, Italy.
Club: Milan.

Baresi was perhaps the greatest in a long line of outstanding Italian sweepers. He began as an attacking midfielder with Milan in the late 1970s and was kept waiting for an international opportunity because of the dominance of Juventus's Gaetano Scirea. Finally, in 1987, Baresi secured a place in the national team, simultaneously providing the defensive foundation on which coach Arrigo Sacchi built Milan's all-conquering club team. While Dutchmen Ruud Gullit and Marco Van Basten were granted much of the glory, discerning observers recognized the enor-

mous influence of Baresi. In the 1994 World Cup Final, Baresi shone like a beacon, despite having undergone knee surgery only two weeks earlier.

Bebeto (full name: Jose Roberto Gama de Oliveira)

Born: February 16, 1964, Brazil.
Clubs: Flamengo, Vasco da Gama (Br), Deportivo (Sp), Vitoria Bahia, Cruzeiro, Botafogo.

Bebeto could have made an international impact earlier in his career, but for a weak temperament and injuries. He was outstanding for Flamengo when they won the Rio championship in 1986 and was the club's top scorer four years in a row. He was trans-

BARESI *Key to Milan's revival*

ferred to Rio rivals Vasco da Gama in 1989 but won Brazil fans over by scoring six goals in his country's 1989 South American Championship triumph. He then moved to Spain's La Coruña and hit three goals in Brazil's 1994 World Cup triumph and three on their way to the 1998 final in France.

Franz Beckenbauer

see Legends (page 76).

Ferenc Bene

Born: December 17, 1944, Hungary
Clubs: Kaposzvar, Ujpest Dozsa.

Bene was a versatile attacker who played center-forward for Ujpest Dozsa but usually outside-right for Hungary because of the presence of Florian Albert. Bene was first capped in 1962 but did not make much impact on the international scene until two years later when he was leading scorer with 12 goals in Hungary's victory at the Tokyo Olympics. Three times Bene was the Hungarian league's leading scorer and he won the championship four times with Ujpest. In the 1966 World Cup Bene was an outstanding member of the Hungarian team which scored a 3–1 victory over Brazil. Hungary fell to the more organized Soviet Union side in the quarter-finals, but Bene's consolation was having scored in each of their four matches.

Dennis Bergkamp

Born: May 10, 1969, Holland.
Clubs: Ajax Amsterdam (Hol), Internazionale (It), Arsenal (Eng).

Bergkamp, a youth product of Ajax, was such a natural that he made his European club debut in a match against Malmö after taking school examinations the previous afternoon. Bergkamp starred for Holland at the 1992 European Championship finals, and Inter beat Barcelona, Juventus and Milan to his $11 million contract signing the following spring. Bergkamp never settled in Italy, and in 1995 he was transferred to Arsenal for £7.5 million, inspiring the club to their league and cup double in 1998. He was one of the stars of France '98, scoring a glorious quarter-final winner against Argentina, and guiding Holland to fourth place.

Orvar Bergmark

Born: November 16, 1930, Sweden.
Clubs: Örebro, AIK Solna (Swe), Roma (It).

Bergmark's record of 94 international appearances stood for years as a Swedish record and established him as one of the great European fullbacks of the 1950s and early 1960s. He began with Örebro in 1949 as a center-forward but quickly switched to full-back and made his debut there for Sweden in 1951. He was voted best right-back at the 1958 World Cup finals, in which his steady play helped the hosts reach the Final against Brazil. Bergmark also had a spell in Italy with Roma before retiring. He was appointed manager of Sweden in 1966 and guided them to the 1970 World Cup finals. One of his players then was Tommy Svensson, who would emulate him as World Cup boss in 1994.

George Best

Born: May 22, 1946, Northern Ireland.
Clubs: Manchester United, Fulham (Eng), Hibernian (Scot), Tampa Bay Rowdies (US).

George Best was perhaps the outstanding British player of all time, despite a career much shorter than it could and should have been. "Wayward genius" is a cliché that cannot be bettered as a description of a player with so many incredible gifts packed into a slight frame: balance, two twinkling feet, a surprisingly high leap, a cold eye for the finishing chance … everything. Best was twice a league championship winner with United, and won both the European Cup and the European Footballer of the Year award in 1968. Then fame and fortune and the temptations of the world beyond soccer all combined to force a sad finale scattered with retirements and comebacks.

Franz "Bimbo" Binder

Born: December 1, 1911, Austria.
Clubs: St Polten, Rapid Vienna (Aus).

Binder was a prolific marksman, either from center-forward or inside-forward, and is popularly considered to have been the first European player to have topped 1,000 goals in his first-class career. When he retired in 1950 to become manager of his old club, Rapid, Binder claimed career

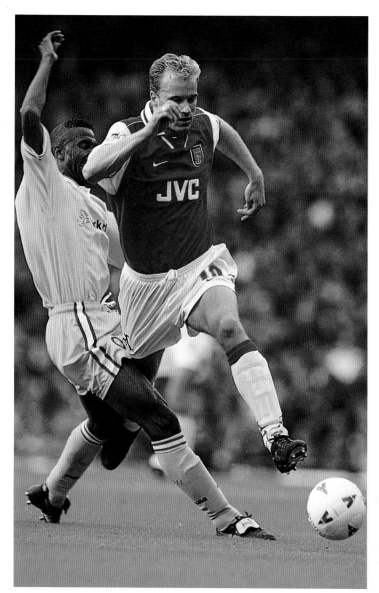

DIFFERENT CLASS *Arsenal's Dennis Bergkamp leaves Leeds' Lucas Radebe behind*

figures of 1,006 in 756 games. Binder was Rapid's greatest player in the 1930s, playing 20 times for Austria before being selected nine times for Greater Germany after the Anschluss of 1938. Binder's greatest achievement for Rapid was in the 1941 Greater German championship play-off, when he scored a hat-trick against Schalke

BEST *So appropriately named*

in Rapid's 4–3 victory. Later he coached not only Rapid but also the Austrian national team.

Danny Blanchflower

Born: February 10, 1926, Northern Ireland.
Clubs: Barnsley, Aston Villa, Tottenham (Eng).

A tactically astute playmaker, Danny Blanchflower was one of the major forces in Ireland's valiant 1958 World Cup side and Tottenham's excellent team of the early 1960s. The League and Cup "double" was followed by another Cup and the European Cup-winners' Cup, with Blanchflower's cerebral approach blending perfectly with the more robust forays of the other wing-half, Dave Mackay. In the

days when few sportsmen appeared on TV, the loquacious Blanchflower was a media darling, always entertaining and forthright in speech or in print. As so often with gifted players, his foray into management, with Chelsea, was an anti-climax. He died in 1993.

Oleg Blokhin

Born: November 5, 1952, Soviet Union.
Clubs: Kiev Dynamo (USSR), Vorwärts Steyr (Austria).

Blokhin was originally an outside-left, but, according to his friend, Olympic sprint champion Valeri Borzov, he could have been a star sprinter. Certainly he used his pace to electric effect, his key role in Kiev's European Cup-winners' Cup triumph of 1975 earning him the accolade of European Footballer of the Year. Blokhin played in the World Cup finals of 1982 and 1986, having by then become the first Soviet player to top a century of international appearances. By the time Blokhin, now a central striker, was "freed" to move west with Vorwärts Steyr of Austria, he had totalled a Soviet record 39 goals in a further record 109 internationals. After retiring he turned to coaching with the Greek champions, Olympiakos of Piraeus.

Steve Bloomer

Born: January 20, 1874, England.
Clubs: Derby, Middlesbrough, Derby.

England's most famous player before the First World War, Bloomer established long-lasting records: his 352 league goals were not exceeded until the 1930s; his 28 goals for his country, in only 23 games, were not surpassed until the 1950s. Bloomer was of medium height and slightly built, often the target for unscrupulous defenders with hard tackles and desperate intent. But he survived, thanks to agility and a sharp brain, through 22 years until the start of the First World War, when he was in his 41st year. Born at Cradley Heath in the West Midlands' "Black Country," he was, nevertheless, a Derby player throughout his career apart from a four-year spell with Middlesbrough. In later years he coached Derby players and did odd jobs at the ground.

Zvonimir Boban

Born: October 8, 1968
Clubs: Dinamo Zagreb (Yug/Cro), Bari, Milan (It)

Boban first made a name as a member of the former Yugoslavia team which won the 1987 World Youth Cup. He became Dinamo Zagreb's

BLOKHIN *Electrifying pace*

youngest-ever captain at 18 and was hailed a local hero after he came to the defence of Croat fans being manhandled by police at a high-tension match against Red Star Belgrade, for which he was given a six-month suspension. It cost him a place with Yugoslavia at the 1990 World Cup finals. His brilliant ball control, astute passing and explosive free kicks were noticed in Italy, however, and Milan snapped him up for $12 million. At the San Siro he has won four championships and a European Cup, playing a major part in the 4-0 final victory over Barcelona in 1994. But the highlight of his career so far is captaining fledgling country Croatia to third place in the 1998 World Cup finals in France.

Zbigniew Boniek

Born: March 3, 1956, Poland.
Clubs: Zawisza Bydgoszcz, Widzew Lodz (Pol) Juventus (It) Roma (It)

Boniek must be considered the greatest Polish soccer player of all time. He was the product of the next soccer generation after the outstanding side of the mid-1970s but his talents shone in World Cups and in European club competition with Juventus. Boniek made his name with Widzew Lodz and his hat-trick against Belgium in the 1982 World Cup finals persuaded Juventus to pay £1.8 million for him – then a record for a Polish player. Boniek scored Juve's winner in the 1984 European Cup-winners' Cup Final defeat of FC Porto and was a member of the side which won the

BONIEK *The greatest Polish player of all time thanks to his feats with Juventus*

European Cup a year later, playing the Final against Liverpool in the shadow of the Heysel disaster. Boniek scored 24 goals in 80 internationals.

Giampiero Boniperti

Born: July 4, 1928, Italy.
Club: Juventus.

Boniperti was the original Golden Boy of Italian soccer. He enjoyed a meteoric rise: within a few months of being signed by Juventus from minor club Momo, in July 1946, he was promoted to the Italian national team and made his debut in a 5–1 defeat by Austria in Vienna. Originally a center-forward, Boniperti later switched to inside-forward and played on the right wing for FIFA's World XI against England in 1953 (scoring twice in a 4–4 draw). Boniperti won five Italian league titles with Juventus, for whom he played a record 444 league games. He was a "father figure" in the Charles/Sivori team of the late 1950s and scored eight goals in 38 internationals. On retiring from

the game he took up a business career which eventually turned full circle when he became a hugely successful president of Juventus in the 1970s and early 1980s under the Agnelli family patronage.

Jozsef Bozsik

Born: September 28, 1929, Hungary.
Clubs: Kispest, Honved.

Bozsik will always be remembered as right-half of the wonderful Hungarian national team of the early 1950s. A team-mate of Ferenc Puskas with Kispest and then Honved, Bozsik was the midfield brains but could also score spectacular goals, including one from 30 yards in the historic 6–3 win over England at Wembley in 1953. Bozsik made his debut for Hungary against Bulgaria in 1947, returned home – unlike teammates Puskas, Kocsis and Czibor – after the 1956 Revolution and combined a career as a soccer player with that of an MP. In 1962 he scored a goal against Uruguay in a friendly to mark

his 100th and last game for his country. Bozsik had been a member of Hungary's victorious side at the 1952 Helsinki Olympics.

Raymond Braine

Born: April 28, 1907, Belgium.
Clubs: Beerschot (Bel), Sparta Prague (Cz), Beerschot (Bel).

Braine was considered the greatest Belgian soccer player until the advent of Paul Van Himst in the 1960s. In 1922 he made his league debut for Beerschot at the age of 15 and was chosen, that same year, for a Belgian XI against Holland. Clapton Orient of London tried to sign Braine in 1928 but could not obtain a work permit for him to come to England, so instead he turned professional in Czechoslovakia with the great Sparta Prague club. The Czechs wanted him to take citizenship and play for them in the 1934 World Cup, but Braine preferred to represent Belgium – and did so at the 1938 World Cup after returning home to Beerschot. Braine's center-forward talents

earned him selection for Western Europe against Central Europe in 1938, and then for Europe against England that same year. He won 54 caps for Belgium.

Paul Breitner

Born: September 5, 1951, West Germany.
Clubs: Bayern Munich (W Ger), Real Madrid (Sp), Eintracht Braunschweig, Bayern Munich (W Ger).

Breitner was a flamboyant virtuoso of a left-back when Helmut Schön brought him into the West German national team in 1971–72. He was a key member of a the new, Bayern-dominated side which also featured Franz Beckenbauer, Sepp Maier, Uli Hoeness and Gerd Müller. Breitner demonstrated his big-match temperament by nervelessly converting the penalty which tied the match for West Germany in the 1974 World Cup Final against Holland. A soccer intellectual, he considered he was being stifled at Bayern and moved forward to midfield on transferring to Real Madrid. A falling-out with the German soccer authorities caused him to miss the 1978 World Cup, but he returned in 1982 and again scored in the Final — this time only the Germans' consolation goal in their defeat by Italy on his old home ground in Madrid. Only four players have scored in two World Cup Finals.

BREITNER *Soccer intellectual*

Billy Bremner

Born: December 9, 1942, Scotland.
Clubs: Leeds United, Hull, Doncaster (Eng).

Bremner made his debut for Leeds at 17, as a winger partnered by Don Revie, a man nearly twice his age. Later midfielder Bremner and manager Revie were outstanding figures as Leeds emerged from decades of mediocrity to be a force feared throughout the game. Bremner's fierce tackling, competitive spirit and selflessness made him a winner of various medals, though the list of second places was much longer. He was not a prolific scorer, but a useful one, providing the winner in each of three FA Cup semi-finals. He also won 55 caps, including three at the 1974 World Cup finals, when Scotland were eliminated, unbeaten, after three matches.

Tomas Brolin

Born: November 29, 1969, Sweden.
Clubs: GIF Sundsvall (Swe), Parma (It), Leeds (Eng), Parma (It), Zurich (Swz), Crystal Palace (Eng)

Brolin had long been considered one of Sweden's outstanding attacking prospects before proving the point by scoring twice on his debut for the senior team in the 4–2 win over Wales in 1990. He followed up with two more against Finland to earn a late call into Sweden's World Cup team. At Italia '90, Brolin's outstanding displays alerted Italian clubs and Parma immediately bought him. He starred for Sweden at the 1992 European Championship – scoring a marvellous solo goal against England – and then helped Parma to success in the 1993 European Cup-winners' Cup. A year later Brolin lead Sweden to third place at the World Cup Finals. But serious injury effectively wrecked his career. He was never the same again, despite stints in Switzerland, England (with Leeds and Crystal Palace) and Italy.

Emilio Butragueño

Born: July 22, 1963, Spain
Clubs: Castilla, Real Madrid (Sp), Celaya (Mex).

Butragueño, nicknamed "the Vulture," was once considered not good enough by Real Madrid's youth coaches. Real's nursery club, Castilla, had second thoughts and Butragueño became "leader" of Madrid throughout the 1980s. His close control and talent as a marksman helped Madrid win the UEFA Cup in 1985 and 1986, and in both years Butragueño won the Prix Bravo as Europe's best young player. He made a scoring debut for Spain in 1984, and in 1986 became a World Cup sensation when he scored four times for Spain in a five-goal thrashing of the well-fancied Denmark in the second round of the finals in Mexico.

TOMAS BROLIN *Rocketed from nowhere to world star in six months in 1990*

C

Rodion Camataru

Born: June 22, 1958, Romania.
Clubs: Universitatea Craiova, Dinamo Bucharest (Rom), Charleroi (Bel).

Camataru was a bluff, determined center-forward who scored more than 300 goals in Romanian league soccer before transferring to Belgium towards the end of his career. In 1986–87 he won the Golden Boot awarded to Europe's top league marksman, albeit in controversial circumstances. Camataru totalled 44 goals but many of them were scored in a string of "easy" matches towards the end of the season and revelations after the collapse of the Communist regime cast doubt on the integrity of the matches. Not that this detracted from Camataru's abilities which were rewarded, even in the twilight of his career, with selection for the 1990 World Cup finals.

Claudio Paul Caniggia

Born: January 9, 1967, Argentina.
Clubs: River Plate (Arg), Verona, Atalanta, Roma (It), Benfica (Por), Boca Juniors (Arg).

Caniggia was one of the most intriguing stars of the 1994 World Cup, having only just completed a 13-month drug suspension in Italy. He scored on his return to international duty in a 3–0 win over Israel, but was injured when Argentina lost to Romania in USA '94. Caniggia began with River Plate, moving to Italy in 1988. His play was one of Argentina's few redeeming features

CAMATARU *Golden Boot-winner*

at the 1990 World Cup, when he scored the quarter-final winner against Brazil and semi-final equalizer against Italy. Caniggia missed the Final through suspension and, without him, Argentina had nothing to offer in attack.

Eric Cantona

Born: May 24, 1966, France.
Clubs: Martigues, Auxerre, Marseille, Bordeaux, Montpellier (Fr), Leeds, Manchester United (Eng).

Eric Cantona's career was a mixture of glorious success and disciplinary muddle. Cantona, born in Marseille, was discovered by Auxerre and sold to Marseille for $3 million in 1988. Two months later he scored on his international debut against West Germany. Later he was banned for a year from the national team for insulting manager Henri Michel, then bounced controversially to Bordeaux, Montpellier and Nîmes before quitting the game after a shouting match with a disciplinary panel. Cantona relaunched his career in England – winning the championship in 1992 with Leeds and four times in five years with Manchester United. A skirmish with a hooligan fan at Crystal Palace cost him a seven-month ban from soccer, but he returned to the field all the more hungry for success. He was voted as Footballer of the Year and then, as captain, sealed United's 1996 "double" by scoring the winning goal in the FA Cup Final against Liverpool. He retired, suddenly, a year later, much to the horror of his fans.

Antonio Carbajal

Born: June 7, 1929, Mexico.
Clubs: España, Leon.

Carbajal set a record, at the 1966 World Cup in England, as the only man then to have appeared in five finals tournaments. A tall, agile goalkeeper, he played for Mexico in Brazil in 1950, in Switzerland in 1954, in Sweden in 1958 and in Chile in 1962. The 1966 finals provided an appropriate retirement point, since Carbajal had made his international debut at the 1948 London Olympics. On his return to Mexico that year he turned professional with Leon and played for them until his retirement in 1966. Later he was presented with FIFA's gold award for services to the world game.

Careca

Born: October 5, 1960, Brazil.
Clubs: Guarani, São Paulo (Br), Napoli (It), Hitachi (Jap), Santos (Br).

Careca was one of the outstanding spearheads in the world game throughout the 1980s and early 1990s. Born in Brazil's Campinas state, he helped unrated Guarani win the 1987–88 national championship and was later sold to São Paulo. Careca missed the 1982 World Cup after being injured in training on the eve of the finals. He made superb amends with five goals in Mexico in 1986, was voted Brazil's Sportsman of the Year and was subsequently transferred to Italy's Napoli. His attacking partnership with Diego Maradona lifted Napoli to the 1989 UEFA Cup and 1990 Italian league titles.

Johnny Carey

Born: February 23, 1919, Rep. of Ireland.
Club: Manchester United (Eng).

Johnny Carey was one of the early all-purpose players, at home as full-back, wing-half, inside-forward, even as deputy goalkeeper. He was a calming influence, short on pace but long on perception. Signed for a modest fee from an Irish junior club he proved a great bargain. He captained Manchester United in the early post-war years, winning League and Cup once each and narrowly missing several more, earned 37 caps, and led the Rest of Europe selection against Great Britain in 1946. Carey later managed

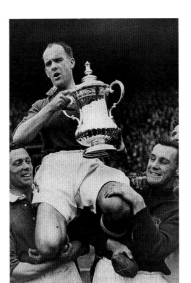

CAREY *One of the great captains*

Blackburn (twice), Everton – until he was fired in the back of a taxi when they were in fifth place in the league – Orient and Nottingham Forest.

Amadeo Carrizo

Born: June 12, 1926, Argentina.
Clubs: River Plate (Arg), Alianza (Peru), Millonarios (Col).

Carrizo set a string of longevity records in a goalkeeping career which lasted from the mid-1940s to the mid-1960s. A dominant character with great personality, Carrizo played 520 Argentine league matches over 21 seasons until he was 44. He won five league championships with River Plate in the early 1950s and played in the 1958 World Cup finals in Sweden. Carrizo was blamed for Argentina's

6–1 defeat by Czechoslovakia but was recalled two years later with great success when Argentina beat England and Brazil to win the 1960 "Little World Cup" in Brazil. After parting company with River Plate he played on in Peru and Colombia before returning home to coach youth teams.

Carlos Caszely

Born: July 5, 1950, Chile.
Clubs: Colo Colo (Chile), Levante (Sp), Colo Colo (Chile).

Caszely was outstanding as a goal-scoring inside-forward in the early 1970s when Colo Colo became the first Chilean club to reach a final of the South American club cup (Copa Libertadores). However, his loudly-proclaimed left-wing political beliefs placed him at risk after the revolution which overthrew President Allende in 1973, and he moved to Spain with Levante. Caszely played for Chile in the 1974 World Cup finals in West Germany and then again eight years later in Spain. By this time, the political situation had eased back home and he had returned to Colo Colo to end his playing days there.

Jan Ceulemans

Born: February 28, 1957, Belgium.
Clubs: Lierse, Club Brugge.

Ceulemans was the central pillar of Belgium's national team throughout the 1980s, first as a striker and then as a midfield general. He began with Lierse and cost Brugge a then record

JAN CEULEMANS *The pillar of Belgium's recent World Cup success*

STÉPHANE CHAPUISAT *Even more famous son of a famous father*

Stéphane Chapuisat

Born: June 28, 1969, Switzerland.
Clubs: FC Malley, Red Star Zurich, Lausanne (Swz), Bayer Uerdingen, Borussia Dortmund (Ger).

Chapuisat, the finest current Swiss striker, is son of a former international, Pierre-Albert Chapuisat, who earned notoriety in his day as a sharp-tempered defender. Son Stéphane, by contrast, not only plays his soccer at the other end of the pitch but has the most even temperament. Chapuisat moved to Germany in 1991 with Uerdingen and transferred to Dortmund a year later. His starring role at the 1994 World Cup finals led to a Footballer of the Year accolade. In 1997, after recovering from injury, he led Dortmund to both the European Champions Cup and World Club Cup.

John Charles

Born: December 27, 1931, Wales.
Clubs: Leeds (Eng), Juventus (It), Leeds (Eng), Roma (It), Cardiff (Wales).

Known as the "Gentle Giant," John Charles allied great skill to an awesome physique, and was good enough to set a Leeds record of 42 goals in one season as a center-forward, while also playing as a dominant central defender for his country. He was one of the first British exports to Italy, in 1957, and probably the best. A then-record transfer fee for a British player, bought Juventus a man who became a legend and helped to win the Serie A title three times in five years, scoring 93 times in 155 games. After some unhappy final seasons he became a non-league manager, publican and shopkeeper.

Bobby Charlton

see Legends (page 77)

Igor Chislenko

Born: January 4, 1939, Soviet Union.
Clubs: Moscow Torpedo, Moscow Dynamo.

Chislenko was one of Europe's most incisive outside- or inside-rights in the 1960s, despite standing only 5ft 7in. He began with the Moscow Torpedo youth section but transferred to Dynamo at 17 and played 300 league games, winning two league titles, with the club. Chislenko, also a good ice hockey player, appeared at the World Cups of 1962 and 1966 as well as in the European Nations Championship in between. He was the best Soviet forward in the 1966 World Cup, and their prospects of reaching the Final disappeared when he was sent off during the semi-final against West Germany.

Hector Chumpitaz

Born: April 12, 1944, Peru.
Club: Sporting Cristal.

Chumpitaz, a powerful, inspirational center-back, starred for Peru in the World Cup finals of both 1970 and 1978. On the first occasion he was a promising youngster, on the second an experienced, resilient organizer of an otherwise fragile defense. Chumpitaz played all his senior career with Sporting Cristal of Lima and appeared around 100 times for his country between his debut in 1966 and the six-goal thrashing by Argentina which controversially ended Peru's 1978 World Cup campaign. Earlier claims that he played 147 full internationals have been discounted, Peru having played "only" 110 matches in that time.

Mario Esteves Coluna

Born: August 6, 1935, Mozambique.
Clubs: Deportivo Lourenço Marques (Mozambique), Benfica (Port).

Coluna was midfield general of Benfica's outstanding club side on the 1960s as well as commander of the Portuguese national team which reached the World Cup semi-finals in 1966. Born in Mozambique, Coluna was the local long-jump record-holder when he was lured away by Benfica to play soccer in 1954. Originally a center-forward, he was converted to inside-left and then midfield by Benfica and won 73 caps for Portugal. In both of Benfica's European Cup Final victories of 1961 and 1962, he scored with typically spectacular long-range efforts. Coluna later turned to coaching and became Sports Minister in Mozambique.

Gianpiero Combi

Born: December 18, 1902, Italy.
Club: Juventus.

Combi was goalkeeper and captain of the Italian team which won the 1934 World Cup, thus pre-dating Dino

---

domestic fee of $500,000 in the summer of 1978. In 1980 he scored 29 of their 76 goals in a league title win and was voted Footballer of the Year for the first time. A year later Ceulemans was poised to join Milan but his mother persuaded him to stay in Belgium, a decision which he never regretted. Ceulemans played with distinction in the Belgian team which finished fourth at the 1986 World Cup finals in Mexico. In 96 internationals – a Belgian record – he scored 26 goals.

Cha Bum Kun

Born: May 21, 1953, South Korea.
Clubs: Darmstadt, Eintracht Frankfurt, Bayer Leverkusen (W Ger).

Thanks to his record at the peak of the European game in West Germany's Bundesliga, Cha ranks as South Korea's finest player. He was a popular fixture from 1978, when he arrived at Darmstadt, until his retirement in 1986 after appearing at his first and only World Cup finals. Cha, who won the UEFA Cup with both Eintracht Frankfurt (1980) and Bayer Leverkusen in 1988, when he scored one of the goals against Espanol, was mystifyingly ignored by his country after moving to Germany. But he used his time well to gain coaching qualifications and he subsequently managed South Korea at the 1998 World Cup Finals in France.

Zoff in that dual role by nearly 50 years. Combi was considered Italy's best goalkeeper until Zoff came along. He started unpromisingly, beaten seven times by Hungary in Budapest in his first international in 1924, and did not gain a regular place in Italy's team until the Paris Olympics of 1928. He was goalkeeper in Juventus's four consecutive league title successes of 1931 to 1934, the year when he retired – immediately after captaining Italy to victory over Czechoslovakia in the World Cup Final in Rome. That was Combi's 47th international.

Bruno Conti

Born: March 13, 1955, Italy.
Clubs: Roma, Genoa, Roma.

Wingers made a comeback on the tactical scene thanks to the displays of Bruno Conti at the 1982 World Cup. Italy's right-winger proved a crucial influence in increasing the momentum of their campaign, which took them past Argentina and Brazil and on via Poland to victory over West Germany in the Final. Conti had struggled to make an impression in the early years of his career but was rescued by Swedish coach Nils Liedholm, who brought Conti back from a loan spell with Genoa and turned him into one of the most consistently effective creative players in *Calcio*. Conti scored five goals in 47 internationals between his debut against Luxembourg in 1980 and the second round defeat by France at the 1986 World Cup.

Henri "Rik" Coppens

Born: April 29, 1930, Belgium.
Clubs: Beerschot, Charleroi, Crossing Molenbeek, Berchem, Tubantia.

Coppens was the *enfant terrible* of Belgian soccer in the 1950s: a center-forward or occasional outside-left of great goal-scoring talent, but one who carried his aggression over into his dealings with teammates, clubs and other officials. Coppens began with Beerschot as a 10-year-old, and on his debut at 16 in a crucial relegation match he scored twice and made Beerschot's two other goals. Three times he was the league's leading scorer and ended his career with a then

CONTI *Outwits West Germany's Uli Stielike in the 1982 World Cup Final*

record total of 217 goals. He once scored six goals in a game against Tilleur. Coppens altogether played 47 times for Belgium.

Alberto da Costa Pereira

Born: 1929, Portuguese East Africa.
Club: Benfica.

Costa Pereira was another of Portugal's great discoveries in the African colonies. He was born in Nacala, Portuguese East Africa, and joined Benfica in 1954. He was a tower of strength in their biggest triumphs, though prone to the odd unpredictable error when the pressure was off. Costa Pereira won seven league titles with Benfica and played in four European Cup finals – the victories of 1961 and 1962 and the defeats of 1963 and 1965. In the latter game, against Internazionale on a quagmire of a pitch in Milan, Costa Pereira was injured early in the game and had to leave the field. He retired soon after to take up coaching. Costa Pereira played 24 times for Portugal, but is not to be confused with the José Pereira who kept goal at the 1966 World Cup.

Johan Cruyff

see Legends (page 78)

Teofilo Cubillas

Born: March 8, 1949, Peru.
Clubs: Alianza (Peru), Basel (Swz), FC Porto (Port), Alianza (Peru), Fort Lauderdale Strikers (US).

Cubillas was a key figure in Peru's greatest international successes, their appearances at the 1970 and 1978 World Cup finals, in which he scored a total of 10 goals. A powerfully-built inside left, he forged an ideal partnership with the more nimble Hugo Sotil in 1970 then, in 1978, emerged as an attacking director. Cubillas also packed a powerful shot, scoring

CUBILLAS *Attacking director*

a memorable goal against Scotland in the 1978 finals. He was not particularly successful in Europe, where he grew homesick. But in Peru he remained a legend after 38 goals in 88 internationals and an appearance for the World XI in a 1978 UNICEF charity match.

Zoltan Czibor

Born: 1929, Hungary.
Clubs: Ferencvaros, Csepel, Honved (Hun), Barcelona, Español (Sp).

Czibor was outside-left in the great Hungarian team of the early 1950s. He had pace and a powerful shot, which he used to great effect in 43 internationals before he moved to Spain following the Hungarian Revolution of 1956. Czibor and teammate Sandor Kocsis were persuaded to sign for Barcelona by Ladislav Kubala and enjoyed five more years in the international spotlight, reaching a climax when Barcelona, most unluckily, lost to Benfica in the 1961 European Cup Final. Czibor had a short spell with neighbors Español before he retired and eventually returned home to live in Hungary.

Kenny Dalglish

Born: March 4, 1951, Scotland.
Clubs: Celtic (Scot), Liverpool (Eng).

Kenny Dalglish is the most "decorated" man in British soccer, having won 26 major trophies as player and manager, in addition to 102 caps (a record for Scotland) and 30 goals (another record, held jointly with Denis Law). Dalglish's signing for Celtic was their other coup – aside from their European Cup triumph – in 1967. He went on to inspire the club to more great deeds before joining Liverpool for $800,000 in 1977. Already a very good player, he became legendary at Anfield, thanks to initial pace, excellent control and an eye for a chance. He won many new friends for his dignified bearing after the disaster of Hillsborough. Those pressures contributed to Dalglish's surprise departure from Liverpool. He returned to manage Blackburn Rovers to the 1995 Premier League title then replaced Keegan as manager of Newcastle United, taking them to the 1998 FA Cup Final. He returned to Celtic as Director of Football in 1999.

Bill "Dixie" Dean

Born: January 22, 1907, England.
Clubs: Tranmere, Everton, Notts Co.

Anybody who begins his international career by scoring 2, 3, 2, 2, 3 deserves a place in the Hall of Fame. Curly-topped Bill Dean was 20 at the time, and still only 21 when he scored his record 60 League goals in

DALGLISH *A winner as player and manager*

one season for Everton, finishing 2, 4, 3 to overhaul George Camsell's 59 for Middlesbrough. Overall, he scored 18 goals in 16 England appearances, 47 in 18 of the other representative matches which were so popular in pre-television days, 28 in 33 Cup ties (one in the 1933 Wembley win), and 379 in 438 League games. All this despite, as a teenager, fracturing his skull.

Luis Del Sol Miramontes

Born: 1938, Spain.
Clubs: Betis Seville, Real Madrid (Sp), Juventus (It).

Del Sol was inside-right in the legendary Real Madrid forward line which won the 1960 European Cup against Eintracht Frankfurt at Hampden. A neat, aggressive midfielder, he had been a wing-half at his hometown club, Betis of Seville, when the Madrid management decided that the great Brazilian, Didi, was not fitting in well enough alongside Alfredo Di Stefano. Del Sol was hurriedly bought in the middle of the 1959–60 season and ran his legs off in support of veterans Di Stefano and Puskas. In 1962 Madrid sold Del Sol to Juventus to raise the cash for a vain attempt to buy Pele from Santos. Del Sol was a pillar of the Italian league through eight seasons with Juventus and two with Roma, before his retirement and return to Spain in 1972.

Kazimierz Deyna

Born: October 23, 1947, Poland. *Clubs:* Starogard, Sportowy Lodz, Legia Warsaw (Pol), Manchester City (Eng), San Diego (US).

Poland's emergence as a world power in the early 1970s owed a huge debt to the skilled grace of Deyna, their midfield fulcrum. Deyna played center midfield, supported by workers such as Maszczyk and Kasperczak, and was constantly creating openings for strikers Lato and Gadocha. He earned a domestic reputation in helping army club Legia win the league in 1969 and was promoted into the national squads when the Legia coach, Kazimierz Gorski, was appointed manager of Poland. Deyna won an Olympic gold medal with Poland in Munich in 1972 then returned to the Olympiastadion two years later to

DIDI *Making the ball "talk" in the 1958 World Cup finals*

celebrate Poland's best-ever third-place finish at the World Cup. He was never quite the same player after moving abroad, first to England and then to the United States, where he died in a car crash. Deyna scored 38 goals in 102 internationals.

Didi (full name: Waldyr Pereira)

Born: October 8, 1928, Brazil.
Clubs: FC Rio Branco, FC Lencoes, Madureiro, Fluminense, Botafogo (Br), Real Madrid, Valencia (Sp), Botafogo (Br).

The success of Brazil's 4–2–4 system, revealed in all its glory internationally at the 1958 World Cup, rested heavily on the creative talent of Didi, one of the greatest of midfield generals. Didi's technique was extraordinary. Teammates said he could "make the ball talk," and drop it on a coin from any distance, any angle. Didi was the first to perfect the "dead leaf" free kick, with which he scored a dozen of his 31 goals in 85 appearances for Brazil. He won the World Cup in 1958 and 1962 and counted as the only failure of his career a spell in between with Real Madrid, where he failed to settle in alongside Di Stefano and Puskas.

Alfredo Di Stefano

see Legends (page 79)

Domingos Antonio da Guia

Born: November 19, 1912, Brazil.
Clubs: Bangu, Vasco da Gama (Br), Nacional (Uru), Boca Juniors (Arg), Flamengo, Corinthians, Bangu (Br).

Domingos was a full-back of the old school, as much a pivoting central defender as a marker in the old-fashioned 2–3–5 formation. His talents earned him transfers all round South America, and he remains less of a legend in Uruguay and Argentina than he is in Brazil. The Uruguayans nicknamed him the Divine Master. Domingos made his debut for Brazil in 1931, was a key member of the team which reached the 1938 World Cup semi-finals, and did not retire until 1948. By this time he had returned to his original club, Bangu. His contemporary, center-forward Leonidas da Silva, once said no defender ever "read a game" better than Domingos.

Dunga (full name: Carlos Bledorn Verri)

Born: October 31, 1963, Brazil.
Clubs: Vasco da Gama (Br), Pisa, Fiorentina, Pescara (It), Stuttgart (Ger), Jubilo Iwata (Jpn).

Dunga, one of the most controversial of modern Brazilian players, obtained the ultimate revenge over his critics when he lifted the World Cup after the victory over Italy in the 1994 Final. Dunga was criticized because, as a defensive midfield player, he was strong and keen in the tackle but slightly slow and relatively clumsy on the ball when compared with his compatriots. But he possessed a strong shot in both feet and 1994 World Cup boss Carlos Alberto Parreira considered Dunga's tactical discipline vital to his strategy. He captained his country at France '98, guiding them to the final, and was named in the team of the tournament before announcing his retirement from international soccer.

Dragan Dzajic

Born: May 30, 1956, Yugoslavia.
Clubs: Red Star Belgrade (Yug), Bastia (Fr), Red Star (Yug).

The British press baptized Dzajic the "magic Dragan" after his left-wing skills helped take England apart in the semi-finals of the 1968 European Nations Championship. Dzajic had pace, skill and intelligence and was perhaps the greatest soccer hero to have emerged in post-war Yugoslavia. He was five times a national champion, four times a cup-winner and earned selection for a variety of World and European XIs on five occasions. Dzajic remained an outside-left throughout a career which brought him 23 goals in 85 internationals, never needing to fade back into midfield like so many wingers who lose the edge of their talent. He retired in 1978 and became general manager of his original club, Red Star.

Duncan Edwards

Born: October 1, 1936, England.
Club: Manchester United.

Duncan Edwards was a giant who is still revered by generations who never saw him play. Comparatively few did, for his career was brief, but his awesome power and genuine all-around skill, as creator as well as destroyer, made him a man apart. At club level, Edwards was the outstanding discovery among Manchester United's Busby Babes. Sometimes he seemed to be a team in himself, as at Wembley in 1957, when 10 men fought bravely in a vain effort against an Aston Villa side set on depriving United of a merited cup and league "double." Having won 18 England caps, Edwards was looking forward to playing a starring role in the 1958 World Cup. His death in the Munich Air Disaster robbed England of one its finest ever players.

Arsenio Erico

Born: 1915, Paraguay.
Clubs: FC Asuncion (Par), Independiente, Huracan (Arg).

The quality of Erico as a center-forward can best be illustrated by the fact that he was the boyhood hero of none other than Alfredo Di Stefano. Born in Paraguay, Erico went to Buenos Aires at 17 to play for a fund-raising team organized by the Paraguay Red Cross during the war with Bolivia. Directors of Independiente

EDWARDS *Epitome of the Busby Babes*

in the crowd were so impressed that immediately after the match they obtained his signature – in exchange for a donation to the Red Cross. Erico started badly, twice breaking an arm, but once he was fully fit he scored goals at a prolific rate and set a record with 47 goals in the 1936–37 league season. Several times he scored five goals in a game before going home to Paraguay in 1941 after squabbling over terms with Independiente. The club persuaded him to return, but knee cartilage trouble forced his premature retirement in 1944.

Eusebio

see Legends (page 80)

Giacinto Facchetti

Born: July 18, 1942, Italy.
Clubs: Trevigliese, Internazionale.

Full-back was never a romantic role until the revolutionary emergence of Facchetti in the early 1960s. He had been a big, strapping center-forward with his local club in Treviso when he was signed by Inter and converted into a left-back by master coach Helenio Herrera. The rigid man-to-man marking system perfected by Herrera permitted Facchetti the freedom, when Inter attacked, to stride upfield in support of his own forwards. Facchetti scored 60 league goals, a record for a full-back in Italy, including 10 in the 1965–66 season. But his most

FACCHETTI *Great attacking full-back*

important goal was reserved for the 1965 European Cup semi-finals when he burst through in the inside-right position to score a decisive winning goal against Liverpool. Later Facchetti switched to sweeper, from which position he captained Italy against Brazil in the 1970 World Cup Final. He would surely have taken his total of 94 caps to 100 but for an injury before the 1978 World Cup finals.

Giovanni Ferrari

Born: December 6, 1907, Italy.
Clubs: Alessandria, Juventus, Internazionale, Bologna.

"Gioanin" Ferrari was inside-left of the Italian team who won the 1934 World Cup and was one of only two team members – the other was Giuseppe Meazza – retained for the 1938 triumph in France. Appropriately, both men made their international debut in the same game against Switzerland in Rome in 1930. Ferrari played then for Alessandria but soon moved to Juventus, with whom he won a record five consecutive league titles. He won further championship honors with Ambrosiana-Inter in 1940 and with Bologna in 1941. He scored 14 goals in 44 internationals and managed Italy at the 1962 World Cup finals in Chile.

Bernabe Ferreyra

Born: 1909, Argentina.
Clubs: Tigre, River Plate.

Nicknamed "the Mortar" for his ferocious shooting, Ferreyra was the

first great hero of Argentine soccer. He scored more than 200 goals for Tigre and then River Plate in the 1930s, having joined River for 45,000 pesos in one of the first formal transfers in Argentina after the establishment of professionalism. In his first season with River, 1932–33, Ferreyra scored a league record 43 goals and was such a regular feature of the weekly scoresheets that one Buenos Aires newspaper offered a gold medal to any goalkeeper who could defy him. Ferreyra played only four internationals before retiring in 1939 and going back to his home town of Rufino. In 1943 he returned to River's front office and in 1956 was honored with a testimonial match in recognition of his loyalty and service to one of Argentina's great club institutions.

Tom Finney

Born: April 5, 1922, England.
Club: Preston.

Moderate in height, thin and fair, Finney was nondescript in appearance, but a player whose versatility was matched by his skill. "Grizzly strong" was the description applied to him by Bill Shankly, who played wing-half behind winger Finney at Preston – "Grizzly" in the sense of bear-like power rather than miserable attitude, for he always had a generous word for opponents as well as a rock-like solidity that belied his frame. Finney was genuinely two-footed, brave as they come, and in his later

TOM FINNEY *Preston plumber equally skilled at dismantling defenses*

years a deep-lying center-forward on Hidegkuti lines. Lack of support left him bereft of honors at club level, his only club was Preston North End, but a 12-year England career, with 76 caps and a then-record 30 goals, earned him a belated knighthood.

Just Fontaine

Born: August 18, 1933, France.
Clubs: AC Marrakesh, USM Casablanca (Mor), Nice, Reims (Fr).

Fontaine secured a place in the history books when he scored a record 13 goals in the 1958 World Cup finals. Yet he was a surprising hero. Born in Morocco, he was a quick, direct center-forward who had played only twice for France before 1958. He had been discovered by Nice, then bought by Reims as replacement for Raymond Kopa, who had joined Real Madrid in 1956. He expected to be reserve to Reims teammate René

FONTAINE *World Cup record*

Bliard at the 1958 World Cup, but Bliard was injured on the eve of the finals and Fontaine took his opportunity in record-breaking style. He owed most of his goals to Kopa's creative work alongside him and the partnership was renewed when Kopa returned to Reims in 1959. Sadly Fontaine had to retire in 1961 owing to two double fractures of a leg. He was twice top league scorer and totalled 27 goals in 20 internationals. Later he was president of the French players' union and, briefly, national manager.

Enzo Francescoli

Born: November 12, 1961, Uruguay.
Clubs: Wanderers (Uru), River Plate (Arg), Matra Racing, Marseille (Fr), Cagliari, Torino (It), River Plate (Arg).

Francescoli followed in a long line of Uruguayan superstars, starting with the heroes of the 1920s and 1930s and continuing through Schiaffino, Goncalves and Rocha. He began with a small club, Wanderers, and then both Uruguayan giants, Penarol and Nacional, were outbid by River Plate of Argentina. Francescoli was top scorer in the Argentine league and voted South American Footballer of the Year before transferring to France with Racing in 1986. Even Francescoli's 32 goals in three seasons were not enough to save Racing from financial collapse. He scored 11 goals in Marseille's championship season of 1989–90 before moving, first, to Italy, then back to River Plate to wind down his career.

Arthur Friedenreich

Born: 1892, Brazil.
Clubs: Germania, Ipiranga, Americao, Paulistano, São Paulo FC, Flamengo.

Friedenreich was the first great Brazilian soccer player and the first officially credited with more than 1,000 goals. His overall total was 1,329. The son of a German father and a Brazilian mother, Friedenreich was also significant as the first black player to break through the early racial/cultural barriers in Brazilian soccer. Nicknamed "the Tiger," Friedenreich began playing senior soccer at 17 and did not retire until 1935, when he was 43. He scored eight goals in 17 internationals for Brazil between 1914 and 1930. His first representative appearance for Brazil was in a 2–0 win against the English club Exeter City on July 21, 1914, when he lost two teeth in a collision with a defender.

Paulo Futre

Born: February 28, 1966, Portugal.
Clubs: Sporting, FC Porto (Port), Atletico Madrid (Sp), Benfica (Port), Marseille (France), Reggiana, Milan (It), West Ham United (Eng), Athletico Madrid (Sp).

Futre was only 17 when he made his international debut and his star continued to shine brightly after FC Porto snatched him away from Sporting to inspire their European Cup victory of 1987. A few weeks later Futre was signed by Atletico Madrid as the first major coup in the controversial presidency of Jesus Gil. Futre

survived all the tempests at Atletico until the start of 1993, when he forced his sale home to Benfica. However, financing the deal proved beyond even Benfica. They sold him to Marseille, who also had to sell him after only a few months to resolve their own cash crisis. Reggiana of Italy paid £8 million to become Futre's fourth club in a year – but he was never the same player after tearing knee ligaments in his first game.

Garrincha (full name: Manoel Francisco dos Santos)

Born: October 28, 1933, Brazil.
Clubs: Pau Grande, Botafogo, Corinthians (Br), AJ Barranquilla (Col), Flamengo (Br), Red Star Paris (Fr).

Garrincha was up there alongside Pele in Brazilian soccer in the 1960s. Born in poverty, childhood illness left his legs badly twisted and the surgeons who carried out corrective surgery thought he would do well merely to walk, let along turn out to be one of the quickest and most dangerous right-wingers of all time. Yet it took a players' deputation to persuade manager Vicente Feola to include him in the 1958 World Cup side in Sweden. Once in, Garrincha was there to stay and was the dominant personality at the 1962 finals after the early injury to Pele. Sadly, his private life was chaotic and he died prematurely of alcoholic poisoning.

Paul Gascoigne

Born: May 27, 1967, England.
Clubs: Newcastle, Spurs (Eng), Lazio (It), Rangers (Scot), Middlesbrough (Eng).

Gascoigne's career has been blighted by his own indiscipline and misfortune with injuries. A powerful midfielder, with a deft touch, he was England's star of the 1990 World Cup. He was memorably inconsolable when his second yellow card ruled him out of the third place game. Gascoigne left Newcastle for Spurs and led them to the 1991 FA Cup Final, where he suffered a bad knee injury making a rash

GARRINCHA *Team-mates' favorite*

of his goals. He scored eight in European matches for his club, a remarkable record for a defender, and two of them were in European Cup Finals. Gemmell crashed one past Internazionale to equalize when Celtic won in 1967, and also against Feyenoord when they lost in 1970. His extroverted style of play was well suited to upsetting foreign defenses during Celtic's greatest years, but he also collected a large haul of domestic honors before a final fling at Forest.

Francisco Gento

Born: October 22, 1933, Spain.
Clubs: Santander, Real Madrid.

Real Madrid's great team of the 1950s and 1960s was more than "only" Di Stefano and Puskas. Tearing great holes in opposing defenses was outside-left Gento, whose pace earned him the nickname of "El Supersonico." Gento began with Santander and was considered a player with pace but little else when Madrid signed him in 1953. Fortunately, he found a marvellous inside-left partner in José Hector Rial, who tutored Gento in the arts of the game. Gento is the only man to have won six European Cup medals. He scored 256 goals in 800 games for Madrid, with whom he won Spanish championship medals on 12 occasions. He played 43 times for Spain despite the challenging rivalry of Enrique Collar, an outstanding left-winger with Atletico Madrid.

Sergio Javier Goycochea

Born: October 17, 1963, Argentina.
Clubs: River Plate (Arg), Millonarios (Col), Racing (Arg), Brest (Fr), Cerro Porteno (Par), River Plate, Deportivo Mandiyu (Arg).

Goycochea earned fame at the 1990 World Cup finals when he stepped into the action during Argentina's match against the Soviet Union after Nery Pumpido had broken a leg. Goycochea's heroics in the penalty shoot-out victories over Yugoslavia and Italy subsequently took Argentina to the Final. Yet he had not played a competitive game over the previous six

GOYCOCHEA *Magic touch in World Cup penalty shoot-outs*

months because of the domestic unrest in Colombia, where he had been contracted to Millonarios of Bogota. After the 1990 World Cup finals Goycochea signed for the ambitious French provincial club, Brest. They soon went bankrupt, however, and he returned to Argentina.

Jimmy Greaves

Born: February 20, 1940, England.
Clubs: Chelsea (Eng), Milan (It), Tottenham, West Ham (Eng).

Greaves was an instinctive goalscorer, whose speed in thought and deed made up for lack of size and power. His 44 goals in 57 full internationals included two hauls of four goals and four threes, and his 357 in League games (all First Division) included three fives. An unhappy interlude in Italy did little to mar his scoring ability, and he gave wonderful value for

money until his closing chapter with West Ham. By then drink had taken a grip, and his overcoming that blight to become a popular television pundit set an inspiring example to others in the same position.

Harry Gregg

Born: October 25, 1932, Northern Ireland.
Clubs: Dundalk (Rep. of Ire.), Doncaster, Manchester United, Stoke (Eng).

Genial, popular Gregg won his first cap after only nine Football League games for Second Division Doncaster, and had established himself as Ireland's first choice before the fateful 1957–58 season. Hardly had he left Yorkshire for Manchester United when, as a survivor of the Munich air crash, he became a hero by helping to rescue some of the injured. Later that year he performed well in helping his club to the FA Cup Final, where they lost 2–0 to Bolton, and the Irish to the quarter-final of the World Cup in Sweden. Injury kept him out of United's FA Cup-winning side in 1963.

John Greig

Born: September 11, 1942, Scotland.
Club: Rangers.

A 16-year spell of hard labor in defense and midfield brought Greig a record 496 League appearances for Rangers and a considerable number of honors, although Celtic were the dominant team in Scotland for a large

tackle. After missing a year through injury he signed with Lazio but played only 42 games in three seasons. He moved to Rangers in 1995, where he won two league titles and was Scotland's Footballer of the Year in 1996, and then joined Middlesbrough in 1998, helping them to win promotion. But "Gazza's" England career looked over when he was sensationally omitted from the 1998 World Cup squad because of his lack of fitness.

Tommy Gemmell

Born: October 16, 1943, Scotland.
Clubs: Celtic (Scot), Nottingham Forest (Eng).

A big and sometimes clumsy fullback who became a folk hero because

TOMMY GEMMELL *Historic goal in the 1967 European Cup Final*

part of that time. He was Footballer of the Year in 1966, the season in which he scored a spectacular goal against Italy in a World Cup qualifier, and won 44 caps, often as captain. Greig also played in two European Cup-winners' Cup finals, losing in 1967 and winning in 1972. Later, he had a spell as manager at Ibrox.

Gunnar Gren

Born: October 31, 1920, Sweden.
Clubs: IFK Gothenburg (Swe), Milan, Fiorentina (It), Orgryte, GAIS Gothenburg (Sw).

Gren, nicknamed "the Professor", claimed Italian attention when in the Olympic Games winning team in London in 1948. His nickname stemmed both from his premature baldness and his astute inside-forward play. Milan won the transfer race and Gren forged, with fellow Swedes Nordahl and Liedholm, the legendary "Grenoli" trio which took Italian soccer by storm. In 1955, after a spell with Fiorentina, he returned home to Sweden and, at 37, helped the hosts to the Final of the 1958 World Cup. That was the last of Gren's 57 internationals. Later he returned to IFK Gothenburg – with whom he had won the Swedish championship in 1942 – as manager of the souvenir shop.

Ruud Gullit

Born: September 1, 1962, Holland.
Clubs: Haarlem, Feyenoord, PSV Eindhoven (Hol), Milan, Sampdoria, Milan, Sampdoria (It), Chelsea (Eng).

Ruud Gullit was Europe's outstanding player in the late 1980s and early 1990s. He began his career as a sweeper, but at PSV he moved forward and after his world record $10 million sale to Milan in 1987 became an out-and-out attacker. A year later he led Holland to victory in the European Championship and won the European Cup with Milan. Serious knee injuries dogged him after that, but after one season at Chelsea in England he was made player-manager and won the FA Cup at the first attempt. His departure, over a wage dispute, in early 1998, rocked English soccer but he returned to manage Newcastle to the FA Cup final in 1999. His tenure in that soccer-mad area ended acrimoniously just four months later.

Gheorghe Hagi

Born: February 5, 1965, Romania.
Clubs: FC Constanta, Sportul Studentesc, Steaua Bucharest (Rom), Real Madrid (Sp), Brescia (It), Barcelona (Sp), Galatasaray (Tur).

Hagi was always destined for stardom. He played for Romania's youth team at 15, was a top-flight league player at 17, an international at 18, and a year later, in 1984, was taking part in the finals of the European Championship. In 1985 he hit 20 goals and in 1986 he 31, after scoring six in one match. Steaua Bucharest virtually kidnapped Hagi from neighbors Sportul without a transfer fee – an escapade approved by the ruling Ceaucescu family, who were Steaua supporters. After the 1990 World Cup Hagi played in Spain and Italy – returning, briefly, to Barcelona after inspiring Romania to reach the quarter-finals of the 1994 World Cup. He also played in the 1998 finals in France, guiding Romania to the second phase.

Helmut Haller

Born: July 21, 1939, Germany.
Clubs: BC Augsburg (W Ger), Bologna, Juventus (It), Augsburg (W Ger).

Haller earned a teenage reputation as an inside-forward in West Germany in the late 1950s, before the advent of full-time professionalism and the Bundesliga. Italian club Bologna gambled on his youth and were

HAMRIN (LEFT) *Drives in a shot despite the close attention of a lunging defender*

HAGI *Accelerates away from Irish defender Paul McGrath*

superbly rewarded: in 1963 Haller's partnership with the Dane Harald Nielsen brought Bologna their first league title in more than 20 years. Later Haller played with further success for Juventus before returning to Augsburg. He will be remembered above all for his outstanding contribution to West Germany's 1966 World Cup campaign.

Kurt Hamrin

Born: November 19, 1934, Sweden.
Clubs: AIK Sola (Swe), Juventus, Padova, Fiorentina, Milan, Napoli, Caserta (It).

Hamrin ranks close behind Matthews and Garrincha among the great outside-rights of the modern game. He was a quick, darting attacker who was not only nimble and clever but one of the most successful goalgrabbers in the history of the Italian league. Hamrin disappointed Juventus and they sold him off after only one year. Once he had adjusted, however, Hamrin proved an irresistible one-man strike force with Fiorentina, with whom he scored 150 goals in nine seasons and won the European Cup-winners' Cup in 1961. At 34, while with Milan, he added a European Cup winners' medal to his collection.

Gerhard Hanappi

Born: July 9, 1929, Austria.
Clubs: Wacker, Rapid Vienna.

Hanappi was one of the most versatile soccer players to be found anywhere

in the world in the 1950s. He played mainly wing-half or occasionally inside-forward for his long-time club, Rapid, but also lined up at center-forward and at full-back in the course of winning 93 caps for Austria. He would have topped a century had it not been for a row with officialdom. Hanappi, an architect by profession, designed a new stadium for Rapid which was, after his premature death, named in honor of his memory. Hanappi was Austrian champion and a cup-winner once each with Wacker then national champion six times and cup-winner once again with Rapid. He played for FIFA's World XI against England in 1953.

Eddie Hapgood

Born: September 27, 1908, England.
Club: Arsenal.

Hapgood was small for a left-back, but as tough as teak. He was an inspiring captain who led England in 21 of his 30 games during the 1930s, with 13 more during the war. In his teens he was an amateur with Bristol Rovers, but was allowed to leave and was with non-league Kettering when Arsenal recruited him. He went on to earn five championship medals and played in three FA Cup finals, winning two. His first international was against Italy in Rome; his first as captain was also against Italy but on his club ground in the infamous "Battle of Highbury" – when he returned to play on after an opponent's elbow had smashed his nose.

After retirement he managed Blackburn and Watford, but with little success.

Ernst Happel

Born: June 29, 1925, Austria.
Clubs: Rapid Vienna, 1st FC Vienna (Aus), Racing Club Paris (Fr).

Happel was a redoubtable center-back with Rapid and Austria in the 1950s, his 51-cap playing career reaching a climax at the 1958 World Cup finals. He possessed a powerful shot and once scored a hat-trick, with free-kicks and a penalty, in an early European Cup tie against Real Madrid. After retiring, Happel became one of Europe's most successful coaches, taking Feyenoord to the World Club Cup and European Cup in 1970. In Argentina in 1978, he was manager of Holland when they reached the World Cup Final, and he had further success in the 1983 European Cup with Hamburg.

HURST *World Cup legend*

Johnny Haynes

Born: October 17, 1934, England.
Clubs: Fulham (Eng), Durban City (SA).

Like Tom Finney, Haynes won precisely nothing in nearly two decades with one club. However, he was the hub of many an England team in a 56-cap career, hitting long passes through a needle's eye and scoring a surprising number of goals with an incredibly powerful shot that belied his comparatively slight frame. As England's first $250-a-week player he often was unjustly criticized, but he earned every penny in the service of Fulham (generally struggling) and England (frequently rampant).

He was England captain from 1960 till a serious car accident in 1962, in a period when, in successive games, England won 5–2, 9–0, 4–2, 5–1, 9–3 and 8–0. The 9–3 result was a slaughter of Scotland, perhaps the best performance of his era. His career might have added up differently if Milan had persisted in their bid for him, or if, after his accident, a record-breaking bid from Tottenham Hotspur had succeeded. He ended his playing career in South Africa, winning a championship medal with Durban City.

Willie Henderson

Born: January 24, 1944, Scotland.
Clubs: Rangers (Scot), Sheffield Wednesday (Eng).

If "Wee Willie" had performed throughout his career as he did in his first few years, he would have been perhaps the best Scottish player ever. Despite persistent foot trouble and far from perfect eyesight, he had won all four domestic honors – league, cup, League Cup and cap – before his 20th birthday. By then Rangers had sold international winger Alex Scott to Everton in order to make room for the kid. Henderson went on to play in 29 internationals and captivate fans with his wizardry, but his career was marred by discontent, and gradually petered out in disappointment.

Geoff Hurst

Born: December 8, 1941, England.
Club: West Ham, Stoke.

A big man who was made for the big occasion, Hurst, strong and deceptively fast, was frequently mundane in West Ham's toils through their League schedule. But when needed in the big events, he was out of the traps like a greyhound. He scored the remarkable total of 46 goals in the League Cup, 23 in the FA Cup (including a fluke in the 1964 Final) and three in the 1966 World Cup Final, when he appeared virtually from nowhere to put the trophy on the nation's sideboard with his hat-trick against West Germany. Like so many big-name players, he became a mundane manager, at Chelsea. Memories of him as a player will last much longer.

Jairzinho (full name: Jair Ventura Filho)

Born: December 25, 1944, Brazil.
Clubs: Botafogo (Br), Marseilles (Fr), Cruzeiro (Br), Portuguesa (Ven).

Jairzinho was the heir to Garrincha's glory, both with Botafogo and with Brazil. He moved from his home town of Caxias to sign professional with Botafogo at 15, and played in the same Brazil squad as his hero at the 1966 World Cup. Four years later Jairzinho made history by scoring in every game in every round of the World Cup on the way to victory. He scored seven goals, including two in Brazil's opening win over Czechoslovakia and one in the defeat of Italy in the Final. He tried his luck in Europe with Marseille but returned home after disciplinary problems to win yet another trophy, the South American club cup, with Cruzeiro at the age of 32.

Alex James

Born: September 14, 1901, Scotland.
Clubs: Raith (Scot), Preston, Arsenal (Eng).

Eight caps were meager reward for the outstanding inside-forward of the 1930s. James began as a fiery attacking player (ejected twice in successive matches at Raith) but

JAIRZINHO *Unique World Cup feat*

changed his style to fit Arsenal manager Herbert Chapman's "W" formation. He scored only 26 League goals in eight years at Highbury, but made countless others with his astute passing from deep to the flying wingers or through the middle. Despite his superb display in the 5–1 rout of England by the "Wembley Wizards," James was often thought too clever by the selectors, though not by fans: at club level he won six major medals and undying fame.

Pat Jennings

Born: June 12, 1945, Northern Ireland.
Clubs: Newry Town (NI), Watford, Tottenham, Arsenal (Eng).

A goalkeeper with character and charm to match his size, Jennings even bowed out of soccer in a big way by winning his 119th cap on his 41st birthday – and in a World Cup, too. Only defeat, by Brazil, marred the occasion. By then Jennings had played well over 1,000 senior matches in a 24-year career, four of them in FA Cup finals. He won with Spurs

PAT JENNINGS *Veteran of more than 1,000 first-class matches*

in 1967 and Arsenal in 1979, lost with Arsenal in 1978 and 1980. Jennings also scored a goal with a punt during the 1967 Charity Shield against Manchester United. He remains one of the finest British goalkeepers ever seen.

Jimmy Johnstone

Born: September 30, 1944, Scotland.
Clubs: Celtic (Scot), San José (US), Sheffield United (Eng), Dundee (Scot), Shelbourne (Ire).

Johnstone was a remarkably talented winger, but infuriatingly inconsistent, as shown by the fact that his 23 caps were spread over 12 years. Small and nippy, he was an old-style "tanner-ball dribbler" and nicknamed The Flea. He won 16 medals with his club – one European Cup, eight league, three Scottish cup, four League Cup. Johnstone also earned a reputation for occasional wayward behavior, on the field and off, but his courage was never in doubt, as many a far bigger opponent found to his cost. He was particularly effective in the 1966–67 season, when Celtic won every competition they entered, culminating in the European Cup Final defeat of Internazionale in Lisbon.

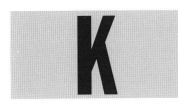

Kevin Keegan

Born: February 14, 1951, England.
Clubs: Scunthorpe, Liverpool (Eng), Hamburg (Ger), Southampton, Newcastle (Eng).

Keegan, the only British player to have won the European Footballer of the Year twice, was a bargain Liverpool signing when he joined from Scunthorpe United in 1971. He was an overnight success, first in his original position of outside-right, then as a free-ranging attacking raider. Keegan won two league titles with Liverpool, leaving for Hamburg after the European Cup victory of 1977. Keegan was a European Cup Final loser with Hamburg against Nottingham Forest in 1980 before breathing new life into first Southampton then Newcastle. Management roles followed with Newcastle, Fulham and, ultimately, England.

Jack Kelsey

Born: November 19, 1929, Wales.
Club: Arsenal (Eng).

Big Jack was beaten five times on his debut for Arsenal in 1951, but he went on to be first-choice keeper for 11 years until a spinal injury, sustained in a collision with Vava of Brazil, forced him to retire. He remained a familiar figure at Highbury as manager of the club shop. He was powerful enough to withstand the challenges of an age when keepers were not well protected, and agile enough to make many remarkable stops, helped by rubbing chewing gum into his palms. Kelsey won 43 caps for Wales and played for Britain against the Rest of Europe in 1955.

Mario Alberto Kempes

Born: July 15, 1952, Argentina.
Clubs: Instituto Cordoba, Rosario Central (Arg), Valencia (Sp), River Plate (Arg), Hercules (Sp), Vienna, Austria Salzburg (Austria).

Kempes, an aggressive young striker with legs like tree trunks, had a first taste of World Cup soccer in West Germany in 1974. He swiftly earned a transfer to Spain with Valencia, where he developed into such a devastating hammer of opposing defenses that he was the only foreign-based player recalled to join the hosts' World Cup squad under Cesar Luis Menotti in 1978. His addition proved decisive: Kempes was the event's top scorer with six goals, including two in the 3–1 defeat of Holland in the Final. Strangely, he was never able to scale those heights again, despite playing once more for Argentina in the 1982 finals in Spain, where he should have felt at home.

Jürgen Klinsmann

Born: July 30, 1964, Germany.
Clubs: Stuttgart Kickers, VfB Stuttgart (Ger), Internazionale (It), Monaco (Fr), Tottenham (Eng), Bayern Munich (Ger), Sampdoria (It), Tottenham (Eng).

Jürgen Klinsmann needed little time before breaking through as the German league's top scorer and the

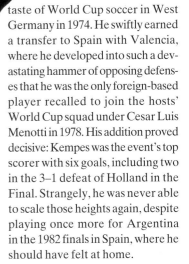

MARIO KEMPES
Argentina's World Cup hammer in 1978

country's Footballer of the Year during his first Bundesliga spell with VfB Stuttgart, whom he also led to the UEFA Cup Final in 1989. He then spent three successful years at Internazionale in Italy before moving to France with Monaco and then to England with Tottenham (where he spent two spells) before returning to Germany and Bayern Munich in July 1995. A year later Bayern won the UEFA Cup with Klinsmann contributing a European club competition record of 15 goals in a season. He won the World Cup with West Germany in 1990 and the European Championships in 1996 before announcing his retirement after scoring three times at France '98.

Ronald Koeman

Born: March 21, 1963, Holland.
Clubs: Groningen, PSV Eindhoven (Hol), Barcelona (Sp), Feyenoord (Hol).

Despite lacking pace, Koeman turned himself into one of the world's best sweepers as well as becoming a free-kick expert. It was from a free kick that Koeman thundered the winner for Barcelona in the 1992 European Cup Final, a trophy he also won with PSV Eindhoven in 1988. Ronald and brother Erwin began with their father's old club, Groningen and were later members together of the Holland side which won the 1988 European Championship in Germany. Ronald won the treble of European Cup, Dutch league and cup in 1988 then moved to Barcelona in 1989, before returning to Holland and Feyenoord in 1995.

Ivan Kolev

Born: November 1, 1930, Bulgaria.
Club: CDNA/CSKA Sofia.

Kolev was the first great Bulgarian soccer player, often compared for control and vision with Hungarian contemporary Ferenc Puskas. Kolev, who could play outside- or inside-left, spent all his career with the Bulgarian army club, variously known as CDNA and then CSKA Sofia. He scored 25 goals in 75 internationals and led Bulgaria on their first appearance at a major soccer tournament in the 1952 Helsinki Olympic Games. With CDNA/

NICE WHILE IT LASTED *Jürgen Klinsmann was a hero in his first season at Spurs*

CSKA he was champion of Bulgaria on 11 occasions and won the cup four times.

Sandor Kocsis

Born: September 30, 1929, Hungary.
Clubs: Ferencvaros, Honved (Hun), Young Fellows (Swz), Barcelona (Sp).

Kocsis was an attacking inside-right for Honved and Hungary in the early 1950s. He and fellow inside-forward Puskas pushed forward while the nominal center-forward withdrew towards midfield, creating gaps for the others to exploit. Kocsis did so to the extent of 75 goals in 68 internationals. He was three times the Hungarian league's top scorer, as well as the leading marksman, with 11 goals, at the 1954 World Cup finals. After the Hungarian Revolution of 1956 Kocsis decided to stay abroad and joined Barcelona with further success, winning the Fairs Cup in 1960. A

year later Kocsis was on the losing side with Barcelona at the European Cup Final against Benfica in Bern.

Raymond Kopa

Born: October 13, 1931, France.
Clubs: Angers, Reims (Fr), Real Madrid (Sp), Reims (Fr).

Born Kopaszewski, the son of an emigrant Polish miner, Kopa gained an added incentive to escape from a mining future when he damaged a hand in a pit accident as a teenager. He was spotted by Angers and then sold on to Reims in 1950. Originally a right-winger, Kopa soon switched to a creative center- or inside-forward role. He led Reims to the first European Cup Final in 1956, being transferred afterwards to their conquerors on the day, Real Madrid. Kopa starred in midfield for third-placed France at the 1958 World Cup, and returned to Reims a year later as

European Footballer of the Year. He played 45 times for France but his playing career ended amid controversy over his outspoken espousal of the cause of freedom of contract.

Johannes "Hans" Krankl

Born: February 14, 1953, Austria.
Clubs: Rapid Vienna (Austria), Barcelona (Sp), 1st FC Vienna (Austria), Barcelona (Sp), Rapid, Wiener Sportclub (Austria).

For Krankl everything happened in 1978. He scored 41 goals for Rapid Vienna, to win the Golden Boot as Euorpe's leading league marksman, and starred for Austria at the World Cup finals in Argentina. He joined Barcelona and inspired their victory in the 1979 European Cup-winners' Cup. Serious injury in a car crash interrupted Krankl's career in Spain and he went home to Austria briefly. Later he returned to Rapid, with whom he became general manager after retiring. Krankl scored 34 goals in 69 internationals and was top league scorer four times in Austria and once in Spain.

Ladislav Kubala

Born: June 10, 1927, Hungary.
Clubs: Ferencvaros (Hun), Bratislava (Cz), Vasas Budapest (Hun), Barcelona, Español (Sp), FC Zurich (Swz), Toronto Falcons (Can).

One of the ironies of 1950s soccer was that Hungary created a great team without one of their very greatest players. Center- or inside-forward Kubala had escaped to the West after having played international soccer for both Czechoslovakia and Hungary in the late 1940s. In exile in Italy, Kubala formed a refugees' team called Pro Patria which played exhibition tours and provided him with the springboard to join Spain's Barcelona. There Kubala was Spanish champion five times and twice won the Fairs Cup. He also gained international recognition with a third country, winning 19 caps for Spain to add to his seven for Czechoslovakia and three for Hungary. He left Barcelona after the 1961 European Cup Final defeat by Benfica, but later returned to coach both Barcelona and the Spanish national team.

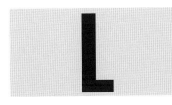

Angel Amadeo Labruna

Born: September 26, 1918, Argentina.
Clubs: River Plate, Platense (Arg), Green Cross (Chile), Rampla Juniors (Uru).

Labruna remains one of the greatest Argentine soccer personalities of all time. Not only was he a great inside-left, but he earned longevity records by playing with River Plate for 29 years and won a reputation as South America's version of Stanley Matthews by playing on until he was 41. At the 1958 World Cup finals in Sweden, Labruna was recalled at the age of 40 to complete an international career which brought him 17 goals in 36 games for Argentina. Labruna began with River Plate when he was 12 and won nine league championships. In the late 1940s he was a member of the legendary "Maquina," or "Machine," forward line. In 1986 Labruna was coach when River at last won the South American club cup.

Marius Lacatus

Born: April 5, 1964, Romania.
Clubs: Steaua Bucharest (Rom), Fiorentina (It), Oviedo (Sp), Steaua.

Tall, slim and sharp in front of goal, Lacatus was a key figure in the Romanian upsurge of the 1980s. Playing nominally as outside-right, he used his pace to great effect to help shoot his country to the 1990 World Cup finals. After the finals, he stayed on in Italy with Fiorentina, and the Romanian federation allocated much of the fee to the redevelopment of sports facilities in the country. Lacatus found it hard to adjust to Italian soccer and later moved on to Spain before returning home in the autumn of 1993.

Grzegorz Lato

Born: April 8, 1950, Poland.
Clubs: Stal Mielec (Pol), Lokeren (Bel), Atlante (Mex).

Lato was a Polish phenomenon, an outstanding striker who later proved equally influential when he moved back into midfield. At the 1974 World Cup finals, Lato was top scorer with seven goals. He had made his debut for Poland against Spain in 1971 and was a member of the squad which won the Olympic gold medal in Munich a year later. Lato became a fixture in the senior national team in 1973, after impressing manager Kazimierz Gorski on a tour of the United States and Canada, and he went on to score 46 goals in 104 internationals, a Polish record. After leading Poland's attack at the 1978 World Cup finals in Argentina, Lato was permitted the "reward" of a transfer to Lokeren in Belgium, and he ended his career in Mexico with Atlante.

Michael Laudrup

Born: June 15, 1964, Denmark.
Clubs: Brondbyernes (Den), Lazio, Juventus (It), Barcelona, Real Madrid (Sp), Vissel Kobe (Jap), Ajax (Hol).

Michael and younger brother Brian are sons of a former Danish inter-

LAUDRUP *Brilliant elder brother*

national, Finn Laudrup, who closely guided their early careers. Michael, as a teenager, attracted scouts from all Europe's top clubs but finally chose Juventus, who loaned him to Lazio before recalling him to replace Poland's Zbigniew Boniek. With Juventus Laudrup won the World Club Cup before moving on to win the European Cup with Barcelona. He starred at the 1986 World Cup finals before falling out with Denmark's national manager Richard Moller Nielsen and thus missing the 1992 European Championship triumph. But he was back for the 1998 World Cup finals in France and was named in the FIFA team of the tournament before retiring.

Denis Law

Born: February 22, 1940, Scotland.
Clubs: Huddersfield, Manchester City (Eng), Torino (It), Manchester United, Manchester City (Eng).

Denis Law and Jimmy Greaves were born within four days of each other, and spent several years as rival scorers and supreme entertainers. Law, of only medium height and slim in build, had a lion's heart and a salmon's leap, scoring many spectacular goals with headers and acrobatic shots. He was also an incisive passer of the ball, and a fierce competitor. Suspensions and injury cost him many more goals. He was European Footballer of the Year in 1964, won two league titles and the 1963 FA Cup, and scored 30 goals in 55 internationals, but missed United's European Cup victory in 1968 through knee trouble.

Tommy Lawton

Born: October 6, 1919, England.
Clubs: Burnley, Everton, Chelsea, Notts County, Brentford, Arsenal.

One of the first soccer players to realize what his market value was, and to work at getting it. Lawton made frequent moves, at a time when there rarely was any percentage for a transferred player. Lawton was a star from his dubbin-smothered toe-caps to the glistening part in his hair. He got a hat-trick on his senior debut aged 16, was the First Division top scorer two years in a row, won a title medal aged 19, scored 23 goals in 22 full internationals, and goals by the dozen

DENIS LAW *The promising youngster in Huddersfield days*

during the Second World War. Lawton was still frightening foes deep into his 30s and pulling in fans everywhere he went.

Leonidas da Silva

Born: November 11, 1910, Brazil.
Clubs: Havanesa, Barroso, Sul Americano, Sirio Libanes, Bomsucesso (Br), Nacional (Uru), Vasco da Gama, Botafogo, Flamengo, São Paulo (Br).

Leonidas was Brazil's 1930s superstar although he played only 23 times for his country. He was the inventor of the overhead bicycle kick, which was unveiled to the international game when he scored twice on his international debut against Uruguay in 1932. The Uruguayans were so impressed he was immediately signed by the top club, Nacional. Later he returned home with Vasco da Gama and was top scorer at the 1938 World Cup with eight goals, including four in a 6–5 victory over Poland. Unfortunately, an overconfident management rested Leonidas from the semi-final against Italy, wanting to keep him fresh for the Final . . . and they lost.

Billy Liddell

Born January 10, 1922, Scotland.
Club: Liverpool (Eng).

An accountant, Justice of the Peace and youth worker, Liddell allied all these activities to soccer. He is still revered as one of the greatest players in Liverpool's history, which is saying a great deal. Liddell missed six years on war service and spent all his career with one club. Apart from the championship in 1947 and a Cup Final defeat three years later, Liverpool achieved little during his 15 years, but he set club records with 492 league appearances and 216 goals, as well as representing Scotland 28 times and Great Britain in two games against the Rest of Europe.

Nils Liedholm

Born: October 8, 1922, Sweden.
Clubs: Norrköping (Swe), Milan (It).

Liedholm played originally at inside-forward, later moved back to wing-half and finally became one of the best of sweepers in his veteran years. He began with Norrköping, winning two championship medals and playing

LITTBARSKI *Testing the resolve of Italian defender Claudio Gentile*

18 times for his country. After helping Sweden win, from outside-left, the 1948 Olympic title, he moved to Italy. There Liedholm formed Milan's celebrated trio with Gunnar Gren and Gunnar Nordahl and he scored 60 goals in 367 league games. At the end of his career Liedholm captained hosts Sweden to runners-up spot at the 1958 World Cup finals. After retiring as a player, he stayed with Milan as a youth coach and later took charge of

the senior team in 1964. He also managed Fiorentina and Roma.

Gary Lineker

Born: November 30, 1960, England.
Clubs: Leicester, Everton (Eng), Barcelona (Sp), Tottenham (Eng), Nagoya Grampus 8 (Jap).

All sorts of records fell to this unassuming son of a market trader, who accepted good and bad with the smiling sincerity that, allied to his skill,

GARY LINEKER *Scoring, against the Irish Republic in the 1990 World Cup, one of his 48 international goals*

made him such a popular figure. This was never more evident than in the desperate days when serious illness struck his first-born son. He went within one goal of England's 49-goal scoring record, ten coming in World Cup final stages, led the First Division marksmen with three different clubs, scored a hat-trick for Barcelona against Real Madrid, and won the FA Cup despite missing a penalty. Lineker retired after two injury-plagued seasons in Japan, and immediately became a broadcaster.

Pierre Littbarski

Born: April 16, 1960, Germany.
Clubs: Hertha Zehlendorf, Köln (Ger), Racing Paris (Fr), Köln (Ger), JEF United (Japan).

Littbarski, an outside-right who later took his dribbling skills back into midfield, shot to prominence by hitting two goals on his debut for West Germany in a World Cup qualifier against Austria in 1981. He joined Köln, the club with which he is most associated, in 1978, played in the 1982 and 1986 World Cup Finals and finally achieved victory in Italy in 1990. Before heading out to Japan to wind down his career, Littbarski described his career ambition as "scoring a goal after beating all 10 outfield players, dribbling round the goalkeeper and putting the ball in the net with a back-heel."

Wlodzimierz Lubanski

Born: February 28, 1947, Poland.
Clubs: GKS Gliwice, Gornik Zabrze (Pol), Lokeren (Bel), Valenciennes, Quimper (Fr), Lokeren (Bel).

Lubanski ranks among Poland's finest players even though injuries were not kind to him. He emerged with the miners' club, Gornik, in the mid-1960s taking over the mantle of inspiration with both club and country from Ernest Pol. Lubanski was four times top league marksman in Poland and captained his country to the 1972 Olympic Games victory in Munich. The following year he suffered a serious thigh injury in a World Cup qualifier against England and missed the finals in which Poland finished third. He returned to national team duty at the 1978 finals in Argentina, before winding down his career in Belgium and France.

Ally McCoist

Born: September 24, 1962, Scotland.
Clubs: St. Johnstone (Scot), Sunderland (Eng), Rangers (Scot).

A powerful striker who survived a disastrous spell in England to become a hugely successful and popular player back in his homeland. McCoist started at St Johnstone, who received a club record fee when selling him to Sunderland in 1981. After 56 games and only eight goals, he was sold to Rangers, and began a decade of almost constant medal-collecting as the club dominated the Scottish game. He won the Golden Boot as Europe's leading league marksman and recovered from a broken leg to smash the legendary Bob McPhail's record of 233 league goals for Rangers. His one disappointment was being left out of Scotland's 1998 World Cup finals squad.

McCOIST *Crowned his goal-grabbing career with the Golden Boot*

Paul McGrath

Born: December 4, 1959, England.
Clubs: Man Utd, Aston Villa, Derby Co.

McGrath was a fine player whose career was dogged by ill-luck and – on occasions – lack of self-discipline. Born in Middlesex of Irish parentage, McGrath had a troubled progress through Manchester United's junior ranks and on into the senior squad, with injuries and authority combining to hinder him. But manager Ron Atkinson kept faith, and took McGrath with him when he moved to Villa. As a club player, one FA Cup win in 1985 – he performed heroically for ten-man United – was poor reward. As an international for the Republic of Ireland, his not inconsiderable skill and total commitment made him a folk hero among the Irish fans during European Championship and World Cup campaigns.

Jimmy McIlroy

Born: October 25, 1931, Northern Ireland.
Clubs: Glentoran (NI), Burnley, Stoke, Oldham (Eng).

If Blanchflower was the key man of

McGRATH *Defied knee injuries*

the Irish World Cup campaign in 1958, Jimmy McIlroy was only a little way behind him. His unhurried, elegant work at inside-forward proved ideal for the tactics devised by team manager Peter Doherty. Altogether McIlroy played 55 games for his country, to go with more than 600 at club level, earning a Championship medal with the attractive young Burnley squad in 1960, and a runners-up medal in the FA Cup two years later – against Blanchflower's Spurs. He later enjoyed a brief but brilliant combination with Stanley Matthews at Stoke.

Sammy McIlroy

Born: August 1, 1954, Northern Ireland.
Clubs: Manchester United, Stoke, Manchester City (Eng).

Another valuable midfielder, like his namesake, but of a totally different type. Sammy McIlroy's all-action style was in complete contrast to Jimmy's deliberate method, but was ideally suited to the hurly-burly of the modern game. It earned him 88 games for his country, spread over 15 years, but only five goals. He also played in three FA Cup Finals with United, losing to Southampton in 1976 and Arsenal in 1979, beating Liverpool in 1977. McIlroy's late equalizer in the 1979 Final seemed sure to take the game to extra time, but Arsenal went downfield to snatch the winner straight from the kick-off.

BILLY McNEILL *Celtic's captain in the glorious 1960s*

Billy McNeill

Born: March 2, 1940, Scotland.
Club: Celtic.

The nickname Caesar suited McNeill. In both size and style he was a big man, and was the hub of the Celtic defense during their great days of the 1960s. He won a host of domestic medals and, in 1967, became the first Briton to lift the European Cup, the most coveted prize in club soccer. He was a soldier's son and educated at a rugby-playing school, but made up for a late introduction to soccer with years of splendid service and a club record number of appearances. His international debut was in the 9–3 mauling by England in 1961, but he recovered to gain 28 more caps. McNeill was later manager of his old club (twice), as well as Aston Villa and Manchester City.

Paul McStay

Born: October 22, 1964, Scotland.
Club: Celtic.

This product of Hamilton played for his country as a schoolboy and at youth level before graduating to the Under-21 team and then to the full national squad. He made his senior debut against Uruguay in 1983 and has plied his creative midfield trade to such good effect that Kenny Dalglish's record of 102 caps might possibly be within his reach. McStay's loyalty to Celtic has been a welcome change in the modern climate of frequent transfers, and he has given good value for his high earnings in a period when his club have been very much overshadowed by Rangers. He sadly missed the 1996 European Championships through injury.

Josef "Sepp" Maier

Born: February 28, 1944, West Germany.
Clubs: TSV Haar, Bayern Munich.

Maier reached the pinnacle of his career in 1974 when he first won the European Cup with Bayern Munich and then, a few weeks later, the World Cup with West Germany on his home ground of the Olympic stadium in the Bavarian capital. He was noted, apart from his goalkeeping talent, for his trademark long shorts and his love of tennis. Maier even opened a tennis school thanks to the money he earned in a 19-year career with Bayern from 1960 to 1979. Maier played 473 league matches, including a run of 422 consecutive games. He made his international debut in 1966, when he was No. 3 goalkeeper in West Germany's World Cup squad in England, and was a member of the European Championship-winning side against the Soviet Union in Brussels in 1972. Maier won the European Cup three times with Bayern as well as the World Club Cup against Atletico Mineiro of Brazil in 1976.

Paolo Maldini

Born: June 26, 1968, Italy.
Club: Milan.

Soccer runs in the family for the fast raiding left-back of Italy and Milan. Paolo's father, Cesare, was a sweeper who captained Milan to their first European Cup success in 1963, played 16 times for his country and, after coaching Italy's Olympic and Under-21 teams, managed the national side at France '98. Paolo, who can play anywhere on defense, began with Milan's youth section and made his first-team debut at 17. He followed in father's footsteps by winning the European Cup in 1989, 1990 and 1994 and was soon acclaimed as one of the finest all-around players in the world when he helped Italy reach the 1994 World Cup Final, only losing to Brazil on penalty-kicks. He was voted 1994 World Player of the Year by *World Soccer* magazine and went on to captain his country, under the manament of his father, at the 1998 World Cup finals in France.

Diego Armando Maradona

see Legends (page 81)

Silvio Marzolini

Born: 1940, Argentina.
Clubs: Ferro Carril Oeste, Boca Juniors.

To many experts, and not only Argentines, Marzolini is the finest full-back of the modern era. He was a left-back who could tackle and intercept with the best of them but also displayed the technique and virtuoso skill of a forward when he had the opportunity to go on attack. At only 13 Marzolini won the Buenos Aires youth title with Ferro Carril Oeste and became a first division regular at 19. In 1960 he was bought by Boca Juniors, winning the

MALDINI *Emulated his father*

league title in 1962, 1964 and 1965. He played in the World Cup finals of 1962 and 1966 – where he rose above all the unpleasant mayhem of the quarter-final defeat by England at Wembley. Marzolini, after retirement, enjoyed some success as a TV and film actor before he returned to Boca as coach and took them to the league title in 1981. He was forced to retire because of a heart condition.

Josef Masopust

Born: February 9, 1931, Czechoslovakia.
Clubs: Union Teplice, Dukla Prague (Cz), Crossing Molenbeek (Bel).

Masopust is the only Czechoslovak player to have won the European Footballer of the Year award, which he collected in 1962 after an outstanding World Cup campaign in Chile. Czechoslovakia finished runners-up to Brazil, and Masopust scored the opening goal in the Final, which they ultimately lost 3–1. Originally an inside-forward, Masopust made his name as a left-half but was, to all intents and purposes, more of an old-fashioned center-half. He preferred to dominate games from a central position in midfield both for Czechoslovakia and the army club Dukla. His intuitive understanding with left-back Ladislav Novak and defensive wing-half Svatopluk Pluskal was renowned throughout the world.

Lothar Matthäus

Born: March 21, 1961, Germany.
Clubs: Borussia Mönchengladbach, Bayern Munich (Ger), Internazionale (It), Bayern Munich (Ger).

Matthäus has been Germany's outstanding leader from midfield – and, latterly, sweeper – since the early 1980s. His career reached its zenith in 1990 when he was not only West Germany's World Cup-winning captain in Rome, but was also voted Player of the Tournament by the world's media. Matthäus was a substitute for the West German side who won the 1980 European Championship and established himself only in 1986, when he scored a magnificent winner against Morocco in the World Cup second round on the way to defeat by Argentina in the Final. He began with Borussia, joined Bayern for $1 million in 1984 and moved to Italy with Inter in 1988 for $3.5 million. Injury kept him out of the 1992 European Championship finals, but he won the 1996 UEFA Cup with Bayern Munich and the 1997 league title and then made a shock international return, aged 37, for the 1998 World Cup finals .

Stanley Matthews

see Legends (page 82)

Alessandro "Sandro" Mazzola

Born: November 7, 1942, Italy.
Club: Internazionale.

Sandro is the son of Valentino, the captain of Torino and Italy who was killed in the 1949 Superga air disaster when Sandro was six. To escape comparisons, he launched his soccer career with Inter rather than Torino, and made his debut in a 9–1 defeat by Juventus – when Inter fielded their youth team in protest at the Italian federation's decision to order an earlier game to be replayed. In 1962–63 Mazzola, a striking inside-forward, scored 10 goals in 23 games as Inter won the league title. In both 1964 and 1965 he won the European Cup and World Club Cup, scoring in the victories over Real Madrid and Benfica. Mazzola reverted to midfield to help Italy win the 1968 European Championship and was outstanding when Italy reached the World Cup Final in Mexico in 1970.

Valentino Mazzola

Born: January 26, 1919, Italy.
Clubs: Venezia, Torino.

Mazzola was an inside-left who was born in Milan, where he played for Tresoldi and then the Alfa Romeo works side. In 1939 he was bought by Venezia, where he struck up a remarkable inside-forward partnership with Ezio Loik – with whom he moved to Torino in 1942. Mazzola captained and inspired Torino to five consecutive league championship victories in 1943 and 1946–49. Before he could celebrate the fifth title, however, Mazzola and 17 of his Torino colleagues had been killed in the 1949 Superga air disaster. Mazzola was the league's top scorer in 1947, and made his Italy debut against Croatia in Genoa in 1942. He scored four goals in 12 internationals and would almost certainly have captained Italy's World Cup defence in Brazil in 1950.

Giuseppe Meazza

Born: August 23, 1910, Italy.
Clubs: Internazionale, Milan, Juventus, Varese, Atalanta.

Only two Italian players won the World Cup in 1934 and 1938: Giovanni Ferrari was one, inside-forward partner Meazza was the other. Meazza was considered the most complete inside-forward of his generation, able both to score goals and create them. Born in Milan, Meazza made his debut with Inter at 17 and scored a then league record 33 goals in 1928–29. He spent a decade with Inter before switching to Milan in 1938, playing wartime soccer with Juventus and Varese and retiring in 1947 after two seasons with Atalanta. Meazza marked his international debut by scoring twice in a 4–2 win over Switzerland in Rome in 1930 and, later the same year, scored a hat-trick in a 5–0 defeat

MEAZZA *Double World Cup-winner*

of Hungary. In all, he scored 33 goals in 53 internationals.

Joe Mercer

Born: August 9, 1914, England.
Clubs: Everton, Arsenal.

"Your legs wouldn't last a postman his morning round" was Dixie Dean's description of Mercer's spindle shanks. But Joe played for a quarter of a century on his odd-shaped pins before breaking one of them and going into management. He won a league title with Everton and two with Arsenal after they had gambled on his durability when he was 32 and had two bad knees. He also won a cup final with the Gunners in 1950 and lost one two years later, when he captained a ten-man team (Arsenal had a player carried off injured and no substitutes were allowed at the time) to a narrow defeat. Mercer repeated his league and cup success as manager of Manchester City, and had a brief spell as England caretaker, manager between Alf Ramsey and Don Revie.

Billy Meredith

Born: July 30, 1874, Wales.
Clubs: Manchester City, Manchester United, Manchester City (Eng).

Meredith won his first medal, for a dribbling contest, at the age of ten, and played his last senior game – a losing FA Cup semi-final – when nearly 50. He was a rugged individual, originally a miner, and a strong union man, often involved in off-field disputes with officialdom. On the field he was rarely in trouble, plying his trade down the right wing with enviable skill and consistency. He won 48 caps (scoring 11 goals) spread over 25 years, with five lost to the First World War, and played around 1,000 first-team matches, in spite of missing a complete season after being involved in a match-fixing scandal.

MATTHÄUS *Proud World Cup-winning captain of West Germany in Italy in 1990*

MICHEL *Grounds Northern Ireland's Kingsley Black with his skill*

Michel (full name: José Miguel Gonzalez Maria del Campo)

Born: March 23, 1963, Spain.
Clubs: Castilla, Real Madrid (Sp), Celaya (Mex).

Michel was one of European soccer's classic midfield operators throughout the 1980s and early 1990s. He made his debut with Castilla, the nursery team of Real Madrid, and was promoted to the senior outfit in 1984. A year later he starred in the UEFA Cup Final defeat of Videoton, scoring Madrid's first goal and making the other two in their 3–0 win in the first leg in Hungary. Michel made his Spain debut in 1985. He was unlucky to be denied a goal at the 1986 World Cup finals when his shot was cleared from behind the line against Brazil, but in 1990 in Italy he claimed a hat-trick against South Korea.

Roger Milla

Born: May 20, 1952, Cameroon.
Clubs: Leopard Douala, Tonnerre Yaounde (Cam), Valenciennes, Monaco, Bastia, Saint-Etienne, Montpellier (Fr).

Center-forward Milla – real name Miller – delighted crowds at the 1990 World Cup with his celebratory dances around the corner flags. His goals, especially the winner against Colombia, made him the first player to become African Footballer of the Year for a second time. Milla played most of his club soccer in France, winning the cup there in 1980 with Monaco and in 1981 with Bastia. He was first voted African Footballer of the Year in 1976. He became, at the age of 42, the oldest player ever to appear in the World Cup finals at USA'94.

Milos Milutinovic

Born: February 5, 1933, Yugoslavia.
Clubs: FK Bor, Partizan, OFK Belgrade (Yug), Bayern Munich (Ger), Racing Paris, Stade Français (Fr).

Milutinovic, a powerful, aggressive center-forward, was head of a famous dynasty of players which has included Bora Milutinovic, coach to the United States' 1994 World Cup squad. Milos began with FK Bor, made his debut for Yugoslavia in 1951 and, the same year, transferred to Belgrade with army club Partizan. He scored 183 goals in 192 games before moving controversially to neighbors OFK, then to Germany with Bayern Munich and finally settling in France. Milutinovic proved a huge success with Racing Paris before injury forced his retirement in 1965. He scored 16 goals in 33 internationals between 1953 and 1958.

Severino Minelli

Born: September 6, 1909, Switzerland.
Clubs: Kussnacht, Servette, Grasshoppers.

Minelli was a steady, reliable right-back with great positional sense who played a then record 79 times for Switzerland during the inter-war years. In 1930 he made his national team debut while simultaneously winning his first league championship medal with Servette of Geneva. In the next 13 years he won another five league medals as well as eight cup finals with Grasshoppers of Zurich. Minelli was a key figure in the "*verrou*" or "bolt" defense introduced by fellow-countryman Karl Rappan, and played to great effect for Switzerland in the World Cups of both 1934 and 1938. One of his finest games was Switzerland's 2–1 defeat of England in Zurich in May 1938.

Luisito Monti

Born: January 15, 1901, Argentina.
Clubs: Boca Juniors (Arg), Juventus (It).

Monti was an old-style attacking center-half in the late 1920s and early 1930s. He was notable for a rugged, ruthless style but was also one of the great achievers of the inter-war years. Monti won an Olympic Games silver medal in 1928 when Argentina lost to Uruguay in Amsterdam and was again on the losing side against the same opponents at the first World Cup Final two years later. In 1931 Juventus brought Monti to Italy. At first he looked slow and vastly overweight, but a month's lone training brought him back to fitness and, little more than a year later, he made his debut for Italy in a 4–2 win over Hungary in Milan. Monti was not only a key figure in the Juventus side which won four successive league titles in the 1930s but he also played for Italy when they first won the World Cup, defeating Czechoslovakia in Rome in 1934.

MILLA *Runs away from Colombian goalkeeper Higuita to score the winner in the 1990 World Cup second round*

MOORE *Leadership by example*

Bobby Moore

Born: April 17, 1941, England.
Clubs: West Ham United, Fulham (Eng), San Antonio Thunder, Seattle Sounders (US).

Bobby Moore was the inspirational, ice-cool captain of England's victorious 1966 World Cup side. Yet an FA Cup, one European Cup-winners' Cup, the 1966 World Cup and 108 England caps (100 of them under Sir Alf Ramsey) represent only part of his value to West Ham and England. Even at 34 he went back to Wembley, for Fulham against his old club, but by then fate was no longer smiling on him. He is likely to remain the only English captain to receive the World Cup trophy. Cruelly he developed cancer, from which he died in 1993, but which he defied with the utmost bravery to the end.

Juan Manuel Moreno

Born: August 3, 1916, Argentina.
Clubs: River Plate (Arg), España (Mex), River Plate (Arg), Universidad Catolia (Chile), Boca Juniors (Arg), Defensor (Uru), FC Oeste (Arg), Medellin (Col).

Many Argentines consider Moreno to have been the greatest player of all time. An inside-right for most of his career, Moreno began with River Plate's youth teams and was a league championship winner in 1936. He won four league titles with River and was a member of the legendary forward line of the late 1940s, together with Muñoz, Pedernera, Labruna and Loustau. Moreno played for España in Mexico between 1944 and 1946, returned to River for two more years, then wandered off again to Chile, Uruguay and Colombia. He scored an impressive 20 goals in 33 internationals.

Stan Mortensen

Born: May 26, 1921, England.
Clubs: Blackpool, Hull, Southport.

As fast over ten yards as any English forward, with finishing skill to round off the openings his pace created, Mortensen scored four times in a 10–0 win over Portugal (away!) in his first international, and his goal in his last England game was his 23rd in 25 appearances. That was against the 1953 Hungarians, a few months after he had become the first man to score a hat-trick in a Wembley Cup Final: his third, after two defeats. Morty loved the FA Cup, scoring in each of Blackpool's first 12 post-war rounds in the tournament and finishing with 28 Cup goals as well as 225 in the league.

Alan Morton

Born: April 24, 1893, Scotland.
Clubs: Queen's Park, Rangers.

"The Wee Blue Devil" was a left-winger with elusive dribbling skill and a waspish shot who had a 20-year career and gained nine championship medals and three for the Scottish Cup. He was a mining engineer who spent several seasons with the amateurs at Queen's Park, before becoming the first signing for new Rangers manager, William Struth, who remained in charge for 34 years. Morton played well over 500 games for Rangers and is reputed never to have appeared in the reserves. He was always very much the gentleman, often appearing for matches in a bowler hat and carrying an umbrella.

Coen Moulijn

Born: February 15, 1937, Holland.
Clubs: Xerxes, Feyenoord.

Moulijn was perhaps Holland's first post-war superstar. A brilliant outside-left, he played 38 times for Holland between his debut in a 1–0 defeat by Belgium in Antwerp in 1956 and his last game, a 1–1 World Cup draw against Bulgaria, in October 1969. That may have been Moulijn's last international, but his final and greatest achievement came the following May when Feyenoord beat Celtic in the European Cup Final in 1970. Moulijn helped Feyenoord go on to beat Estudiantes de La Plata in the World Club Cup and retired in 1972 with five league championships to his name. At the insistence of the Dutch federation, Feyenoord had inserted a clause in Moulijn's contract that he should never be sold abroad.

Gerd Müller

Born: November 3, 1945, Germany.
Clubs: TSV Nordlingen, Bayern Munich, Fort Lauderdale (US).

Coach Tschik Cajkovski was not impressed when Bayern bought a stocky new center-forward in 1964. "I can't put that little elephant in among my string of thoroughbreds," said Cajkovski. But once he had done so, Bayern never looked back. Müller not only had the opportunist's eye for goal, but he was a powerful header of the ball. His goals shot Bayern out of the regional league to victory in the European Cup-winners' Cup in little more than three years. He went on to score well over 600 goals, including a record 365 in the Bundesliga and an astonishing 68 in 62 internationals for West Germany. Müller once scored four goals in a victory over Switzerland, but his most famous goal was his last, the one with which the Germans beat Holland in the 1974 World Cup Final. Müller won the European Cup three times and was also a European Championship winner in 1972.

MÜLLER *Volleys the dramatic winner against England in 1970 in Leon*

José Nasazzi

Born: May 24, 1901, Uruguay.
Clubs: Lito, Roland Moor, Nacional, Bella Vista.

Nasazzi was one of the great captains in soccer history. He led Uruguay to their victories in the 1924 and 1928 Olympic Games and then to the 1930 World Cup. Nasazzi was nicknamed "The Marshall" for his organizational ability at the heart of defence from right-back, though he also played occasionally at center-half and at inside-forward. Nasazzi was also a South American champion on four occasions in his 15-year, 64-game international career and was a key member of the Nacional team which so dominated the league championship in 1934 that it became nicknamed "The Machine."

Zdenek Nehoda

Born: May 9, 1952, Czechoslovakia.
Clubs: TJ Hulin, TJ Gottwaldov, Dukla Prague (Cz), SV Darmstadt (W Ger), Standard Liège (Bel), FC Grenoble (Swz).

Nehoda, a skilled, mobile general of a center-forward was the first – and last – Czechoslovak player to go anywhere close to a century of caps. He scored 31 goals in 90 internationals, of which the highlight was the European Championship victory over West Germany in Belgrade in 1976. Nehoda was three times a champion of Czechoslovakia with the army club, Dukla Prague, twice a domestic cup-winner and was twice voted his country's Footballer of the Year, in 1978 and 1979. Nehoda's international reputation also earned him selection for a Europe XI against Italy in 1981.

Johan Neeskens

Born: September 15, 1951, Holland.
Clubs: Haarlem, Ajax (Hol), Barcelona (Sp), New York Cosmos (US).

Neeskens was an aggressive, sharp-tackling midfielder who fitted perfectly into the "total football" pattern set by Ajax and Holland in the early

NEESKENS *Goes past Argentina's Ardiles in the 1978 World Cup Final*

1970s. Neeskens provided the steel which supported the more technical gifts of teammates Cruyff, Keizer and Van Hanegem. He scored 17 goals in 49 internationals and earned a place in history by converting the first-ever World Cup Final penalty against West Germany in Munich in 1974. With Ajax, Neeskens won hat-tricks of victories in the European Cup, the Dutch league and the Dutch cup. In 1974 he moved to Barcelona, with whom he won the Spanish cup in 1978 and the European Cup-winners' Cup in 1979. After a spell in the North American Soccer League he attempted a comeback, in vain, in Switzerland.

Oldrich Nejedly

Born: December 13, 1909, Czechoslovakia.
Clubs: Zebrak, Rakovnik, Sparta Prague.

Nejedly was inside-left for the Sparta club which dominated the Mitropa Cup for much of the 1930s and for the Czechoslovak national team which reached the 1934 World Cup Final. His skills were described as "pure as Bohemian crystal," and his partnership with outside-left Antonin Puc was one of the best of its kind in Europe in the inter-war years. Nejedly scored twice in the 3–1 defeat of Germany in the semi-finals but could make no headway against Italy in the Final. Nevertheless he was the World Cup's top scorer with five goals. A broken leg against Brazil in 1938 ended Nejedly's dream of revenge over Italy. He scored 28 goals in 44 internationals and was chosen for Central Europe against Western Europe in 1937.

Igor Netto

Born: September 4, 1930, Soviet Union.
Club: Moscow Spartak.

Netto was a left-half in the 1950s who captained the Soviet Union from 1954 to 1963, leading by example and winning what was then a

NEHODA *Provokes unorthodox attention from Italian defender Collovati*

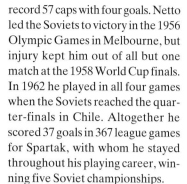

record 57 caps with four goals. Netto led the Soviets to victory in the 1956 Olympic Games in Melbourne, but injury kept him out of all but one match at the 1958 World Cup finals. In 1962 he played in all four games when the Soviets reached the quarter-finals in Chile. Altogether he scored 37 goals in 367 league games for Spartak, with whom he stayed throughout his playing career, winning five Soviet championships.

Gunter Netzer

Born: September 14, 1944, West Germany.
Clubs: Borussia Mönchengladbach (Ger), Real Madrid (Sp), Grasshoppers (Swz).

In the late 1960s and 1970s, West Germany had a surfeit of outstanding midfield generals. Netzer was at his best in the West German side which won the 1972 European Championship, forging a marvellously refined partnership with sweeper Beckenbauer behind him. He lost his place in the national team to Wolfgang Overath after transferring to Spain with Real Madrid, and never regained it on a permanent basis, although he made an occasional appearance. He was twice West German champion with Borussia, twice Spanish champion with Real Madrid, and a cup-winner once in each country. Netzer was also once West German Footballer of the Year before, as manager, masterminding Hamburg's 1989 German championship.

Gunnar Nordahl

Born: October 19, 1921, Sweden.
Clubs: Degerfors, Norrköping (Swe), Milan, Roma (It).

Nordahl was the most famous of five first division brothers. He was born in Hornefors in northern Sweden and scored 77 goals in 58 games with local Degerfors. Next came 93 goals in 92 games which brought Norrköping four championships in a row. A fireman by training, Nordahl gave that up in 1948 when, after Sweden's Olympic Games victory in London, he was lured away to Milan. There Nordahl formed the central spearhead of the "Grenoli" trio (with Gunnar Gren and Nils Liedholm). Five times he was the Italian league's leading scorer, and by the time he retired in 1957 he had totalled 225 goals in 257 Italian league matches.

Bjorn Nordqvist

Born: October 6, 1942, Sweden.
Clubs: IFK Hallsberg, Norrköping (Swe), PSV Eindhoven (Hol), IFK Gothenburg (Swe), Minnesota Kicks (US), Orgryte (Swe).

For some time in the mid-1980s, Nordqvist was the world's longest serving international with 115 caps. He played in three World Cups, in 1970, 1974 and 1978, and, with Norrköping, was twice champion of Sweden and once a cup-winner. Having taken the plunge to turn full-time professional in 1974, Nordqvist immediately won the Dutch league championship with PSV Eindhoven and later tried his luck briefly with Minnesota in the North American Soccer League. Surprisingly, considering his century of caps, Nordqvist had to wait a year between his first cap in 1963 and the second.

Ernst Ocwirk

Born: March 7, 1926, Austria.
Clubs: FK Austria (Austria), Sampdoria (It).

Ocwirk, nicknamed "Clockwork" by the British for his consistent creativity in midfield, was the last of the old-fashioned attacking center-halves – a role for which he was ideally suited, with both technical and physical strengths. Ocwirk began with FK Austria of Vienna, made his debut for his country in 1947 and appeared at the 1948 Olympic Games in London. Three years later he was back at Wembley, captaining an Austrian side which thoroughly deserved a 2–2 draw against England. In 1953 the stopper center-back had taken over throughout Europe and Ocwirk was selected at wing-half in the Rest of the World team which drew 4–4 with England in a match played to celebrate the 90th anniversary of the Football Associ-

ation. In 1956, at the advanced age of 30, he undertook the Italian adventure with Sampdoria with whom he spent five seasons before returning for one last campaign with FK Austria. Later he coached FKA to league titles in 1969 and 1970.

Raimundo Orsi

Born: December 2, 1901, Argentina.
Clubs: Independiente (Arg), Juventus (It).

Vittorio Pozzo, Italy's manager in the 1920s and 1930s, had no hesitation in picking imported South Americans such as Orsi for his team. "If they can die for Italy," said Pozzo, "they can play soccer for Italy." Orsi played outside-left for Argentina in the 1928 Olympic Final against Uruguay before switching, amid controversy, to Juventus. He spent six months kicking his heels before finally making his Juventus debut. Within four months he was playing for Italy and scoring twice on his debut in a 6–1 win over Portugal in November 1929. Orsi was one of the exceptional players who won five successive league titles with Juventus in the early 1930s. For good measure, he scored Italy's all-important equalizer on the way to an extra-time victory over Czechoslovakia in the 1934 World Cup Final.

Wolfgang Overath

Born: September 29, 1943, Germany.
Club: Köln.

Overath, an old-style inside-left and then a left-footed midfield general, was one of the most admired members of the West German

sides which featured in starring roles at the World Cups of 1966, 1970 and 1974. Overath played all his senior club career for Köln and scored 17 goals in 81 internationals between 1963 and 1974. He was a World Cup runner-up in 1966, scored the goal against Uruguay which earned West Germany third place in 1970, and won a personal duel to oust Gunter Netzer as midfield commander for the World Cup victory of 1974. Overath then retired from the national team, though he was selected for the World XI which played Brazil in Rio de Janeiro in 1968. The latter years of Overath's Köln career were sadly marred by disagreements with opinionated coach Hennes Weisweiler.

Antonin Panenka

Born: December 2, 1948, Czechoslovakia.
Clubs: Bohemians Prague (Cz), Rapid Vienna (Austria).

Panenka was a throw-back in style, a languid, skilled, dreamer of a midfield general who might have appeared more at home in the central European game of the 1930s than in the increasing hurly-burly of international soccer in the 1970s. He spent most of his career in the Czech shadows with Bohemians, from which the national manager, Vaclav Jezek, rescued him for the 1976 European Championship finals. Panenka was influential in midfield and struck the decisive blow in the Final when his penalty shot, stroked so deliberately past Sepp Maier, brought Czechoslovakia their shoot-out triumph. Later he spent several successful years in Austria with Rapid Vienna. Panenka's 65 caps including helping Czechoslovakia finish third, this time after a penalty shoot-out against Italy, in the 1980 European Championship.

Jean-Pierre Papin

Born: November 5, 1963, France. *Clubs:* Valenciennes, Club Brugge (Bel), Marseille, Milan (It), Bayern Munich (Ger), Bordeaux.

Papin was one of the outstanding strikers of the game. He began his career with

PAPIN *French goalscoring ace*

Valenciennes and played in Belgium with Brugge before returning to France to become captain and the attacking inspiration of Marseille. Papin was top scorer in the French league for four successive seasons before joining Milan in the summer of 1992. A year later he found himself appearing as a substitute for Milan against Marseille in the Final of the European Cup, which the French club won 1–0. That was Papin's second European Cup Final defeat, for he had been on the losing side in a penalty shoot-out when Red Star Belgrade beat Marseille in Bari in 1991. His consolation was in being voted European Footballer of the Year later that year. Injury upset his career after a 1994 transfer to Bayern Munich.

Daniel Passarella

Born: May 25, 1953, Argentina.
Clubs: Sarmiento, River Plate (Arg), Fiorentina, Internazionale (It).

Passarella belongs to that select band of heroes who can claim to have received the World Cup as winning captain. His moment of triumph came in the River Plate stadium – his own home club ground – in 1978. Passarella thoroughly deserved the honor of holding the cup aloft, since he had guided, controlled and commanded Argentina from central defense. Time and again Passarella powered up into midfield to serve Ardiles and Kempes, while his vicious free-kicks and strength in the air at

PASSARELLA *Argentina's inspiration*

corners added to the pressure on opposing defenses. He ended his career as a goal-grabbing defender with Fiorentina and Inter in Italy, before returning to River Plate as coach. He later guided Argentina to the quarter-finals of France '98 after taking over the national side.

Adolfo Pedernera

Born: 1918, Argentina.
Clubs: River Plate, Atlanta, Huracan (Arg), Millonarios (Col).

Pedernera was a great center-forward turned rebel. He made his debut for River Plate in 1936 and won five league championships in 11 years. In the late 1940s Pedernera led the legendary "Maquina," or "Machine," attack with Munoz, Moreno, Labruna and Loustau. River sold him, perhaps prematurely, to Atlanta and he joined Huracan just before the Argentine soccer players' strike of 1948. Millonarios of Bogota, from the pirate Colombian league, signed up Pedernera not merely as a player but as "liaison officer" to lure away other top Argentines, including his center-forward successor at River Plate, Alfredo Di Stefano. Later Pedernera returned to Argentina as coach of Gimnasia y Esgrima, Boca Juniors, Huracan and Independiente. He played 21 times for Argentina.

Pele

see Legends (page 83)

Roger Piantoni

Born: December 26, 1931, France.
Clubs: Nancy, Reims.

Piantoni was one of the last great European inside-forwards, before the "old" positions were wiped out by the advent of the 4–2–4 and 4–3–3 formations, with their new roles and terminology. Piantoni, who was born at Etain, in the Meuse, built his reputation with Nancy and transferred to Reims in 1957. He played in the World Cup finals of 1958 – when France finished third – and in the European Cup Final of 1959 (which Reims lost to Real Madrid). Piantoni played 38 times for France, having made a scoring debut in a 1–1 draw against the Irish Republic in Dublin in 1952. He also scored in his last international, nine years later, against

PIRRI *From striker to captain to club doctor with Real Madrid*

Finland. Piantoni's left-wing partnership, for Reims and France, with outside-left Jean Vincent was famed throughout the continent.

Silvio Piola

Born: September 29, 1913, Italy.
Clubs: Pro Vercelli, Lazio, Torino, Juventus, Novara.

Piola was a tall, strong, athletic, aggressive center-forward who scored 30 goals in 24 internationals between his debut against Austria in 1935 – when Piola scored both Italy's goals in a 2–0 win – and his last game, a 1–1 draw against England in 1952. Piola, a World Cup-winner in 1938 when he scored twice in the 4–2 Final defeat of Hungary, would have collected even more goals and won more caps

had it not been for the war years. As it was he played on until he was 43 in a prolific career which included his fair share of controversy – such as the goal he later admitted he punched against England, nearly 50 years before Maradona's Hand of God repetition. Piola scored six goals in Pro Vercelli's 7–2 win over Fiorentina in 1933–34.

Pirri (full name: Jose Martinez Sanchez)

Born: March 11, 1945, Spain.
Club: Real Madrid.

Pirri epitomized the spirit of Spanish soccer during his 15 extraordinary years with Real Madrid between 1964 and 1979. He began as a goal-grabbing inside-forward, then shifted back successively to midfielder and central defender in a glittering career which brought honors flooding in – eight Spanish championships, three Spanish cups and the European Cup in 1966. Pirri played 44 times for Spain between 1966 and 1978 and was twice selected for Europe XIs, first against Benfica in 1970, then against South America in 1973. After retiring, Pirri completed his studies to qualify as a doctor and was appointed to the Real Madrid medical staff.

Frantisek Planicka

Born: June 2, 1904, Czechoslovakia.
Clubs: Slovan Prague, Bubenec, Slavia Prague.

Planicka was Central Europe's finest goalkeeper of the 1930s, a great personality as well as an outstanding and courageous player in the World Cups of both 1934 – when Czechoslovakia lost the Final 2–1 to Italy – and 1938. In the latter competition, long before the days of substitutes, Planicka played the last half of the quarter-final draw against Brazil despite the pain of a broken arm. Planicka won more honors than almost anyone in the history of the Czechoslovak game. He was a domestic league champion nine times with the great Slavia club, and won the cup six times and the Mitropa Cup – forerunner of today's European club competitions – in 1938. Planicka played 74 times for his country between 1925 and 1938.

Michel Platini

Born: June 21, 1955, France.
Clubs: Nancy-Lorraine, Saint-Etienne (Fr), Juventus (It).

Platini was the greatest achiever in international soccer in the early 1980s. He first appeared on the international stage at the 1976 Olympic Games in Montreal, and two years later, at his first World Cup in Argentina, gave an indication of the great things to come. In 1982 Platini inspired France to fourth place at the World Cup when he was man of the match in the dramatic semi-final defeat by West Germany in Seville. After the finals Platini was sold to Juventus, with whom he was three times the Italian league's top scorer. He also converted the penalty kick which brought "Juve" their long-awaited European Cup victory in 1985 (albeit overshadowed by the Heysel tragedy). After retiring, Platini concentrated on commercial interests and TV work until he was persuaded to become national manager and took France to the finals of the 1992 European Championship. France disappointed, and Platini left the job to become joint head of the team set up by the French federation to organize the 1998 World Cup.

Ernst Pol

Born: November 3, 1932, Poland.
Clubs: Legia Warsaw, Gornik Zabrze.

Pol was the first great Polish soccer player of the post-war era. He played center- or inside-forward and scored 40 goals in 49 internationals – then a Polish record – between 1950 and 1966. He was a complete player, with ball-control, good passing and tactical ability and an accurate shot. Pol won the Polish championship twice with the army club Legia, then five times with Gornik, the Silesian miners' club. He once scored five goals in an international against Tunisia in 1960, and had the consolation of scoring a marvellous individual strike for Gornik in their 8–1 thrashing by Tottenham in the European Cup in 1961. It was Pol's ill fortune that eastern European players were not allowed transfers to the professional west. His total of 186 Polish league goals stood as a record for 20 years.

Ferenc Puskas

see Legends (page 84)

Helmut Rahn

Born: August 16, 1929, West Germany.
Clubs: Altenessen, Olde 09, Sportfreunde Katernberg, Rot-Weiss Essen, Köln (W Ger), Enschede (Hol), Meiderich SV Duisburg (W Ger).

Rahn was anything but a typical outside-right, being heavily built and tall, but his power carried him through many a defence and his right-foot shot was ferocious. Hungary discovered this to their cost in the 1954 World Cup Final, when Rahn struck the equalizer at 2–2 and then the winner with only eight minutes remaining. Yet Rahn, "enfant terrible" of the German game, might not have even been in Europe: shortly before the finals he had been on a South American tour with Rot-Weiss and was in negotiations with Nacional of Uruguay when national coach Sepp Herberger sent a telegram to summon him home. In 1958 Rahn was far from either his best form or his best playing weight, and could not repeat his World Cup feats. Altogether he scored 21 goals in 40 internationals.

Antonio Ubaldo Rattin

Born: May 16, 1937, Argentina.
Club: Boca Juniors.

Rattin was a midfield pillar with club and country in the 1950s and 1960s. He made his league debut in 1956 and played 14 inspiring seasons with Boca Juniors, setting a club record of 357 league appearances and winning five championships. Rattin was also a key figure in the Boca side – along with Silvio Marzolini and Angel Rojas – which lost narrowly to Pele's Santos in the final of the South American club cup in 1963. Born in the Tigre delta outside Buenos Aires, Rattin played 37 times for Argentina. His most unfortunate game is, however, the one for which he is best remembered. This was the 1966 World Cup quarter-final against England at Wembley, when Rattin's refusal to accept expulsion by German referee Kreitlein very nearly provoked a walk-off by the entire Argentine team. Rattin always insisted he was an innocent victim of dark circumstances.

Thomas Ravelli

Born: August 13, 1959, Sweden.
Clubs: Oster Vaxjo, IFK Gothenburg, Tampa Bay (US).

Ravelli and twin brother Andreas, a midfielder, are both internationals, but Thomas has been by far the most successful – with a world record number of 138 caps. Ravelli's parents emigrated to Sweden from Austria, and Thomas made his reputation with Oster Vaxjo. In 1989 he joined IFK Gothenburg, Sweden's leading club, as successor to Tottenham Hotspur-bound Erik Thorstvedt. Early in his career, Ravelli's temperament was considered suspect: for example, he was sent off for dissent during a 2–0 defeat in Mexico in November 1983. Ravelli learned his lesson to inspire Sweden to reach the semi-finals of both the European Championship in 1992 and, two years later, the World Cup. In June 1995 he overtook Peter Shilton's record of 125 international caps, although he has failed to achieve his ambition of playing his club soccer outside Sweden.

MICHEL PLATINI *More successful as France's captain than manager*

Frank Rijkaard

Born: September 30, 1962, Holland.
Clubs: Ajax (Hol), Sporting (Port), Zaragoza (Sp), Milan (It), Ajax (Hol).

Rijkaard has been one of the most universally-admired and versatile players over the past decade at both club and international level. He turned professional under Johan Cruyff at Ajax in 1979 and made his Holland debut at 19 despite Ajax protests that he was "too young." In 1987 Rijkaard fell out with Cruyff and had brief spells in Portugal and Spain before committing the key years of his career to Milan with

whom he won the World Club Cup and the European Cup twice apiece. Rijkaard played in midfield for Milan, but usually in central defense for Holland, with whom he won the 1988 European Championship. Following Milan's defeat by Marseille in the 1993 European Cup Final he returned to Ajax, and was a vital member of their victorious 1995 European Cup and Dutch title-winning teams, after which he retired.

Luigi "Gigi" Riva

Born: November 7, 1944, Italy.
Club: Cagliari.

Riva is remembered as one of the finest strikers in Italian soccer history. Orphaned in early childhood, he made a teenage reputation with Third Division Legnano as a left-winger and was signed

RAVELLI *World record international*

by Second Division Sardinian club Cagliari in 1963. Riva's formidable left foot and nose for goal sent Cagliari rocketing out of the shadows to league championship success in 1970. Riva was top league marksman three times, including the 1969–70 season when he scored 21 goals in 28 games. His 35 goals in 42 internationals meant Riva bore much of the responsibility for Italy's World Cup challenge in 1970. He scored three times in the quarter- and semi-final defeats of Mexico and West Germany before Italy's defeat in

the Final. Complications stemming from two broken legs ultimately enforced a premature retirement.

Roberto Rivelino

Born: January 1, 1946, Brazil.
Clubs: Corinthians, Fluminense.

Rivelino was originally the deeply-lying left-winger who filled the Zagalo role in Brazil's 1970 World Cup-winning side. He was not particularly quick, but was possessed of a super technique which made him a perpetual danger with his banana-bending of free-kicks and corners. Rivelino later moved

RIJKAARD *One of the greats*

into center midfield and was influential in the third-place finish of 1978. Rivelino is credited unofficially with the fastest goal in soccer history: scored in three seconds with a shot from the starting pass after he noticed the opposing goalkeeper still concentrating on his pre-match prayers.

Gianni Rivera

Born: August 18, 1943, Italy.
Clubs: Alessandria, Milan.

The "Bambino d'Oro," the Golden Boy: that was Rivera in the early 1960s. As a creative inside-forward, he had the lot: skill, pace and a deft shot, plus the rare natural gift of grace. Rivera in full flight was soccer poetry in motion. Milan paid Alessandria a huge fee for a half-share in the 15-year-old Rivera and signed him "for real" in 1960. In 16 years with the "Rossoneri" he was twice a winner of the World Club Cup, the European Cup and the Italian league, as well as three times an Italian cup-winner and once European Footballer of the Year, in 1969. Rivera became a controversial figure, however, as successive national managers struggled to build teams around him. Thus he played only the last six minutes of the 1970 World Cup Final – although his Italy career produced 14 goals in 60 games. On retiring Rivera turned to politics and became a member of the Italian parliament.

Bryan Robson

Born: January 11, 1957, England.

Clubs: West Bromwich, Manchester United, Middlesbrough.

A considerable part of English soccer in the 1980s was played to the accompaniment of breaking bones, many of them Bryan Robson's. Despite his season ticket to the surgery he won an impressive list of honors, with 90 caps (often as captain), three FA Cup medals, European Cup-winners' Cup in 1991, and inaugural Premier League championship in 1992–93. Robson was an inspiring, driving force in midfield and a believer in the value of an early strike: three of his England goals were in the first minute. He broke a leg twice as a teenager with West Bromwich, and then broke the transfer fee record when Manchester United bought him for £1.5 million. He moved into management in 1994, immediately leading Middlesbrough into the Premier League.

Pedro Rocha

Born: December 3, 1942, Uruguay.
Clubs: Penarol (Uru), São Paulo (Br).

Rocha was far removed from the typical image of angry, temperamental Uruguayans. A statuesque inside-left of great skill to match his height, he was surprisingly quick and soon became a local hero after joining mighty Penarol of Montevideo at 17. Seven times in the next nine seasons Rocha was a champion of Uruguay, and he inspired Penarol to victory both home and away over Real Madrid in the 1966 World Club Cup final. He captained Uruguay into the 1970 World Cup finals but was injured in the first match. Fit again, he moved to Brazil and led São Paulo to victory in the Paulista state championship in his debut season. Rocha won 62 caps for Uruguay.

Romario da Souza Faria

Born: 29 January, 1966, Brazil.
Clubs: Vasco da Gama (Br), PSV Eindhoven (Hol), Barcelona (Sp), Flamengo (Bra), Valencia (Sp), Flamengo (Bra).

Romario has been arguably the finest attacker in the world game in the 1990s. Discovered by Vasco da Gama, he was still a teenager when he began to establish a reputation for controversy after being banished from Brazil's World Youth Cup

BRYAN ROBSON *Manchester United and England's often injured captain*

squad for flouting a hotel curfew. After starring at the 1988 Seoul Olympics, he transferred to PSV Eindhoven. There he clashed with coaches and teammates, yet still totaled 98 league goals in five seasons to earn a $4.8 million sale to Barcelona in the summer of 1993. Simultaneously, he was recalled for USA'94 by Brazil after almost a year in the wilderness. Romario scored five crucial goals and followed Brazil's World Cup triumph by returning home to Flamengo.

Ronaldo (full name: Ronaldo Luiz Nazario da Lima)

Born: September 22, 1976, Brazil.
Clubs: Sao Cristovao, Cruzeiro (Br), PSV (Hol), Barcelona (Sp), Inter (Ita).

Ronaldo has been the most talked about player in Europe in the 1990s – a status underlined by his award as the 1996 and 1997 FIFA Player of the Year. He was compared favorably with Pele at his age by the likes of past Brazilian heroes as Zico and Tostao. Ronaldo grew up in a working class district of Rio. He failed a trial with Flamengo but was signed by minor club Sao Cristovao where his potential was discovered by 1970 World Cup star Jairzinho – who then sold Ronaldo on to Cruzeiro of Belo Horizonte. In his first year he scored 54 goals in 54 games. Ronaldo then moved to PSV Eindhoven and joined Barcelona in 1996 for $20 million. He ended his first season in Spain as the league's top scorer with 34 goals. He was on the bench when Brazil won the 1994 World Cup, but scored four goals in

France '98 as Brazil reached the final, losing to France. But he was also the center of controversy after playing in the final despite being unfit, hav-

PAOLO ROSSI *Stranger than fiction*

ing suffered a convulsive fit before the game.

Paolo Rossi

Born: September 23, 1956, Italy.
Clubs: Prato, Juventus, Como, Lanerossi Vicenza, Perugia, Juventus, Milan.

Paolo Rossi's story is more fantastic than fiction. As a teenager Juventus gave him away because of knee trouble. Later, when they tried to buy him back, they were outbid by provincial Perugia, who paid a world record $5.5 million. Rossi, a star already at the 1978 World Cup, was then banned for two years for alleged involvement in a betting-and-bribes scandal. Juventus finally got him back, but he was only three matches out of his ban when Italy took him to the 1982 World Cup finals, where he top-scored with six goals and collected a winner's medal from the Final victory over West Germany. Rossi was only 29 when he retired into legend.

Karl-Heinz Rummenigge

Born: September 25, 1955, West Germany.
Clubs: Lippstadt, Bayern Munich (W Ger), Internazionale (It), Servette (Swz).

Rummenigge was one of the great bargains of German soccer. Bayern Munich paid Lippstadt just $7,000 for their young, blond right-winger in 1974 and sold him to Italy a decade later for more than $3 million. In between Rummenigge had won the

RUMMENIGGE *Twice best in Europe*

World Club championship and the European Cup and had twice been hailed as European Footballer of the Year. The former bank clerk, who first impressed Internazionale officials with a World Cup hat-trick against Mexico in 1978, developed

into a central striker, as his career progressed. Injuries reduced his effectiveness in the early 1980s, and controversy lingered over whether national manager Jupp Derwall was right to play his injured captain from the start in the 1982 World Cup Final defeat by Italy.

Ian Rush

Born October 20, 1961, Wales.
Clubs: Chester, Liverpool (Eng), Juventus (It), Liverpool, Leeds, Newcastle

Rush was the goal-scorer supreme in modern British soccer, but he would have been a great player even if he had never hit a net. His off-the-ball running and excellent passing were bonuses to go with his acutely developed finishing ability. Rush was only 18 when Liverpool had to pay $500,000 to get him, but the fee was repaid many times over. In two spells at Anfield, interrupted by a none-too-happy Italian adventure, he broke scoring records for club, country and FA Cup Finals (five goals in three winning appearances), with medals for five league titles and four League Cups as well. Released on a free transfer in 1996, he was snapped up by Leeds and later Newcastle Utd.

IAN RUSH *One of the great bargains, at $500,000 from Chester*

Hugo Sanchez

Born: June 11, 1958, Mexico.
Clubs: UNAM (Mex), Atletico Madrid, Real Madrid (Sp), America (Mex), Rayo Vallecano (Sp).

Hugo Sanchez was top league goalscorer in Spain five seasons in a row in the late 1980s and early 1990s. His 230-plus goals in Spain left him second overall behind Bilbao's Telmo Zarra and underlined his claim to be considered one of the great strikers of the modern game. Each one of Sanchez's goals was followed by a celebratory somersault, taught him originally by a sister who was a gymnast in Mexico's team for the 1976 Olympics in Montreal – at which Hugo made his debut on the international stage. Despite a World Cup finals debut as far back as 1978, Sanchez totalled only around 50 games for Mexico – his many absences caused either by club commitments in Spain or by disputes with Mexican soccer bureaucracy.

Leonel Sanchez

Born: April 25, 1936, Chile.
Club: Universidad de Chile.

Leonel Sanchez was the outstanding left-winger in South America in the late 1950s and early 1960s. He was perhaps neither as fast as Pepe of Brazil, nor as intelligent a player as another famous Brazilian, Zagalo, but he was certainly much more forceful when it came to making his presence felt in the penalty box. Sanchez was a star of the Chilean side which finished third as hosts in the 1962 World Cup, but he also featured in controversy: earlier in the tournament he somehow escaped punishment from the match referee for a punch which flattened Humberto Maschio in the so-called Battle of Santiago against Italy. Sanchez played 106 times for Chile, though only 62 of those appearances may be counted as full internationals. He was seven times national champion with "U," his only club.

José Emilio Santamaria

Born: July 31, 1929, Uruguay
Clubs: Nacional (Uru), Real Madrid (Sp).

Santamaria was a ruthless centerback whose finest years were spent at Real Madrid in the 1950s and early 1960s, closing down the defensive gaps left by great attacking colleagues such as Di Stefano, Puskas and Gento. Santamaria was first called up at 20 by Uruguay but missed the 1950 World Cup finals because his club, Nacional, refused to let him accept the inside-forward spot allocated to him in the squad bound for Brazil. Four years later Santamaria was one of the stars of the 1954 World Cup, this time in his traditional place in the center of defense. Madrid brought him to Europe in 1957 and, having played 35 times for Uruguay, he collected another 17 caps in the service of Spain, including the 1962 World Cup. He was a World Club championship and triple European Cup winner with Real Madrid and later managed hosts Spain at the 1982 World Cup finals.

Djalma Santos

Born: February 27, 1929, Brazil.
Clubs: Portuguesa, Palmeiras, Atletico Curitiba.

Djalma Santos is considered a cornerstone of the Brazil side which won the World Cup in 1958 and 1962 and lost it in 1966. Yet, in Sweden in 1958, he was brought in only for the

DJALMA SANTOS *A great survivor who earned two World Cup winners' medals for Brazil*

GAETANO SCIREA *Skilled contrast to the rugged sweepers before him*

Final because manager Vicente Feola considered his acute soccer brain and positional sense would make him more effective against Swedish left-winger Skoglund than regular right-back Nilton Di Sordi. In due course he became the first Brazilian player to reach an official century of international appearances, though he was well past his best when – to his own surprise – he was recalled by Feola for the 1966 World Cup finals in England. He played for the World XI against England in 1963 in the match which celebrated the 100th anniversary of the FA.

Nilton Santos

Born: May 16, 1927, Brazil.
Club: Botafogo.

Nilton Santos was a left-back and, though no relation to Brazil partner Djalma Santos, equally outstanding. Nilton Santos played 83 times for his country between 1949 and 1963, having made his Brazil debut just a year after signing for his only club, Botafogo of Rio. He loved nothing more than powering forward in support of attack, a tactic which surprised the opposition and owed everything to the new free-dom afforded "wing backs" by the advent of 4–2–4. Santos was a World Cup-winner in 1958 and 1962 and was immensely respected by teammates and officials. He led the player delegation which, in Sweden in 1958, crucially persuaded coach Vicente Feola to call up his Botafogo teammate, the match-winning right-winger Garrincha.

Gyorgy Sarosi

Born: September 12, 1912, Hungary.
Club: Ferencvaros TC (Hun).

Sarosi, one of the world's greatest soccer players between the wars, died in 1993 in his adopted home of Genoa, Italy, aged 81. Sarosi was born in Budapest, where he duly played both at center-forward and center-half for FTC (Ferencvaros), scoring 349 goals in 383 games. He won the Hungarian championship eight times, the cup once and the Mitropa Cup once. In internationals Sarosi scored 42 goals in 75 appearances, and captained Hungary to the 1938 World Cup Final. Doctor, lawyer and magistrate, he made his debut for Hungary in a 3–2 defeat by Italy in Turin in November, 1931. When the Communists took over in Hungary in 1947, Sarosi fled to Italy, where he coached Padova, Lucchese, Bari, Juventus (winners of the 1952 championship), Genoa, Roma, Bologna and Brescia. He also coached Lugano in Switzerland.

Hector Scarone

Born: June 21, 1898, Uruguay.
Clubs: Sportsman, Nacional (Uru), Barcelona(Sp), Ambrosiana-Internazionale, Palermo (It).

Scarone was Uruguay's inspiring inside-forward in their greatest era of the 1920s and early 1930s. He won the Olympic gold medals in Paris in 1924 and in Amsterdam in 1928 – in between playing in Spain for Barcelona – and was top scorer at both the 1926 and 1927 South American Championships. He then led Uruguay to victory at the inaugural World Cup finals on home soil in Montevideo in 1930. Inevitably, his talents drew more offers from Europe, but he insisted on waiting until after that World Cup before returning, this time to Italy with Ambrosiana-Inter. Later he went back to Spain in the early 1950s as coach to Real Madrid before making a playing comeback in Uruguay with Nacional and retiring finally at 55 – a South American and probably a world record.

Juan Alberto Schiaffino

Born: July 28, 1925, Uruguay.
Clubs: Penarol (Uru), Milan, Roma (It).

"Pepe" Schiaffino always wanted, as a boy, to play center-forward, but youth coaches with Penarol of Montevideo, his first club, considered him too thin and fragile. They switched him to inside-forward and, at 20, he was playing for Uruguay at the South American Championship and top-scoring with 19 goals in Penarol's league-winning side. In World Cup terms, Schiaffino peaked in 1950 when he scored Uruguay's equalizer at 1–1 on the way to their shock victory over Brazil. After starring again at the finals in 1954, he was sold to Milan for a world record transfer fee, and is regarded as one of the

DARTING IN *Two Uruguayans can't stop Uwe Seeler getting in a header*

ENZO SCIFO *A mixture of loyalties between soccer in Belgium, Italy and France*

greatest players ever to have graced *Calcio*. He wound down his career with Roma, after narrowly failing to lead Milan to victory over Real Madrid in the 1958 European Cup Final, when, despite Schiaffino's fine solo goal, they lost 3–2.

Peter Schmeichel

Born: November 18, 1963, Denmark.
Clubs: Hvidovre, Brondbyerenes (Den), Manchester United (Eng).

Schmeichel very nearly came to England in 1987, after Newcastle sent spies to watch him. Although he was then considered too inexperienced for the English First Division, Manchester United landed a bargain when they bought him for $1.2 million in 1991. Later, he was one of the heroes in Denmark's astonishing triumph at the 1992 European Championship finals in Sweden. Schmeichel's saves at crucial moments against Holland in the semi-final and Germany in the Final helped secure him the accolade of the world's Best Goalkeeper. He won the English league and Cup "double" in 1994 and 1996 and the fabulous "treble" – adding European Cup glory in 1999.

Karl-Heinz Schnellinger

Born: March 31, 1939, West Germany.
Clubs: Duren, Köln (W Ger), Mantova, Roma, Milan (It).

Schnellinger, a left-back who later played in most other defensive positions, was to be found at the heart of the international action throughout the 1960s. He stood out not merely for his blond hair and bulky frame but for his power, pace and will to win. He made his World Cup finals debut at 19 in Sweden and was a key member of the West German sides which reached the quarter-finals (1962), the Final (1966) and third place (1970) over the next 12 years. His injury-time goal in the 1970 semi-final with Italy, which forced extra time, typified his fighting spirit. Roma took him to Italy but had to sell him to Milan to overcome a cash crisis. Their loss was Milan's gain as Schnellinger's steel lifted them to victory in the 1969 European Cup. This was the peak of a career which also earned success in the German and Italian championships and the Italian cup, three selections for World XIs and four for Europe Selects. He was West German Footballer of the Year in 1962.

Vincenzo "Enzo" Scifo

Born: February 19, 1966, Belgium.
Clubs: Anderlecht (Bel), Internazionale (It), Bordeaux, Auxerre (Fr), Torino (It), Monaco (Fr), Anderlecht (Bel).

Born in Belgium of Italian parents, Scifo joined Anderlecht as a teen-ager after scoring hatfuls of goals at junior level for La Louvière. In 1984 he chose to take up Belgian citizenship just in time to play for his country at the finals of the European Championship in France. His Latin technique and vision earned an almost instant transfer to Italy, but he was really too inexperienced to cope with the challenge of running Inter's midfield. A spell in France and appearances at the 1986 and 1990 World Cups (and later the 1998 finals, too) revived Italian interest and he joined Torino but, after Scifo schemed them to the 1992 UEFA Cup Final, he was sold to Monaco.

Gaetano Scirea

Born: May 25, 1953, Italy.
Clubs: Atalanta, Juventus.

Scirea was "the sweeper with charm," a skilled, graceful performer very different to the sort of ruthless "killers" employed by many Italian clubs in the 1960s and 1970s. Scirea began with Atalanta as an inside-forward and later became the defensive cornerstone of the all-conquering Juventus side of the 1980s. His central defensive partnership with Claudio Gentile was one of the most effective in the international game, as they proved at the heart of Italy's World Cup-winning defense in Spain in 1982. Scirea's sustained brilliance – he was seven times Italian champion with Juventus in 11 years – long thwarted the international ambitions of Milan's Franco Baresi. Sadly, soon after retiring, he was killed in a car crash in Poland while on a scouting mission for Juventus.

Uwe Seeler

Born: November 5, 1936, West Germany.
Club: Hamburg.

Seeler, son of a former Hamburg player, was so much the central figure in West German soccer in the 1960s and early 1970s that the fans used his name – "Uwe, Uwe" – as their chant at international matches. He made his full senior debut in a 3–1 defeat by England at Wembley in 1954 when still only 18. Seeler captained West Germany in their World Cup Final defeat at Wembley in 1966, but gained a measure of revenge by scoring a remarkable back-headed goal when Germany won 3–2 in extra time in the dramatic 1970 quarter-final. He scored 43 goals in 72 internationals: he and Pele are the only men to score in four World Cups. Seeler played for Hamburg throughout his career from 1952 to 1971, loyally rejecting a string of offers from Italy and Spain.

Alan Shearer

Born: August 13, 1970, England.
Clubs: Southampton, Blackburn Rovers, Newcastle United (Eng).

Shearer became the heir-apparent to Gary Lineker as England's top international marksman when he scored a record 13 goals in 11 matches for the under-21s and then collected a superb goal on his senior national team debut against France at Wembley in February 1992. Unfortunately, a serious knee injury cost Shearer a place alongside Lineker in England's attack at the European Championship finals in 1992. That same summer Blackburn signed Shearer for $5 million. He was their joint top scorer with 22 goals in his first season at Ewood Park. The top scorer at Euro 96 with five goals, Shearer was transferred to Newcastle in 1996 for $23 million. An horrific ankle injury disrupted much of 1997, but he captained England in the 1998 World Cup finals, scoring twice.

Peter Shilton

Born: September 18, 1949, England.
Clubs: Leicester, Stoke, Nottingham Forest, Southampton, Derby, Plymouth, Bolton Wanderers, West Ham United.

Shilton was only 20 when first capped, and nearly 41 when he made his 125th and last appearance for England, during the 1990 World Cup. That was his 17th game in such competitions, a record for a Briton. He conceded only 80 international goals, every one of them a dreadful blow to such a perfectionist. Shilton's awesome pursuit of personal fitness and elimination of error were renowned throughout the game. He played in an FA Cup Final with Leicester, who lost, when he was 19, but never appeared in another. Only with his move to Forest, and their brief dominance of England and Europe, did club honors flow. He played on well into his 40s, after entering management for a controversial spell with Plymouth.

Nikita Simonian

Born: October 12, 1926, Soviet Union.
Clubs: Kirilia Sovietov, Moscow Spartak.

Simonian, one of the few Armenian soccer players to have succeeded in the Soviet game, was small for a center-forward but skilful and quick – talents which brought him a then record 142 goals in 265 league matches in the 1950s. Three times he was leading scorer in the Soviet Supreme league, and his 1950 haul of 34 goals set a record that was not overtaken until the emergence of Oleg Protasov in the 1980s. Simonian began his career on Georgia's Black Sea coast, moved to Moscow with Kirilia Sovietov, or "Wings of the Soviet," and, three years later in 1949, joined Spartak. He won the league four times and the cup twice, and scored 12 goals in 23 internationals before retiring. Later he was coach to Spartak, then joint manager of the Soviet national team at the 1982 World Cup Finals in Spain.

SKUHRAVY *Outpaces Austrian defender Pecl in the 1990 World Cup*

Agne Simonsson

Born: October 19, 1935, Sweden.
Clubs: Orgryte (Swe), Real Madrid, Real Sociedad (Sp), Orgryte (Swe).

The Swedish team which reached the 1958 World Cup Final on home soil leaned heavily on foreign-based veterans but they, in turn, depended for the injection of a decisive attacking edge on Simonsson, the splendid center-forward from the Gothenburg club of Orgryte. Simonsson enhanced his reputation by leading Sweden to victory over England at Wembley in 1959 and was signed the following summer by Real Madrid. They envisaged Simonsson becoming the successor to the ageing Alfredo Di Stefano, but Simonsson failed to adjust to life and soccer in Spain and, in any case, Di Stefano was not ready to go. After a spell with Real Sociedad, Simonsson returned to Orgryte and played again for Sweden, but never quite recovered his earlier spark.

Matthias Sindelar

Born: February 18, 1903, Austria.
Clubs: FC Hertha Vienna, FK Austria.

Nicknamed "the Man of Paper," for his slim build, Sindelar was the very spirit of the Austrian "Wunderteam" of the 1930s as well as their center-forward and attacking leader. Born and brought up in Kozlau, in Czechoslovakia, he was discovered by a minor Viennese club, Hertha, in 1920, and joined neighboring giants FK Austria a year later. Twice he won the Mitropa Cup – the interwar forerunner of the European Cup

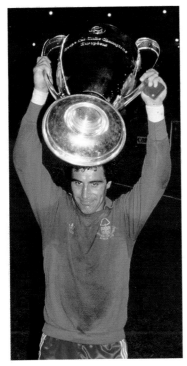

SHILTON *European Cup-winner*

– with FK Austria in the 1930s and added 27 goals in 43 internationals to his list of honors. Those 27 included two hat-tricks against old rivals Hungary in 1928 and the two goals which beat Italy in the newly-built Prater Stadium in Vienna in 1932. Sindelar scored in both Austria's classic matches against England in 1932 and 1936 and led Austria to the World Cup semi-finals of 1934. Depressed by the 1938 Anschluss, when Austria was swallowed up into Hilter's Greater Germany, he and his girlfriend committed suicide together in January, 1939.

Omar Enrique Sivori

Born: October 2, 1935, Argentina.
Clubs: River Plate (Arg), Juventus, Napoli (It).

Sivori was nicknamed "Cabezon" – Big Head – by his admirers in Argentina and Italy, because his technical virtuosity prompted him to humiliate and embarrass opposing defenders in the most outrageous ways. An inside-left with great talent and a quick temper, Sivori put fire into the Juventus attack of the late 1950s alongside the coolness of John Charles and the experience of veteran Giampiero Boniperti. He cost Juventus a then world record fee and repaid them with 144 goals in eight seasons before falling out with Paraguayan coach Heriberto Herrera and sulking off to Napoli, where his partnership with Milan outcast José Altafini produced the sort of fervour seen in the 1980s for Maradona. Sivori played 18 times for Argentina, as well as nine times for Italy, and was European Footballer of the Year in 1961.

Tomas Skuhravy

Born: September 7, 1965, Czechoslovakia.
Clubs: Sparta Prague (Cz), Genoa (It), Sporting Lisbon (Por), Genoa.

Tall, gangling Skuhravy earned instant acclaim when he opened up his 1990 World Cup finals campaign by scoring a hat-trick in the Czechoslovaks' 5–1 defeat of the United States. He finished the tournament as second-top scorer, with five goals, behind Toto Schillaci and with a lucrative new contract from Genoa in his pocket.

Skuhravy's partnership there with the Uruguayan, Carlos Aguilera, brought Genoa a measure of success in the league and the UEFA Cup before a succession of injuries took their toll. Skuhravy, who invested his money in an old prince's castle in Italy, always insisted that he would have preferred to star in Formula One motor racing rather than in soccer.

Graeme Souness

Born: May 6, 1953, Scotland.
Clubs: Tottenham, Middlesbrough, Liverpool (Eng), Sampdoria (It), Rangers (Scot).

Souness walked out of Spurs without playing in the first team in a League game, though he did appear for them in a European tie in Iceland. Even as a teenager, he was a player who knew his own value. He developed into a world-class midfielder, winning 54 caps and a string of honors with Liverpool, where he was an influential player and captain. Despite his abrasive style, he then became a great favorite with Sampdoria in Italy, but returned to become player-manager of Rangers. His huge spending ensured a string of titles for the club in the small arena of Scottish soccer, but he was less successful after his return to Anfield, where he succeeded his old friend Kenny Dalglish as Liverpool manager, and he lasted less than three seasons.

Neville Southall

Born: September 16, 1958, Wales.
Clubs: Bury, Everton, Port Vale (on loan), Everton (Eng).

A fiery character, Southall played Welsh League soccer at 14 and worked as a dish-washer, brick-layer and garbage man before joining Bury. He was then 21, and shortly afterwards was signed by Everton. A moderate start and a brief loan period were forgotten after his return, when he suddenly hit the form that established him as one of the world's top goalkeepers. He won two championship medals, two FA Cups, and one European Cup-winners' Cup medal, and was voted Footballer of the Year in 1985. After passing the Welsh record of 73 caps, ironically he made an expensive error in the defeat that prevented his country from qualifying for the 1994 World Cup.

STOICHKOV *Specially recommended to Barcelona by Johan Cruyff*

Jürgen Sparwasser

Born: June 14, 1948, East Germany.
Club: Magdeburg.

Sparwasser was one of the few outstanding players produced by East Germany in its 40 years of independent soccer existence. Sweeper Hans-Jürgen Dorner and center-forward Joachim Streich both earned a century of caps, but the most memorable achievement fell to Sparwasser at the 1974 World Cup finals. An excellent attacking midfield player, Sparwasser scored the historic goal in Hamburg which beat World Cup hosts West Germany in the first and last meeting between the two states at international level. Sparwasser's career featured 15 goals in 77 internationals and a European Cup-winners' Cup medal after Magdeburg's victory over Milan in Rotterdam in 1974. Later he fled East Germany by taking advantage of his selection for a veterans' tournament in West Germany.

Pedro Alberto Spencer

Born: 1937, Ecuador.
Clubs: Everest (Ecu), Penarol (Uru), Barcelona Guayaquil (Ecu).

Spencer is probably the greatest Ecuadorian player of all time. He scored a record 50-plus goals in the South American club cup (Copa Libertadores), though all in the service of the Uruguayan club, Penarol, who dominated the event's early years in the 1960s. Spencer helped Penarol win the World Club Cup in 1961 and 1966 and earned such status on the field that, with his business interests, he was created Ecuadorian consul in Montevideo. Uruguayan officials so coveted Spencer's talents that he was called up to lead Uruguay's attack against England at Wembley in 1964, and scored their only goal in a 2–1 defeat. But protests from Ecuador and other South American nations ensured that this remained his one and only appearance for the "Celeste."

Hristo Stoichkov

Born: August 2, 1966, Bulgaria.
Clubs: CSKA Sofia (Bul), Barcelona (Sp), Parma (It), Barcelona (Sp), CSKA (Bul), Kawisa Reysol (Jpn).

Stoichkov built a reputation as one of Europe's finest marksmen since being reprieved from a six-month suspension after a controversial Bulgarian cup final between his army team, CSKA, and old Sofia rivals Levski-Spartak in 1985. Stoichkov then so impressed Barcelona they bought him for a Bulgarian record $3 million in 1990. Stoichkov rewarded coach Johan Cruyff's personal recommendation by scoring more than 60 goals in his first three seasons in league and European competition for the Catalan giants. He also led them to their long-awaited European Cup victory in 1992 and was the inspiration for Bulgaria's fourth place in the 1994 World Cup. He was European Footballer of the Year in 1994 and also played, with little impact, in the 1998 World Cup finals in France.

Luis Suarez

Born: May 2, 1935, Spain.
Clubs: Deportivo de La Coruna, Barcelona (Sp), Internazionale, Sampdoria (It).

Suarez was born and brought up in La Coruña, where he was discovered by Barcelona. The Catalans insisted on buying him immediately after he had earned a standing ovation in their own Nou Camp stadium, playing against them at 18 in 1953. Suarez was hailed as the greatest Spanish player of all time, a midfield general who was later the fulcrum of the Internazionale team which dominated world club soccer in the mid-1960s. Suarez's ability to transition defence into attack with one pinpoint pass suited Inter's hit-and-hold tactics admirably. Injury, significantly, prevented Suarez lining up against Celtic when Inter lost the 1967 European Cup Final in Lisbon. Later Suarez managed Spain at the 1990 World Cup finals.

Frank Swift

Born: December 26, 1913, England. *Club:* Manchester City.

Big Frank was a personality among goalkeepers, who enjoyed a joke with opponents and referees, but

SAFE KEEPING *Neville Southall, long-serving keeper for Everton and Wales*

was deadly serious at stopping shots. He stood in the crowd and watched Manchester City lose the 1933 FA Cup Final, then played for them when they won a year later, fainting at the finish as nervous exhaustion overcame him. During the war his entertainment value became even greater, and he won 19 caps while in his 30s – only twice on the losing side. After his retirement he became a journalist, and was one of those killed in the Munich air crash in 1958.

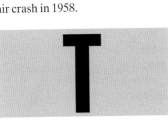

T

Marco Tardelli

Born: September 24, 1954, Italy.
Clubs: Pisa, Como, Juventus, Internazionale.

Tardelli was a utility defender or midfielder who was seen to best effect playing for Juventus and Italy in the first half of the 1980s. With both club and country Tardelli succeeded the more physical Romeo Benetti in midfield, though his Azzurri debut, against Portugal in Turin in 1976, was at right back. Tardelli is one of the very few players to have won every major prize in the modern domestic and European game, from the World Cup to the 1985 European Cup with Juventus. He scored six goals in 81 appearances for Italy and was voted official Man of the Match in the 1982 World Cup Final defeat of West Germany in Madrid.

Tostao (full name: Eduardo Goncalves Andrade)

Born: January 25, 1947, Brazil.
Clubs: Cruzeiro, Vasco da Gama.

Tostao, a small, nimble center-forward, was already nicknamed "the White Pele" when he made his World Cup debut for Brazil at the

MARCO TARDELLI
One of the elite few who have won a World Cup-winner's medal plus every major prize in European club soccer

1966 finals in England. He scored Brazil's consolation goal in their 3–1 defeat by Hungary. It nearly became his only World Cup appearance when, in 1969, he suffered a detached retina during a South American cup tie against Millonarios in Bogota. Tostao underwent specialist surgery in Houston and recovered to become one of the heroes of Brazil's World Cup victory in Mexico a year later. However Tostao, a qualified doctor, recognized that the longer he played on, the greater the risk of permanent injury, and retired at 26 in 1973 … to become an eye specialist.

V

Jorge Valdano

Born: October 4, 1955, Argentina.
Clubs: Newell's Old Boys (Arg), Alaves, Zaragoza, Real Madrid (Sp).

Valdano has proved a rare personality in the world game: an author, poet, polemicist, coach and World Cup-winning player. Born in Las Parejas, he left Argentina for political reasons as a teenager and built his playing career in Spain. His success in winning the UEFA Cup twice in the mid-1980s with Real Madrid earned him selection for Argentina, and his positional and tactical skills were massive influences in the 1986 World Cup victory in Mexico. Originally an outside-left, Valdano was converted by Argentine coach Carlos Bilardo into a roving link between midfield and attack. He was later struck down by hepatitis, struggled in vain to make a World Cup comeback in 1990 and retired to become a journalist, an analyst and a successful coach with Tenerife before going back to Real as coach.

Carlos Valderrama

Born: September 2, 1961, Colombia.
Clubs: Santa Marta, Millonarios, Atletico Nacional (Col), Montpellier (Fr), Valladolid (Sp), Medellin, Atletico Junior Barranquilla (Col), Tampa Bay Mutiny (US), Miami Fusion (US).

Carlos Valderrama was voted South American Footballer of the Year in 1987 after guiding Colombia to a fine third place at the Copa America. The combination of frizzy hairstyle and all-around skill earned him the nickname of "the South American Gullit," and he shared South American Cup glory with Atletico Nacional before trying his luck in Europe with Montpellier of France and Valladolid

VALDERRAMA *Compared to Gullit for both hairstyle and talent, Valderrama dances past a Bolivian opponent*

of Spain. He failed to impress, but played well as Colombia reached the second round of the 1990 World Cup finals and rediscovered his touch after returning to Colombia in 1992. He was South American Footballer of the Year in 1994, after masterminded Colombia's sensational 1994 World Cup qualifying campaign (including a 5-0 win over Argentina). And, at the age of 36, he also played in the 1998 World Cup finals in France.

VAN BASTEN *Cruyff's protégé*

Marco Van Basten

Born: October 31, 1964, Holland.
Clubs: Ajax Amsterdam (Hol), Milan (It).

Marco Van Basten contributed one of the all-time great international goals when he volleyed home a long, looping cross in the 1988 European Championship Final in Munich. That was Van Basten just reaching his peak, one year after graduating from Ajax Amsterdam to Milan. Tall and angular, Van Basten made his international debut at the 1983 World Youth Cup and scored 128 league goals for Ajax before joining Milan for a mere $2 million in 1987. With Ajax he had won the European Golden Boot (37 goals in 1985–86) and the European Cup-winners' Cup, but with Milan he added even more honors – including FIFA, World and European Player of the Year awards plus World Club and European Cup medals. Sadly, ankle trouble wrecked the latter years of his career.

Paul Van Himst

Born: October 2, 1943, Belgium.
Clubs: Anderlecht, RWD Molenbeek, Eendracht Aalst.

Van Himst, the manager who guided Belgium to the 1994 World Cup finals, is still regarded as his country's greatest player. He joined the Brussels club Anderlecht at the age of nine and, at 16, was playing center-forward in the first team. He was to be Belgian champion eight times, a cup-winner four times, league top scorer three times and was four times Footballer of the Year. Van Himst scored 31 goals in 81 internationals between 1960 and 1979, which included the 1970 World Cup finals and a third-place finish as hosts at the 1972 European Championship. Later he coached Anderlecht to victory in the UEFA Cup before being appointed manager of Belgium after the qualifying failure in the 1992 European Championship.

Odbulio Varela

Born: September 20, 1917, Uruguay.
Clubs: Wanderers, Penarol.

Varela was captain of the Uruguayan team which shocked Brazil by beating their hosts in Rio's Maracana stadium in the 1950 World Cup "Final" (the deciding match of the final pool). Varela was an old-style attacking center-half and a captain who led by example. He had made his league debut with Wanderers at 21 and had already played for Uruguay before joining local giants Penarol in

1942. Twice he won the South American Championship with Uruguay but the 1950 World Cup saw him at his zenith, driving his team forward with every confidence even after Uruguay went 1–0 down early on. Varela was outstanding again, even at 37, in the 1954 World Cup finals in Switzerland. He retired immediately afterwards and was briefly coach to Penarol.

Vava (full name: Edvaldo Izidio Neto)

Born: November 12, 1934, Brazil.
Clubs: Recife, Vasco da Gama (Br), Atletico Madrid (Sp), Palmeiras, Botafogo (Br).

Vava may not have been one of the most refined center-forwards in soccer history, but he was one of the most effective when it mattered. Originally an inside-left, Vava was switched to the center of attack by Brazil at the 1958 World Cup to allow Pele into the line-up. He scored twice in the 5–2 Final victory over Sweden to earn a transfer to Spain with Atletico Madrid. The hawk-nosed Vava was successful and hugely popular in Spain, but his family grew homesick. Returning home in time to regain his Brazil place for the World Cup defence in Chile in 1962, he scored another of his typically vital goals in the 3–1 Final victory over Czechoslovakia. In all, Vava scored 15 goals in 22 internationals spread over 12 years between 1952 and 1964.

VALDANO *Sprinting into the clear*

Fritz Walter

Born: October 31, 1920, Germany.
Club: Kaiserslautern.

Fritz Walter and center-forward brother Ottmar starred with Kaiserslautern in the late 1940s and early 1950s and were World Cup-winners together against hot favorites Hungary in the 1954 Final in Bern, Switzerland. Yet that triumph came late in a career which was cut in two by the war. Walter scored a hat-trick on his Germany debut in his favourite position of inside-left in a 9–2 thrashing of Romania in July 1940. After soccer was halted Walter was called up as a paratrooper, but his wartime flying experiences led him to refuse to fly to games in later, peacetime years. On the resumption of international soccer, Walter was restored as captain by long-time admirer and manager Sepp Herberger with success in the 1954 World Cup. Walter retired from the national team but was persuaded by Herberger to return in 1958 when, now 37, he led his team to the semi-finals. Walter, who scored 33 goals in his 61 internationals, later wrote successful soccer books.

George Weah

Born: October 1, 1966, Liberia.
Clubs: Young Survivors, Bonrang, Mighty XI, Monrovia (Lib), Tonnerre (Cam), Monaco, Paris St Germain (Fr), Milan (It).

Weah began playing the back streets of Liberia's capital, Monrovia, yet rose to become FIFA's World Footballer of the Year in 1995 as well as a special ambassador for Unicef. He was a star, aged 15, in Monrovia and was signed by Tonnerre of Cameroon. Arsene Wenger took him to France and Monaco, where Weah demonstrated his potential as a world star. Weah then joined Paris Saint-Germain, where he spent three highly successful years before transferring in the summer of 1995 to Milan. Weah has invested his multi-million earnings wisely – his family live in New York – and he has put thousands of dollars

WALTER *1954 World Cup-winner*

into Liberian soccer, sponsoring their 1994 World Cup entry.

Ernst Wilimowski

Born: June 23, 1916, Poland.
Clubs: Ruch Chorzow (Pol), PSV Chemnitz, TSV 1860 Munich, Hameln 07, BC Augsburg, Singen 04, Kaiserslautern (Ger).

Wilimowski wrote his name into World Cup history when he scored four goals against Brazil in a first-round tie in France in 1938 – yet still finished on the losing side after a 6–5, extra-time defeat. He totalled 21 goals in 22 games for Poland, where he won five league titles with Ruch Chorzow. For years, Wilimowski's name was omitted from Polish sports records – because, after the German invasion, he continued his career in Germany and scored 13 goals in eight games for Greater Germany. In 1942 he scored for 1860 Munich's in their 2–0 defeat of Schalke in the Greater German cup final. After the war he played on in Germany with a string of regional league clubs before retiring at 37 in 1953. Ironically, Wilimowski made his Poland debut playing against Germany in 1934.

Billy Wright

Born: February 6, 1924, England.
Club: Wolverhampton Wanderers.

A lively wing-half who moved into the center of defense and – by reading play superbly, timing tackles well and leaping to remarkable heights for a smallish man – he extended his career for years and years. Two League titles and one FA Cup went his way, plus the little matter of 105 caps (the majority as captain) in 13 seasons (out of a possible 108). He was the first in the world to reach a century of caps, and might have had more, even at 35, but for ending his career at virtually a moment's notice, in response to being left out of his club side for a lesser player. Later he managed Arsenal with little success, and then became a TV executive. He died in 1994.

BILLY WRIGHT *First Englishman to win 100 international caps*

Lev Yashin

see Legends (page 85)

Rashidi Yekini

Born: October 23, 1963, Nigeria.
Club: Kaduna (Nga), Vitoria Setubal (Por), Olympiakos (Gr), Gijon (Sp), Zurich (Swz).

Yekini was, more than any other player, responsible for Nigeria's sensational first finals appearance at the 1994 World Cup. He had made his international debut 10 years earlier yet did not become a regular until the 1992 African Nations Cup when he scored four goals in a qualifier against Burkina Faso, then the winner in the third-place play-off against Cameroon. Yekini was eight-goal top scorer in the African qualifiers of the 1994 World Cup then led in scoring again with five goals at the 1994 African Nations finals, and collected a winners' medal into the bargain. Yekini, the 1993 African Footballer of the Year, made history when he scored – against Bulgaria – Nigeria's first-ever goal in the World Cup finals. Following the finals, he then left Setubal for Olympiakos but ran out of luck, both losing form and suffering a serious knee injury.

Zico (full name: Artur Antunes Coimbra)

Born: March 3, 1953, Brazil.
Clubs: Flamengo (Br), Udinese (It), Flamengo (Br), Kashima Antlers (Jap).

The youngest of three professional soccer brothers, Zico was at first considered too lightweight by Flamengo. Special diets and weight training turned him into the wiry attacker who scored with one of what became his speciality free-kicks on his Brazil debut against Uruguay in 1975. Injury and disagreements over

POWER PLAY *Rashidi Yekini inspired Nigeria's first World Cup finals appearance*

tactics spoiled the 1978 and 1986 World Cups for Zico, and he was thus seen at his best only in Spain in 1982. At club level he inspired Flamengo's victory in the 1981 Copa Libertadores and their demolition of European champions Liverpool in Tokyo in the World Club Cup final. That was the start of Zico's mutual love affair with Japan which was resumed when, after a spell as Brazil's Minister of Sport, he joined Kashima Antlers to lead the launch of the professional J.League. He was assistant to Brazil coach Mario Zagallo for the 1998 World Cup finals in France.

Zinedine Zidane

Born: June 23, 1972, France
Clubs: Cannes, Bordeaux, Juventus (It)

Zidane proved himself to be one of the world's greatest midfielders when he scored twice in the 1998 World Cup final for France. He became a national hero as he masterminded a 3–0 victory over Brazil and lived up to his reputation as the new Platini.

The playmaker began his career at French club Cannes and made his name at Bordeaux (where he was named France's Player of the Year in 1996) before moving to Juventus.

Dino Zoff

Born: February 28, 1942, Italy
Clubs: Udinese, Mantova, Napoli, Juventus

Zoff is Italy's record international, with 112 appearances, of which the 106th was the World Cup final defeat of West Germany in Madrid in 1982. In 1973–74 he set a world record of 1,143 international minutes without conceding a goal. He won European trophies both as player and coach at Juventus.

Andoni Zubizarreta

Born: October 23, 1961, Spain.
Clubs: Bilbao, Barcelona, Valencia (Sp).

Zubizarreta was probably the finest product of the remarkable Basque school of goalkeeping which produced internationals such as Carmelo, Iribar, Artola, Arconada and Urruti. Zubizarreta was discovered by Bilbao in 1981, while playing for Alaves, and helped Bilbao win the league and cup double a year later. In 1986 he cost Barcelona a then world record fee for a goalkeeper of $1.8 million.

Zubizarreta overtook Jose Camacho's record of 81 caps for Spain in a 1993 World Cup qualifier against the Republic of Ireland in Dublin, and went on to top 100 appearances. He later left Barcelona for Valencia after a dispute with coach Johan Cruyff.

RECORD MAN *Andoni Zubizarreta defied opposition forwards – and Barcelona coach Johan Cruyff*

U.S. INTERNATIONAL RESULTS 1916–1999

Date	Opponent	Venue	Result
1916			
Aug 20	Sweden	Stockholm	3–2
Sep 3	Norway	Oslo	1–1
1924			
May 25	Estonia	Paris	(OGF) 1–0
May 29	Uruguay	Paris	(OGF) 0–3
Jun 10	Poland	Warsaw	3–2
Jun 16	Ireland	Dublin	1–3
1925			
Jun 27	Canada	Montreal	1–0
Nov 8	Canada	Brooklyn	6–1
1926			
Nov 6	Canada	Brooklyn	6–1
1928			
May 30	Argentina	Amsterdam	(OF) 2–11
Jun 10	Poland	Warsaw	3–3
1930			
Jul 13	Belgium	Montevideo	(WF) 3–0
Jul 17	Paraguay	Montevideo	(WF) 3–0
Jul 26	Argentina	Montevideo	(WF) 1–6
Aug 17	Brazil	Rio de Janeiro	3–4
1934			
May 24	Mexico	Rome	(WQ) 4–2
May 27	Italy	Rome	(WF) 1–7
1936			
Aug 3	Italy	Berlin	(OF) 0–1
1937			
Sep 12	Mexico	Mexico City	2–7
Sep 19	Mexico	Mexico City	3–7
Sep 26	Mexico	Mexico City	1–5
1947			
Jul 13	Mexico	Havana	0–5
Jul 20	Cuba	Havana	2–5
1948			
Aug 2	Italy	London	(OF) 0–9
Aug 6	Norway	Oslo	0–11
Aug 11	N. Ireland	Belfast	0–5
1949			
Jun 19	Scotland	New York	0–4
Sep 12	Mexico	Mexico City	(WQ) 0–6
Sep 12	Cuba	Mexico City	(WQ) 1–1
Sep 12	Mexico	Mexico City	(WQ) 2–6
Sep 12	Cuba	Mexico City	(WQ) 5–2
1950			
Jun 25	Spain	Curtiba	(WF) 1–3
Jun 29	England	B. Horizonte	(WF) 1–0
Jul 2	Chile	Recife	(WF) 2–5
1952			
Apr 30	Scotland	Glasgow	0–6
Jul 16	Italy	Tampere	(OF) 0–8
1953			
Jun 8	England	New York	3–6
1954			
Jan 10	Mexico	Mexico City	(WQ) 0–4
Jan 14	Mexico	Mexico City	(WQ) 1–3
Apr 3	Haiti	Pt-au-Prince	(WQ) 3–2
Apr 4	Haiti	Pt-au-Prince	(WQ) 3–0
1955			
Aug 25	Iceland	Reykjavik	2–3
1956			
Nov 28	Yugoslavia	Melbourne	(OF) 1–9
1957			
Apr 7	Mexico	Mexico City	(WQ) 0–6
Apr 28	Mexico	Long Beach	(WQ) 2–7
Jun 22	Canada	Toronto	(WQ) 1–5
Jul 6	Canada	St. Louis	(WQ) 2–3
1959			
May 28	England	Los Angeles	1–8
Oct 8	Mexico	Mexico City	(OQ) 0–2
Nov 22	Mexico	Los Angeles	(OQ) 1–1
1960			
Nov 6	Mexico	Los Angeles	(WQ) 3–3
Nov 13	Mexico	Mexico City	(WQ) 0–3
1961			
Feb 5	Colombia	Bogota	0–2
1963			
Apr 20	Chile	Sao Paulo	(WQ) 2–10
Apr 22	Argentina	Sao Paulo	(WQ) 1–8
Apr 28	Brazil	Sao Paulo	(WQ) 0–10
May 2	Uruguay	Sao Paulo	(WQ) 0–2
1964			
Mar 16	Surinam	Mexico City	(OQ) 0–1
Mar 18	Panama	Mexico City	(OQ) 4–2
Mar 20	Mexico	Mexico City	(OQ) 1–2
May 27	England	New York	0–10
1965			
Mar 7	Mexico	Los Angeles	(WQ) 2–2
Mar 12	Mexico	Mexico City	(WQ) 0–2
Mar 17	Honduras	S Pedro Sula	(WQ) 1–0
Mar 21	Honduras	Tegucigalpa	(WQ) 1–1
1967			
May 21	Bermuda	Hamilton	(OQ) 1–1
May 27	Bermuda	Chicago	(OQ) 0–1
1968			
Sep 15	Israel	New York	3–3
Sep 25	Israel	Philadelphia	0–4
Oct 17	Canada	Toronto	(WQ) 2–4
Oct 20	Haiti	Port-au-Prince	6–3
Oct 21	Haiti	Port-au-Prince	2–5
Oct 23	Haiti	Port-au-Prince	0–1
Oct 27	Canada	Atlanta	(WQ) 1–0
Nov 2	Bermuda	Kansas City	(WQ) 6–2
Nov 10	Bermuda	Hamilton	(WQ) 2–0
1969			
Apr 20	Haiti	Pt-au-Prince	(WQ) 0–2
May 11	Haiti	San Diego	(WQ) 0–1
1971			
Jul 18	El Salvador	Miami	(OQ) 1–1
Jul 25	Barbados	Miami	(OQ) 3–0
Aug 15	El Salvador	San Salvador	(OQ) 1–1
Aug 22	Barbados	Bridgetown	(OQ) 3–1
Sep 18	El Salvador	Kingston	(OQ) 1–0
1972			
Jan 16	Jamaica	Kingston	(OQ) 1–1
Jan 23	Mexico	Guadalajara	(OQ) 1–1
Apr 16	Guatemala	Guatemala C	(OQ) 2–3
Apr 25	Guatemala	Miami	(OQ) 2–1
May 10	Mexico	S Francisco	(OQ) 2–2
Jan 16	Jamaica	St. Louis	(OQ) 2–1
Aug 20	Canada	St. John's	(WQ) 2–3
Aug 27	Morocco	Augsburg	(OF) 0–0
Aug 29	Malaysia	Ingolstadt	(OF) 0–2
Aug 29	Canada	Baltimore	(WQ) 2–2
Aug 31	W Germany	Munich	(OF) 0–7
Sep 3	Mexico	Mexico City	(WQ) 1–3
Sep 10	Mexico	Los Angeles	(WQ) 1–2
1973			
Mar 17	Bermuda	Hamilton	0–4
Mar 20	Poland	Lodz	0–4
Aug 3	Poland	Chicago	0–1
Aug 5	Canada	Windsor	2–0
Aug 10	Poland	San Francisco	0–4
Aug 12	Poland	New Britain	1–0
Sep 9	Bermuda	Hartford	1–0
Oct 16	Mexico	Puebla	0–2
Nov 3	Haiti	Port-au-Prince,	0–1
Nov 5	Haiti	Port-au-Prince	0–1
Nov 13	Israel	Tel Aviv	1–3
Nov 15	Israel	Beersheba	0–2
1974			
Sep 5	Mexico	Monterrey	1–3
Sep 8	Mexico	Dallas	0–1
1975			
Mar 26	Poland	Poznan	0–7
Apr 4	Italy	Rome	0–10
Apr 20	Bermuda	Hamilton	(OQ) 2–3
Apr 27	Bermuda	S Francisco	(OQ) 2–0
Jun 24	Poland	Seattle	0–4
Aug 19	Costa Rica	Mexico City	1–3
Aug 21	Argentina	Mexico City	0–6
Aug 25	Mexico	Toluca	(OQ) 0–8
Aug 25	Mexico	Mexico City	0–2
Aug 28	Mexico	Wilmington	2–4
1976			
Sep 24	Canada	Vancouver	(WQ) 1–1
Oct 3	Mexico	Los Angeles	(WQ) 0–0
Oct 15	Mexico	Puebla	(WQ) 0–3
Oct 20	Canada	Seattle	(WQ) 2–0
Nov 10	Haiti	Port-au-Prince	0–0
Nov 12	Haiti	Port-au-Prince	0–0
Nov 14	Haiti	Port-au-Prince	0–0
Dec 22	Canada	Pt-au-Prince	(WQ) 0–3
1977			
Sep 15	El Salvador	San Salvador	2–1
Sep 18	Guatemala	Guatemala City	1–3
Sep 25	Guatemala	Guatemala City	0–2
Sep 27	Mexico	Monterrey	0–3
Sep 30	El Salvador	Los Angeles	0–0
Oct 6	China	Washington	1–1
Oct 10	China	Atlanta	1–0
Oct 16	China	San Francisco	2–1
1978			
Sep 3	Iceland	Reykjavik	0–0
Sep 6	Switzerland	Lucerne	0–2
Sep 20	Portugal	Benfica	0–1
1979			
Feb 3	Soviet Union	Seattle	1–3
Feb 10	Soviet Union	San Francisco	1–3
May 2	France	East Rutherford	0–6
May 23	Mexico	Leon	(OQ) 2–0*
Jun 3	Mexico	New York	(OQ) 2–0*
Oct 7	Bermuda	Hamilton	3–1
Oct 10	France	Paris	0–3
Oct 26	Hungary	Budapest	2–0
Oct 29	Rep. Ireland	Dublin	2–3
Dec 2	Bermuda	Hamilton	(OQ) 3–0
Dec 12	Bermuda	Ft Lauderdale	(OQ) 5–0
1980			
Mar 16	Surinam	Orlando	(OQ) 2–1
Mar 20	Costa Rica	San Jose	(OQ) 1–0
Mar 26	Costa Rica	Edwardsville	(OQ) 1–1
Apr 2	Surinam	Paramaribo	(OQ) 4–4
Oct 5	Luxmbourg	Dudelange	2–0
Oct 7	Portugal	Lisbon	1–1
Oct 25	Canada	Ft Lauderdale	(WQ) 0–0
Nov 1	Canada	Vancouver	(WQ) 1–2
Nov 9	Mexico	Mexico City	(WQ) 1–5
Nov 23	Mexico	Ft Lauderdale	(WQ) 2–1
1982			
Mar 21	Trin & Tob	Port of Spain	2–1
1983			
Apr 8	Haiti	Port-au-Prince	2–0
1984			
May 30	Italy	East Rutherford	0–0
Jul 29	Costa Rica	Palo Alto	(OF) 3–0
Jul 31	Italy	Pasadena	(OF) 0–1
Aug 2	Egypt	Palo Alto	(OF) 1–1
Sep 29	Net. Antilles	Curaçao	(WQ) 0–0
Oct 6	Net. Antilles	St. Louis	(WQ) 4–0
Oct 9	El Salvador	Los Angeles	3–1
Oct 11	Colombia	Los Angeles	1–0
Oct 14	Guatemala	Guatemala City	0–4
Oct 17	Mexico	Mexico City	1–2
Nov 30	Ecuador	Long Island	0–0
Dec 2	Ecuador	Miami	2–2
1985			
Feb 8	Switzerland	Tampa	1–1
Apr 2	Canada	Vancouver	0–2
Apr 4	Canada	Portland	1–1
May 15	Trin & Tob	St. Louis	(WQ) 2–1
May 19	Trin & Tob	Torrance	(WQ) 1–0
May 26	Costa Rica	Alajuela	(WQ) 1–1
May 31	Costa Rica	Hawthorne	(WQ) 0–1
Jun 16	England	Los Angeles	0–5
1986			
Feb 5	Canada	Miami	0–0
Feb 7	Uruguay	Miami	1–1
1987			
May 23	Canada	St. John's	(OQ) 0–2
May 30	Canada	St. Louis	(OQ) 3–0
Jun 8	Egypt	Seoul	1–3
Jun 12	South Korea	Pusan	0–1
Jun 16	Thailand	Chongju	1–0
Sep 5	Trin & Tob	St. Louis	(OQ) 4–1
Sep 20	Trin & Tob	Port of Spain	(OQ) 1–0
Oct 18	El Salvador	San Salvador	(OQ) 4–2
1988			
Jan 10	Guatemala	Guatemala City	0–1
Jan 13	Guatemala	Guatemala City	1–0
May 14	Colombia	Miami	0–2
May 25	El Salvador	Indianapolis	(OQ) 4–1
Jun 1	Chile	Stockton	1–1
Jun 3	Chile	San Diego	1–3
Jun 5	Chile	Fresno	0–3
Jun 7	Ecuador	Albuquerque	0–1
Jun 10	Ecuador	Houston	0–2
Jun 12	Ecuador	Fort Worth	0–0
Jun 14	Costa Rica	San Antonio	1–0
Jun 16	Soviet Union	Seoul	0–1
Jun 19	Nigeria	Kwangju	2–3
Jul 13	Poland	New Britain	0–2
Jul 24	Jamaica	Kingston	(WQ) 0–0
Aug 13	Jamaica	St. Louis	(WQ) 5–1
Sep 18	Argentina	Taegu	(OF) 1–1
Sep 20	South Korea	Pusan	(OF) 0–0
Sep 22	Soviet Union	Taegu	(OF) 2–4
1989			
Apr 16	Costa Rica	San Jose	(WQ) 0–1
Apr 30	Costa Rica	St. Louis	(WQ) 1–0
May 13	Trin & Tob	Torrance	(WQ) 1–1
Jun 4	Peru	East Rutherford	3–0
Jun 17	Guatemala	New Britain	(WQ) 2–1
Jun 24	Colombia	Miami	0–1
Aug 13	South Korea	Los Angeles	1–2
Sep 17	El Salvador	Tegucigalpa	(WQ) 1–0
Oct 8	Guatemala	Guatemala C	(WQ) 0–0
Nov 5	El Salvador	St. Louis	(WQ) 0–0
Nov 14	Bermuda	Cocoa Beach	2–1
Nov 19	Trin & Tob	Port of Spain	(WQ) 1–0
1990			
Feb 2	Costa Rica	Miami	0–2
Feb 4	Colombia	Miami	1–2
Feb 13	Bermuda	Hamilton	1–0
Feb 24	Soviet Union	Palo Alto	1–3
Mar 10	Finland	Tampa	2–1
Mar 20	Hungary	Budapest	2–0
Mar 28	E Germany	Berlin	2–3
Apr 8	Iceland	St. Louis	4–1
Apr 22	Colombia	Miami	0–1
May 5	Malta	Rutgers	1–0
May 6	Canada	Burnaby	0–1
May 9	Poland	Hershey	3–1
May 10	Mexico	Burnaby	0–1
May 30	Liechtnstein	Eschen-Mauren	4–1
Jun 2	Switzerland	St. Gallen	1–2
Jun 10	Czech.	Florence	(WF) 1–5
Jun 14	Italy	Rome	(WF) 0–1
Jun 19	Austria	Florence	(WF) 1–2
Jul 28	E Germany	Milwaukee	1–2
Sep 15	Trin & Tob	High Point	3–0
Oct 10	Poland	Warsaw	3–2
Nov 18	Trin & Tob	Port of Spain	0–0
Nov 21	Soviet Union	Port of Spain	0–0
Dec 19	Portugal	Porto	0–1
1991			
Feb 1	Switzerland	Miami	0–1
Feb 21	Bermuda	Miami	0–1
Mar 12	Mexico	Los Angeles	2–2
Mar 16	Canada	Los Angeles	2–0
Apr 7	South Korea	Pohang	0–2
May 5	Uruguay	Denver	1–0
May 19	Argentina	Palo Alto	0–1
Jun 1	Rep. Ireland	Foxboro	1–1
Jun 29	Trin & Tob	Pasadena	2–1
Jul 1	Guatemala	Pasadena	3–0
Jul 3	Costa Rica	Los Angeles	3–2
Jul 5	Costa Rica	Los Angeles	3–2
Jul 7	Mexico	Los Angeles	2–0
Aug 28	Romania	Brasov	2–0
Sep 4	Turkey	Istanbul	1–1
Sep 14	Jamaica	High Point	1–0
Oct 19	North Korea	Washington	1–2
Nov 24	Costa Rica	Dallas	1–1
1992			
Jan 25	C.I.S.	Miami	0–1
Feb 2	C.I.S.	Detroit	2–1
Feb 12	Costa Rica	San Jose	0–0
Feb 18	El Salvador	San Salvador	0–2
Feb 26	Brazil	Fortaleza	0–3
Mar 11	Morocco	Casablanca	1–3
Apr 4	China	Palo Alto	5–0
Apr 29	Rep. Ireland	Dublin	1–4
May 17	Scotland	Denver	0–1
May 30	Rep. Ireland	Washington	3–1
Jun 3	Portugal	Chicago	(UC) 1–0
Jun 6	Italy	Chicago	(UC) 1–1
Jun 13	Australia	Orlando	(UC) 0–1
Jun 27	Ukraine	East Rutherford	0–0
Jul 31	Colombia	Los Angeles	0–1
Aug 2	Brazil	Los Angeles	0–1
Sep 3	Canada	St. John's	2–0

Date	Opponent	Venue	Result		Date	Opponent	Venue	Result		Date	Opponent	Venue	Result		Date	Opponent	Venue	Result
Oct 9	Canada	Greensboro	0–0		**1994**					Jul 20	Brazil	Maldonado	(CA) 0–1		**1998**			
Oct 15	Saudi Arabia	Riyadh	0–3		Jan 15	Norway	Phoenix	2–1		Jul 22	Colombia	Maldonado	(CA) 1–4		Jan 24	Sweden	Orlando	1–0
Oct 19	Ivory Coast	Riyadh	5–2		Jan 22	Switzerland	Fullerton	1–1		Aug 16	Sweden	Norrkoping	0–1		Feb 1	Cuba	Oakland	(GC) 3–0
1993					Jan 29	Russia	Seattle	1–1		Oct 8	Saudi Arabia	Washington	4–3		Feb 7	Costa Rica	Oakland	(GC) 2–1
Jan 30	Denmark	Tempe	2–2		Feb 10	Denmark	Hong Kong	0–0		**1996**					Feb 10	Brazil	Los Angeles	(GC) 1–0
Feb 6	Romania	Santa Barbara	1–1		Feb 13	Romania	Hong Kong	1–2		Jan 13	Trin & Tob	Anaheim	(GC) 3–2		Feb 15	Mexico	Los Angeles	(GC) 0–1
Feb 13	Russia	Orlando	0–1		Feb 18	Bolivia	Miami	1–1		Jan 16	El Salvador	Anaheim	(GC) 2–0		Feb 21	Holland	Miami	0–2
Feb 21	Russia	Palo Alto	0–0		Feb 20	Sweden	Miami	1–3		Jan 18	Brazil	Los Angeles	(GC) 0–1		Feb 25	Belgium	Miami	0–2
Mar 3	Canada	Costa Mesa	2–2		Mar 12	South Korea	Fullerton	1–1		Jan 21	Guatemala	Pasadena	(GC) 3–0		Mar 14	Paraguay	San Diego	2–2
Mar 10	Hungary	Nagoya	0–0		Mar 26	Bolivia	Dallas	2–2		May 26	Scotland	New Britain	2–1		Apr 22	Austria	Vienna	3–0
Mar 14	Japan	Tokyo	1–3		Apr 16	Moldova	Jacksonville	1–1		Jun 9	Rep Ireland	Foxboro	(UC) 2–1		May 16	Macedonia	San Jose	0–0
Mar 23	El Salvador	San Salvador	2–2		Apr 20	Moldova	Davidson	3–0		Jun 12	Bolivia	Washington	(UC) 0–2		May 24	Kuwait	Portland	2–0
Mar 25	Honduras	Tegucigalpa	1–4		Apr 24	Iceland	San Diego	1–2		Jun 16	Mexico	Pasadena	(UC) 2–2		May 30	Scotland	Washington	0–0
Apr 9	Saudi Arabia	Riyadh	2–0		Apr 30	Chile	Albuquerque	0–2		Aug 30	El Salvador	Los Angeles	3–1		Jun 15	Germany	Paris	(WF) 0–2
Apr 17	Iceland	Costa Mesa	1–1		May 7	Estonia	Fullerton	4–0		Oct 16	Peru	Lima	1–4		Jun 21	Iran	Lyon	(WF) 1–2
May 8	Colombia	Miami	1–2		May 15	Armenia	Fullerton	1–0		Nov 3	Guatemala	Washington	(WQ) 2–0		Jun 25	Yugoslavia	Nantes	(WF) 0–1
May 23	Bolivia	Fullerton	0–0		May 25	Saudi Arabia	East Rutherford	0–0		Nov 10	Trin & Tob	Richmond	(WQ) 2–0		Nov 6	Australia	San Jose	0–0
May 26	Peru	Mission Viejo	0–0		May 28	Greece	New Haven	1–1		Nov 24	Trin & Tob	Pt of Spain	(WQ) 1–0		**1999**			
Jun 6	Brazil	New Haven	(UC) 0–2		Jun 4	Mexico	Pasadena	1–0		Dec 1	Costa Rica	San Jose	(WQ) 1–2		Jan 26	Bolivia	Santa Cruz	0–0
Jun 9	England	Foxboro	(UC) 2–0		Jun 18	Switzerland	Detroit	(WF) 1–1		Dec 14	Costa Rica	Palto Alto	(WQ) 2–1		Feb 6	Germany	Jacksonville	3–0
Jun 13	Germany	Chicago	(UC) 3–4		Jun 22	Colombia	Pasadena	(WF) 2–1		Dec 21	Guatemala	San Salvador	(WQ) 2–2		Feb 21	Chile	Fort Lauderdale	2–1
Jun 16	Uruguay	Ambato	0–1		Jun 25	Romania	Pasadena	(WF) 0–1		**1997**					Mar 11	Guatemala	Los Angeles	(US) 3–1
Jun 19	Ecuador	Quito	0–2		Jul 5	Brazil	Palo Alto	(WF) 0–1		Jan 17	Peru	San Diego	(UC) 0–1		Mar 13	Mexico	San Diego	(US) 1–2
Jun 22	Venezuela	Quito	3–3		Sep 7	England	London	0–2		Jan 19	Mexico	Pasadena	(UC) 0–2		Jun 13	Argentina	Washington	1–0
Jul 10	Jamaica	Dallas	1–0		Oct 19	Saudi Arabia	Dhahran	1–2		Jan 22	Denmark	Pasadena	(UC) 1–4		Jul 24	New Zealand	Guadalajara	(CC) 2–1
Jul 14	Panama	Dallas	2–1		Nov 19	Trin & Tob	Port of Spain	0–1		Jan 29	PR Chi	Kunming	1–2		Jul 28	Brazil	Guadalajara	(CC) 0–1
Jul 17	Honduras	Dallas	1–0		Nov 22	Jamaica	Kingston	3–0		Feb 1	PR Chi	Guangzhou	1–1		Jul 30	Germany	Guadalajara	(CC) 2–0
Jul 21	Costa Rica	Dallas	1–0		Dec 11	Honduras	Fullerton	1–1		Mar 2	Jamaica	Kingston	(WQ) 0–0		Aug 1	Mexico	Mexico City	(CC) 0–1
Jul 25	Mexico	Mexico City	0–4		**1995**					Mar 16	Canada	Palto Alto	(WQ) 3–0		Aug 3	Saudi Arabia	Guadalajara	(CC) 2–0
Aug 31	Iceland	Reykjavik	1–0		Mar 25	Uruguay	Dallas	2–2		Mar 23	Costa Rica	S. Jose, C.R.	(WQ) 2–3		Sep 8	Jamaica	Kingston	2–2
Sep 8	Norway	Oslo	0–1		Apr 22	Belgium	Brussels	0–1		Apr 20	Mexico	Foxboro	(WQ) 2–2		Nov 17	Morocco	Marrakech	1–2
Oct 13	Mexico	Washington	1–1		May 28	Costa Rica	Tampa	1–2		Jun 4	Paraguay	St Louis	0–0					
Oct 16	Ukraine	High Point	1–2		Jun 11	Nigeria	Foxboro	(UC) 3–2		Jun 17	Israel	Jacksonville	2–1					
Oct 23	Ukraine	Bethlehem	0–1		Jun 18	Mexico	Washington	(UC) 4–0		Jun 29	El Salvador	S. Salvador	(WQ) 1–1					
Nov 7	Jamaica	Fullerton	1–0		Jun 25	Colombia	Piscataway	(UC) 0–0		Aug 7	Ecuador	Baltimore	0–1					
Nov 14	Cayman Is.	Mission Viejo	8–1		Jul 8	Chile	Paysandu	(CA) 2–1		Sep 7	Costa Rica	Portland	(WQ) 1–0					
Dec 5	El Salvador	Los Angeles	7–0		Jul 11	Bolivia	Paysandu	(CA) 1–0		Oct 3	Jamaica	Washington	(WQ) 1–1					
Dec 18	Germany	Palo Alto	0–3		Jul 14	Argentina	Paysandu	(CA) 3–0		Nov 2	Mexico	Mexico C.	(WQ) 0–0					
					Jul 17	Mexico	Paysandu	(CA) 0–0		Nov 9	Canada	Vancouver	(WQ) 3–0					
						(U.S. won 4–1 in penalty shoot-out)				Nov 16	El Salvador	Foxboro	(WQ) 4–2					

KEY

* = U.S. was awarded the Olympic Games Qualifying matches by forfeit (2–0) over Mexico because Mexico illegally used professional players. The U.S. lost the actual matches 0–4 (Leon) and 0–2 (New York).
WQ = World Cup Qualifier
WF = World Cup Finals
OQ = Olympic Games Qualifier
OF = Olympic Games Finals
CC = CONCACAF Gold Cup
GC = FIFA Confederations Cup
UC = Nike U.S. Cup
CA = Copa America

NORTH AMERICAN SOCCER LEAGUE CHAMPIONS

1968	Atlanta Chiefs
1969	Kansas City Spurs
1970	Rochester Lancers
1971	Dallas Tornado
1972	New York Cosmos
1973	Philadelphia Atoms
1974	Los Angeles Aztecs
1975	Tampa Bay Rowdies
1976	Toronto Metros
1977	New York Cosmos
1978	New York Cosmos
1979	Vancouver Whitecaps
1980	New York Cosmos
1981	Chicago Sting
1982	New York Cosmos
1983	Tulsa Roughnecks
1984	Chicago Sting

MAJOR LEAGUE SOCCER CHAMPIONS

1996	Washington D.C. United
1997	Washington D.C. United
1998	Chicago Fire
1999	Washington D.C. United

PHOTO CREDITS

The publishers would like to thank the following sources for their kind permission to reproduce the pictures in this book:

Allsport UK Ltd./Simon P Barnett, Al Bello, Shaun Botterill, Clive Brunskill, Simon Bruty, David Cannon, Chris Cole, Stephen Dunn, David Durochik/MLS, Stu Forster, Elsa Hasch, Tom Hauck, Mike Hewitt, Hulton Getty, Jed Jacobsohn, Vincent Laforet, David Leah, Gray Mortimore, Doug Pensinger, Ben Radford, Richard Steinmetz, John Van Woerden/MLS
Colorsport
Corbis/UPI
Hulton Getty
National Soccer Hall of Fame, Oneonta, New York
National Soccer Hall of Fame, Oneonta, New York/CSU
National Soccer Hall of Fame, Oneonta, New York/Jerry Liebman Studio
Popperfoto
Sporting Pictures (UK) Ltd.

Every effort has been made to acknowledge correctly and contact the source and/copyright holder of each picture, and the publisher apologises for any unintentional errors or omissions which will be corrected in future editions of this book.